14D

Jumpin' Jack Flash

D0861128

FEB 16 2017

Jumpin' Jack Flash

David Litvinoff and the Rock'n'Roll Underworld

Keiron Pim

JONATHAN CAPE
LONDON

5 7 9 10 8 6

Jonathan Cape, an imprint of Vintage Publishing,
20 Vauxhall Bridge Road,
London SW1V 2SA

Jonathan Cape is part of the Penguin Random House group of companies whose addresses can be
found at global.penguinrandomhouse.com.

Copyright © Keiron Pim 2016

Keiron Pim has asserted his right to be identified as the author of this Work in accordance with the
Copyright, Designs and Patents Act 1988

First published by Jonathan Cape in 2016

www.vintage-books.co.uk

A CIP catalogue record for this book is available from the British Library

ISBN 9780224098120

Typeset in Adobe Caslon by Palimpsest Book Production Ltd, Falkirk, Stirlingshire

Printed and bound by Clays Ltd, St Ives plc

Penguin Random House is committed to a sustainable future for our business, our readers and our
planet. This book is made from Forest Stewardship Council® certified paper.

Contents

For Brian Case,
who started me writing
and kept me reading
– with my thanks and respect.

List of Illustrations

'Grown older since those days, I understood how much disappears when such a man drops out of his place in the world, were it only because, amid the daily increase in hopeless monotony, the unique grows continually more precious.'

Stefan Zweig, *Buchmendel* (1929)

'The only performance that makes it, that really makes it, that makes it all the way, is the one that achieves madness. Right? Am I right? *You with me?*'

Turner, played by Mick Jagger, in *Performance* (1970), directed by Donald Cammell and Nicolas Roeg

Introduction

He opened his front door and felt a fist in his face, then nothing until a strange vision appeared: the coloured roofs of cars and buses, distant pedestrians on the pavement below, the broad grey sweep of Kensington High Street. David Litvinoff had awoken in a few odd places before but this was something different. Ropes constrained his back tight against the wooden chair, which itself hung secured to the railings of his balcony, and as consciousness seeped back with every heartbeat, with it came sensation: the cold ooze of blood dripping from his head down to the street, the lattice of scratches across his scalp, the chill gusts of breeze scouring his naked body. He coughed and felt a metallic tang fill his mouth, strained to look around, his sore eyeballs dimly registering. . .what? The night's last stars being absorbed into the morning light? Traffic growling down the road past Derry & Toms? The ancient souls of holy Jews floating across the sky in spectral transit to Jerusalem?

No sudden movements. He squinted downwards. His heart thudded in his throat. He brooded and waited, his quiet groans melding with the wind's soft moan as it buffeted the Victorian block. . .and now he heard something. He glanced along the road. Down beyond the department store he saw the beginnings of a crowd, saw them approach with the slow intent of a protest march. The first faint calls were unclear, just vocal percussion echoing back and forth, then as they grew near they coalesced: 'Ban the bomb, *ban the bomb*, ban the bomb, *ban the bomb*. . .' Over and over, louder and louder until they reached a raucous crescendo as the protestors tramped by beneath him: Aldermaston marchers, some carrying trade union or CND banners, others strumming guitars and hollering, most focused on the road ahead. Any member of this moving audience whose gaze had shifted upwards for a few moments would have seen the sallow smudge of a man's body twisted like a Francis Bacon nude against the red background of the building's facade: but twitching, animated now, as very gently he reached back to the balcony and clenched his fist around a slender iron railing. With his other hand he tried the ropes around his chest, teasing at them, testing which he could ease loose and which were keeping the chair suspended. He slackened a couple, squirmed, wriggled, and in a firm deft movement swung around and grasped the bar across the top of the railings, his taut triceps flexing as he hauled himself up and over and back with a stumble on to the balcony and into his flat.

Bloodstains, scattered clothes and broken possessions covered the carpet. Drawers hung out and empty, cupboards gaped open, crinkled wallpaper peeled from the walls. He staggered into the bathroom and stood at the mirror, dazed for a moment by the man who peered back at him: his head was shaved and gashed, his eyes blackened and his nose broken. He had a good idea who was responsible but that could wait. What was this now? Faint strains of song drifted into the flat. He returned to the balcony. Somewhere from deep within the long trail of trudging humans arose plangent voices in rough union:

> *Corrina, Corrina, where you been so long?*
> *Corrina, Corrina, where you been so long?*
> *I been worried about you,*
> *Ever since you been gone.*

He wandered back inside and collected his thoughts. He'd call in on Joan Wyndham and Shura Shihwarg and tell them what had happened, just as he would tell anyone who cared to listen for the rest of his life, the story mutating and improving with every rendition – switching between Kensington High Street and the Fulham Road, from his home to a friend's, from his balcony to a roof garden, having him being helped down by a passer-by who wiped away a raindrop and saw it was red, or by his borrowing a window cleaner's ladder to descend to the pavement, or by freeing himself, running into the flat and down to the street only to realise he was naked, at which moment an *Evening Standard* vendor at the bottom of the block asked: 'Would you like to borrow my overcoat, sir?' – a story that grew in other people's minds and mouths, metamorphosing its way around the city over the decades until it attained the form you have just read.

'He said to me once, "I only want two pieces of paper that record my life: my birth certificate and my death certificate." Everything else was an avoidance.'

Nigel Waymouth skipped back almost half a century to the years when the posters he painted and clothes he sold helped define the

'Swinging London' aesthetic: back to when he co-founded the King's Road vintage fashion boutique Granny Takes a Trip, to when he and a friend merged their artistic and musical talents and named themselves Hapshash and the Coloured Coat, to when his and David Litvinoff's lives overlapped. We sat in a patisserie by Holland Park Tube, Waymouth's perky tones competing with the hiss and clatter of an espresso machine as he traced his old friend's progress from Brick Lane to the Shropshire seat of Lord Harlech, and tried to establish Litvinoff's relationships with his family, friends and rivals: musicians such as Mick Jagger and Keith Richards, artists including Lucian Freud and Francis Bacon, film-makers such as Donald Cammell, with whom he created one of the great British movies; criminals from Jack 'Spot' Comer through to the Kray twins, writers such as his half-brother Emanuel, or Manny to friends and family, the doyen of Anglo-Jewish literature.

'He doesn't get credit for *Performance,*' said Nigel, 'or he probably does now, posthumously, but everything was in the shade. He was never ambitious in that sense.

'He wanted the freedom. That's what made him so appealing in many ways. Because he wasn't about to do you down, he wasn't competitive in that way at all. He wanted to enjoy life. What's fascinating is he used to bring Manny round sometimes when he was living at my studio, this elder brother, elder statesman, and they were chalk and cheese. Manny was quite fond of David, wasn't he? I know David was the black sheep of the family and was a disappointment in many ways, but then he was a bit of an outlaw and that didn't fit everybody else's aspirations or lifestyles. There was this fondness. David was so proud of his elder brother who was a man of letters, who had stood up to T. S. Eliot's anti-Semitism in public. He knew Manny was a man of substance and strength. When he came round Manny was always very polite and quiet and reserved, and David was like a boy, you know. It was very sweet, very tender.'

After an hour's conversation that took us from the 1950s' shadows into the luminous 1960s and on to the hungover early 1970s, Waymouth had a small epiphany. 'I suppose it's just occurred to me what it was about him, in a nutshell: no matter where you were or who you were with, if David walked into the room he'd be the strongest personality in that room – and yet he was not a man of substance. You couldn't say "That was David Litvinoff the banker", or "the famous artist", "the great writer". There was nothing there.'

Who was David Litvinoff? This is the story of a multifaceted character – to some people a humble visionary intent on using his vast knowledge and diverse connections to catalyse other lives, to some a storytelling jester at the court of Swinging London whose jokes, like a Shakespearian Fool's, contained insights beyond the wit of the cast's leading characters, to many the funniest man they ever knew, to others little more than a self-aggrandising crook capable of severe premeditated violence – and of my attempt to mould every discordant perspective I could find into a coherent whole, ushering into the daylight a man most at home in the crepuscular hinterlands of mid-twentieth-century London. It wouldn't always be easy, but the quest would introduce me to an array of intriguing personalities, from rock stars, pop artists, photographers and film actors to louche aristocrats and sandpaper-throated retired gangsters, all of whom had their own stories to tell: ones in which Litvinoff usually played a decisive role before slipping out of their lives again.

Stories were his primary form of capital. He lived by words, traded in gossip and intrigue, tapped the river of London life and sluiced information to all who would listen. His legendary *spiels* weren't so much a stream of consciousness as a churning torrent. He drew audiences wherever he chose to perform: he'd begin talking in a noisy Chelsea pub and before long all other voices fell silent, faces turned his way. His magnetism could interfere with the moral compass of those in his vicinity who were susceptible. The lexicographer Jonathon Green labelled him 'a seeker after reflections'[1] and Litvinoff's is indeed a tale of looking-glass worlds offering complex symmetries, divided by social membranes through which he had the requisite knowledge or *chutzpah* to pass. He functioned as a conduit, a go-between. . .a procurer, to allude to his 1954 portrait by Lucian Freud, a painting that, as we will see, had a serious impact on his life. He died in 1975, leaving almost no physical legacy. As I was born three years later I had no purchase on his era. I had to begin encircling his ghost from a distance. Coaxing out the memories of old friends and relatives, searching for film and photographs and tape recordings, for official documentation, for lingering evidence of a man who shunned the attention of straight society and stepped back into the shadows at the faintest drone of a police siren. His afterlife consists of tangents, passing references, colourful digressions; let the footnote become the main text, I thought. His friends wished me luck. I realised soon that this was no platitude but a measure of the task. Timothy Whidborne, a society portraitist who befriended Litvinoff in 1953, cautioned me that 'to try to capture David's personality is rather like trying to net a butterfly'. Litvinoff seemed evanescent: his spectre materialises here and there in brief visitations on the pages of others' autobiographies. Variations on the phrase 'I ever met' recur where he is remembered. Recalling their time at the Pheasantry on the King's Road, Eric Clapton wrote of him as 'the most colourful character in our midst. . .one of the most extraordinary men I've ever met'.[2] To Mervyn Peake's daughter Clare he was 'the most hilarious person I had ever met', with 'the quickest wit and the sharpest tongue'.[3] In his memoir *Owning Up*, George Melly called Litvinoff 'the fastest talker I ever met, full of outrageous stories, at least half of which turned out to be true, a dandy of squalor, a face either beautiful or ugly, I could never decide which, but certainly one hundred per cent Jewish, a self-propelled catalyst who didn't mind getting hurt as long as he made something happen, a sacred monster, first class'.[4]

Litvinoff branded such an imprint on to dozens of minds, whether through intimate friendships or brief intersections, a warp to their weft; where the entanglements were transient they were all the more exciting for it. As Melly suggests, people were transfixed by his near-ugliness, some of it innate, some acquired. He looked like a once-handsome man whose features had been manipulated as if cast in putty: the nose pulled, the ears tweaked up, the brow flattened. This ever-animated countenance hinted of anti-Semitic caricature made flesh, his nose blooming out from between his sunglasses' lenses in an arc that curved to a downward-pointing tip, the long nostrils like horizontal commas. Flickering eyes with pale blue irises, the pupils twin black holes sucking light into an avaricious mind. High cheekbones, a sharp jawline, thin lips that often assumed a pursed half-smile. Atop this singular assembly of angles and curves lay a severe comb-over of wavy dark brown hair, reminiscent of a slipped wig. Unsparing as it is, the Freud portrait lacks a later-acquired characteristic of the subject's physiognomy mentioned by all who knew him in the 1960s, the scars running from the corners of his mouth: underworld justice done and seen to be done.

David Litvinoff.

Melly's, Peake's and Clapton's memoirs' detailed descriptions of this peculiar figure are unusual. More often the same small narratives are repeated, reworded but never expanded; take the aforementioned incident that left him dangling naked and shaven-headed from a balcony over Kensington High Street. Colin MacCabe touches on that affair in his book on *Performance*, but in a footnote concedes that 'the full details. . .involve too many living performers for me to desire to achieve complete accuracy'.[5] He goes on to call Litvinoff 'one of the great mythic characters of '60s London' and reaches a tantalising conclusion: 'A monomaniacal fantasist who made up believable fictions as easily as he recounted unbelievable truths, it is more than difficult to discover the real facts of his extraordinary life.'

To explore this life is to journey from Hare Marsh to Cheyne Walk, from the Pale of Settlement to the Garden of England, from the East End underworld to bohemian Chelsea, and from the intensity of Soho to suburban fringes where the idea of London begins to dissolve. His daily adventures marked on the *A–Z* would resemble the scrawlings of an irate toddler. I spent days retracing his paths through the city, along Brick Lane, down the Old Kent Road, through old Chelsea with my soles rubbing at pocked and whorled flagstones; to Camera Place, to Hans Crescent, to Kensington High Street and down the King's Road (Litvinoff: 'Apostrophise the King's would you please, between "g" and "s"'); through Notting Hill and Ladbroke Grove, from Fleet Street to Dalston, around Piccadilly and St James's; and time and again through Soho: Dean Street, Archer Street, Denman Street, D'Arblay Street, where white lamplight glistened on the wet pavement as snowflakes met their swirling shadows. In other hours, walking alone, I sloped down dark alleys and beneath black-brick railway arches that once formed East End tribal thresholds, leaving no footprint on the dry summer pavement, unnoticed when I slipped cross-current through a crowd, the rhythm of my footsteps inculcating the notion I was floating. Once I ran a fingertip down the cool roughness of an old wall and felt a moment's surprise that my hand didn't simply pass through, sensing then how the city makes ghosts of its inhabitants in life, if not in death. There were moments in pursuing Litvinoff when turning back seemed preferable – through concern that the man might not match up to the myth, though it turned out he always did, or because wisdom dictated I shouldn't chase the story any further down certain passages having glimpsed a shadowy figure waiting at the other end – but a creeping obsession took hold. I had to know everything possible. I explored more dead ends than I care to recall, launched countless letters and emails into the abyss, but over time the investigation developed a kind of fractal proliferation: most branches unfurled new shoots, corners turned into tighter corners, people passed me on to ever-more obscure contacts. I experienced the sensation too of wading through a vast breeding-ground for myths, as if London were an immense Petri dish in which cells of story self-replicated and mutated into contagious new forms. In his day Litvinoff carried as many as he could and spread them far and wide. Iain Sinclair titled his most substantial account of Litvinoff's legend 'Who Cares for the Caretaker?' Who tells the storyteller's story? This is the story of my attempt to do so.

* * *

Iain Sinclair's attempt to consolidate this ethereal figure forms a beguiling chapter in his and Rachel Lichtenstein's book *Rodinsky's Room*. The 'Chelsea chancer',[6] as he terms him, proves elusive: rumoured acquaintances clam up at the name's mention, trails run cold in the Carpenter's Arms but, via a mutual friend named Gerry Goldstein, Sinclair lays his hands on an audio tape of the man in full flow. Edited excerpts from the transcript weave through the first part of the book you're reading. It is September 1968 and Litvinoff is in conversation with John Ivor Golding, a Welsh derelict who has no idea he is being recorded, though 'conversation' sounds too mutual: Golding speaks more but Litvinoff is in control. It could more accurately be described as an imbalanced exchange of the former's plaintive rants and the latter's surrealist barbs (cueing Golding up, putting him down). It sounds like a rehearsal for a Harold Pinter dialogue that never reached the stage. Litvinoff guides Golding to expound his preoccupations: medieval philosophy, immigration, drink, the underrated aspects of Nazism. His provocations display an intellect as sharp as a cut-throat razor; Golding's retorts betray flaws in the wiring, synaptic misfires that would have perplexed Pavlov. Litvinoff's allusions come laced with surreal menace: apparent non sequiturs reveal a seed of weird logic under scrutiny. There is a grip on syntax that hints at the writer he might have been, or rather the spoken word artist he was. There are these 'strange twists and whips of language that you get in Pinter,' said Sinclair, 'the general sentences that have a twist of the arm at the end of them. But there's also an East End Jewish thing of being fast-witted. Psychological warfare.'

Golding relates his life in the past conditional tense, offering a narrative of 'could have been's sculpted by memories of aborted futures, one with which his interlocutor must, by 1968, have empathised more than he let on. But here Litvinoff inhabits what he terms 'the predatory tense', a phrase that would serve well as the play's title. He is merciless when the Welshman propounds his rehearsed discourse on race relations and in particular the relative merits of black and Jewish people ('The difference is the yid has intellect!'). If there's a single comment in the hour-long conversation that is Litvinoff encapsulated – a savage contempt for prejudice issued via vice-tight phrases laden with subtexts and sarcasm – it is this: 'I must say one thing about these sheenies, they do hold on to their money, don't they? The devil's work. Speaking as a good democrat, I must say that I do feel sometimes that they are emissaries of the devil.' Golding doesn't dismiss the idea. After I met Sinclair at his home in Hackney he was kind enough to share this tape and another of Litvinoff's furtive recordings, a conversation with an art dealer named Philip Laski. We watched *The Cardinal and the Corpse*, a short film that Sinclair made with Chris Petit for Channel 4 in 1992 ('Wouldn't get made now,' he murmured afterwards), in which an ensemble of bibliophiles peruse the mystery of 'David Litvinov', some pursuing a rumoured set of revelatory Litvinoff journals. He hooked on to Litvinoff as a figure who bore analogy with another of his obsessions, David Rodinsky. *Rodinsky's Room* describes his and Lichtenstein's efforts to dredge up the life of this eccentric autodidact, a linguist and cabbalist who lived above the synagogue at 19 Princelet Street until vanishing in 1969 apparently without trace, leaving a chamber that formed an undisturbed time-capsule – porridge on the stove, the impression of a head on the pillow – when unlocked in 1980.

'The great thing is they are unknowable,' said Sinclair in a soft Welsh lilt that grew almost incantatory as he mined deeper into the seam. 'They are these Jewish shape-shifting characters who live in a landscape which is itself unknowable and shape-shifting. There is a very strong sense of plural time, of being able to reach it and lose it.' There would be many instants when I felt that sensation. He likened Emanuel Litvinoff's *Journey Through a Small Planet*, an evocative, bittersweet recollection of growing up in Whitechapel, to 'a fictional novel of his own memoir' and argued that 'David, I think, did a similar thing, but it was verbal: he didn't write things down.' He placed David Litvinoff as a performer who prefigured the artists who now inhabit his old terrain. 'It's this performance artist tradition. Provocation, gambling, mystery, making his own life the work of art – so in a sense he anticipates Gilbert and George, who move into that territory later with the invasion of the culture classes into [Whitechapel], these guys who become the performers of their own life.' In fact nowadays 'the whole area is occupied by extremely wealthy millionaire artists who are trading on their personalities, like Tracey Emin living in Princelet Street,' he said, and Litvinoff is 'ahead of them, he's anticipating them – but it's much more high risk, because the kind of people he gets involved with treat him in a very vicious way: he's a kind of court jester who can be attacked. There's the gay underworld, the highlife-lowlife, and all those things make him a really significant figure in that era. The East End is this fashionable art and culture zone, and the taproots of that run right down into that time. It was discovered by people from the West End as a sort of off-limits sexual paradise, somewhere where you go off the radar into this other landscape of these particular drinking cultures and gambling cultures. You could go to a pub, the Old Horns or somewhere, and there's Judy Garland or Sonny Liston with the Krays, and it's all of a mix and it's like a strange dream where anything could happen in this night: it could end up in a murder in Stoke Newington, it could end up in an orgy in a block of flats, it could be Tom Driberg, it could be anybody. It's fantastic.

'Litvinoff is the person who tells the tales. A storyteller. People who knew him keep talking about the way he disappeared, which again is like Rodinsky. You'd know him, he'd be around, he'd be charming and over-the-top and then he'd disappear to somewhere.'

Litvinoff was too wary of becoming definable, of leaving a paper-trail, just as he'd told Nigel Waymouth. Not for him the constrained condition of Joseph Roth's archetypal twentieth-century stateless Jew, whose prospect of an at best restricted liberty lay in his treasured clutch of papers.* Among Litvinoff's multiple contradictions is that he was a salty, physical character whose potency pervaded any room he entered, yet he proved too ephemeral to leave a tangible mark on the world. Sinclair prefaced 'Who Cares for the Caretaker?' with a quotation from Paul Celan: 'no more than a breath between / there and not there'. Litvinoff's ghost stands on that cusp. To grasp at it is to delve into an assortment of long-vanished interdependent milieus – of West End *spielers*, Notting Hill slum landlords, dubious art dealers, Chelsea dinner parties, trad jazz bands playing bare-chested through the night in sweat-soaked Soho basements, macho gangsters who combed London's boxing gyms and nocturnal streets for sexual 'prospects' – all of which existed between the mid-1950s and early 1970s, thus resurrecting a figure whose story traces a twenty-year line of engagement between the realms of bohemia and criminality. 'Those worlds represent a very real fiction,' said Sinclair, 'a legendary mythology of place, and he's the one person amid it all who's not out to make his own

---

*   'The presence or absence of papers is a leitmotif throughout Roth's work. At the end of Gabriel Dan's westward return from his Siberian imprisonment, he encounters a hostile local police force and reaches unconsciously for his passport. He asks the constant question for all Central Europeans: "Do I have my passport? Do I exist without it?" The same is true of Joseph Kargan and Andreas Pum and even the pious Hebrew teacher Mendel Singer in *Job*. They cannot move without the appropriate documents. If legitimate papers are not immediately available, then someone must counterfeit them.' *Wandering Jew: the Search for Joseph Roth*, by Dennis Marks (Notting Hill Editions, 2011), pp. 64–5.

career as a writer or artist, but as a pre-conceptual artist, as a forerunner of the era of performance and conceptualism and personality. It's the prophecy come to pass, with Litvinoff out ahead of them.'

In his novel *White Chappell, Scarlet Tracings*, Sinclair investigates a Victorian surgeon named James Hinton who, in the words of a contemporary who introduced his collected letters, was not so much 'a man of science, but a philosopher. Science was to him the servant of philosophy. He felt himself to be an interpreter of nature; not in the Baconian sense by the collection and arrangement of facts, the sequences of causes and effects, but, like the Hebrew seer of old, penetrating through appearances to their central cause.'[7]

The comparison is reminiscent of an eerie brilliance attributed to Litvinoff by many of his friends. Juno Gemes, a multimedia artist and photographer whose generosity, wisdom and encouragement would prove fundamental to my completing this book, called him 'a kind of relentless seer' with 'the most profound and immediate understanding of human being'. A Hebrew seer of old, a performance artist ahead of his time. Litvinoff layered paradox upon contradiction. But amid the mythology of his story, for all the discord between his associates' perspectives, for all that his worlds invite speculation and the perpetuation of London fable, and allowing that the 'truth' is often political and warped by the fallibility of half-century-old memories, it became apparent that dogged investigation could reassemble his life. The place to begin was with those two pieces of paper that Nigel Waymouth mentioned over coffee in Holland Park: the places and dates of birth and death created two straight routes through space and time from which to make the first forays. The birth certificate is archived at the Tower Hamlets register office, the death certificate in Tonbridge, Kent. The former document states:

When and where born: Third February 1928, 54 Fuller Street
Name, if any: David
Sex: Boy
Name, and surname of father: Solomon LEVY
Name, surname and maiden name of mother: Rose LEVY late
    LITVINOFF formerly MICHAELSON
Occupation of father: Tailor (Journeyman)
Signature, description and residence of informant: S Levy, Father, 54
    Fuller Street, Bethnal Green E2.

Nothing is truly discrete; everything merges, everything connects. When the rising sun fires its first shafts flat across the city, the shadow of Christ Church Spitalfields' spire reaches for an instant from Commercial Street to Notting Hill. Litvinoff eschewed boundaries and discretion, becoming an analogue for the city itself, an embodiment of its grime and brilliance, its violent congestion and bursting fluidity, its urbanity and sordidness, its dazzling light and disturbing darkness. Consider this book an attempt to pin him in place so that he occupies at last his own space in pop culture's display case: or better yet, to draw this performer in from the shadowy wings, to stand for a moment in an ellipse of limelight at centre stage. Doing so took five years throughout which Colin MacCabe's warning in his book on *Performance* often haunted me: 'it is more than difficult to discover the real facts of his extraordinary life.'[8] But more often still those words felt akin to a business proposal from a pair of identical, stocky, sharp-suited men staring at you across a desk in a poky office in 1960s London just after one of them has locked the door: dangerous to accept, impossible to resist.

The Predatory Tense:
or, *We'll All Have Lunch,*
a Dadaist comedy in three acts,
by David Litvinoff

Scene: split between the Basil Street Hotel in Knightsbridge, the Pheasantry on the King's Road, and a red telephone box in Oxford Circus.

Characters:

DAVID LITVINOFF, a performer, provocateur, procurer, London operative.

JOHN IVOR GOLDING, an alcoholic vagrant seeking a home and a drink and an audience for his philosophies.

MARTIN SHARP, an Australian pop artist domiciled at the Pheasantry.

London, September 1968. The newspapers are full of the British government's quandary over the secessionist Nigerian state of Biafra. DAVID LITVINOFF and JOHN IVOR GOLDING are speaking on the telephone. LITVINOFF, his friend Gerry (aka Joey) Goldstein and GOLDING met at Victoria station the day before. GOLDING, a man of no fixed abode, sees LITVINOFF as his conduit to the stars, the one who could bring an overlooked street philosopher his due acclaim. What follows amounts to one of the strangest house-share interviews imaginable. GOLDING believes he is applying to live with LITVINOFF and Goldstein. His strident Welsh-accented voice registers hurt, melancholy, flashes of anger; he abandons syntax when he is impassioned, which is often. LITVINOFF's suggests an amphetamine-fuelled Laurence Olivier, a Radio 4 play broadcast with the tape running a little fast. The call connects and a few moments later, we join the conversation as LITVINOFF activates his tape recorder.

<u>Act One, Scene One:</u>

Spotlights up. We see two men holding telephone receivers.
Stage right, a scruffy, ruddy-faced man standing in a red
phone box. Stage left, a puckish, wiry character sitting
on a chair by a slowly whirring reel-to-reel tape player.

JOHN IVOR GOLDING: Why did you not answer my telephone
    calls, when I lost one and six last night?

**DAVID LITVINOFF: Well, John, I didn't know you were
    ringing.**

JIG: Oh yes, I rang you and an American, Tony, answered
    the phone and said he'd pass the message on to Mick.*
    A Tony from America answered the phone at 6.35pm last
    night. You know the number you gave me?

DL: I didn't get the message.

JIG: Well I did telephone—

**DL: I think you may consider yourself hired. And I'll
    fix you up with adequate references too.**

JIG: Oh good! Can I come round now?

**DL: Yes. But can you just tell me a couple of things
    about yourself on the telephone?**

JIG: Good gracious. Well, you know I'm from South Wales
    originally, and at the same time I have a good commer-
    cial background, Allied Control Commission at Nuremberg
    Trials, the Board of Trade and Ministry of Food.
    Bachelor, 44—

DL: What are your philosophical views?

JIG: They vary from A to Z. They are more comprehensive
    than Brigitte Bardot, Professor Barnard of South Africa,
    and I'm also prepared to be a James Joyce with *Pravda*
    at a thousand roubles a week where a misdemeanour took
    place with our own William James Joyce.

*   Litvinoff's friend Mick Jagger.

DL: Indeed. I have no problem with that. You're not a married man are you?

JIG: My God, I wish I was. . .that's my downfall, you see. My God. You'll see I'm very reserved and have a sense of proportion. A calibre of celibacy better than the Pope of Rome. You liked that articulation, didn't you?

DL: I adored it.

JIG: You enjoyed that better than your breakfast this morning?

DL: I had no breakfast this morning.

JIG: Very well. When I've given you a call, might you have something to eat? Let me cook it for you.

DL: What else has happened to you lately that's amusing?

JIG: Well, as I say, I am an ex-contributor to *Picture Post*. The Hulton Press.

DL: Oh yes, Edward Hulton.

JIG: That's quite correct.

DL: The Welsh are wonderful people. What do you think to Welsh policemen, though?

JIG: The point is this, I hold a demarcation line there, I hold a tremendous demarcation line—

DL: So do I . . . Good God. I have *got* to see you. And I want to know about your attitude towards the police, because I hate them.

JIG: Well, they're more iceberg to me than what is in the Antarctic which killed Captain Falcon Scott.

DL: It did indeed. It didn't do much good for Admiral Byrd* either.

---

*   American naval officer and aviator Rear Admiral Richard Byrd (1888–1957), whose claims to have made the first flights to the North and South Poles are generally considered dubious.

JIG: Well there you are. Now do you want me to have rum and breakfast with you?

DL: **Yes, but this is the point: I am flying at the moment to Stamford Hill by helicopter. I shall be back later on this afternoon. I'm going to address a meeting of Biafrans.**

JIG: Can I have a drink with Joey in the meantime? Which pub shall I meet him at?

DL: **Joey? I think the Chelsea Potter. But I think it would be much better if we met this evening. I can give you some money. . . But I must make absolutely certain that you're not a policeman.**

JIG: Ah, David, you've got my word for that. I hope you've tape-recorded every bit of this conversation on the phone.

DL: **Oh no, I'd never do that!**

Part One

Chapter 1

A Modest Unassuming Young Hebrew Boy

'What have I in common with Jews? I have hardly anything in common with myself. . .'
Franz Kafka, *The Diaries of Franz Kafka: 1910–23*, trans. Martin Greenberg and Hannah Arendt

In a book-lined flat in Mecklenburgh Square, east of Coram's Fields on the northern fringes of Bloomsbury, I sat looking into a ninety-five-year-old pair of eyes and thought of all they had seen. In 1951 they stared out towards T. S. Eliot as the mouth a few inches below nervously declaimed a poem decrying his anti-Semitism. During the Second World War they surveyed Italian POWs in Sierra Leone, in the 1930s they channelled hallucinatory visions that transported their owner's troubled mind to the nineteenth century, and in the 1920s they ingested the sights of Whitechapel, where Yiddish-speaking tailors hunched over rattling machines and Galician matriarchs dipped callused fingers in barrels of pickled herring. Now those eyes peered through thick spectacles, over my shoulder and across the room. 'Well, David was a dubious character,' said Emanuel Litvinoff, his half-brother. 'I mean his name was David Levy, he called himself David Litvinoff. The point about David was that he was totally ridiculous, only in the sense that he was inventing roles for himself that didn't have any reality.'

Why did he change his name from Levy, I wondered. Lodged in a rare space on a bookshelf was Manny's likeness in bronze hewn by a sculptor whose style owed something to Jacob Epstein; above his head was an oil-painted portrait showing him as a serious but faintly amused man of letters in late middle age; all over the shelves, atop and before volumes by Graham Greene, T. S. Eliot, Alexander Solzhenitsyn, tiny faces smiled from framed family photographs.

'Because it sounded more romantic,' he explained. 'To be David Levy was commonplace, to be David Litvinoff made him sound more interesting, you see.'

What age was he when he did that? 'He must have been about seventeen, something like that.'

Emanuel's fifty-eight-year-old wife, Mary McClory, called across the room from the kitchenette in a sharp Northern Irish brogue: 'Emanuel, was David caught up with the Krays?'

'Oh, he was very much involved with those people, he was fascinated by them and he used to associate with them quite a lot. So, he was involved in some way with the Krays, but I don't think he was involved in . . .you know, he was first of all too unsophisticated as far as they were concerned. They didn't need him.'

They did for a time, I would later learn, though not as much as he needed them. He savoured the cachet, the frisson of association. David Litvinoff broke into their realm with ease; there was no door in London he couldn't prise open by virtue of his wit or ability to procure what his mark most desired, though more often than not he would eventually find himself kicked out again. Perhaps it was a theory suggested by Emanuel's T. S. Eliot connection but I suspected at first that David's beginning might lie in his end. Emanuel mentioned a telephone call in April 1975 during which David asked him to come to Kent the coming weekend.

'I always remember he wanted me to come and visit him in the country, where he was, and I wasn't keen to go and visit him in the country anyway, but I did have good reasons for not accepting this invitation of his . . .and the next thing I knew, a younger member of the family had gone, and he had loaded all his property on to this particular person.'

'I remember when I met you,' Mary interjected, 'you used to tell me that with hindsight, you were sorry that you hadn't gone, because that very weekend he committed suicide.'

'I didn't particularly like going out to the country to visit,' continued Emanuel, 'and he would have given me all his property, which he did to whoever came, and then he committed suicide. David was an unfortunate character altogether.'

If there was any guilt, it arose from decency rather than culpability. It is the family's and friends' natural instinct in the wake of a suicide: could we have done more? But relations were strained beyond redemption by then. No one knew what to believe. Emanuel mentioned another conversation in which an agonised David spoke of his girlfriend being ill – 'and this girlfriend of his was a boy,' he said. 'I knew very well it couldn't be a girl. I had already picked up that David was gay.'

Emanuel wrote acclaimed novels, television plays, thoughtful yet steely reviews. His books rarely satisfied his political urges so he dedicated much of his time to editing his newsletter *Jews in Eastern Europe*, which exposed the USSR's anti-Semitic persecutions throughout the second half of the twentieth century, and helping Soviet Jews to flee the country. But his fiction and verse countered prejudice where they could. He wrote 'To T. S. Eliot' circa 1950 in dismay that, even as the ash lay across Eastern Europe like a faint grey snowfall, the eminent poet should have chosen to republish* early works such as 'Burbank with a Baedeker: Bleistein with a Cigar', which includes lines infected by the endemic casual anti-Semitism of the 1920s.

The rats are underneath the piles.
The Jew is underneath the lot.
Money in furs. The boatman smiles. . .

In 1951 Emanuel received an invitation to read two poems at the recently opened Institute of Contemporary Arts (ICA). The anarchist publisher and art critic Sir Herbert Read chaired the event; 'he had recently allowed himself to be knighted,' Emanuel wryly noted in a 1998 interview with the Museum of London. 'Now when I was called to read my poems, I had read the first one, which was absolutely innocuous, and I had just announced the title of the second one, "To T. S. Eliot", and Herbert Read said: "Oh good, Tom has just come in." Eliot apparently had arrived with an entourage and I felt dreadful about reading it, I felt very, very nervous and I thought to myself, "Well look, the poem is entitled to be read," and I read it with a trembling voice that gave it an extraordinary power.'[1]

Standing before a silent, crowded hall, he enunciated a brave and substantial riposte. 'I am not one accepted in your parish,' he stated. 'Bleistein is my relative and I share / the protozoic slime of Shylock, a page / in *Sturmer*, and, underneath the cities, / a billet somewhat lower than the rats.' In a final stanza he counselled Eliot to 'Let your words / tread lightly on this earth of Europe / lest my people's bones protest.'

As he sat down chaos broke out across the room. Emanuel reflected on the episode in the Museum of London interview: 'When I finished reading it Herbert Read said to me "If I had known that you were going to

---

* *Selected Poems*, by T. S. Eliot (Penguin, 1948).

3 1326 00528 2837

read such a poem I would never have allowed it," and I thought "Eh? And you're an anarchist?"

'Then hell broke loose and I remember particularly Stephen Spender getting up and saying: "As a poet as Jewish as Litvinoff, I'm outraged by this unwanted, undeserved attack on my friend T. S. Eliot."' But Litvinoff's friend Dannie Abse heard Eliot, his head resting on the back of the chair in front, mutter to his friends: 'It's a good poem, a very good poem.'[2]

David Litvinoff agreed. An insatiable reader, he also absorbed his esteemed older half-brother's other best-known work, *Journey Through a Small Planet*, and admired the writings of Emanuel's brother Barnet, whose histories and biography of David Ben-Gurion established him a similarly respected position in the ranks of Anglo-Jewish literature. This was the familial context, the line against which David's exponentially disparate trajectory might be measured by the mid-1970s. Barnet's son Miles Litvinoff remembered his father trying to maintain a meaningful connection with David towards the end, to no avail.

The September light flooding in from the window overlooking Mecklenburgh Square softened as the afternoon passed. Emanuel had the visage of an amiable retired hawk, spending most of the time perched on a wooden armchair; if he hadn't stayed in he might have spent it on his favourite bench in the square. Smoke-grey hair wisped at his temples. He was frail now, diminished, his smart jacket and trousers hanging baggy. His voice issued from the back of his throat and had that near-nasal note characteristic of the old Jewish East End, a warped mirroring of the plum-in-the-mouth at the other end of the social spectrum. He wheezed a laugh now and then, repeated himself as ninety-five-year-olds will, drifted out at times but still snapped back in acerbic tones – did he have a photograph of David, wondered Mary? 'I don't think I ever had a photograph of him, why the hell should I?'

'Well, you're his half-brother I guess. . .'

'Yes, but I didn't have photographs of my brothers necessarily.'

Mary remarked on the growing number of people who were inter-ested in him: Emanuel replied that 'he was an attractive character, David, but totally untrustworthy'. Did you see much of him as an adult? I asked. 'Did I see much of David? Well, first of all I didn't approve of him.' You didn't feel too drawn to go and see him? 'No, I wasn't enamoured of him. . . In any case he was only a half-brother, he was a child of my stepfather so I wasn't very close to him anyway.' Mary pointed out that he was close to other half-brothers such as Gerald Levy, known as Jack. Emanuel said Jack was a very different kind of character.

'There was always this sort of thing hanging over David,' Mary said. 'There's this shadow, a dark umbrella I would call it. Because we don't really know what he got up to, and I think some of whatever he was up to, Emanuel wasn't approving of.'

'Well, he was involved with the Krays, to some extent,' Emanuel repeated. I pressed him for detail: did he know what David actually did for them? A long pause. 'I think he enjoyed that kind of thing, and they were, you know, definitely not respectable. And as far as Dave was concerned, that was an asset.'

Maksim and Rose Litvinoff left Odessa when the pogroms and poverty grew intolerable. This wild and cosmopolitan port city perched over the Black Sea at the far fringes of the Russian Empire, spawning in its lawless atmosphere a Jewish gangland culture preserved in the terse, lugubrious stories of Isaac Babel and a vicious anti-Semitism that produced some of Imperial Russia's ghastliest pogroms, which is no small claim. When refugees' children prised open their traumatised parents' cache of recollections they acquired second-hand memories* of babies being torn apart by screaming mobs, women being raped and disembowelled, Jews of all ages being hurled from high windows, a mother tied by her feet to a ceiling and left dangling to look down at her six children's corpses arrayed on the floor. Between the spasms of bloodletting were stretches of grim deprivation. Joseph Roth evoked a sepulchral landscape in *The Wandering Jews*, his

---

* Or as the Columbia University academic Marianne Hirsch terms it in an essay on the post-Holocaust generation, 'postmemory': she writes that their parents' 'experiences were transmitted to them so deeply and affectively as to seem to constitute memories in their own right. Postmemory's connection to the past is thus not actually mediated by recall but by imaginative investment, projection, and creation. To grow up with such overwhelming inherited memories, to be dominated by narratives that preceded one's birth or one's consciousness, is to risk having one's own stories and experiences displaced, even evacuated, by those of a previous generation' ('The Generation of Postmemory', by Marianne Hirsch, in *Poetics Today*, vol. 29 no. 1, 2008, pp. 106–7). Imaginative projection and creation were David Litvinoff's forte. The risk of having his own stories displaced was not one he had any intention of allowing to materialise. In Ukraine Jewish gravestones became paving slabs: memory worn away by foot, erasure implanted into the towns' unthinking daily business. Jewish texts vanished in fires across Eastern Europe, as they had periodically since medieval times. Litvinoff intuited that the spoken word cannot be broken or burned.

missive from Eastern Europe during the last years of the Weimar Republic. With hindsight the twilit tone prefigures the dark night that would soon fall. 'I suspect that the Jewish proletarian is worse off than any other,' Roth concluded.

> I had my most depressing experience during a tour of the Jewish quarter of Odessa, known as the Moldovanka. The evening there is a curse, the rising moon a mockery. A thick fog presses down like a condemnation. Beggars are not merely the public face of the town, they are beggars three times over, because they are the residents. Every house comprises five, six or seven tiny stores. Every store doubles as an apartment. Behind each window, which also serves as a door, is the workshop; behind that is the bed. Over the bed are the children, suspended in bassinets, which misery rocks to and fro. . . All the workers labour until late at night. The windows leak a drab yellow light. A strange light that doesn't spread brightness but a kind of gloom with a pale kernel. Unrelated to any sacred flame. The soul of darkness . . .[3]

Like many, the Litvinoffs had designs on reaching America, and, like many, their steerage-class tickets took them no further than London, a halfway-house that became a home. Between 1881 and 1919 the Jewish population of England increased from around 60,000 to 250,000, swelled by the arrival of impoverished *ostjuden* who had to counter the disdain of both gentiles and the embarrassed ranks of established Anglo-Jewry. 'My mother and father left the Ukraine, Odessa, in early 1913 and stopped over in Brussels and they came over just before the war began. . .and they settled in East London,' Emanuel told an interviewer. 'My older brother was just born there too and then I was born about fifteen months later.

'My grandparents. . .on my mother's side had a rather interesting sort of history,' he digressed. 'When they were relatively young they lost one of their children. . .and they decided that it was because they had been sinful. So they gave everything they had away and they built themselves a. . .shelter open to the sky and they ceased to have marital relations and they used to see the souls of holy Jews being carried through the sky to Jerusalem. And apparently they became known in the district as holy people and even non-Jewish peasants would come to see them.'[4]

Every immigrant household in this seething, dilapidated patch of London imported its particular potent blend of family lore and horror stories.

The place felt discrete, unique within the city. To Emanuel's mind the Whitechapel of the 1920s and 1930s always had a quality of temporal and spatial dislocation. It was a place where 'people spoke of Warsaw, Kishinev, Kiev, Kharkov, Odessa as if they were neighbouring suburbs',[5] a square mile of great integrity whose residents felt a closer proximity to Eastern Europe than to west London. I asked him about his and his brothers' shared urge to escape the East End, and why he had found success despite a difficult childhood while David had not. To him the similarities were minimal.

'Yes, but it was quite different because I had talent, and David didn't have any talents. In other words he was playing roles, whereas I was genuinely writing things and publishing them and getting known as a young writer.'

David spoke admiringly of his big brothers Manny and Barney, recommending their books, proud of the connection. David looked up to Manny, Manny looked askance at David: he was a poseur, one who lacked the abilities to pursue a worthwhile calling and instead struck a series of postures, none of them resonant or plausible. It wasn't that Manny couldn't empathise to some degree: he understood mental fragility, having endured 'total depression' and 'some kind of a nervous breakdown'[6] in his down-and-out days during the desperate 1930s and burned an early novel through embarrassment. By the Brune Street Soup Kitchen for the Jewish Poor, whose ornate terracotta facade today adds allure to a set of £1 million flats, he once believed himself to have slipped into Victorian London, looking up to see the cars gone and horse-drawn carts in their place. 'In this condition,' wrote Patrick Wright, 'he saw Jewish immigrants arriving from Russia, and tenements melting away mysteriously, to be replaced by older cottages with little gardens. He remembers asking a man the date and, on being told it was 1890, going into a haberdashery shop and looking at children's exercise books for verification.'[7]

He worked hard to build a life for himself, though, and overcame his frailties. Knowing this, knowing how tenuous his existence was in those times and how strained the tether between his body and soul, it was moving to think of how that vulnerable youth had ultimately prospered, that someone who had barely escaped the Depression era should still be among us in the twenty-first century. Our interview drew to a close. Mary showed me a photocopy of a photograph, a double-refracted ersatz memory, depicting Emanuel around ninety years earlier, his silken hair and smooth oval face contrasting with the wizened and angular figure who sat beside me.

After an hour and a half in their company I emerged to find Mecklenburgh Square soaked in the ochre tones of an autumn evening. The clouds were lead and mauve and tinged with amber, the tree trunks bordering Coram's Fields gnarled like knuckles. I was warmed by the encounter but mingled with this was a colder sense of how hard it would be to piece together David Litvinoff's life. I suspected that if I were to achieve any kind of truthful conclusion, I had to go back to the very beginning, back to before the reinvention began, and with it the assumption of roles that had no reality.

By the 1970s the Spitalfields Great Synagogue had become a mosque serving the Bangladeshi community. Built in 1743–4 as a Huguenot Protestant chapel, it provides a much-cited physical metaphor for the evolution of East End immigrant life, one that is almost too neat, betraying our fondness for imposing three-act narratives on to a messy world, in this instance trying to impose order on the whole chaotic flux of London's most protean square mile. Despite all the changes in meaning held by this red-brick Georgian building, a melancholic continuity exists in the vertical sundial that has always traced the daylight's transit across its southern wall, bearing a Latin inscription from Horace. 'UMBRA SUMUS', it reminds all those who walk by. *We are but Shadows.* Today the Islamic call to prayer sings out from an illuminated ninety-foot minaret, the mournful melody recalling the song of the cantors that once echoed within the synagogue's cavernous interior. Muslim men in traditional dress, City workers on their lunch breaks and hipsters with ironic haircuts move past one another without appearing to engage, as if existing in distinct dimensions. Very rarely, one still sees a black-hatted Hasidic Jew drift by the former *shul*, a study in ghostly self-containment, his greying beard, black suit and white shirt lending him the look of a silent film character flickering through Technicolor Whitechapel. As the Jewish East End recedes from view the place's uncanny richness of atmosphere only intensifies. Mysticism presents a stronger than usual challenge here to the most ardent rationalist: one could be forgiven for feeling that places that have long been densely inhabited retain an electrical residue of so many humans' presence, some kind of charge lingering in the atomic mesh. The brickwork's palette emphasises the sense of decline and disappearance; even in rising spring the unpainted umber, tan and russet tones are redolent of autumn leaves.

Fuller Street ran north from Cheshire Street, which spears east from the top of Brick Lane. Thirty years before David Litvinoff's birth, Charles Booth had coloured the area dark blue on his Poverty Map of

London, denoting it as 'Very poor, casual. Chronic want', with dashes of black, the bottom of the scale: 'Lowest class. Vicious, semi-criminal.' To begin grounding Litvinoff in context I felt I should walk the length of Brick Lane, this spinal column of Spitalfields, exploring the ribs that protrude east and west as I ascended north. Princelet Street, where David Rodinsky sequestered himself in the synagogue's attic, and where in 1887 seventeen people were crushed to death fleeing a fire in a Yiddish theatre. Thrawl Street, by which ran the now-vanished Flower and Dean Street with its Rothschild Buildings and Nathaniel Dwellings tenements, until their demolition in the 1970s. Fournier Street, with its Huguenot silk weavers' houses, their architecture preserved and gentrified. For generations the gentile populace were pulled between a pair of mighty conducting rods placed there and 200 yards up the Lane: Christ Church Spitalfields tugged at the sacred in their souls, the Truman Brewery chimney at the profane. Buxton Street and Quaker Street, their names a remnant of the Society of Friends' historic association with what became a Jewish quarter. Here the connection felt personal. My mother is Jewish, my father a lapsed Quaker, and Quaker benefactors eased my maternal grandparents' entry into England from Vienna in 1939. Having been born a mile east from here at the Mile End Hospital, to me these streets come to embody my own history, even though I had never called Brick Lane home.

On my wanderings I carried a copy of Bill Fishman's book *The Streets of East London*. Aside from suggested walks and local history its pages contain affecting photographs of East End Jews crowded by shop doorways, queuing for the Brick Lane 'vapour baths', congregating before the Yiddish theatre, assembled in a cramped tailor's workshop to face the camera for a restless moment; all were taken when a photograph was an event, the attendant illusion of arresting time a novel phenomenon, just like pictures of the lost pre-war central Europe I've seen salvaged from drawers in the homes of deceased elderly relatives.* Unidentified exuberant figures on a family outing to the seaside, others in heroic pose against alpine scenery; all exude a strain of pathos unknown to humanity before

---

* Marianne Hirsch: 'Even for the familial second. . .generation, pictures are no more than spaces of projection, approximation and affiliation; they have retained no more than an *aura* of indexicality' (Hirsch, p. 122). The camera never lies, it just offers a selected half-truth. A decontextualised snapshot offers material for our fictions: old photographs of ourselves prompt wistful edited memories, and we conjure speculations from pictures of strangers.

Louis Daguerre offered his first images for public inspection in 1839. For an instant we think that the moment has been caught, then we remember that it is irretrievably gone, and in this glint of realisation teeters an ambivalent melancholy. Whose faces were these? Where had they been that day, what became of them? The scope of possibilities is infinite. Just trying to contemplate the extent of what one does not know is enough to induce a feeling akin to vertigo. So much appears to be lost. I feared that David Litvinoff would elude me as he had those who previously tried to pin down his story. I reminded myself, though, of the wondrous discovery my mother made when clearing my late grandmother's house in 2007: not just the expected trove of unfathomable photographs, but something more magical still. My grandfather, Josef Meller, had died in 1985, when I was seven and he was sixty-four. Such conception as I had of him was drawn from a few thin flashes of memory, some photographs and silent home movies, and a stern charcoal portrait sketched by the expressionist painter Ludwig Meidner when the two men were interned as enemy aliens on the Isle of Man. He remained present also through his absence: for years after he died my grandmother kept his beloved turntable and amplifier (German-made, always) in their living room, though covered by white drapes so they looked like cubist ghosts. My childhood was populated by elderly Jewish relatives whose minds had accommodated sadnesses beyond my comprehension; it was only later that I realised I had mingled with actors performing the closing scenes of a play whose opening act was tragedy, and whose subject was the possibility of recovery from unimaginable loss. David Litvinoff was of the same generation; viewed within the context of the Holocaust's aftermath, his desire to remain undocumented, to elude authority and have the freedom to disappear when necessary takes on a less mystical hue.

I became gradually aware of the long psychic undulations discernible through immigrant families' history, as generations drift away from and veer back towards the cultural lode. Often we see the same pattern: the newly arrived 'aliens' entrench within the enclave and cleave to the security of those who share their past, talking of the old country; the second generation tries to scrub off the ghetto and create a new world; to the second's bemusement the third generation feels a cultural estrangement that elicits an impulse towards the places and customs their parents laboured to leave behind. Rachel Lichtenstein chronicled her reclamation of her past in *Rodinsky's Room*, journeying from her grandparents' Whitechapel back to Eastern Europe in the process. As I grew conscious of a similar urge, I appreciated one of the many aspects of what had been lost with my grand-father's passing: the chance for me to ask him questions about his life and my ancestors' origins. Knowing he was from Vienna, I assumed that his family had lived there for generations, were respectable *mitteleuropean* Jews – I had nothing to suggest otherwise and no prospect of ever having my questions answered. Then my grandmother died suddenly and my mother excavated her childhood home; she found a document dedicated to my sister, my cousin and me.

'14th April 1982,' it began. 'BEFORE THE APOCALYPSE. An account of growing up in Central Europe in the twenties and thirties of the twentieth century for Keiron, Laura and Daniel, to give them some idea of the background of one quarter of their ancestry.'

Had this been a book or a movie, my good fortune would have seemed implausible, a *deus ex machina* act that would render any plot ridicu-lous. But here it was, here it all was: a narrative history interspersed with anecdotes and irreducible facts, the genealogy detailed back through three wide generations. My grandfather's Hebrew name was Ephraim Josef ben Menachem Mendel ben Mordechai, and back in the 1890s his parents Mendel and Liebe were born in Cieszanów in Poland and Mościska in the Ukraine, the same country as Rose and Maksim Litvinoff. Not high Viennese Jewry as I had arrogantly surmised in the absence of evidence to the contrary, not fastidious assimilated middle-class Austrians, but *ostjuden*, impoverished *yidden* from the Galician *shtetls*. Terror drove them to Vienna, my teenaged great-grandfather having survived a pogrom in which a pistol was held to his head while Cossacks ransacked the family shack in futile pursuit of the hoard of coins and jewels that surely every Jewish home contained somewhere. It taught me something about the poignant futility of snobbery among Jews and reminded me of how in anti-Semites' eyes all are equal, from the Rothschilds and Montefiores all the way down to David Litvinoff. It also showed me that the world could be beautiful even when it seems unremittingly sad, and that time can cough up remnants of the past that we thought were buried in unreachable depths.

Now modern apartments squat across the old tenements' footprints: affluent tenants ghost through the space once occupied by blackened bricks and greasy glass, across kitchens where mothers tended their bubbling broths and bawling infants, their pots pluming tendrils of steam that entwined with tobacco-smoke spectres twisting over from the dining table where bearded fathers sat up late chattering in Yiddish and smacking down dominoes. Air-conditioning has desiccated a viscous atmosphere once coarse with *schmaltz* and onion, with the scent of the drains, with the sweet meaty reek of childbirth hanging in the bedroom while next door the old widower sat *shiva* with his mirrors to the wall. The intensity of aspiration was visceral, the dreams palpable. Whether in the crowded flats or the jostling street market at Petticoat Lane, voices cut across voices in a bid for attention. Read of any given home, tailor's shop or cafe and one gains the impression of a dozen plays performed simultaneously on the same small stage, every actor speaking ever-louder in trying to make himself heard. Almost all are silent now, Emanuel Litvinoff among them. He died aged ninety-six in September 2011, a year after we met. One relative remembered him resenting the possibility that for all his good work he'd be remembered as 'David Litvinoff's brother'. The obituaries focused on the T. S. Eliot affair and *Jews in Eastern Europe*; David didn't get a mention.

What remains of the Jewish Brick Lane? Little aside from a beigel bake and Epra Fabrics, run by Leo Epstein. A. Elfes' monumental stonemasons recently vacated its premises at number 17 after half a century. A few glimpses persist despite the city's perpetual exchange, despite all the sediments that have settled and the layers scoured away. Chaim N. Katz's string and paper bag shop closed in the 1990s, and his name remains in peeling black capitals on a white-painted window arch. A dark Star of David glints when the sun catches the black-painted ironwork at the top of a drainpipe on the frontage of Christ Church School, and certain doorways to Bengali businesses retain a little *mezuzah*, containing a hidden scroll inscribed with the *shema* prayer: 'Hear, O Israel, the Lord our God, the Lord is One', it begins. All else proved transient, if not reversed. Time mirrors itself. Eighty years ago some residents obeyed the graffiti advising 'yids' to 'go back to Palestine'; now the charge is that their grandchildren should leave, the latest choreographic instruction for the long Jewish dance around the world. Where once impoverished mothers dressed their children in patched-up old hand-me-downs, today students advertise their awareness of a broader historical context than the present by wearing 'vintage clothing' from Whitechapel's numerous retro fashion stores.

One such outlet occupies an externally grimy old warehouse that sits opposite the Carpenter's Arms in the north-eastern corner of a small yard, an aborted deviation from the main thrust of Cheshire Street, an excrescence of grey space too short to be called a cul-de-sac. Hare Marsh.

There's nothing to see here but a glimpse of railway track and a wall decorated with teenage psychic effluvium (tags, cartoons, street philosophers' dicta), but to the initiated the street sign is a relic that summons wild vistas in the mind's eye: first of the bucolic landscape that has gradually yielded to roads and buildings and railway tracks since Georgian times,* then of the teeming locality that was known by this name. Turn back to Cheshire Street and look left: one can almost summon the image of Fuller Street Buildings,† a rackety assemblage of thin-walled flats where eighty people shared three outside toilets, and where in 1918 Rose Litvinoff took possession of two rooms in which to house herself, three sons and the fourth child she expected later that year. Like many 'alien' men in Whitechapel, her husband had been hauled back to Russia to help the Tsar's army fight the First World War; then the Russian Revolution sucked him into its vortex. As part of a gang that minted money and stole horses he headed for Archangel, a bastion of the anti-Bolshevik White Army, where they booked themselves on an early-morning boat to London. The ship set sail but Maksim Litvinoff was not on board. His companions stood on deck watching his diminishing figure arrive at the quayside and wave desperately in a bid to draw the vessel back to shore. Back in Whitechapel Rose received letters for a time, then they stopped arriving.

Solomon Levy was known as 'the Englishman' as he was born in England, a distinguishing characteristic among Jewish adults in early-twentieth-century Whitechapel. Emanuel described his stepfather's arrival into the family in *Journey Through a Small Planet*. Around eight years after Maksim went to fight for the Tsar, the family heard confirmation that he would never return. One of his friends, an Alec Roitman, came back to Fuller Street at last and held a homecoming party, at which he took Rose aside, placed an arm on her shoulder and, while friends bellowed raucous songs in the next room, told her gently of her husband's death. By then she already knew that her parents and siblings had been murdered by the Bolsheviks. In her late twenties she faced the prospect of raising four boys as a widow, supported only by what

---

*   See the excellent Great Wen blog for a summary of its disappearance: http://greatwen. com/2010/02/16/hare-marsh-and-rabbit-marsh-fact-and-fiction-in-bethnal-green/.
†   Nothing remains of Fuller Street Buildings nor even of Fuller Street, which ran from Cheshire Street through to Bacon Street. Standing in the way now is an imposing yellow-brick residential building called Fuller Close.

she earned as a seamstress and perhaps assistance from the Jewish Board of
Guardians. Her friends urged her to consider remarrying: a chubby, little,
bespectacled upholsterer named Berl Paisky was said to be *meshugge* for her.
Rose and her sons were introduced to him at Roitman's neighbouring flat in
Fuller Street Buildings. 'See, a wonderful family!' Roitman said to Paisky as
they entered the room where he sat. 'Four lion cubs, eh, Paisky? If you tried
for a hundred years could you make such boys?' This Paisky smiled and 'a
gold tooth twinkled in the ruined cavern of his mouth', Emanuel recalled.[8]
'*Nu, kinder?*' he said. So, children? He waved a glinting sixpence as an entice-
ment and asked the boys to give him a kiss. Abraham, Rose's eldest, leapt up
and grabbed it before puckering his lips and wincing for a moment. Young
Barnet hid in his mother's skirt. Emanuel demurred, hesitated at the offer of
a shilling, then braced himself when the payment rose to two shillings; but
an unknown man wearing Norfolk tweeds and gleaming oxblood brogues
interjected in an English accent: 'Half a crown if you don't kiss him.' Emanuel
took the money home, received a slap from his mother for accepting money
from strangers, then had to share it with his brothers.

The infatuated Paisky pursued Rose a while longer, turning up at
the house proffering gifts: sweet Russian halva, a box of face powder,
balloons for the boys. 'You shouldn't, Mr Paisky,' she'd say, meaning it. The
affair came to an unpleasant culmination. The scene was another party at
the Roitmans' next door, and as Rose's boys lay in their beds they could
hear their mother's urgent tones through the walls. 'Please, Mr Paisky! The
children are sleeping! Go away, Mr Paisky, please!'

Emanuel and Abraham burst through to find this flush-faced man
– gold-framed glasses askew, lank strands of hair slipping from his pate –
clutching their mother's arms and beseeching her: 'Rosa! Rosale! *Oy*,
Rosale!' The boys launched themselves at him, punching his fleshy backside and calling for help. Roitman arrived and yanked his friend away by
the collar, ripping the fabric. '*Schweig!*' he shouted – be quiet! – and Paisky
fell away, permitting Roitman to escort him from the room. Others drifted
from the scene, leaving only Rose, Abraham, Emanuel and the dapper
stranger again. 'It's all right, kids,' he told them. 'You go back to sleep.'
They returned to their room, leaving their mother with him, and soon after
they could no longer hear her crying.

He was distinct from most Jewish men in the East End, not only by
virtue of having been born there. Solly was of different stock: his mother was
from Amsterdam (one of nineteen children) and his father was English-born;

his paternal grandfather was a peasant from Bessarabia named Levi Gorabinski, who on arriving in London tried to explain his name to an uncomprehending immigration official and was registered with the surname Levy. Solly was one of nine children, spending part of his childhood in Blossom Street and later a tenement called Carmel House in Cheshire Street, then known as Hare Street. He signed up with the army in 1914, fought at Gallipoli in 1915, was mentioned in dispatches for his bravery at the Somme in 1916 and the following year, with shrapnel still embedded in his leg and gas damage in his lungs, joined the Royal Fusiliers' 38th Battalion, one of five that formed the Jewish Legion. With them he was posted to Palestine. After the war he managed a hotel in Johannesburg and prospected for diamonds on the veld. The man who entered the Litvinoff boys' world in the early 1920s had a verve that set him apart from the other men whom Emanuel saw around Whitechapel and Bethnal Green, the 'soft-bellied tailors stooped from working with the needle, slow-moving men who hewed at wood, workers in fur who sneezed and coughed through all the seasons'.[9] He'd stride down Cheshire Street twirling a Malacca cane, while hushed women turned their heads as he walked by. He was handsome, moustachioed, regal in bearing, and a self-declared freethinker, though as he spent more time around Rose he acquired her habit of ending sentences with 'please God': 'We'll go to the seaside sometime, please God!' He was two years younger than her and his friends thought him crazy to court an older widow with four sons, but he was smitten. He began spending more evenings at Fuller Street Buildings than elsewhere. One warm night after a walk with Rose, he slipped into the boys' room to find Emanuel and Abraham awake. He gave them each sixpence to call him 'Uncle Solly'. Not long afterwards, their mother announced that his relation to them had changed: 'Uncle Solly is your new father, *kindelech*.'[10]

They married on 12th February 1924. Together Rose and Solly would have five children whom Solly helped to raise, while contending with his stepsons' ambivalence at his uninvited entrance into their lives. Emanuel characterised him as a dashing but feckless gambler whose glamour faded a little every time he moped home from the racetrack bemoaning his misfortune. A quick detour on his return from work turned into a long night in which he lost a week's wages at a game of rummy. The atmosphere the next morning blended silence and fury. 'You won't even let me explain," he murmured to his wife. 'Ask him, somebody,' she said, 'can I pay the rent collector with explanations? Will explanations perhaps buy a piece of meat? What do I put on my children's feet – shoes or explanations?'[11] He held down his job as a tailor, which induced a slight stoop and a sag in his hitherto taut frame; but he dreamed of becoming a bookmaker, one who would earn his new family such wealth that they'd relocate to the promised land of Stamford Hill. The opportunity came with the death of a bookie named Rosenbloom who had a stand at Harringay greyhound track. Solly and his brother Hermy took over the pitch. When Solly departed for his first day in business, his moustache trimmed, chest puffed out again and clad in a wide-lapelled checked blazer, the children spent hours dreaming of bicycles and a bigger house, expectantly awaiting the return of a figure whose pockets sagged with coins. It was past 11pm when he and Hermy came home. Hushed mutters in the kitchen stirred the boys into eavesdropping. If a favourite hadn't let them down, Solly was whispering, 'we'd-a been laughing'. Instead they were £14 down and grimacing. It would develop into a pattern that caused growing consternation in the household. 'Money doesn't come from the sky,' Rose told him. 'Maybe you'll learn it at last.'[12]

By summer 1927 she was pregnant with her seventh child, Solly's third, whom they named David when he was born the following February. There was already a daughter, Sonya, and a son, Gerald, along with Pinchus, Barnet, Emanuel and Abraham, the eldest at fourteen years old: so none had yet left home, and the introduction of another wailing, hungry child into this fraught space was a mixed blessing. Easing the financial pressure was the fact that the baby's arrival came as the oldest boys began to bring home wages: Abie was earning a pound a week. At last, after fifteen years in Fuller Street, came the long-awaited move upwards. In 1930 they left for Mare Street, Hackney, where two more sons were born, Frank and Philip. The house was at the back of a tobacconist and sweet shop, and had a cement-floored kitchen. The rent was a pound a week. Solly worked long hours to provide for his family, all the while contending with his lung damage from the war. His children had a different perspective from the one conveyed in *Journey Through a Small Planet*. 'I didn't expect perfection from my dad because times were very hard in those days,' said Philip, who was known as Phil. 'He did the right thing by his family. He made sure that we were looked after. We didn't see a lot of him. He was always a tailor. And a very good tailor as well. As indeed I was! We were *schneiders*,* as Germans would say.' Solly worked for Hector Powe, a maker of quality garments with factories nationwide, and fought hard on behalf of his colleagues.

---

*   Yiddish for tailor, from the German, literally meaning 'cutter'.

Though Rose kept a kosher household and maintained Jewish traditions, visits to synagogue were rare. Solly preferred to read secular books rather than pore over the Talmud. A favourite was Anatole France's 1908 novel *Penguin Island*, a satirical socialist history of Europe in which a near-blind missionary monk finds himself washed up on an island populated by great auks which he mistakes for humans. France lampooned the Dreyfus Affair and the aristocracy in a way that would have appealed to any working-class socialist Jew such as Solly, who was an organiser for the National Union of Tailors and Garment Workers during the industrial strife of the 1930s. 'When they came out on strike for trade union recognition,' said Phil, 'I remember I used to take him sandwiches when he was on the picket line, and there were blacklegs coming to work in boarded-up taxis, with a policeman next to the driver. It was a different world. The strike was successful and he was the first shop steward there. He was telling me once, as soon as he was made shop steward, the boss invited him into the office and said: "Would you like a drink?" and he said: "No, I'll have a cup of tea if one's going," and the boss turned around to him and said: "Solly, tell me, are you going to take their money or mine?" And my father was disgusted. He was a man of principle. And he stood up and said: "Until you speak to me in a proper manner I have no wish to stay here." And he walked out.'

Solomon Levy.

The family moved house again in the mid-1930s, this time to 109 Sandringham Road, and David was selected for entry into the Hackney Central School on Cassland Road. The London County Council created 'central schools' in 1911 for bright children from families who could not afford school fees and who had not won a scholarship. The headmaster, a Mr Chew, said they 'were intended to put boys and girls on the road they could travel best',[13] guiding them towards vocations rather than success in examinations: shorthand, typing and bookkeeping featured in the curriculum. The young David certainly had the requisite intelligence but it was soon plain that he had little interest in their vision of his future. School's main appeal was as a way of attracting attention and making his friends laugh. 'He used to wear a cap with a peak,' said Phil, 'like schoolboys used to wear, and he refused to take it off on one occasion. And the teacher said: "Remove that cap straight away," so he lifted the peak, and written across the peak was "ON STRIKE". That's the sort of thing he used to do. It was worth a laugh at the time. But it used to get him into trouble, a lot.'

A school photograph of the young David Levy.

His parents were beginning to find him as difficult as his teachers. He couldn't keep still, never knew when to stop, had a tendency to walk around 'stark bollock naked' in Phil's words, and would do anything to prevent the risk of boredom setting in. Aged eleven, he was sitting by the fireside at Sandringham Road with Phil when he took a burning piece of wood, lifted it to his head and set his hair alight, to see what would happen. What happened was that their mother came rushing through with a pail of water which she poured over him. He embraced any excuse for a bit of danger or excitement, the more so if it brought a sense of defending his people. When fascism arrived in the East End many hitherto friendly non-Jewish neighbours turned malign overnight: adolescent boys with whom one had loitered in the street suddenly appeared in black uniforms and heavy boots, marching down the Roman Road yelling: 'We gotta get rid of the yids, the yids, we gotta get rid of the yids!' On one such occasion the baying crowd of demonstrators contained a young David hurling bricks at them.

Soon both his family and his school had an enforced break from trying to handle him. In September 1940 the authorities began evacuating inner cities and moving children to safer places, far from the German bombs that would soon litter the East End with craters and reduce buildings to rubble, among them the school on Cassland Road. Much later David told friends that he had never been happier than during the Blitz. In razing London's buildings the bombs also levelled its social hierarchy, if only for a while. He'd set out on solo excursions from Hackney over to Mayfair and Belgravia to investigate the ruins, and look on as elderly gents poked around the rubble of their historic homes, an antique barometer or oil painting visible here and there on a standing wall. Suddenly you could talk to anyone, he discovered; or rather, in these extraordinary circumstances, anyone would talk back to you, even if you were an impudent cockney Jew-boy with no apparent respect for the established order. The ever-present threat of death proved also a sexual liberation for many Londoners: Sylvia Scaffardi, founder of the National Council for Civil Liberties, recalled that 'Sex became an expression and proof of the vitality of life . . . When you are uncertain of whether you were going to die that day, what did the occasional fuck in a doorway with a stranger during black-out matter?'[14] The adolescent David revelled in the possibilities that the wartime city offered: and then he was swept off with Phil and Frank to a household miles away in Amersham, Buckinghamshire. This supposed refuge turned out to present its own dangers, as the parents were both paedophiles and began to abuse Phil and David. The boys soon left, though the experience must have left psychological scars.

'We ran away and it took us three days to get back to London,' said Phil. 'We had no food or anything and David looked after me as best he could.' They slept in fields, where they lay on their backs watching German bombers soar overhead towards London. When Phil complained of feeling cold, David removed several items of clothing and dug out his handkerchiefs, arranging them across his little brother as a makeshift blanket.

'When we finally got to the outskirts of London, around Harrow, he said: "We're going to find a police station and I'm going to try and get some support, but keep your mouth shut – I'll do the talking."

'So we went to this police station and spoke to this Jack Warner type,* and David said he gave them a cock and bull story: "We live in the East End and we took a bus, and then we took another bus, and then another bus, and we find we've spent all our money. We need to get home." So we had a lecture from this man but he gave us the fare to take us home. And when we got to Bishopsgate we had to change buses and David decided he wanted to go into the Geffrye Museum.† He stayed there for four or five hours on an empty stomach and he left me and Frank to carry on home on our own.

'Our parents weren't expecting us, we never told them why we'd run away, because in those days you just didn't [talk about sexual abuse]. So my mother gave me some hot soup, I remember, very painful to swallow, and then David turned up. My father was very angry – because of the Blitz they didn't want us in London at all, and we were both evacuated again immediately.'

This time their destination was very different. Habonim (meaning 'the builders'), a Socialist-Zionist youth movement, had set up three evacuation hostels in south Devon. The aim was to instil left-wing Zionist values and train children as the future leaders of *kibbutzim* or *moshavim*, this being eight years before the establishment of modern Israel. Asher (né Arthur) Tremberg was an East Ender in his early twenties who served as one of the mentors, living with his young charges twenty-four hours a day. On later moving to Israel he took the Hebrew surname Tarmon. As a ninety-two-year-old in 2012, living on a *moshav* called Kfar Vitkin near Natanya, he remembered David Levy all too well.

---

*   Jack Warner OBE, 1895–1981, the actor who played Dixon of Dock Green.
†   Opened by the London County Council in 1914 in the early eighteenth century as almshouses of the Ironmongers' Company, and turned into a furniture museum at the behest of members of the Arts and Crafts movement.

'He was one of the older inmates of the Dawlish Hostel and was in my group and I was his mentor (*madrich*),' wrote Tarmon. 'There is no doubt he was the brightest in intelligence, but very voluble, aggressive, self-confident to a high degree and hard to work with. He liked outshining others.'

Of the 150-odd children who stayed in the three hostels, Tony Landaw was there the longest, staying from 1940 to 1945. He remembered David as a boy who would regularly beat him at chess and who relished showing other children that he was brighter than them. The children learned folk dancing and gardening, studied Jewish history, performed dramas, sang Hebrew songs and played musical instruments, though to his annoyance David was barred from trying the violin. 'David was always in trouble there, he was always against authority,' said Phil. 'And he took the mickey out of everything. He was a rebel. That would be the description.'

He was seen as a disruptive influence and separated from Phil and Frank, which meant he 'had a miserable, miserable time; it wasn't very good,'[15] in Emanuel's words. They were there for a couple of years off and on. One photograph shows a camping party in the woods, with David lounging on the ground, staring at the camera; in another from 1941, the Levy boys sit in chairs in a garden with towels around their necks having their hair cut. Frank sits in the background laughing while a mentor named Wolf pretends to trim Phil's hair with a pair of shears. Asher holds a pair of clippers over David, who is puffing his cheeks, pulling out his ears and sticking out his tongue.

Haircut day at the Habonim hostel in Dawlish, Devon, 1941.

By the time they returned to London David was over fourteen so his schooling, such as it was, came to an end. He re-enrolled instead in the university of the East End streets, where the dons were master pickpockets and off-course bookies, graduating with what Nigel Waymouth would later describe as 'a PhD with honours in street savvy'. He'd roam the city meeting strangers, befriending them, seeking to understand them and himself, exploring his growing feelings for other boys, picking up stories and weaving them into his own fictionalised autobiography. Thirty years later he would lie on a sunlit lawn in Sydney, Australia, with a joint in one hand and a half-empty bottle of wine before him, and cast his mind back to his adolescent wanderings during a long *spiel* to camera given for an experimental documentary. The interviewer, a recently acquired friend named Albie Thoms, began to mention Walt Disney when David cut in: 'Walt Disney was an anti-Semitic fascist, did you know that? He employed 17,000 animators in the heyday of the late '30s and not one was a Jew.*. . . And that made *Snow White and the Seven Dwarves* for me – because I learned that fact at quite an early age – "Well all right then, I'll laugh at the fucking thing!". . . It's analogous to the kind of feeling I felt when I used to get a kick looking at the very fantastically beautiful, in obviously fascist parts of the East End, young boys and girls. I used to get very hot for them, all these fascist-looking boys with their uniforms and all that. A real Genet trip for me!† Well, eventually I satisfied the object of my curiosity because I got into two fascist guys and had a total trip with them. And it kind of made me understand my Jewishness all the more.'[16]

Those who reached maturity as the war ended began their adult lives by setting out into an austere world. The East End was as bleak as anywhere. Bomb sites, displaced pensioners, orphans, rationing, making-do, dereliction. The elements chafed at the broken cityscape: sun-glints on fractured windows, gales blowing through abandoned drawing rooms, rain softening brown rubble. Children scurried and hid in craters, buried shells blew them apart. David's older half-brothers were beginning to establish themselves: Emanuel had risen to the rank of major during the war and published his first poetry collection in 1942, Barnet emerged from three years as a POW to pursue his

---

*   Not a fact at all, though Disney was known to hold anti-Semitic views.

†   'With fanatical care, "jealous care", I prepared for my adventure as one arranges a couch or a room for love; I was *hot* for crime.' *The Thief's Journal*, by Jean Genet, trans. Bernard Frechtman (Penguin, 1967), p. 8.

calling as a historian. David tried to cultivate a profession too: he was taken on by a West End chartered accountancy firm but faltered when it became necessary for him to pay to gain qualifications, which his family could not afford. He considered pursuing religion, having evidently eschewed his father's atheism and scorn for antiquated ritual: Margaret Levy, Phil's ex-wife, remembered that her 'late father-in-law Solomon Levy told me that David was normal until he did not get the job that he desperately longed for [as] secretary to the local synagogue – who knows?' Maybe, though one suspects that by then Solly had little understanding of what was going on in his second son's head. He briefly had a job with a pen-making business, and spent a day cutting up animal skins in an East End furrier's, which he later proclaimed put him off work for life. He undertook some training as a journalist and, like Emanuel, began contributing to the *Jewish Standard*, a weekly newspaper that propounded the Revisionist Zionism conceived by the Odessa-born Vladimir Jabotinsky. This school of thought saw the fight for a Jewish state as analogous to the biblical revolts of the Maccabees, who battled the Greeks for independence. Britain's worst ever anti-Semitic rioting came in 1947, when David was nineteen, in the aftermath of the Irgun's killing of two British soldiers. To the *Standard* the Irgun and the Stern Gang were laudable modern warriors, Britain was the new Greece and moderate Zionists such as David Ben-Gurion were tantamount to Hellenised Jews, too ready to compromise and betray their people. During the summer of 1949 the *Jewish Standard* carried a couple of articles that are probably by the twenty-one-year-old David, neither of them overtly political. One is an enthusiastic review, bylined 'David Levy', of a play by Emanuel's friend Dannie Abse. The other is a sadder piece of work that purports to be reportage but seems to have been smoothed into a story, one written by an earnest young man who has plainly already come to see the world as a stage and 'being as playing a role',* however tenuous that role's relation to others' perception of reality. Its headline, 'Six Days to Sunday', smacks of a kitchen-sink drama but this effect is undone by the blunt sub-heading: 'Jew-baiting in Ridley Road'. The scene is, in the author's words,† 'a working-class market selling many varied commodities', which 'is open for business for

---

* To take Susan Sontag's well-known phrase from her 'Notes on Camp'.
† It is bylined only 'D. L.', but is almost certainly him owing to a combination of the date – 3rd June 1949, a few weeks before the Abse review – the lack of any other contributors with those initials at that time, the location near the family home in Sandringham Road and similarities to his tone and phrasing.

six days and is closed on Sunday, but [where] each Sunday a new type of salesman makes his appearance – a salesman of hate. His shop is the roof of a loudspeaker van – ironically draped with the Union Jack. His goods cost you nothing but your conscience. He hopes that his wares will be bought everywhere, when he will declare a dividend on his sales – a dividend of death.'

The reporter looked on as a warm spring Sunday soured into a 'vapid, close' evening, and the 'sky, previously blue and serene, seemed threatening and overcast. There was an end-of-day atmosphere. The cinema queues were crawling slowly into the theatres. The barrow-boys were shouting the praises of their wares in hoarse, desperate voices. The streets were emptying of people. From a nearby shop-basement came the sound of raucous dance-band music.'

He moved on, looking through windows with melancholic detachment, while inside 'the public houses people laughed, simulating gaiety. Outside, young factory girls with pretty painted faces lounged negligently. I sauntered past the half-deserted market square. Opposite the public lavatory a platform was erected. Men were standing round it muttering aggressively and excitedly. Nearby policemen stood bored and apathetic to what was going on.'

Here he saw a young demagogue in 'khaki battledress' standing on the platform with an aura of conquest, seemingly 'in a trance as he stood feet astride, hands on hips, jaw projected. Lips compressed. The Führer complex. Clipped, abrupt speech. In a hysterical falsetto, he shrieked of alien mongrels, Jew-bossed finance, Sydney Stanley,* Yids who seduced young Christian girls, others who foreclosed mortgages on workers' houses, and foreign, un-British Asiatic refugees.' He watched the spectacle until the meeting closed, whereupon the speaker and his aroused acolytes made their way towards a nearby pub; but they were distracted en route by 'a young zoot-suited Jewish lad [who] unwittingly encountered them at the corner of the alley'. As he retreated they recognised him as a Jew. 'A pug-ugly middle-aged man with an Irish brogue urged his comrades to "Do the little Yid-bastard." This cry was taken up by others in the bunch and they all formed a circle around the boy.' They yelled abuse as they closed in, jabbing and grasping at his jacket. A policeman finally wandered over only to find 'a battered, blood-stained youth, his clothing torn, moaning and sobbing like a child'.

---

* A Polish-born bankrupt Jewish businessman whose frauds, lack of ethics, likely role as a spy for the Irgun and attempted corruption of British politicians were seized upon by anti-Semites as confirmation of their prejudices.

Though it sounds foolhardy, as he too looked recognisably Jewish, what occurs next would be entirely characteristic given David's blend of bravado and appalled, sexualised fascination with these characters ('a real Genet trip', indeed). The report describes following the assailants into the 'hot steamy atmosphere of the pub' where, their bloodlust sated and energies spent, they were now

feeling deflated and moody. They shouted to the barmaid for speedier service. They talked thickly and gloomily of their return to work the next morning. 'Roll on next week-end,' said one. 'Blimey, Bert,' replied another, 'Six days to Sunday, you know.'

Outside in the empty market square, the light was growing dim. It was starting to rain. Unread and unwanted pamphlets were lying in the gutter. A shabbily-dressed old woman was half-heartedly poking through the market garbage for food. The rain brought the cold wind and the end of the one-act play.

As news of the Holocaust reached post-war London, many East End Jews living in this climate thought 'Never again'. The 43 Group largely comprised Jewish ex-servicemen who had returned from helping defeat fascism abroad to find it resurgent at home, and were determined to fight it wherever and however they could: breaking up hundreds of rallies such as the one described above, deploying gentile friends as infiltrators and spies, punching and coshing Mosleyites in the street. Financial support came from sources as diverse as the businessman Sir Charles Clore, comedian Bud Flanagan and Jack 'Spot' Comer, a notorious racketeer and slasher of rival thugs' faces, who liked to mythologise his violence as being honourably anti-fascist. He often described his influential part in the Battle of Cable Street but others noted, perhaps not to his face, that his tales of laying into the blackshirts on that fabled day back in 1936 didn't tally with reality: most of the fighting was between anti-fascists and the Metropolitan Police.

David used his oratorical skills to good effect as a 'left-wing rabble rouser', Phil recalled, addressing anti-fascist meetings during this time. The period forged his character. Writing of his experiences for a Jewish readership in the *Standard* offered no prospect of changing his enemies' thinking. Inhaling the East End's poisonous atmosphere day after day seems to have given his personality a tint of jaundice, shaping him into a man who was primed for violence: not only eager to fight back against anti-Semites or anyone else who threatened him, but to land the first punch. However unpalatable his adolescent strain of Zionism might seem to twenty-first-century liberal sensibilities, it was an extreme yet comprehensible response to a youth steeped in local hostility, his apprehension of a more decorous disapproval common among the middle and upper classes, the new horror stories reaching London from across the Channel and the old family tales of Odessa. George Orwell caught David's generation's position with typical acuity in 1945 when he wrote:

> In theory a Jew suffered from no legal disabilities, but in effect he was debarred from certain professions. He would probably not have been accepted as an officer in the navy, for instance, nor in what is called a 'smart' regiment in the army. A Jewish boy at a public school almost invariably had a bad time. He could, of course, live down his Jewishness if he was exceptionally charming or athletic, but it was an initial disability comparable to a stammer or a birthmark. Wealthy Jews tended to disguise themselves under aristocratic English or Scottish names, and to the average person it seemed quite natural that they should do this, just as it seems natural for a criminal to change his identity if possible. . .
>
> The working-class attitude was no better. The Jew who grew up in Whitechapel took it for granted that he would be assaulted, or at least hooted at, if he ventured into one of the Christian slums nearby, and the 'Jew joke' of the music halls and the comic papers was almost consistently ill-natured.[17]

Who can know the particular expressions of mid-twentieth-century English anti-Semitism David encountered or to which he grew accustomed? But we can imagine that from fascists' fists to schoolteachers' barbs the hostility would prove formative:* he would have been expected to reply with little

---

* Anthony Julius identifies a kind of Anglo-Jewish psychological relationship with anti-Semitism that I suspect Litvinoff experienced: 'To understand anti-Semitism is to understand yourself as a Jew, even as a human being. You become inward with it. . .you regard anti-Semitism as an important, perhaps the most important, question in your life. You *commit* yourself to studying it, and in the intervals when it does not actually pose any immediate threat to you, you address anti-Semitism in its historical and theoretical aspects. You work to refute its calumnies; your encounters with it will be high points in the psychodrama of your life. You take it seriously. In due course, anti-Semitism will contribute to defining the person that you are.' *Trials*

hesitation when pointedly asked his 'Christian name'; to swallow accumulated minuscule slights and reminders of his status as a suffered guest, to acknowledge 'Jew' as a synonym for 'miser', to become inured to the tag 'Christ-killer' as it was hurled across the street by gangs of London Irish boys; and even among some of his more genteel peers to show due gratitude for, as Betty Miller wrote in her 1941 novel *Farewell Leicester Square*, '[t]heir damned shallow self-satisfied *tolerance!*'[18] He would have developed an eye for that just-perceptible wrinkling of the English middle-class nose, become familiar with the grudging admission that Jews had suffered of late but they ought really to consider why their history contained such episodes, and with the suspicion that they answer to their own kind ahead of gentiles. Growing up he would have been advised to keep his head down, his voice subdued, his mannerisms refined; to fit in, to keep his Jewishness as discreet as his sexuality. He would fail on all counts quite gloriously. Nigel Waymouth remembered the delight he took years later in defying such prejudices: he'd bowl into the Picasso cafe on the King's Road and greet the gathered English public schoolboys with a cry of: 'Hello, I'm David Litvinoff – I'm Jewish and homosexual!'

The war's desolate aftermath brought grief as well as an embittering realisation of his social position. After thirty years' hard work keeping the family together, leaning over a sewing machine, worrying over money, scolding and protecting her children like a lioness, Rose Levy began experiencing severe pain. She was diagnosed with cancer. She died at the age of fifty-four a fortnight after David turned nineteen. He lived with her until the end. Soon after the family traipsed eastward out of the city to the marshes at Rainham, where her body was laid to rest in a rapidly expanding Jewish cemetery. Soon the widowed Solomon Levy would move to north London, while David's obligatory two years' National Service, spent as a clerical worker in the RAF, served to detach him further from east London. It also marked the first sign of a determination to live a life without trace.

'He told me something about his National Service,' said Julian Lloyd, who knew him later in Chelsea. 'He told me: "All I want, man, I just want to be anonymous. When I was discharged on my last day, I went back. I knew where the office was and I went back in and I got all my papers, all

---

of the Diaspora, by Anthony Julius (Oxford University Press, 2012), p. lii. Julius himself, however, noted in an email to me that he 'expressly reject[s] this particular path to Jewish self-understanding'.

my records, and I got them out and tore them up and threw them away so there would be no record of me.'"

After that he had neither a reason nor the inclination to settle back in the East End. Its rugged streets had already shaped him, their pungency and repartee infusing his character, and he would always return regularly to recharge on its illicit energies. In his 1991 book *Limehouse Days*, Daniel Farson discussed leaving Kensington for Narrow Street in the 1950s, noting that 'Though it is hard to credit today when the East End seems so familiar and accessible, then it was a foreign territory, as if I had passed an invisible frontier post at Tower Bridge.'[19] By the time of Farson's move David had long been pushing back and forth through this threshold at will, but from the late 1940s his focus veered west, drawn by the more salacious thrills that post-war Soho had to offer, thrills that obscured any sentimental tie to his home turf. Besides, one can imagine his intuition that for anyone of common *ostjuden* stock who occupied an East End 'billet somewhat lower than the rats', the idea of attachment towards one's birthplace was nuanced: by the inherited momentum of a kinetic history, by exposure to local fascism, by a deeper recognition of a location-based identity's susceptibility to the movement of borders that dragged back and forth like the tide across late-nineteenth to mid-twentieth-century Eastern Europe. One's only reliable home was one's head, one's surest identity was as a Jew and a human being. David refused to be defined by his context and hauled himself upwards and outwards by dint of a very deliberate self-reinvention. He'd listen to LPs of Laurence Olivier performing until he'd got the voice just so, modulating his cockney accent into something befitting a Chelsea dining room. He abandoned the common-place name Levy and, without asking them, pinched the distinctive surname of his older half-brothers; and this at a time when Jews were more likely to anglicise their names to avoid unwanted attention. While his oldest sibling, Abraham, began calling himself Alf Lister, he became David Litvinoff, a young man whose name and appearance could hardly be more Jewish but whose voice exuded upper-middle-class Englishness.

In 1951 Alf and his young family moved from Hackney to St Ann's Road in Tottenham and for a time Litvinoff stayed with them, using the house as a base from which to head down to Soho, where, courtesy of his younger brother Phil, he had discovered the joys of long nights dancing in tumultuous trad jazz clubs.

'He used to drive my parents potty,' said Alf's daughter Anne, 'getting home late from the West End and then singing very loudly. They put up with the noise but my mum drew the line when he was featured on the front page of the *Tottenham Herald*, along with our address, [after] he was found guilty of stealing £25 (probably about five weeks' salary at the time). My mum insisted that he found somewhere else to live.'

So he moved on, though he would often return. Alf, an accountant, was proud of having ascended to a relatively well-to-do (and largely gentile) area of Tottenham and once, after a calm and amicable visit, his younger daughter Gail watched her uncle depart via the front garden with a sudden yell: 'Do your neighbours know you're Jewish?' He took a flat at 21 Queensborough Terrace in Paddington but left for a houseboat moored at Chelsea Reach in 1953, which was when he met Timothy Whidborne, who'd just bought a house nearby at 122 Cheyne Walk, on the corner of Blantyre Street in the World's End, the 'wrong end' of Cheyne Walk at the time. Whidborne was a tall, elegant artist who had been a pupil of the modern realist painter Pietro Annigoni in Florence for three years and whose closest friend at Stowe School was George Melly. From his vantage point on the houseboat Litvinoff had spied Whidborne gradually equipping the empty house; one day this 'rather dishevelled young man met me at the front door', Whidborne recalled. Litvinoff had arranged for an Indian cook to make a large curry for a group of friends and wondered whether they could use the newly installed cooker if he paid for everything. 'There was something fascinating about him,' said Whidborne, 'and as the house was deserted, not much damage could be done so I said "All right" . . . We sat on the uncarpeted staircase with about fifteen guests eating curry.' The house began to attract a disparate cast of characters from around west London, some of them scuffling a living, others seeming to float without effort: the languorous Whidborne had his rooms and studio on the top floor; when in London, his mentor Annigoni would visit and work on his portrait of the Queen; Monty Sunshine, Chris Barber's clarinettist, was on the first floor; a couple of young women from Israel and Lebanon named Orna and Nadia lived on the ground floor; and an Old Etonian by the name of Andy Garnett shared the damp basement with a succession of flatmates until Melly moved in and became a permanent fixture, later joined by his fiancée, Vicky Vaughan. 'There was always a terrible racket going on in our flat with all my jazz set staying,' Melly wrote. 'Andy was wonderfully relaxed. Once he came in and there were mattresses everywhere. He pulled back the sheets and looked at the naked bodies. He turned to me and shouted, "What do these animals eat in the morning, George? Hay?" It was a bit like the 1920s, when after the First World War people reacted with short skirts and the Charleston. This was only ten years after the Second World War.'[20] Melly had left his job as assistant at the London Gallery, run by the English surrealist Roland Penrose and the Belgian Dadaist E. L. T. Mesens,* in order to sing with Mick Mulligan's Magnolia Jazz Band, which meant that he was often away on tour. Garnett was rarely alone, however, for as he recalled in his book *Memories of a Lucky Dog*, 'David Litvinoff had squeezed himself into the house in capacity as rent collector and factotum and he brought an astonishing variety of people, some nice, some tedious, some fun, some tiresome and some villainous.'[21]

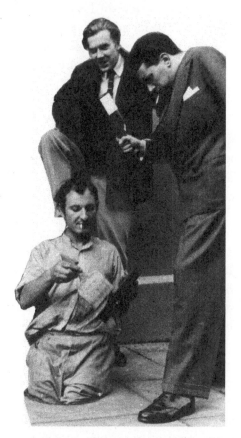

Litvinoff, Timothy Whidborne and George Melly outside the house in Cheyne Walk.

*   Melly saw Litvinoff as 'more a Dadaist than a surrealist', a creator of situations who had 'terrific chutzpah', and grew 'very much to appreciate his lunacy', as he said when the actor Patrick Kennedy interviewed him.

Among those who began to frequent the house was a talented young portraitist whom Whidborne had met a few months earlier. He was in a King's Road art gallery when he overheard a self-assured eighteen-year-old making disparaging comments about the works on show. They fell into conversation and this cocksure character said he was an artist himself, had won the gold medal for art at Westminster School and, like Whidborne, had studied under Annigoni in Florence. After a while he mentioned that he'd fallen for a beautiful girl but couldn't take her back to his parents' house nearby. Whidborne invited the two of them to share a room with him and his girlfriend at their large rented studio in the Italian Village on Fulham Road: so Donald Cammell moved into Whidborne's circle, and now at Cheyne Walk grew friendly with Melly, Garnett and particularly Litvinoff, with whom he had already hung around as a schoolboy in Soho. Cammell took a studio in nearby Flood Street, where Augustus John, the archetypal bohemian Chelsea painter, had founded a short-lived art school fifty years earlier; owing to Cammell's charisma it became a locus for the most beautiful and well-connected young people in Chelsea, among them his wife, the actress Maria Andipa, whom he left when she bore him a son, and Antony Armstrong-Jones. Whidborne and Litvinoff were passing a cinema one chilly day in 1953 when they found Cammell's sixteen-year-old brother David, who had just emerged from seeing Dr Seuss's film *The Five Thousand Fingers of Dr T.* and was now standing outside without a jacket on. 'Aren't you cold?' Litvinoff asked him. David Cammell agreed that he was rather, and the next day Litvinoff appeared unannounced at the parental home with a gift: a beautiful blue paisley-patterned coat, which the younger Cammell wore with pride. Five years later, at the end of a party he picked it up and prepared to leave, whereupon another guest eyed it with admiration and said: 'You know, I used to have a coat just like that but it went missing.'

Another regular at Cheyne Walk was Philip Laski, son of the judge and Anglo-Jewish figurehead Neville Laski, nephew to the socialist thinker Harold Laski and brother of the novelist and critic Marghanita Laski. He and Litvinoff had a certain amount in common: both were gay Jewish men with a roguish streak who were growing estranged from their more respectable older relatives. Indeed Laski's distant cousin Anthony Blond, the publisher and author, recalled in his autobiography *Jew Made in England* that he 'even dressed like a black sheep: a walking stick, a fancy waistcoat, a buttonhole, and a velvet collar covered with dandruff. He was full of deceit and extraordinary tales, having married a Bourbon princess in

Barcelona Cathedral during the war, and astonishing connections, like ringing up Laurence Olivier from my office. He was a fixer. The family tried to have him certified just after the war, but he seduced the psychiatrist with petrol coupons for his Rolls-Royce.'[22]

Laski became a distinctive and familiar sight around Chelsea and Soho, mincing around in a cape and pursing his 'small wet mouth' as Litvinoff's friend Christopher Gibbs put it, adding that 'the boys in the pinball arcade called him Princess Wetlips'. He was an early example of the eccentric specimens with whom Litvinoff would surround himself, simultaneously amused by and mocking them. 'Philip Laski used to visit from time to time,' said Whidborne, 'and he and David made a point of the difference between Spanish Jews – Sephardic, like Laski – and Russian ones, Ashkenazi like David, Laski claiming his sort superior or grander* which opinion David would rubbish.'

While Litvinoff proved the kind of sidekick Whidborne needed as landlord of this unruly household – in his memoir *Slowing Down* Melly wrote that he 'came down [to the basement] very strictly to get the rent, part of the gas bill etc.'[23] – his own finances were chaotic. Andy Garnett had a girlfriend named Helen Peaker until she ended the relationship in a letter complaining about his and Litvinoff's callous behaviour, in which she mentioned in passing 'David has had a lot of writs lately concerning his bills in various places'.[24] Over the next two decades Whidborne would prove to be one of Litvinoff's few enduring stable influences: patient, long-suffering, indulgent, usually ready to bail him out when he was broke. He remembered him with a wearied but amused affection: there was the time Litvinoff dyed all his shirts pink in the bathtub and then climbed in and dyed himself pink too; the time they went to a restaurant and he ordered his dinner in reverse, beginning with a syrup pudding; the times when he disappeared leaving Whidborne to clear up his chaos. Another young artist who began visiting the house at this time would prove a more tempestuous presence in Litvinoff's life.

---

*   An attitude satirised by the Whitechapel-raised author Israel Zangwill in his novella *The King of Schnorrers*, in which he has the Sephardi beggar Manasseh da Costa loftily inform the Ashkenazi businessman Joseph Grobstock: 'Ours have been the poets and scholars in Israel. You cannot expect that we should recognise your rabble. . .We made the name of Jew honourable; you degrade it. You are as the mixed multitude which came up with our forefathers out of Egypt.' *The King of Schnorrers*, by Israel Zangwill (William Heinemann, 1931), p. 13.

Act One, Scene Two. The next day.

JIG: I was down there and I waited a whole hour, I thought Gerry would have turned up.

DL: Didn't he turn up?

JIG: Nooo. . .

DL: Monstrous.

JIG: Well, there you are, and that's what made me lose confidence for the rest of the day you see. I would have liked to have come to your Biafra meeting.

DL: Oh God, yes. It would have been wonderful, we had wine and cheese and jambalaya.

JIG: Where was that?

DL: It was in a hall in north London.

JIG: What time did it start?

DL: It started at about five o'clock and went on 'til about eight. We had that Colonel Ojukwu there.

JIG: And then from eight o'clock I could have come back with you, couldn't I?

DL: Yes, and there was lovely Biafran wine, which is very powerful stuff.

JIG: Good gracious. Well, look, can I spend the rest of the day with you?

DL: Yes, starting this evening. I'll take you out to eat and we'll give you some. . .loot. Bread. Gazooma. Lolly. Spondulicks. Money.

JIG: Yes, yes. Shall I come along right away?

DL: No, dear, because I've got to go and have lunch with my wife, and it's one of those awful chores.

JIG: What do you suggest then?

DL: I suggest I meet you later. But I must say I've been ruminating on some of the things you said yesterday, they're very profound. Beautifully articulated.

JIG: Whereabouts, David, do you want to meet me?

DL: I suppose we could meet at a restaurant and then come on to my place. Have you been in touch with Mick Jagger or not?

JIG: Well, only what I told you yesterday. But have you spoken to him about me?

DL: Yes I have, I saw him yesterday.

JIG: What did he say? What did he think of me?

DL: He thought it was absolutely a heaven-sent opportunity, you know, because he hasn't really met many people, and lives a rather quiet, withdrawn life. And every fresh face brings a ray of hope, you know.

JIG: Now whereabouts shall I meet you?

DL: Before the end of the conversation I'll make a definite arrangement with you for a couple of hours' time. Then we'll go to have something to eat and go to the cinema. How about that?

JIG: Very good indeed.

Chapter 2

Mirrors and Mergers

'I cannot tell whether I should call him a foolish wise man or a wise foolish man, for undoubtedly he beside his learning had a great wit, but it was so mingled with taunting and mocking that it seemed to them that best knew him, that he thought nothing to be well spoken except he had ministered some mock in the communication.'
Sir Thomas More (1478–1535), described by his contemporary Edward Hall

In 1954 Lucian Freud walked into Esmeralda's Barn, a smart nightclub in Knightsbridge, for the first time to hear a barman asking a customer: 'Is that on your bill, Mr Freud?'

'When I got to the bar,' Freud later recalled, 'I said, "Excuse me, who was that just buying a drink?" and the barman said, "Oh, that's Mr Lucian Freud."'[1]

Litvinoff and Freud's facial features shared a common angularity, though Freud's were arranged into a cruel beauty whereas Litvinoff's had an indefinable strangeness ('a face either beautiful or ugly, I could never decide which', as Melly put it).[2] The similarity was sufficient to enable Litvinoff to pass himself off as the artist in the clubs and bars of Soho and Chelsea, charging drinks to Freud's accounts. 'It turned out he'd been me for quite a while,' Freud said many years later.[3] Now he had been caught in the act, but Freud's response demonstrated typical caprice: while he had an urge to hit Litvinoff, he had a stronger one to paint him. He invited Litvinoff to sit at his studio in Paddington for what the art critic William Feaver called a 'proxy self-portrait', inspired by Freud's own observations about its genesis. His subject was, he wrote, 'possibly the most revolting person that I had ever seen in my life. Repulsive. So then I took some trouble – though none was needed – to get to know this horrible man. And that was David Litvinov [*sic*]. I thought, well, I can do a self-portrait without all the bother of looking in the mirror.'[4] It was as if by scrutinising the twenty-six-year-old Litvinoff's already battered physiognomy Freud saw his own face in a fairground mirror; and as if in doing so, whether or not he'd admit it, he saw certain of his own qualities reflected back at him. 'There was something of David in Lucian, and something of Lucian in David,' confirmed their mutual friend Michael Caborn-Waterfield, aka Dandy Kim. Like Litvinoff, Caborn-Waterfield operated on the cusp between art and criminality; the pair conspired with George Melly to steal Annigoni's 1954–5 portrait of the Queen from the studio at 122 Cheyne Walk and demand a ransom from its commissioners, the Worshipful Company of Fishmongers, but Melly had second thoughts and the chance vanished when it was taken away for varnishing.

By then Freud was ascending fast through London's art world. This *enfant terrible* had graduated from Cedric Morris' East Anglian School of Painting and Drawing with a reputation as a meticulous draughtsman whose invigorating personality combined an intense focus with a propensity for wild behaviour. Rumours abounded about the fire that destroyed the college and of how he'd earlier been expelled from Bryanston School in Dorset. This grandson of Sigmund Freud had arrived in England aged ten after his family fled Berlin in 1933, an exile precipitated by Nazi persecution. Even during his infanthood in Germany his pathological detachment had been apparent. Freud's first word to his mother was '*allein*', a request that she leave him alone. While he was witty, charismatic and knowledgeable on topics from art history to boxing, that single-minded streak remained apparent for another eight decades, until his death in 2011 at the age of eighty-eight. As a youth he seemed to revel in creating a disturbing frisson; his love of animals inspired his habit of carrying a small hawk with him as he travelled on the Underground. In the mid-1940s he fell for his first love, Lorna Wishart. She had previously been living with Laurie Lee, who wrote on losing her to Freud that: 'This mad, unpleasant youth appeals to a sort of craving she has for corruption.'[5]

When his path crossed with Litvinoff's, he was thirty-one, recently divorced from Sir Jacob Epstein's daughter Kitty Garman, the subject of his first great paintings, and newly married to Timothy Whidborne's cousin Lady Caroline Blackwood, hence his visits to 122 Cheyne Walk. He was living and working at 20 Delamere Terrace in Paddington, the cheap and shabby area of west London he'd called home for a decade: like Litvinoff he needed the vital within his grasp, to feel himself close to sources of danger and sensation. In the critic John Russell's evocative description, the post-war Paddington into which Freud immersed himself was 'a neigh-bourhood worthy of an up-dated *Lower Depths*. The law was not so much disobeyed as disregarded. People came and went without regular hours or avowable occupations. Identities were changed like number-plates. As a background, there were the great run-down porticoed terraces, the dank and silent canal, the bizarre, overbearing, unvisited Victorian parish churches, and the blank spaces rubbed out at random by German bombers.'[6]

Both men had a self-absorption that could border on selfishness, and both were incorrigible scrutinisers of the human animal, by turns enthralled and appalled by the congregation of bodies that swam around them in the midst of the dirty crowded capital. 'My idea of travel is downward travel really,' Freud once said. 'Getting to know where you are better and exploring feelings that you know more deeply.'[7] Depth of knowledge was everything. From displaying an almost chilling precision in depicting the weave of basketwork in an early pencil drawing, in his maturity he developed a profound ability to convey insights into a sitter's personality, to penetrate through appearances to the central cause, displaying a clinical scrutiny that invites too-easy comparisons with his famous grandfather. Freud would later become well known for the number and duration of sittings he required of his subjects, and by 1954 that exacting streak was already in place: he paid Litvinoff to sit for him around thirty times during the course of the year, which seems especially excessive for a painting measuring only $12^3/_4$ inches by $8^3/_4$ inches until you learn that the original work was substantially bigger and then trimmed to form a tight enclosure around Litvinoff's sullen face. The portrait lies within the pivotal phase in his development. In the late 1940s and early 1950s his style was smooth and precise yet stylised: subjects such as Charlie Lumley and Kitty Garman were rendered with oversized almond eyes, the artist deploying a Flemish-toned palette; then he exchanged small soft sable brushes for coarser ones of hog's hair, which later he would load with mixtures rich in the Cremnitz White paint that imbued his nudes with the cadaverous tone that became his hallmark. Here in 1954 he is beginning to loosen up and blend fine observation with more expressive brushstrokes.

When Christie's sold the painting in 1999 to a private buyer for £1,156,500 the catalogue notes spoke of its 'medieval quality', how with his 'weather-beaten head...wrapped in a coarse scarf' the subject 'could easily be a character out of a Breughel [*sic*] snow-scene'. (The headscarf had practical as well as artistic value, Freud explained: 'I put a blanket over his head because he had horrible grease from the kitchen in his hair, which really stank.'[8]) The effect, the notes averred, is to 'capture the verisimilitude of the human face and the personality within' to a degree that achieves an 'almost unreal intimacy': and they added to the unreality by ushering Litvinoff further into obscurity. So well does Freud seem to know his subject's face 'that the painting has even been thought to be a self-portrait rather than the face of a forgotten figure that Freud had perhaps encountered in a London Soho drinking den'.[9] Forgotten? Freud remembered Litvinoff all too well. A year before he died I contacted him via his daughter Esther Freud, whom I had previously met; the message came back that Lucian most certainly did not want to discuss him. The more I learned of their relationship the less I was surprised.

During the year he painted Litvinoff, the Slade School of Fine Art employed Freud as a visiting tutor, though his own work remained his focus: and his evolving attitude towards it became explicit in the midst of the painting's creation when he wrote an 800-word article for *Encounter*, the literary magazine founded the previous year by his friend Stephen Spender. 'My object in painting pictures is to try and move the senses by giving an intensification of reality,' he wrote.*

> Whether this can be achieved depends on how intensely the painter understands and feels for the person or object of his choice. Because of this, painting is the only art in which the intuitive qualities of the artist may be more valuable to him than actual knowledge or intelligence...
>
> The aura given out by a person or object is as much part of them as their flesh. The effect that they make in space is as bound up with them as might be their colour or smell. The effect in space of two different human individuals can be as different as the effect of a candle and an electric light bulb.
>
> Therefore the painter must be as concerned with the air surrounding his subject as with that subject itself. It is through observation and perception of atmosphere that he can register the feeling that he wishes his painting to give out.[10]†

---

*   As Sir John Richardson noted in conversation with Freud in 2009, his paintings at this time were 'more real than the real thing' and Freud thus fulfilled the original intention of 'sur-realism' as defined by the poet Guillaume Apollinaire, rather than the 'surrealist' dreamlike explorations of the unconscious initiated by Max Breton, who removed the hyphen and shifted the movement's direction. Ref: http://www.bridgemanimages.com/en-GB/search?filter_text=DDS780468 & filter_group=all.

†   Marina Warner on Freud in 1988: 'He has written almost nothing about his art, and now

The portrait was one of the first he produced standing up, a development that freed him to paint with a new dynamism: we can imagine him looming over Litvinoff, twists of black lustrous hair surrounding Freud's lean cheekbones and sharp nose, now stooping to scrutinise some detail of Litvinoff's face from two inches' distance, now leaning back to transfix his model with a macabre bulge of the eyeballs, the better to pin him in space and to canvas. Freud's distaste for the air surrounding Litvinoff radiated from the paint. It took another four years before the picture reached the market, at which point it became apparent that the artist had abandoned its working title: *Portrait of a Jew*.

The inhabitants of 122 Cheyne Walk oscillated between Chelsea and Soho, growing known for their wildness in both locales. Parties at home would see Melly leave the room for a moment and return naked, posing with flexed biceps like an old-fashioned weightlifter and declaiming in a deep voice: 'I'm a man!' before disappearing again only to prance back in, genitals tucked between his legs, and squeaking: 'I'm a woman, a lovely, lovely woman!' Finally he'd crawl along the floor emitting loud barks and growls – 'I'm a bulldog! Woof!' – with his testicles protruding like a dog's, a sight that a few years later would shock even Lenny Bruce at a party held during his residency at the Establishment Club. Litvinoff more than matched Melly in energy and disregard for respectable mores. While walking down the street he'd hook a foot and arm around a lamp post and swing himself round and round while hollering at the top of his voice: 'I'm just a crazy mixed-up yid!' but a more outrageous display came in 1955 at the ICA at 17–18 Dover Street, where Emanuel had confronted T. S. Eliot four years earlier. Melly had been invited to give a lecture on 'Erotic Imagery in the Blues', a rich subject in which he might have cited Bessie Smith's 'Need a Little Sugar in my Bowl' ('I need a little hotdog *between* my roll'), Joe Williams' 'I Want It Awful Bad' ('Look pretty mama what you done done, you squeezed my lemon, caused my juice to run') or anything by Bo Carter, best known for his 1931 side 'Banana in Your Fruitbasket'. Feeling anxious at the prospect of addressing a learned audience and chairmen in the form of the jazz critics Charles Fox and Vic Bellerby, Melly had prepared diligently and

---

abjures a statement he made in *Encounter* in 1954, that the "intensification of reality" at which he aims depends on how intensely the painter understands and feels for the person or object of his choice.' It felt true when he wrote it, false later. From http://www.nytimes.com/1988/12/04/ magazine/lucian-freud-the-unblinking-eye.html?src=pm&pagewanted=3.

structured the talk under headings such as 'The Machine as a Sexual Image' and 'Animal Symbolism in Erotic Blues', each of which he would illustrate by playing records. Three-quarters of the audience consisted of the ICA's regular attendees – 'self-righteous in their socks and sandals', [11] as Garnett put it – and the remainder were a boisterous crew of Melly's friends for, in a unfortunate piece of scheduling, the event coincided with his stag do. His marriage was to take place the next day in Scotland. As he took to the stage Mick Mulligan handed him what appeared to be a glass of water, which he downed in one. It contained four shots of gin. After he'd been introduced, Melly began preparing to speak when Litvinoff raised his hand, stood up and politely asked for clarification on an important matter: 'Is it permitted for the audience to wank during the recital?' Most people turned to glower or looked away in silent embarrassment, the rest howled with laughter. Melly launched into his lecture but Mulligan kept passing him gins: soon he was singing merrily along with his records, and before long he was incoherent and barely able to stand. The ICA, Melly declared, was the 'Institute of Contemporary Arseholes', and when a trad jazz clarinettist named Ian Christie took issue with a Bessie Smith song Melly offered to throw him down the stairs. The gathering descended from rowdiness into chaos, with the stag party knocking over chairs and grabbing Dubuffet sculptures from display shelves. Litvinoff manhandled the chairmen from the stage, stripped naked and belted out his adaptation of the blues standard 'You've Been a Good Old Wagon': 'Looka here, Daddy, I want to tell you, please get out of my sight. / I'm playin' quits now, right from this very night. / You've had your day, don't sit around and frown. / You've been a good old chairman, Daddy, but you done broke down.' Later they carried the incapacitated Melly out of the building and loaded him into Garnett's van for the journey to King's Cross station. On the platform Mulligan's band played a dirge as Garnett hauled Melly aboard the sleeper train to Edinburgh, gave the porter a hefty tip to look after him and installed him in his bunk for the long journey north.

Despite their diverse backgrounds – Melly, the Jewish Liverpudlian who'd attended Stowe School; Garnett, the Old Etonian who rebelled against his terrifying mother and sought out the company of bohemians and villains; Litvinoff, the reinvented cockney – all were equally at home in Soho. This area made a virtue of its cosmopolitan population and formed a base for revivalists of the music they all revered: the jazz and blues recorded in the American Deep South twenty to thirty years earlier. Soho had long been the city's acknowledged wild zone, a place where the only recognised crime was to be dull. Eccentrics and mavericks congregated in search of kindred spirits, many of them artists, writers or musicians, some finding that rubbing against other abrasive personalities sparked their creativity, some hoping that their work might be illuminated by association with more famous friends, many resenting said friends' success, many realising too late that they'd spent their critical moments railing and boozing and pissing their talent away in the French House or the Colony Room. The reputation was enshrined by the 1940s, when Julian Maclaren-Ross, dandy habitué of the northern bloc known as Fitzrovia, recorded an exchange with Meary James Tambimuttu. 'Tambi' was the editor of *Poetry London* and the man who in 1943 would help bring Lucian Freud's work into view by commissioning him to illustrate a poetry collection.*

'Only beware of Fitzrovia,' Tambi said. . . 'It's a dangerous place, you must be careful.'

'Fights with knives?'

'No, a worse danger. You might get Sohoitis you know.'

'No I don't. What is it?'

'If you get Sohoitis,' Tambi said very seriously, 'you will stay there always day and night and get no work done ever. You have been warned.'[12]

By the mid-1950s cases of Sohoitis languished in pubs and bars from Regent Street to Charing Cross Road. Iron Foot Jack[†] was a classic specimen, a sturdy elderly man who wore a homburg hat over his mane of grey hair, a black cape over a black shirt, a cerise satin cravat around his neck and a tall iron shoe filling the gap between his right leg and the Soho pavement. His disinclination to wash meant he had plenty of room even in crowded, smoky cafes such as the French, where he would hold court as the self-styled King of the Bohemians and foist handwritten screeds of memoir and poetry upon those he managed to ensnare. Litvinoff and Garnett found him an amusing curio and befriended him. Jack wrote Garnett a letter from his home at 28 Blantyre Street (he was by now another Sohoite cross-pollinating with Chelsea) in which he relates the impossibility of subsisting in the old ways. He could no longer sell clutter 'as every market I go I have to pay for a stall and 5/- to stand you don't know how happy I am to say goodbye to this noncence [*sic*]'. He could no longer 'get a living out of fortune telling as I did in the old days as the

---

*   *The Glass Tower* by Nicholas Moore.

†   Born Jack Neave or Neaves in Sydney, Australia, *c.*1886 but brought up in London.

coppers will not let me stand eneware'. He'd modelled for artists – Tim Whidborne painted a full-length portrait – given numerology forecasts for sixpence, slept in the workhouse, prison and the Royal Hotel. But he'd just been to Petticoat Lane to flog copies of his pamphlet 'The Drama of Life' with encouraging results, and had confidence that 'this little game. . .will get me money for food and fags for the rest of my life'. Beleaguered, defiant characters such as Jack helped maintain Soho's reputation as London's most idiosyncratic quarter. Local traders decided to capitalise on this by launching a week-long summer fair, both to draw in tourists and give the resident bohemians a chance to flaunt their vibrancy in the midst of the austere 1950s. The first Soho Fair was held from 10th to 16th July 1955, and anyone wandering that week through the grimy grid of streets – their strange kinks tracing the boundaries of medieval fields bought one at a time by seventeenth-century property speculators – might have seen a Caribbean band playing Latin American rhythms, flamenco dancers, a roaming accordionist, an ornate Dutch street organ filling Golden Square with music, carnival floats adorned with shimmying, scantily clad cabaret girls, or a lone woman sitting in Shaftesbury Avenue working at a spinning wheel. 'We've tried to cater for all tastes,' said Gaston Berlemont, the impressively moustachioed landlord of the York Minster (later renamed the French House) and instigator of the fair. 'Some people like poetry, just as some like elephant's foot steak. Personally I like neither.'[13]

Pathé News set out from its office in Wardour Street to document the festivities, titling the resulting two-minute film *Soho Goes Gay*. 'All the world lives in Soho,'* declared the plummy narrator over footage of crowds milling down Dean Street, 'even including some English, so when it decides to hold a fair, it's a fair – and no messing!' Cut to Iron Foot Jack standing outside a cafe in conversation with a younger man, then to the waiters' race, in which dozens of white-jacketed, black-bow-tied men dash through Soho Square, each balancing a tray bearing a bottle of champagne and a glass. Litvinoff had various jobs as a waiter – he and his friend Hilary Gerrard supposedly once set up a short-lived 'fish restaurant' in which one took orders at the tables and relayed them to the other, who would nip out the back and buy the meal from a nearby chip shop† – but there is no sign of him here. . . and then there he is: the film flicks to the fair's carnival parade, and a white

---

* 'So-*ho*' in his mid-twentieth-century pronunciation, a since-vanished relict of the word's origin as a cry yelled by the huntsmen who pursued hares and foxes there hundreds of years ago.
† A story also attributed to Iron Foot Jack, another magnet for mythology.

Messerschmitt bubble car rolls by with Andy Garnett sitting hunched inside, the exterior decorated by Tim Whidborne with geometric patterns and the legend 'CHELSEA MEATCUTTERS' on the bonnet, and Litvinoff sitting on the boot wearing a bearskin hat, military tunic and skimpy black shorts, clicking his fingers to the music and turning to glance at the camera. A man dances alongside waving a placard that reads '3rd Prize – Soho Fair'. Two seconds on screen, then he's gone, though a photographer caught him a couple of times that day. In one picture Iron Foot Jack is in a wheelchair, smiling as Litvinoff, Whidborne and friends connect it by tow-rope to the back of the bubble car; in the other Litvinoff is leading a marching jazz band down Bloomsbury Street where it passes Bedford Avenue, clutching a drum major's baton, his shoulders back, chin jutting under the weight of his busby, bare striding legs cutting a crisp V-shaped shadow on the sunlit road, while behind him a column of trumpeters and trombonists fires a barrage of blue notes at his back and over his shoulders into the warm London air.

Litvinoff leading the band at the 1955 Soho Fair.

* * *

The same summer provided a reminder that Maclaren-Ross's wariness about 'fights with knives' was not misplaced. August 1955 saw the tensions within London's underworld burst into public view in an incident on Frith Street. The city's criminal realm was in the control of two different men, Billy Hill and Jack 'Spot' Comer, so-called either because of the mole on his cheek or (his version) because whenever there was trouble he was always on the spot. Comer was born Jacob Comacho in 1912 in Fieldgate Mansions on the Jewish side of Whitechapel's Myrdle Street, and by the age of seven had himself a gang of fellow 'Jew-boys' whose chief rivalry was with the Catholic lads from the Irish side of the road. By the time Litvinoff was growing up everyone in the East End knew of 'Spotty', not least for his anti-fascist activities but also for his control of the lucrative illegal off-course betting business, and for allegedly being behind a £1.25 million robbery at London Airport (now Heathrow) in July 1948 that was intercepted by the Flying Squad, which left Spot a free man but several of his henchmen with long prison sentences. From the mid-1940s Spot and Hill had worked in tandem to siphon off the immense profits to be made across the West End demi-monde, from drinking clubs, brothels and the shabby gaming rooms known as *spielers*, all the while taking 'protection' money from businesses across the city. Hill was in prison during the airport heist but by 1952 he was free again and resurgent, while Spot's power was in decline, his position fatally weakened by the decline of the off-course betting industry and the younger Hill's determination to usurp him at the apex of London criminality. In 1955 Hill published an autobiography titled *Boss of Britain's Underworld*, which described his career and his working methods. He often 'striped' his victims with a blade or 'chiv', cutting them down the cheek – always downwards, never upwards or across, he explained in his book: 'So that if the knife slips you don't cut an artery. After all, chivving is chivving, but cutting an artery is usually murder. Only mugs do murder.'[14] Spot was similarly handy with a knife and adept with his fists too. He once described his preference for punching men as they stood at a pub's urinals: 'Bump, down he goes, into the piss.'[15]

One of Hill's trusted men was Albert Dimes, or 'Italian Al', a bookmaker who had sought to take over Spot's lucrative betting pitches at Epsom racecourse a few days earlier. Dimes was walking down Frith Street when Spot set upon him with a blade as a revenge attack against Hill's mob for trying to put him out of business. Dimes ran into a nearby greengrocer's but Spot followed him inside, stabbing him again and shouting, 'You want to be a tearaway? How do you like this?'; Dimes won the knife from him and fought back, inflicting serious wounds on Spot too. The greengrocer, Hyman Hyams, and his formidable wife Sophie looked on aghast at the carnage unfolding in their shop: then Mrs Hyams brought it to a sudden halt by setting about the two men with a pair of metal scale pans. Both fled and ended up in hospital, where their lives were thought to be in danger, but they survived to be taken to trial. At the Old Bailey Spot was described as a turf accountant of Hyde Park Mansions, Marylebone, whereas Dimes was a commission agent of River Street, Finsbury. Both men faced charges of wounding with intent to cause grievous bodily harm, possession in a public place of an offensive weapon, and fighting and making an affray. Both were found not guilty, for which feat Spot hailed his barrister, Rose Heilbron, as 'the greatest lawyer in history'. It was an incident conducted in broad daylight in busy Soho in which two men stabbed each other and yet somehow neither was guilty: the press soon dubbed it 'The Battle that Never Was', and in retrospect it is seen as the pivotal moment between two criminal eras.

While Spot walked free, his time had passed. In 1956 he received a beating from a team of Hill's men led by an up-and-coming south Londoner known as 'Mad' Frankie Fraser, in the course of which it was suggested that the forty-four-year-old should consider taking early retirement. He did so and lived out his remaining forty years an impotent and subdued figure. Hill remained a feared criminal but one who divided his time between a flat in Bayswater and Spain, from where he continued to exert a powerful influence within the underworld. Back in London there was a vacuum to be filled. A pair of twin brothers from Bethnal Green were now casting their eyes over the relatively open criminal field that lay before them, and began their careers in earnest. Every punch they landed and face they sliced represented a small step in the bloody business of terrorising their way to the top.

Spot and Hill knew the Kray twins already. Reggie Kray would later write that Hill was his criminal role model: 'When I was in my early twenties, the man I wanted to emulate most of all was the former gang boss of London's underworld, Billy Hill. The prime reason for my admiration was, that apart from Billy being very physical and violent when necessary, he had a good, quick-thinking brain and this trait appealed to me most of all.'[16]

For Jack Spot they had less admiration. In 1955 Ronnie and Reggie Kray agreed to protect him at the Epsom spring race meeting, another occasion when he was being threatened by Italian rival bookmakers.

'It wasn't that we liked him,' said Reggie. 'We despised him really. We just turned out with Spotty to show everyone that we was the up-and-coming firm and didn't give a fuck for anyone. Old Spotty understood. Whatever else he may have been he wasn't stupid. He knew quite well that though we were there in theory as his friends, we meant to end up taking over from him.'[17]

The twins were five years younger than Litvinoff, and began their move west across the city around five years after him. In 1956 they took on their first involvement in a West End business, a Cambridge Circus drinking club called the Stragglers owned by their friend Billie Jones, a docker. It was a good club but had lately been plagued by fighting, which left Jones concerned for its reputation: he needed some feared characters on the door to restore order. Taking on the job expanded the Krays' criminal scope, revealing the possibilities that London offered. It also created a substantial overlap between their world and that of David Litvinoff.

Litvinoff and Garnett embarked on various 'tinpot adventures', the most successful of which – not financially but in terms of their desire to give London a good shake-up – involved holding a drink-soaked party for their friends among the 'Chelsea Set', the cohort of wealthy young upper-class bon vivants (languid bohemians to some, spoilt layabouts to others) who whiled away their days sipping crème de menthe in pubs such as the Markham Arms. That in itself was not unusual but the location was. Other than on 4th October 1936, when it went down in history as the site of London's best-known battle between the Metropolitan Police and anti-fascist demonstrators, Cable Street had always been a tough, bleak, largely overlooked strip running from the southern fringe of the East End towards the Isle of Dogs. Back then it was one of the city's few reliable sources of cannabis, which Litvinoff would buy from West African merchant seamen. Litvinoff 'introduced me to the world of Cable Street and gave me the self-confidence to hang around that rather menacing part of London', Garnett recalled. One one occasion they ended up in an all-night club called Al Capone's on the adjoining Swedenborg Square, whose formerly splendid early-eighteenth-century buildings had once housed wintering

Swedish mariners but were now perilously dilapidated and only a few years from the wrecking ball. The last time they visited Cable Street they found the owner, Mrs Bah, in the Magpie and Stump pub, bemoaning that she was in rent arrears as her husband had been sent to prison. The club was on the first floor of one of the old houses, accessible from a courtyard via a steep iron staircase. Garnett and his friend Peter Prowse took it on with the aim of creating the most exciting venue in town for 'a clientele of Africans, West Indians and inhabitants of faraway places like Kensington and Chelsea'.[18] The first step was to redecorate, so they brought in a friend named Angel, who normally painted the faces of the Soho working girls in Archer Street but was now commissioned to paint the walls of Al Capone's. Within a fortnight the two rooms were covered with images such as a voluptuous woman with bats flying out from between her legs, and a blue sky with a cloud bearing a black baby and a signpost reading 'Heaven Five Miles Up'. Entertainment would be provided by Ransford Boi and his Exotic Highlife Rhythm, a troupe of oiled, muscular, bare-chested West African hand-drummers, nourishment in the form of an infamously hot fish curry concocted by a Caribbean cook named Carey, and guests would bring their own drink. Keeping order on the door would be the imposing figure of 'Boxer Gold', who had black ringlets and a Star of David tattooed across his chest; he formed part of a tradition of east London Jewish boxers who often began as street scrappers responding to anti-Semitic jibes, many of whom had trained at the Judean Soul and Athletic (Temperance) Club elsewhere in the square.

The grand opening night was to be on 12th May 1956. Invitations were sent to 150 people, among them Lady Arabella Stuart, Sally Spencer-Churchill, a great-niece of Sir Winston Churchill, and the young Lord Montagu, not long out of jail after a twelve-month imprisonment for 'homosexual offences', an affair that came to symbolise the oppressive atmosphere in which gay and lesbian people then existed. In this paranoid Cold War climate the Conservative Home Secretary, Sir David Maxwell Fyfe, promised to 'rid England of this plague' of 'male vice' and told his colleague Robert (later Lord) Boothby that 'I am not going down in history as the man who made sodomy legal', to Boothby's disappointment.[19] Alan Turing was hounded to apparent suicide in 1954, John Gielgud devastated and humiliated after his 1953 arrest for cottaging in a Chelsea public toilet. In such circumstances life for gay men necessarily involved a degree of performance, whether by struggling to suppress their desires or by reacting with defiance and accentuating their sexuality. In Litvinoff's case, his quickfire transformations between queeny aesthete and street-hustling procurer blended with his Jewish heritage to provide an unusually broad repertoire of preordained roles to adopt – the pitiable *schlemiel*, the mendicant *schnorrer*, the intimidating *shtarker*, the performing *badchen* – and then to discard as necessary, the better to elude definition.

When the night came Litvinoff stepped aside. He'd opened the door for his friend but didn't need to follow him through, and probably 'had other fish to fry', said Garnett. At first it seemed no one else would bother to make the trek east across the city, and then they all arrived. The rooms seemed to grow ever smaller and hotter as dozens of young aristocrats poured in, along with black kids from local immigrant families, all jiving and drinking until the rooms were 'crammed tight with a mixture of people from every sort of background, and the music, shouting and noise [became] a frantic crazy kaleidoscope'.[20] Garnett heard banging from below and thought the floor was giving way, then realised it was the residents downstairs. He and Gold scurried down the iron steps and through the door to see drips splashing into a washing-up bowl and an angry man yelling at them: 'I'm telling you, there's urine coming through the ceiling.' Garnett took a sip from the bowl. 'That's not urine, that's whisky,' he informed them, and headed back upstairs. There was Vere Harmsworth, later Viscount Rothermere and owner of the *Daily Mail*, opening a wine bottle by smashing its neck against a railing; a robed African man was whirling a pretty debutante around in an exuberant dance while her forlorn partner from Kensington looked on; and somewhere in the mêlée Sally Spencer-Churchill's handbag containing £850 worth of jewellery was being stolen. When the rooms finally emptied in the early hours, the detritus told its own story: broken cups, broken bottles, odd shoes littered around and a discarded pair of knickers. Garnett handed Mrs Bah a cash-filled envelope and informed her that his tenancy of Al Capone's was over.

The next day's newspapers were full of it. 'AN ORGY' AS MAYFAIR NECKS IN DOCKLAND, blared the *Sunday Pictorial*. DEBUTANTES AMONG THE DUST BINS, said the *Evening Standard*. An East End Labour MP was promising to ask questions in the Commons: 'What Action By The Police?' asked the indignant subheading.

All in all it had been quite a success. Disparate elements of London had been dropped into a test tube with explosive results, respectable folk were outraged and the press had picked up on it, which would have amused Litvinoff no end. At this time he began to revive his journalistic connections, switching from the *Jewish Standard* to something more mainstream in the form of various newspapers around the lower end of Fleet Street. Many among his Chelsea friends were dabbling with the press in some form. Melly wrote a satirical cartoon in the *Daily Mail* titled 'Flook'; Garnett adopted a feminine guise and became 'Prue Dent', gossip columnist for the *Fulham Gazette*, interviewing characters from Iron Foot Jack to Allen Ginsberg when he was in town making a recording of 'Howl'; and Litvinoff inveigled himself into contributing to the *Daily Express*'s William Hickey diary column, while also supplementing his living by selling stories to other papers. Diarists such as Ray Nunn could be relied upon for a lavish lunch on expenses, and the titbits that Litvinoff and company fed them helped concoct the fiction of the Chelsea Set, which Garnett fingers as a 'creation of these desperate gossip columnists' that 'grew and grew, and even people in Chelsea began to believe in it'. The columns' trademark breathless witter and chatter conveyed a world of debutantes' presentations through the London Season, theatrical openings, engagements between members of the upper classes, and revelations about which colour hat the deb of the moment had worn to a garden party at the weekend: a realm far removed from that of most of the newspapers' readers, but one with which Litvinoff had grown intimate (though in the model and socialite Suna Portman's words, 'He seemed to know all of us rather better than we knew him'). His Chelsea connections meant that he could file a steady stream of such hard-hitting reportage, but his friendships with artists and writers there and in Soho gave him a more interesting source of stories. The playwright Bernard Kops was a friend of Emanuel Litvinoff and thus acquainted with David.

'David was on the make, but we all were on the make so I can't vilify him for that,' Kops said. In 1956 he was a young writer living with his wife Erica and their baby son Adam, scraping a living by running a bookstall in Cambridge Circus. His prospects were looking up though. His first play, *The Hamlet of Stepney Green*, was gaining attention and one day the telephone rang: it was the Arts Council informing him of a £500 award so he could concentrate on his writing. He and Erica met to celebrate at Cafe Torino on the corner of Old Compton Street and Dean Street, where their buoyancy jarred with the more jaded bohemians' air of bitterness: as Kops arrived he waved the cheque at her through the window, which attracted baleful glances from within. 'Be careful,' said Erica as he joined her at a table in the corner. 'Our good news is another nail in their coffin.'

Then Litvinoff appeared and made a beeline for them. What were they looking so happy about? he wondered, and was overjoyed by the explanation. He jotted down notes while Erica continued to chide Bernard, saying: 'People don't want to know your good news, it's only human.'

'I want to know your good news,' Litvinoff said. 'I want to do a story. Don't you want to be in the newspapers? Lovely photo: both of you and Adam.'

'Yes,' said Bernard. 'Please, yes.'

'No,' said Erica. 'Please, no.'[21]

But the two men talked her into consenting. 'Great!' said Litvinoff. 'I can just see the story all over page two. Impoverished Jewish genius discovered in Soho. Runs pathetic bookstall in Cambridge Circus and suddenly writes a masterpiece.'

'No,' said Erica. 'If you print that, I'm walking out right now.'

Soon afterwards their photograph was on the front page of the *News Chronicle*, a left-leaning paper that in 1960 would 'merge' with, or rather be swallowed without trace by, the *Daily Mail*. Kops was thrilled with Litvinoff's article, which triggered a flurry of attention: 'It was the usual Fleet Street tale,' Kops wrote, 'the one they never tire of using: rags to riches, the sudden journey from obscurity to fame. They didn't mention the drugs, the addiction, the psychosis after my mother died. Apparently I had just appeared, as if conjured up by Houdini.'[22]

The play's success saw Kops placed into the coalescing movement of 'kitchen sink' dramatists who were emerging in the late 1950s, feeling to him as if they were 'the first bubbles on the boiling surface of social change that was taking place'.[23] Litvinoff helped usher him into view, then slipped away. He seemed to be of 'another world', Kops said. Litvinoff, the remade cockney, seemed out of place in Soho by virtue of his immersion in upper-class Chelsea circles. 'I always felt that he didn't quite fit in with the other bums and bohemians in Soho. He was better dressed. There was something about him. Maybe he had heard of my success, or my success that could be. . . He did a big splash about me, which I think was the first time I had been in the newspapers. He was quite flattering, which was also something I hadn't experienced.

'He wrote this article about me that really emphasised the poverty we were going through and extolling the fact that I was going to have a big success in New York.

'The world looked very stark, bad news on the political front, this terrible Cold War going on. So basically I met him, he came around occasionally; he was high, his eyes were sometimes glazed over. He had a handsome demeanour but there was something you couldn't quite trust about him. I have got an idea that he was the scapegoat of the family. . . I felt that he was out on a limb. He was in Soho in that period.'

Our conversation came at the beginning of my investigation. I knew then that Litvinoff was a familiar figure in Chelsea but not that he was simultaneously identified with Soho. 'Well, yes. . .people who were in Soho *and* Chelsea were usually not to be trusted,' said Kops, with a small laugh.

Journalism: a moral endeavour so often perverted to immoral ends, a high trade or a low profession, a bridge between subjects and readers, offering its exponents privileged access into rarefied or dangerous realms. Its appeal to Litvinoff is obvious. It enabled him to burrow deep into London's substrata and ascend to vertiginous heights, leaving the privations of an East End childhood far behind. His press pass and the promise of a review (which rarely materialised) won him free entry to galleries, exhibitions, debutantes' balls at the Grosvenor Hotel in Park Lane and Soho's jazz clubs, often with an impressed younger relative in tow. Gossip was his lifeblood and in many senses he had excellent journalistic credentials: a colourful but precise grasp of the English language, an unshockable nature, an incorrigible inquisitiveness, an ability to project authority on a matter he'd only just read about, an uncanny empathy with what people were feeling (and an antenna for their particular weaknesses), an instinct for what made a story and, as important as anything, a flair for making one happen rather than waiting passively for it to land in his lap. Nothing happening in town tonight? He'd gather a group of debutantes and pile them on to the Underground with a table and some glasses of champagne, then inform his readership the next morning that those frivolous young people from the Chelsea Set had held a riotous drinks party on the Circle Line, sipping their fizz and lighting up the suburban commuters' evening while the train trundled along its slow loop around subterranean London. Such inventions only served to realise the 'fiction' of the Chelsea Set, showing Litvinoff operating at the interface between myth and reality, blurring the border, creating facts that would seed other people's improvisations. The William Hickey column proved a perfect receptacle. Tom Driberg established it in May 1933, having for some years written pseudonymous diaries for the *Daily Express* titled 'The Talk of London' and 'These Names Make News. . .' Under Lord Beaverbrook's instruction this new feature was to be about interesting people doing important things – Canadian businessmen running newspaper groups, for instance – rather than the old simpering fare: 'Social chatter about the eccentricities of gilded half-wits is dead,' Driberg proclaimed in launching the column, which took its byline from a debauched diarist of Georgian London. As a member of the Communist Party Driberg had an ideological sympathy with the shift away from bolstering aristocratic egos, though, as his biographer Francis Wheen points out, his claim that earlier incessant reports of their foibles served subtly to undermine them and thus advance the class struggle smacks of self-justification, when in truth he rather enjoyed their company.

After being expelled from Lancing, known as a liberal public school (Wheen: 'One might as well speak of a comfortable dungeon or a palatable Liebfraumilch'[24]), and three hedonistic years reading Classics at Christ Church, Oxford, during which he intensely discussed modernist art and poetry and fellated innumerable men but neglected to gain a degree, Driberg found himself a niche in journalism at the same time as agitating for communism. In 1942 he became the Independent MP for Maldon in Essex, and was later re-elected as a Labour candidate. He was already notorious in certain circles and would become, in Christopher Hitchens' description, 'indubitably the most consecrated blow-job artist ever to take his seat in either House'.[25] This insatiable desire led him into every corner of society and he cultivated connections along the way from Bob Boothby to denizens of London's underworld. Litvinoff likewise found that having illicit sexual urges compelled him towards shady social spaces where other prohibited activities also congregated; in the 1950s it would have been hard to be homosexual in London and not associate with criminals, in Litvinoff's case for instance at the twenty-four-hour Lyons Corner House in Bethnal Green or the E&A Salt Beef Bar in Stamford Hill, run by his friend Jack Herman. Though their paths would cross later, by the time Litvinoff came to write for the Hickey column Driberg had moved on and its content had returned to the frothy aristocratic gossip to which Lord Beaverbrook had once been so opposed.

Litvinoff during his time working for the *Daily Express*.

Take a couple of random articles from 1957, when Litvinoff had begun contributing as the *Express*'s 'man about town'. As the column was pseudonymous we cannot know whether he penned these, but they are entirely of the world in which he was moving. A photograph showed the Duke of Edinburgh sporting a new beard while on a trip to Tristan da Cunha, 'the world's loneliest island', commented Hickey. 'What we are wondering: Will he shave it off before he comes home?'[26] Or another: 'CALL them "The Reluctant Bachelors." No tender trap can close on them. First: Billy Wallace,* who doesn't want it to. Rumour has seethed through London's drawing-rooms, restaurants, and night-clubs for three days that he really is going to marry Miss Joanna Smith-Bingham. He really isn't. We talked to him as he worked at his airline desk yesterday. He was firm. "You can say I have no intention of getting engaged to anyone for the moment. And while you're at it you can flatly deny rumours that I may marry Princess Margaret."'[27]

That much was true. It was a typical example of the society diarist currying favour with his sources, playing the traditional journalistic game of give-and-take, finding common interest in their distinct agendas. Litvinoff could get people into or keep them out of the papers, with or against their will.

---

*   William Euan Wallace (1927–77), Old Etonian, stylish society figure and friend of Princess Margaret's.

Newspapers' payments for stories became one form of revenue, those from publicity-shy individuals whose sexual proclivities he'd threatened to expose were another. Journalism became a way of toying with the city: he played London like a musical instrument, where other people's lives were his notes and he improvised for his own amusement. He manipulated himself into becoming a mediator, a trader channelling diverse forms of capital – cash, information, boys – while tightening the tensions of the city's financial matrix. (Saul Bellow in 1957: 'Money surrounds you in life as the earth does in death . . . Who is free? No one is free. Who has no burdens? Everyone is under pressure.'[28]) He preferred not to become the story himself – authoring others' from the shadows was far preferable – except when it suited his own agenda.

Readers of the *Daily Express* on 25th March 1958 would have turned to the Hickey column to be confronted with David Litvinoff's face, though he did not return their gaze: his eyes were averted downwards, guiding the reader towards his splayed nose and pursed lips. Lucian Freud's portrait was ungenerous but it was its new title that caused its subject more discomfort. 'About this portrait: The man in it rows with Freud', read the headline, and the story itself drew the *Express*'s readership into the scene:

> A row blew up at the smart Bond-street opening of an exhibition of paintings by Lucian Freud, grandson of the pioneer of modern psychology and estranged husband of the sister of Lord Dufferin and Ava.
>
> It was all over a picture called 'The Procurer' – reckoned to be one of the best of the 24 on view.
>
> The subject of the picture is David Litvinoff, who is 29, independent, and one of the Chelsea set. Mr Litvinoff, who was not at last night's preview, used to be Lucian Freud's secretary. Mr Freud's painting of him was originally to be called 'Portrait of a Jew'.
>
> But a little while ago, said Mr Litvinoff, he permitted Mr Freud in a signed statement, to rename the painting as the artist wished.
>
> 'But never in my wildest dreams did I imagine that he would call it "The Procurer",' said Mr Litvinoff.
>
> 'That's going a bit too far. Though I have been a friend of Freud's, and hope I still am, I have to consult my solicitor.'

The solicitor, Mr Ellis Lincoln, went to the preview at the Marlborough Fine Arts Gallery last night – and saw the picture.

He said later: 'There is no doubt as to who it is. I have seen Mr Litvinoff, and he has given me instructions.'

Lucian Freud, who is 35, and a teacher at the Slade School, waited around shyly at the preview.

Three of his pictures were sold in minutes. . . Mr Freud does not like them to be known as portraits. His titles are anonymous. 'I regard them as subjects,' he said.

Of *'The Procurer'* he said: 'It was a title which I chose. I believe it fits the picture. Litvinoff gave me a signed statement, allowing me to call it whatever I wished.

'I know him very well. And he told me he did not even trust himself not to sue. That is why I got him to give me the statement.'

'About this portrait: The man in it rows with Freud',
by 'William Hickey', *Daily Express*.

According to William Feaver, Freud's friend and biographer, the article was inaccurate in saying that Litvinoff had been Freud's secretary. He also said: 'Lucian told me that after threatening to sue, [Litvinoff] wrote a letter swearing that he wouldn't and Lucian took this to be enough to stop him suing. There was nothing paid as far as I know and no undertaking.'

Instead Litvinoff claimed compensation in his own way, if Freud is to be believed. A stuffed zebra's head had served as Freud's model for his 1943–4 oils *Quince on a Blue Table* and *The Painter's Room*. Freud had left it on the landing at Delamere Terrace, and according to the artist Litvinoff soon absconded with it. 'He said he wouldn't sue over the title [of the painting], then he stole the zebra head,' Freud told Feaver. 'Everything about him was fake.'[29]

Lucian Freud c.1943 with his stuffed zebra head.

The contretemps came in the midst of a particularly turbulent time in Freud's life. Charlie Lumley, his studio assistant in the 1950s, recalled that after Lady Caroline Blackwood divorced him in 1957, his friends such as Francis Bacon feared he was suicidal. Feaver described Lady Caroline's departure as 'an abandonment: and he abandoned himself – he got into fights, he went wilder'.[30]

He provoked those he detested, whether by walking up to them and kicking them hard in the shins or giving their portrait a defamatory title. The Conservative MP Michael Astor bought *The Procurer* but disliked the name almost as much as its subject did, thinking it 'seedy or suggestive', said Feaver. That was Freud's aim entirely. Feaver wrote that 'it referred to Litvinov's [*sic*] habit of bringing girls round to Delamere Terrace, which Freud rather resented'.[31] One such girl was his niece Vida, Emanuel's daughter, who was introduced to Freud as a fourteen- or fifteen-year-old, as her sister Sarah recalled. 'Vida was a wild child and didn't get on with my father, and at one point she ran away and turned up at David's. David took her in. He introduced her to Lucian Freud, because he said he would want to paint her. Now my sister was very beautiful and even at that age she had a wonderful pneumatic older woman's figure, she was very well built. But it turned out that Lucian Freud wasn't remotely interested in painting her and she felt that David had set her up; he was pimping her out to Lucian Freud. He was basically giving him a gorgeous young girl. But nothing happened. And then David told her, in typical David fashion, that Lucian Freud was actually her real father. And I know my mother never met Lucian Freud. . . It was one of the reasons that my mother absolutely loathed David and didn't want me to have anything to do with him.'

It was the kind of behaviour that proved the worst connotations of Freud's title were well merited, though much later the artist would give Julian Lloyd a more generous explanation.

'There was a time when I used to go to parties in London and meet Lucian on and off and I asked him about David,' said Lloyd. 'And he did not speak unkindly about David. We had quite an affectionate reminisce about him. He was a little bit guarded but he wasn't outspoken or derogatory about him. And he said there was that painting of him, which Lucian said he called *The Procurer* because. . .when he came round to you, David would always bring a gift or a present or something to eat or a book or some person he thought you might like to meet. And Lucian said, "Do you remember how he always used to do that?" and I said, "Of course," and he said, "So that's why I called it *The Procurer*."'

Either account would be accurate, as Litvinoff had become a procurer in both senses of the word. By the time Freud met him he was ensconced in his life's business: the recirculation of property and information, of material and immaterial goods. If there was a gap in any market he could procure the necessary goods to fill it: an example would be the 1950s labour shortage, which presented the opportunity to establish a dubious employment agency. At first it was located in Wealdstone, where his father was living, then he decided to move it to 'within walking distance of Paddington Station, to attract the Irish navvies', as Andy Garnett recalled. Litvinoff offered two main sources of work: building work for labourers and film extra roles for handsome young actors. However, when any of the latter arrived, Litvinoff would inform him that unfortunately the parts had already been filled – but he was *perfect*, had just the Greek profile that directors wanted these days, and if he would just accept a short-term labouring job for now, Litvinoff would keep him on the books and put him first in line for the next movie role that arose. The man would begin work on the site but would hear nothing more of his cinematic career and eventually walk away, by which time Litvinoff had his commission from the builders. Another brief source of revenue came from working in a Jewish bookshop on Charing Cross Road, though this terminated abruptly when he was found *in flagrante* with his boss's wife. No matter: he just moved on to something else and retained the knowledge for his own freelance efforts at book-dealing, procuring fine old volumes for his Chelsea friends. Freud's reputation rested on his uncanny ability to capture a sitter's character in paint, but where Litvinoff was concerned he managed also to do so with language.

One black loafer on the Knightsbridge pavement, the other on a pedal of the bicycle that propelled him on his missions around the city. He would

In Hans Crescent, 1957.

never learn to drive, or not legally at least, though he was once stopped by police in possession of a stolen car; he plucked a name from the air and told them he'd bought it from Jeffrey Bernard, who was hauled off to Scotland Yard for questioning. Leaning on the bike exposes a flash of red tartan sock, and with his striped buff blazer and neatly knotted tie, arms casually crossed and a hint of a smile on his lips, he looks like a man-about-town with London at his feet, his jauntiness accentuated by the twist of the bike wheel. The photograph was taken on Hans Crescent, just next to Harrods, where he'd taken a new flat in which he cohabited with a bush baby.* The locale may have been smart but the lifestyle that the walls now enclosed remained chaotic and bizarre. Discarded Vicks inhalers lay scattered around, Litvinoff having removed the internal swab of Benzedrine-soaked cotton wool and jammed it up his nose. He'd boil a few chickens at once and keep them in the cupboard, breaking off a congealing wing or a drumstick to gnaw on when he was hungry. When his brother Phil and his new wife Margaret paid a visit, Margaret had already been warned by his sister Sonya that 'David should be kept at a distance', she remembered, adding that Sonya's 'husband Les found David quite outrageous. My father said he was "no good". Needless to say I was intrigued by this information... My first meeting with David will never be forgotten. He called me "sweetie", but then, male or female, we were all "sweetie", which I recall made Les squirm, Les always being terribly correct...

'A never-to-be-forgotten evening was at David's flat in Hans Crescent. I offered to make tea. "Where are the cups and saucers?" I asked David. "Jam jars," came the reply. David's pet bush baby lived in a wicker cage suspended from the ceiling. From time to time the bush baby urinated, David being quite oblivious to the stream of urine trickling across the lovely wood flooring.'

Such moments only served to emphasise the gap between Litvinoff and his respectable relatives, as did another occasion when he went to visit a newly-wed brother. So, how was married life? he enquired of his sister-in-law as she made tea in the kitchen. 'Oh very nice, very nice,' came the answer: evidently a bit bland for Litvinoff's tastes, so he stirred things up a little with his reply: 'Well, you get a good fuck when you want one, don't you?'

---

* Perhaps purchased from the store's famous zoological department, where one could buy any pet from a mouse to a lion.

More disturbing, though, was the incident at a family party when a young mother asked him to keep an eye on her child who was sitting on a potty, while she left the room to take a telephone call. As soon as she'd gone Litvinoff took the potty to the lavatory, where he sat on it himself and released a huge bowel movement before nipping back to seat the child in place again. When the mother returned to find what her toddler had apparently produced she was beside herself. In later years he would complain to friends of a lack of support from his family but if some relatives began to keep their distance, one can understand why.

I began to sense I'd grown too obsessed around the time I first felt an urge to dial KEN 2942 and see whether my call was answered by David Litvinoff in 1957. This curious dead man had insinuated his way into my subconscious and hunkered down to stay. The only way I might exorcise him was to write him out; but instead the opposite occurred. The book became a trap, biographical quicksand: the harder I dug into his life, the more I became ensnared. Litvinoff showed no sign of moving on. Everything began to connect, or rather held the promise of connection if I would only look hard enough. I converged with Patrick Kennedy, who had begun his own pursuit of Litvinoff a decade earlier and then stepped back owing to an ascending career as an actor and a deteriorating relationship with Litvinoff's friends Gerry and Patricia Goldstein, whose behaviour in addiction singed a whole network of their associations. The balance tilted for Patrick but Litvinoff continued to haunt him. We met at the French House, a little warily; by the end of a long lunch we'd agreed to keep in touch, each bemused and amused to meet a man of the same age with the same fixation on what felt then like a maddening, untellable story. Between us we might pinpoint his ghost by triangulation. Patrick taught me a new word, apophenia, the experience of perceiving meaningful patterns in random phenomena: finding faces in clouds, say, or ghostly figures from light and shadow in photographs. This was some comfort. I'd been developing forms of behaviour that, in my more lucid moments, I could see were unusual. I'd browse any bookstall I spied – in London, in Wales – searching for his signature in the inside front covers. Every time I stepped on to a Tube train I'd notice the Metro-Cammell footplate and feel it a part of the story's background scenery. I'd watch endless silent footage of mid-twentieth-century London street scenes and crowded pubs in the hope of that he'd been caught on celluloid for a moment, however fleeting: was that a two-second glimpse of his nodding face, half out of shot and part obscured by a female friend's wavy blonde hair, in an unidentified Soho bar in 1958? By the twentieth replay I was convinced. I played his telephone recordings over and over again to try to determine indecipherable phrases: press play, listen and frown, pause, rewind, listen again until the sounds yielded meaning or all language began to sound meaningless. . .walk away, suppress the urge to scream, walk back and listen again. There were other tapes I suspected existed but couldn't find, worse still ones that I had located but whose owners had signally failed to grasp the benefit to global culture of granting me access, letters I hadn't read, any of which might contain a clue that solved one of Litvinoff's mysteries. His story tormented me. . .or stories, rather: here was a man to whom contradictory myths swirling around the city accrued like flies to flypaper. The interviewees' fields of memory differed wildly but gradually it seemed I could thread a narrative through the overlaps. Beside the overlaps, though, lay the chasmic gaps into which his experiences had fallen beyond recovery. Like the drop either side of a high wire the absences seemed to render what remained terrifyingly minute: and yet just enough to tread the course of his life.

Act One, Scene Three.

DL: And what do you feel about the sexual and political state of people today? You're a man of the world.

JIG: Well I'm coming to that, David, it's like this. What makes me, shall we say, act careful at times—

DL: You're very *reserved*—

JIG: It's all right if you meet the right company, and you could get me into the right company, you see.

DL: I'll *do my best*.

JIG: The point is this. When you mention the law, I don't trust them.

DL: No, I'm afraid I have fair grounds for distrust myself.

JIG: I'm going to be quite frank about it—

DL: They're frustrated tailors: they're always stitching up.

JIG: They're always asking 'When are you going to pay the rent on the locker?'. . . And the point is this, why, all of a sudden, don't they know the difference between a *bona fide* citizen and an undesirable?

DL: Yes! That's a very interesting distinction, because you're one of the most *bona fide* citizens that I've seen.

JIG: The point is I'm very reticent towards them, and they know that. In other words it will take more than two dozen cases of brandy and whisky before I will give them a thought. . . Do you understand what I mean, David?

DL: I do indeed, yes.

JIG: And then, in other words, I can be a Heydrich, who was the SS for Czechoslovakia, in 1941.

DL: What about Seyss-Inquart* and Baldur von Schirach?†

JIG: Very good indeed, very good indeed.

DL: Yes. Freedom fighters.

JIG: Especially when he said, every time he did enquire about your exile, he was always deceived by the Gestapo.

DL: Which exile?

JIG: Well, when he always enquired where he was, in Bohemia and Moravia and Austria—

DL: Because he was the Gauleiter of Vienna?

JIG: Quite correct—

DL: Sent all those trains off with those Jews. . .

---

*   Arthur Seyss-Inquart (1892–1946), Austrian Nazi who facilitated the Anschluss, served as Reichskommissar to the Netherlands and was hanged at Nuremberg for crimes against humanity.

†   Baldur von Schirach (1907–74), leader of the Hitler Youth and, as Litvinoff says, the Gauleiter of Vienna.

JIG: . . .Well he was always deceived by the Gestapo—

DL: Yes, they were fibbers.

JIG: —and that was the point with the law. You get these copper narks, and I can pick them out like A, B, C, do you know what I mean, David? I know the copper narks that walk about here in London, and I drop them like the atomic bomb that went on Nagasaki and Hiroshima!

DL: Beautiful!. . . You're a man of splendid bearing.

JIG: I know a lot of people say 'There's Heydrich walking by', and I don't worry about their remarks like that.

Chapter 3

The Man Who Laughed

My house is a decayed house,
    And the jew squats on the window sill, the owner,
    Spawned in some estaminet of Antwerp,
    Blistered in Brussels, patched and peeled in London.
                   From 'Gerontion', by T. S. Eliot

The coming years grew pregnant with the 1960s as a new London took shape through three Acts of Parliament: the 1957 Rent Act, the 1959 Street Offences Act and the 1960 Betting and Gaming Act. Legislation formulated and passed in the elevated surrounds of Whitehall and Westminster would re-route the disreputable careers of Litvinoff and his associates in Soho, Notting Hill and Belgravia, creating new boundaries to push against. When the Rent Act removed controls on rental rates, enabling landlords to charge far higher amounts to new tenants than were paid by the current residents, the less scrupulous reacted by kicking out the occupants as soon as possible and getting new ones in; and if they were disinclined to move on, then they would need encouragement. Joan Wyndham's diaries record a party at which a gatecrasher was 'thrown out by David Litvinoff who works for Rachmann [*sic*], an evil property tycoon who puts rats painted with fluorescent paint through letter-boxes to flush out sitting tenants'.[1]

    Perec Rachman was born in 1919 in Poland, the son of a dentist. Having spent part of the war in a concentration camp and the rest fighting for the Allies, he arrived in Britain as a stateless refugee, whereupon he adapted his first name to Peter. After working in the East End he took a job with an estate agency in Shepherd's Bush; then he went it alone, having spotted the lucrative opportunity presented by a combination of the post-war housing shortage and the arrival of migrants from the Caribbean. Borrowing £220,000 from the newly established Eagle Star Building Society, Rachman responded to the Act by buying around eighty large, dilapidated Victorian terrace houses around Notting Hill, Paddington, North Kensington and Ladbroke Grove. Most were formerly grand buildings that seemed to embody the decline from London's imperial Victorian days to the Suez Crisis era's forfeit of global influence. The tall stuccoed terraces around Powis Square, for instance, had been built in the 1860s and were first occupied by professionals – stockbrokers, doctors, lawyers and retired army officers – but the growth of the Portobello food market and the commuting possibilities into central London created by the new Hammersmith and City Line stations at Ladbroke Grove and Westbourne Park attracted a poorer demographic of traders and manual workers. After the First World War Kensington Borough Council divided most of Powis Square's four- or five-storeyed houses into flats, then further still into bedsits, until by 1922 only five continued to have a single occupancy. The early 1950s' influx of immigrants into this area consolidated a Caribbean presence dating from that post-First World War decade; the area had since housed a rich commingling of ethnicities and lifestyles, also combining Russian and Polish Jews, Irish and English people who'd left deprived areas up north to seek a better life in the capital. 'Many of the people who lived there became legends, people who made their names into real folk myths,' reported the *International Times* much later. 'Eccentrics, madmen, political radicals, poets and artists: Chicago Kate (who lived in Basing Road), the Englisher (a British-born Jew),' proving that Litvinoff's father Solly's nickname was not unique, 'the Presser (the quiet communist theoretician), Schmooser, the best dancer in Notting Hill. Stallholders in Portobello Road for generations, many of them still represented; Rosie, an Irish woman who kept a vegetable stall and who spoke fluent Yiddish.'[2]

Rachman's office was at 91–3 Westbourne Grove, where Litvinoff was a regular presence according to his friend David Gittleman. 'Although he would claim he was always in Chelsea, he was usually either in Soho or to be found in Westbourne Grove – nobody wanted to admit to being in Westbourne Grove, it was really the pits! He did some sort of rent-collecting [for Rachman] and I think he kept his hand in the till.' The hub of Rachman's empire lay around Powis Terrace and Powis Square, which had long been a haunt of prostitutes and pimps. This suited him as he could also use his properties as brothels. Methods that he deployed to persuade sitting tenants to move on, it was said, included initially offering them a cash inducement, then letting out adjoining properties to his associates who would hold noisy all-night parties and make life unbearable. If that didn't work, agents were sent in to sabotage the locks, damage the shared toilets, or leave itching powder or the aforementioned rats in people's beds. The sculptor and drug-smuggler Francis Morland commented that since Litvinoff 'could hold sophisticated intellectuals spellbound with his wit', it was 'doubly surprising then that he made his living as an enforcer for Rachman, evicting his tenants by puncturing header tanks to flood houses or installing a Jamaican jazz band in the house with instructions to practise late at night'. Some tenants took Rachman to rent tribunals, such as the one in 1959 which ruled that his properties at 31, 32, 44 and 45 Powis Square were 'scruffy, dirty and unfit for human inhabitation';[3] most, however, had little option but to pack their cases.

While he went down in history as the archetypal malevolent slum landlord, many people looking back now argue that Rachman received an unfair press. They invert the notion that he simply exploited newly arrived Caribbean families and point out that he at least gave them somewhere to live when other tenements around the capital bore signs reading 'No Irish, no blacks, no dogs'. Certainly many of his tenants felt gratitude towards him. Stories about his methods of moving people on were exaggerated for dramatic effect, they say, and as a personality he was largely affable and generous.

Litvinoff's old friend David Cammell is among those who take this stance. In 1956 Rachman put up the money for his Lebanese-born associate Raymond Nakachian, aka Raymond Nash, to open a nightclub and asked Cammell to furnish it. They called it Le Condor,* a play on the ribald French 'con d'or', and Cammell fitted it with canopies to resemble the interior of a circus tent while his brother Donald designed the neon sign that glowed over Wardour Street, depicting 'a rogueish looking bird holding a champagne glass'.

'Rachman made three mistakes,' Cammell said. 'One was to go around in the long coat and dark glasses and drive everywhere in his Rolls-Royce, which made him look like a gangster. The second thing he did, and the reason he was vilified, was that he betrayed the property racket because when the blacks came over he gave them rooms to live in, and that lowered the value of the properties.

---

* David Cammell: 'It's always referred to in books as El Condor, as if it were Spanish, and I'd like to set the record straight on this. Late one night Raymond Nash said to me, "What do you think of calling it Le Condor? It has a special meaning in French"...and as I speak French I knew right away what he meant.'

'He wasn't a rogue. If an old lady was struggling with the rent he'd reach in his pocket and give her a fiver. He'd been through a lot, been in a concentration camp during the war. The third mistake he made was to die.'

Rachman only entered the public eye after his death from a heart attack in November 1962. Ben Parkin, the Labour MP for Paddington North, raised concerns in the House of Commons about his constituents' living conditions and suggested that this dubious character Rachman had faked his own death to escape justice; from there the press picked up the story and other politicians pursued the cause.* The Profumo affair brought to light lurid stories about his relationships with Mandy Rice-Davies and Christine Keeler, the latter's reputation as the embodiment of the emerging 'permissive society' fixed by Lewis Morley's famous photograph. A caricature replaced the complex and in some ways sympathetic character who was a product of his times: as his biographer Shirley Green wrote, 'Had there never been a war, Rachman might still have been alive; a gentle, well-liked family dentist. And although he may not have proved worthy of compassion, ironically, his name derives from the Hebrew root, *Rachamim*. Nearest translation – the abstract noun, Pity.'[4]

If his death was his third mistake, his fourth was to have been born Jewish: there was more than a hint of anti-Semitism in his depiction when the story broke in early 1963. Litvinoff certainly felt the coverage was prejudiced. Four years later, in a conversation with Philip Laski, he would decry the way the newspapers revelled in Rachman's misdeeds and his demise 'during the Robert Jacobs† post-Rachman episodic treatment; week-by-week another thrilling instalment', he recalled, showing 'How International Jewry was Flouted'.

Lynn Lewis was a Fleet Street journalist in the early 1960s and came across Litvinoff as he attempted to establish a connection between Rachman and the Kray twins, whose activities were beginning to attract the attention of the Metropolitan Police and in turn the newspapers.

---

* Harold Wilson raised the matter in the House of Commons on 22nd July 1963, urging Harold Macmillan's government to 'take immediate and drastic action to restore security for threatened tenants'. 'Sometimes,' Wilson declared, 'one turns over a stone in a garden or field and sees the slimy creatures which live under its protection. . . But the photophobic animal world has nothing to compare with the revolting creatures of London's underworld, living there, shunning the light, growing fat by battening on human misery.'

† A property dealer who bought numerous ex-Rachman properties on Powis Terrace after Rachman's death.

'I remember meeting him on the King's Road with Ronald Maxwell;* I think [Ronald] knew David Litvinoff from some previous incident,' said Lewis. 'So when we were put on to the Krays story he was one of the first people we wanted to see. We met him in a bar on the King's Road, sat on the pavement and talked. . . We had a couple of conversations with him. He clearly wasn't going to get mentioned.

'We had been investigating the Rachman empire. Once we got info about his bodyguards and hangers-on, we knew a lot of the crime scene and followed it through for the next two or three years.

'Did he talk? Very much so. He was talking to us very easily, very freely. I think he told us about the guys who we wanted to know about who were very low in the Rachman empire: people like Freddie Rondel, "Freddie the Earbiter". David Litvinoff told us about people like him.'

Norbert Friedrich Rondel was a former kindertransportee from Berlin and rabbinical student who had a spell in the Maudsley psychiatric hospital before trading his studies for a career in professional wrestling, in the course of which he met fellow Rachman enforcer Bert Assirati. It was Assirati who had to drum into 'Mad Freddie' that wrestlers did not actually deliberately injure one another, they only pretended to do so. Rondel earned his other nickname in 1959 when he received a grievous bodily harm conviction for cutting off a man's ear in a fight. He then tried to sue his barrister for negligence on the basis that he had not been properly defended: he hadn't used a blade, he argued. He had actually used his teeth. Rondel and Assirati were joined among Rachman's enforcement crew by a fellow wrestling friend, Peter Rann, and a young Trinidadian man who'd arrived in London in 1957. Michael de Freitas first met Rachman when burgling his office; Rachman's reaction was to offer him a basement flat in Powis Square, which de Freitas turned into a noisy gambling joint. Later he would convert to Islam and, under the name Michael X, become a campaigner for black civil rights, a darling of the hippie counterculture whose commitment to racial equality led them to overlook his sadistic streak. The worst of the excesses attributed to Rachman's agents – setting dogs on white tenants to scare them out of their flats, for instance – are often now held to have been de Freitas' work. While it would be naive to swing the pendulum too far regarding Rachman's reputation – the initial funds for his business came from the proceeds of prostitution, and the

---

* A reporter with the *Sunday Mirror*.

eloquent and beguiling Litvinoff is said to have added to his coffers by perpetrating insurance scams on his behalf – he was an intelligent, nuanced character rather than a caricature; and besides, while he operated on a grander scale than most, hustling a living was far from unusual during Britain's gradual emergence from the economic rupture of war, when many people did whatever it took to get by. Leslie Payne, who would apply his unscrupulous intellect to running the Kray twins' numerous fraudulent businesses a few years later, once recalled his days as a door-to-door vacuum cleaner salesman after being demobbed from his wartime service.

'I earned well doing legitimate business but, as in the army, I found I could do better on the fiddle,' he said. 'There was nothing extraordinary about this. Many working men in post-war England were busy at some kind of fiddle or other, and the vast majority of the respectable classes profited by it. Black market or underground commerce was essential to make life possible in the jungle of shortages, restrictions, permits, licences and prosecutions. As times got better most people gave it up as a major occupation, but a few went on to make it their career. I was one of these.'[5]

So was Litvinoff, who likewise found a variety of markets and loopholes to exploit. One lucrative scam drew from an ever-reliable source, male sexual stupidity, and propelled a new moral panic in the late 1950s. Pathé News outlined the growing popular concern about the seedier side of London in a 1958 newsreel titled *Clubs Galore!* 'This is Soho, catering for all tastes – low included. Even the cats are a bit furtive,' the narrator intoned as a skinny tabby-and-white feline scurried down a gaslit pavement. Only a stone's throw from theatreland, where unsuspecting, respectable people could be found enjoying wholesome entertainment on any given evening, it became apparent that there existed a shadier realm of pornographic bookshops, of striptease clubs in which tantalised middle-aged men peered through perspiration-flecked spectacles at lissom dancing girls, of dark streets where bored women in long coats twirled their keys and tapped stiletto-clad feet while awaiting passing trade, and of cynical establishments that found another way of squeezing money out of male folly.

'In the dingy streets are the cellars of the one-room clubs,' warned the narrator, 'where the seamy side of life is even more blatant than in the street above. A drinking club can be opened just by filling up a form and paying five shillings. They're found not only in London – they've even sprung up in provincial cities too. Is it not time now that something was done about it?'

Something was soon done about the prostitution. While in 1958 around 5,000 women worked the streets of central London from Powis Square to Soho, the next year's Street Offences Act saw them vanish – but this legislation only pushed the problem behind closed doors and up flights of steps into shabby backrooms whose use was advertised at street level in discreet cards offering 'French Lessons' or a 'Large Chest for Sale'. Meanwhile the dubious drinking clubs still flourished, as did the membership scams; Litvinoff's friend Douglas Villiers recalled him opening one such establishment, signing members up on standing orders and still receiving money some years later from men who hadn't cancelled their payments. Many such places were 'near beer' clubs selling drinks containing less than two per cent alcohol, which meant that the owners did not require a liquor licence. A number of these were 'clip joints', 'so-called because their conductors join in clipping the purses of unsuspecting visitors',[6] as a peer put it during a House of Lords debate about the problem. Litvinoff worked on the door of a clip joint called Midnight Follies, on Denman Street just off Piccadilly Circus. The routine was familiar: passing men would get lured over the threshold either by a seductive woman or a plausible-seeming man on the street, who would collar them, ask if they were looking for somewhere to drink and, as if doing them a favour, chaperone them to the newest 'place to be seen'. There would be vague intimations of glamour, sophistication, the possible sexual encounters within; but as Dan Farson recalled from bitter experience, there was a sharp disjunction between the promise and the reality. The tout who'd intercepted him on Wardour Street 'seemed genuinely helpful as he told me of a club which had just opened, for which he didn't ask for money, nor did he stop for a drink,' Farson wrote. 'He left me at the foot of a dimly lit staircase where a man demanded a membership fee. I flattered myself on this "discovery" until I reached the upstairs room and was overwhelmed by depression. The darkness did not conceal the shabbiness and through the gloom several ill-at-ease faces stared at me, recognising a fellow fool.'[7]

There the punter would find himself seated at a table with a hostess, who would order them expensive drinks – usually cocktails such as the one Farson sampled, which was 'a nauseating mixture of Coca-Cola, ginger wine and a touch of peppermint cordial'. The ingredients cost a few pence; put together they sold for five shillings. The girls were paid by the number of cocktail sticks they'd collected from their punters' glasses by the end of the night, and their earnings could amount to around £20 a week.

'After a while,' said Andy Garnett, 'the girls, who were all sixteen to eighteen, would prod them in the groin and say: "I'd do you – but we can't do anything here, the manager don't like it." So they'd say: "Meet me in ten minutes at the entrance to Leicester Square Tube," but of course there are about ten entrances all crowded with people. . .and the girls wouldn't turn up, and sometimes the men would then come back to the club and try to get in again.

'And Litvinoff would grab them by the collar, shouting up close so he was spitting in their face: "I know your type! You want to come here and have your pornographic ways with these teenage girls! Well, I know Inspector Huggins of Wealdstone Police and I'm going to tell him to come down to Soho, and if we see you again he'll give you a frontal lobotomy!"'

It normally did the trick, though Litvinoff wasn't averse to impersonating a police officer himself if necessary: he kept a policeman's helmet handy and would sometimes appear wearing it in order to scare off the irate suburban businessmen, American soldiers et al. who had been duped into visiting the bar and wanted their money back.

Another haunt at this time was the Temperance Billiard Hall back in Chelsea (built in the Queen Anne style *c*.1912 as part of the movement offering alternatives to the pub), on the corner of the King's Road and Flood Street. There he loitered with an artist called Brian Messitt, who renamed himself Masset out of frustration at people laughing at his surname,* a handsome young Irishman called Eddie Dylan and a tough guy named Tommy Waldron, aka Cholmondeley. Emilio 'Mim' Scala was a young theatrical agent at the time and used to see them on the King's Road, where they stood out as anachronisms who 'bought all their clothes from Ryder's, an old-fashioned glass-fronted shop occupying a large corner site in Pimlico' and 'dressed like Victorians, like they'd come from the nineteenth century'. Scala makes Litvinoff sound more than ever like a character from *London Labour and the London Poor*, the astonishing collection of rogues and itinerants and unfortunate souls that Henry Mayhew and two colleagues interviewed on the capital's streets in 1851, none of them named but only identified by their trade: the Street Seller of Birds' Nests, the Jew Old Clothes Man, the Bone Grubber, the Street Telescope Exhibitor, the London Scavenger, the Sewer Hunter.

---

* And who met a sorry end in 2005 on a street in Swiss Cottage, when he was almost decapitated with an axe by a former friend who was later sent indefinitely to a psychiatric hospital.

Consciously or otherwise Litvinoff's friends often reached for a Victorian stereotype in trying to describe him: the adjective that they most often employed was 'Faginesque'. Alexander 'Shura' Shihwarg, for instance, met him around this time, when Litvinoff gatecrashed a party and stole two high-quality cameras; despite this, Shihwarg and his wife Joan Wyndham 'liked him – though like a pet hedgehog, we were always wary of his spines. . . He was truly a Fagin character,' said Shihwarg, who usually saw him accompanied by an entourage of lawless street kids. 'It's a pretty accurate comparison.' The actor James Fox applied it too, having first set eyes on Litvinoff in Soho around this time, teaching a gang of schoolboys how to steal cigarettes. The Krays' biographer John Pearson reached for a different Dickensian comparison in *The Cult of Violence*. Litvinoff, he said, was akin to the fat boy in *The Pickwick Papers* who tells old Mrs Wardle: 'I wants to make your flesh creep.' Pearson was referring particularly to Litvinoff's disturbing humour, and the relish he took in relaying developments from London's shadiest corners back to captivated friends in Chelsea dining rooms.

When he wasn't guarding the door of the clip joint, every night in Soho offered new possibilities. Some nights he'd go to Humph's, Humphrey Lyttelton's place at 100 Oxford Street, but more often he could be seen at the raucous Cy Laurie's Jazz Club down in the heaving, sticky basement of 41 Great Windmill Street, where he could jive and gyre and rap away all night, whipping a bottle of poppers from his jacket and taking a snort whenever he felt his tempo slowing. The beat poet Michael Horovitz remembered him as a 'wild and voluble' character there; Melly said he 'lived on Benzedrine' and 'never went to bed as far as I could see', while his friend David Gittleman recalled sampling some of Litvinoff's amphetamine: 'I couldn't sleep for four days and when I closed my eyes I could see through my eyelids.' The uppers twisted reality to his preferred speed and texture: existence italicised, and if it's a clockwork universe, at least swing the pendulum hard. Walk fast, talk faster, keep heaving at time's boundary; anything to avoid the still, silent moments when momentum would accede to inertia. Between Cy's and the nearby Harmony Inn on Archer Street – main clientele speeding jazzers and white-faced nocturnal prostitutes retouching their make-up – they'd push on through the night, emerging with dry eyes and cigarette-roughened throats, jaws grinding and ears ringing, into the scouring light of dawn. No sleep and the long day ahead: how to contend with the comedown? Keep going, head up to London Zoo, give your gaggle of hungover friends an expert guided tour: 'And these are the bumming-birds,' Litvinoff informed jazz musician Eric Jackson as they reached the aviary, displaying something less than the devastating wit that made his reputation. Other nights he'd go jiving to the new rock'n'roll that blasted from jukeboxes in the all-night cafes that had sprung up between the bombsites, often partnered by Nicolette Meeres, who was at that time an art student at the Slade, where Lucian Freud was teaching. 'David was a fantastic and very energetic dancer, and knew all the moves,' she said. She found his face mesmeric and painted him in less exuberant, more furtive mode in the Granada Cafe on Berwick Street, sitting between a pair of teddy boys known as the Bailey brothers. As in the Freud portrait he avoids the viewer's eye, again looking frustrated by being rendered static in paint, seeming as if he might at any moment leap to his feet and bustle out of the scene in search of something more exciting to do.

Litvinoff and the Bailey brothers in the Granada Cafe, c.1958,
by Nicolette Meeres.

Attending one of his friends Mariella Novotny and Hod Dibben's sex parties, say, or drinking with Francis Bacon and Lucian Freud at the Colony Room. The sticky green walls of the club upstairs at 41 Dean Street enclosed a garrulous assembly of dissolute talents, all overseen by the formidable Muriel Belcher, who was precisely Litvinoff's kind of woman: strong, funny, Jewish, perceptive, ribald, unshockable (though when the brilliant but poisonous photographer John Deakin put it around that her charity balls for disabled children were a means of lining her own pockets the limits of her tolerance were revealed). The poet Paul Potts summarised her power and allure in a letter to Daniel Farson, calling her 'a natural procurer whether it be the Bacon for the eggs or a date for a girl friend'.[8]

While Litvinoff had an involvement in various kinds of 'moral menace' within Soho, from feckless boozing and casual violence to the burgeoning sex industry, at the same time over in the more ostensibly genteel parts of town he was embroiled in another trend that was bothering the Metropolitan Police. Illegal *chemin de fer* parties were proliferating around Chelsea and Belgravia, run by people such as John Aspinall, who over the past year had found it possible to avoid prosecution through a combination of guile and bribery. There was nothing illegal *per se* about 'chemmy', a form of baccarat in which six packs of cards are combined and dealt from a shoe (originally of iron, hence *chemin de fer* or 'iron road', the French term for 'railway'), and hosts were allowed to take a five per cent cut on private parties they held for invited guests. The law defined an illegal gaming house as one where gambling had taken place more than three times: so Aspinall rented a series of smart addresses and was careful never to host more than three chemmy parties at each, while his mother, Lady Osborne, helped keep the law's suspicion at bay by paying off police officers. After a time, however, Lady Osborne persuaded her son to settle on a fixed location, so they rented a flat in her name. Before long 1 Hyde Park Street became known as a place where high-stakes card games were held every Thursday night. Aspinall's games saw gamblers stake £1,000 per hand, around £20,000 today, and with each hand lasting around thirty seconds, fortunes were won and lost within minutes. Waiters in white tie and tails would serve his wealthy friends chilled champagne, caviar and Lady Osborne's game pie, and from 11pm until they emerged blearily at dawn to be chauffeured home, they would spend their nights in convivial company frittering away tens of thousands of pounds: sums that would seem huge to the man in the street but that only rarely placed these people in financial difficulty. The police began to observe the property and in January 1958 Aspinall and his mother, along with their associate John Burke, found themselves confronted by the law after a policeman clambered up a drainpipe and dangled himself down from the edge of a fire escape to squint through a gap in the curtains. He saw the players sitting at the green baize tables with their piles of chips and Aspinall acting as croupier, dealing cards from the shoe: enough to warrant a raid. Chief Superintendent Richard Rogers banged on the door, his team of officers were let in by a boy from the kitchen, and they proceeded to interrogate the host, who countered their accusations by saying that all present were his good friends there at his invitation. What game were they playing and how much was the bank worth? 'You know what it is' and £500 came the answers. Aspinall, Burke and finally Lady Osborne were charged with running a common gaming house, at which she took great umbrage. The story that Aspinall liked to tell later was that she'd responded: 'This is absurd. All these people are friends of ours and none of them is common. Young man, there was nothing common here until you walked in.'[9]

When it went to court the prosecuting QC's case rested on his ability to prove that their use of the flat for unlawful gaming was both habitual and 'for gain or lucre' as expressed in the statute of Henry VIII. Parties were held on two occasions three weeks apart around Christmas, but it was the festive season and 'no judge or jury in the world could conceivably say that was habitual', submitted Gilbert Beyfus QC for the defence. His argument succeeded. The trio walked free from court and their victory prompted an escalation in the number of chemmy games occurring nightly around south-west London. From Pont Street and Sloane Gardens in Chelsea to Eaton Place and Grosvenor Crescent in Belgravia, a couple of dozen people at a time would congregate at an agreed address and play cards through the night. Regulars at the tables included Freud, Bacon, assorted aristocrats such as Mark Sykes and Mark Birley, Billy Hill and his underworld associates, and David Litvinoff; where protection was needed, the Kray twins offered their services. Mark Sykes' games were a tier down from Aspinall's in prestige but still saw fortunes change hands in an evening; over a double vodka and tonic in the Antelope pub in Belgravia the raffish Sykes, sporting a blazer and polka-dotted navy cravat and a few days' stubble, told me that he paid Litvinoff a commission for introducing wealthy new players. The morning after one of his chemmy parties in summer 1959 Litvinoff offered to clean his house and left it spotless, though in doing so he also tidied away the transcripts of a court case in which Sykes appeared as a witness – a society scandal concerning young heiress Katherine Dowsett and her would-be husband, Edward Langley, who had disobeyed a restraining order brought by her father – and promptly sold the story to the *Daily Express*. The chemmy scene assumed an untenable place somewhere between legality and illegality and this, coupled with the absurd situation in which OAPs playing bridge in a village hall had to decamp elsewhere to settle up, made it plain that the archaic gambling laws needed to change. So it was that, as the Krays' associate Leslie Payne put it, 'the unbelievably inept' 1960 Betting and Gaming Act became law. From 1st January 1961, gambling for small sums would become legal for games of skill. 'Its intention', Payne wrote, 'was to legalise the harmless games of bingo played in church halls and at Women's Institute meetings up and down the country; its effect was to start a mad scramble of unscrupulous gambling club operators.'[10]

By now the Kray twins had expanded their business from protecting other people's venues to running their own. Their first was a billiard hall off the Mile End Road, which Ronnie and Reggie followed with the Double R club in Bow Road. In the spring of 1960, thanks to some deft work by his solicitor, Reggie emerged early from an eighteen-month prison sentence for making threats connected to a protection racket, and the reunited twins teamed up with Payne, who, along with the equally shrewd fraudster Micky Fawcett, lent their activities a sophistication of which they alone would have been incapable. 'Payne the Brain', as he was known, was a softly spoken, meticulous character usually to be seen in a lightweight suit and polka-dotted blue bow tie. While he was not an aggressive man by nature, his horrendous wartime experiences fighting in Italy meant he was unfazed by the persistent petty violence surrounding his new colleagues: it was tiresome rather than appalling. After his release Reggie asked Payne to contact a man named Stefan de Fay, the owner of the nightclub Esmeralda's Barn, which since the early 1950s had attracted a glamorous crowd of debutantes and their friends. The club at 50 Wilton Place in Knightsbridge had been run by Esmeralda Noel-Smith until her sudden death from carbon monoxide poisoning. Pietro Annigoni and Tim Whidborne had created a mural peopled with characters after William Hogarth and Thomas Rowlandson that made the main room look like an eighteenth-century country barn, the gentle lighting cast a sympathetic glow over the well-to-do members, and the Guyanese singer Cy Grant crooned Caribbean folk songs. Each of the club's three floors had a different purpose. At the bottom was the Cellar Club, run for a lesbian clientele by a woman named Ginette; then there was a smart dining room; and now at the top, owing to de Fay's eagerness to exploit the new atmosphere surrounding gambling, there was a casino with chemmy tables and a roulette wheel. It was Rachman who had alerted the Krays to the Barn and de Fay's vulnerability, as he owed them a favour: when they harangued him for protection money he wrote them a cheque that bounced, then vanished when they came looking for him. This spurred the twins to set their enforcers on his men in Notting Hill: as Reggie said, they 'were big but our boys were bigger'.[11] Rachman needed to sweeten them with a major gesture. Also vital was the encouragement of Billy Hill, who knew the opportunity meant they would be preoccupied at a safe distance from the more lucrative gambling scams he was perpetrating in Mayfair.

Esmeralda's Barn in Knightsbridge.

It was autumn 1960 when Payne phoned de Fay to invite him over to his office for a chat about a business proposal. Payne sounded amiable enough, as indeed he was when de Fay first stepped into his office. It was the two silent, besuited men sitting alongside him who lent a charge to the atmosphere. Payne proceeded to reveal methodically his detailed under-standing of the Barn's cashflow and management structure. De Fay could only nod as Payne informed him that during the last three months the Barn had raked in an average of £7,250 per month, and that while de Fay was one of four investors in the club, overall control lay in the hands of a holding company titled Hotel Organisation Ltd; and only one man owned Hotel Organisation Ltd: Stefan de Fay. It must be a great responsibility for one man, he intimated. Ultimately he made it sound as if these kindly gentlemen were proposing to do him a favour and lighten his burden in life.

'You will simply be relieved of all the worries you must have, running such a vulnerable club as this,' he said.

'Worries?' replied de Fay. 'But I have no worries.'

Payne said nothing, only turned to look at the twins, whose eyes were fixed on de Fay.

'I wouldn't be so sure,' said Payne. Their offer was £1,000. De Fay had no option but to accept.

Billy Wallace's assertion via the Hickey column that he would not marry Princess Margaret was proved true in February 1960 when she announced her engagement to Antony Armstrong-Jones, with whom Litvinoff had been acquainted since Donald Cammell's days in Flood Street. The world's press were beside themselves at the prospect of the Queen's sister getting married, and to a commoner too. A hack from United Press International's London bureau went door-knocking at his former address and duly reported that 'Ethel Wright, the cleaning woman at Armstrong-Jones' old flat, clucked: "Princess Margaret will have to persuade Tony to be tidier – he used to let his place get into an awful mess." Armstrong-Jones now rides in a Rolls-Royce, another significant change in his mode of living. A neighbour at his old flat, David Litvinoff, said: "He often used to travel on his old motorcycle."'[12]

While Litvinoff evidently had a flat near Armstrong-Jones' in Pimlico Road at this time, the London telephone directories record that he remained at 14 Hans Crescent from 1957 to 1959; then in 1960 he pops up at 219a Kensington High Street, listed between his half-brothers Emanuel, Barnet and Pinchus, who were living in Ealing, Hampstead and Golders Green respectively. While he was often seen now with gay, Jewish East End friends such as Lionel Bart and Harry Bidney, a notorious masochist who would later form the 62 Group,* he remained close to friends such as George Melly, Tim Whidborne, Andy Garnett and Donald Cammell. Cammell left London in late 1959 for New York, by which time Litvinoff, with typical hyperbolic wordplay, observed that 'Donald had tried every drug, and every known combination of drugs, known to man'.[13] He grew closer to the twins, in particular Ronnie, who usually called him 'Litz', but his fascination with the workings of the mind led him also to cultivate connections with those who displayed a gentler kind of madness, such as Michael Cross, who typed Litvinoff long screeds of his arcane philoso- phising and who in Garnett's words 'had string tied between furniture legs in his room to project his power to give Princess Margaret an immaculate conception'. These letters suggest Litvinoff had interviewed him with the intention of writing about him. Cross became another of Litvinoff's pet eccentrics and grotesques, the latest addition to a fast-expanding collection.

Esmeralda's Barn symbolised the Krays' brusque grope into society's upper reaches, and soon came to embody everything that Ronnie Kray wanted in his life. Now they were company directors in formal control of a significant Knightsbridge venue, stretching still further the East End's westwards grasp: they were as imperious here and in Soho as they were in Bethnal Green. Kenny Cantor, a nightclub entertainer, recalled the twins' presence in the lounge of the Raymond Revuebar: 'If they laughed, everyone laughed.'[14] At the Barn the scowling Ronnie, now styling himself 'the Colonel', could survey his newly won empire and bask in the reflected glory every time someone such as Armstrong-Jones glided in to be greeted by their respectable frontman, Lord Effingham. To Payne the two ends of the social spectrum seemed made for each other: 'Aristocrats and successful criminals have a great deal in common: boredom and selfishness, ample money and free time and a complete lack of interest in conventional, cautious bourgeois morality.'[15]†

---

*   A revival of the 43 Group intended to combat the resurgent anti-Semitic fascism propounded by Colin Jordan's National Socialist Movement – and here with Bidney, just as in the late 1940s, Litvinoff was again involved in tracking down and confronting anti-Semites.
†   Not a phenomenon unique to 1960s London but one apparent in various culturally fruitful times. Jazz clarinettist Mezz Mezzrow on playing at Luigi's Cafe during the Jazz Age in 1920s Detroit: 'It struck me funny how the top and bottom crusts of society were always getting together during the prohibition era. In this swanky club, which was run by the head of the notorious Purple Gang, Detroit's bluebloods used to congregate – the Grosse Pointe mob on

The Barn brought to Ronnie Kray's life a touch of glamour, a chance to meet wealthy and powerful people, to entertain boys, to make substantial amounts of money without lifting a finger. No need to 'chiv' anyone, wave a Luger around or perpetrate the usual manipulations by which they did someone an unsolicited favour then declared him in their debt. If you ran a casino it appeared that wealthy people would queue up to pour their money into your pockets. It formed a prominent stage, too, for them to indulge their taste for the sinister, the dim spotlights over the smoke-clouded tables creating a room full of shadows and intrigue.* Then there was the exotic sophistication, the way that his favourite croupier, a former stable boy named Bobby Buckley, enunciated the French terms when running a chemmy game: *banco*, or *banco suivi*, he'd lisp, or *avec la table*, depending on how large a bet the player wished to place. In Mim Scala's words, Buckley was 'a pretty leprechaun of an Irish boy with a slight stammer but as hard as nails'.[16] Micky Fawcett was one of the twins' most trusted associates by then, and would later run the Barn himself for a spell.

---

the slumming kick, rubbing elbows with Louie the Wop's mob. That Purple Gang was a hard lot of guys, so tough they made Capone's playmates look like a kindergarten class, and Detroit's snooty set used to feel it was really living to talk to them hoodlums without getting their ounce-brains blown out.' *Really the Blues*, by Milton 'Mezz' Mezzrow and Bernard Wolfe (The Jazz Book Club/Secker and Warburg, 1959), p. 92. Cultural historian Mark Donnelly offered these thoughts on 'how and why high society rubbed shoulders with the underworld in the 1960s', saying, 'without generalising too crudely, there does seem to be an individualist reaction in the 1960s against the collectivism and group mentality of wartime, and against the new social discipline of the welfare state – personified by housing officers, welfare bureaucrats, teachers, and so on. You can track a pop culture language of individualism through things like Elvis's rock'n'roll, Marlon Brando and James Dean films, British kitchen sink dramas with the non-conformist anti-heroes – and of course there was a growth in advertising that positioned people as discerning and empowered consumers. . . There's also a lot of political and media talk in the mid-1960s about "classlessness", pushed in particular by Harold Wilson's election campaign to create a newly "meritocratic" Britain, freed from class snobbery and the power of old school tie networks. That's probably why Wilson gave the Beatles MBEs in 1965, because they symbolised social mobility.'

*   Micky Fawcett noted how Ronnie in particular relished creating a macabre effect, whether on show in the Barn or at home in Bethnal Green. 'Barney Ross, an old world-champion boxer, was among those who visited Vallance Road and got a tour of the tiny streets packed into that area of the East End. I was charged with getting him there. "Bring him all the way through Spitalfields Market," said Ronnie, "in the dark." It was that theatrical side coming out again. He knew that the deserted rows of stalls at night would be a delightfully spooky way to greet the visitor.' *Krayzy Days*, Chapter Five, 'Having a Quiet Drink at the Hammer Club'.

He remembered Ronnie salivating over Buckley, always 'taking him off' by copying the way he spoke. The fact he worked there at all resulted from a pair of manoeuvres that won 'the Colonel' the prize he coveted, while simultaneously emphasising that the growing ranks of weaker subordinates under his dominating control included David Litvinoff.

Bobby Buckley and Ronnie Kray.

* * *

After the 1960 Act casinos became a newly designated, formalised zone in which those who were drawn to risk naturally congregated, and thus a natural intersection point between the spheres of art, aristocracy and criminality. When a book called *The New London Spy* was published six years later, the un-bylined author of the section on gambling theorised about the psychological urges propelling this behaviour. 'Why do they do it? Some are sadists, enjoying it best when other losers squirm; others are masochists, squirming with pleasure when they themselves lose.'[17] Further to that he or she quoted the novelist Simon Raven's observation: 'In one's childhood, Mummy and Nanny said it was wrong to get something for nothing. Obsessive gamblers have a subconscious desire to be punished.'

For men such as Litvinoff, Freud and their mutual friend Francis Bacon (who preferred roulette, which correlated with his painting's obsession with chance and accident), at some level, conscious or otherwise, the addiction to gambling manifested a deep-seated obsession with, and even an urge towards, the painful sensation of loss. Freud found casinos appealing only when they had the ability to ruin him. 'Gambling is only exciting if you don't have any money,' he told Geordie Greig in 2009, by which time it had long lost its thrill. 'It just no longer interests me as I have enough money to lose without it ever hurting me. The only point of gambling is to have the fear of losing and when I say losing I mean losing everything. It has to hurt.'[18]

Gambling at Esmeralda's Barn brought a very real risk of being hurt. David Somerset, the Duke of Beaufort, recounted in the BBC documentary *Lucian Freud: Painted Life* how Freud appeared at his home one morning requesting a £1,500 loan after crossing the Krays. Somerset asked why he needed such a large sum at such short notice. 'He said because if I haven't produced it by twelve o'clock they're going to cut my tongue out.'[19] Lord Rothschild recalled Freud telling him: 'I'm in trouble with pressing debts to the Kray brothers. If I do not give them £1,000 they will cut my hand off.'[20*]

Rothschild gave him the money, though Litvinoff is said by one friend to have interceded with the twins regarding this affair, explaining that such a talented artist was of far more use to them with his hands intact. But regarding his own debts, there was no one to mediate and no prospect of raising the necessary sum by selling a portrait. His only resources were his wit, a potent but ephemeral kind of capital that invariably only kept people at bay for so long, and his ability to exert leverage by ensuring that his creditors were in other ways in his debt. One thing was certain: he would never gamble his way out of arrears, or at least not for long, for if by chance he found himself in the black, the masochist in him would soon rectify the situation. Whidborne, who'd tired of the Barn when it became a casino and now preferred the bohemian atmosphere of the Pheasantry on the King's Road, said that Litvinoff 'was always hoping to win money gambling, and on occasions would give me several hundred pounds' which Whidborne would stow away in a small safe in his wall. 'A few days later he would frantically call round to pick the cash up so that he could continue his winning streak – sure enough the next time I saw him it would all have been lost.'

* * *

---

*   The twins were not the only gangsters to whom he owed gambling debts. Michael Caborn-Waterfield was accustomed to Freud knocking on his door at 4am and asking him to act as a go-between and give a 'marker' (IOU) to Billy Hill or Tommy Falco, Albert Dimes' bookmaker colleague, in lieu of debts incurred at *spielers*.

Bobby Buckley was a sparky and engaging ex-jockey and stable boy, who in John Pearson's words was 'immensely charming, and charm was rare around the twins'.[21] Frankie Fraser remembered him as 'a very good driver'; that is to say, one who knew all the best getaway routes rather than one who'd memorised the Highway Code. In late 1962 he could often be found at David Litvinoff's flat in Ashburn Place off Cromwell Road; at around a decade older, Litvinoff seemed to Micky Fawcett to have become Buckley's sugar daddy. Litvinoff had been working as a greeter schmoozing guests at the club while also frequenting the chemmy tables with associates such as Freud. He had known the Barn since its time under Esmeralda Noel-Smith's management; when the twins redecorated it to their tastes he visited with Fawcett and looked around in despair: 'What have they done? They've turned it into a fucking Maltese restaurant!' That he was able to gamble there at all marked it out as somewhere outside the top echelon of gaming houses, which at that time comprised Crockfords, the Curzon House, Quents and John Aspinall's new venture, the Clermont Club, all of them in Mayfair. 'What we're looking for are people who are nicely behaved and who have some money,' Tim Holland, the chairman of Crockfords, told *The New London Spy*. 'By nicely behaved I mean they don't pick their noses or swear at the table. What we want is a first-class chap. As for money, it's no use anybody earning say £2,000 a year wanting to join. In fact, we don't really want *anybody* on a salary. Someone on a fixed salary only gets into trouble when things go wrong.'[22]

People without a salary *or* a private income got into deeper trouble still. When Litvinoff was in funds he was characteristically generous, meaning that he was soon broke again. Around this time he often saw his niece Anne, Alf Lister's (aka Abraham Litvinoff's) daughter. They'd go to jazz clubs or wander down Oxford Street together, on one occasion her uncle approaching every person he saw who looked vaguely Semitic and one after another saying a little rhyme to them: 'Hello, I'm a Jew – are you one too? Hello, I'm a Jew – are you one too?' In 1962 Anne married her fiancé, John Moore. 'When I was planning my wedding, [David] told me to go into any shop in London and choose the clothes I wanted,' she said. 'He would then go and pay for them for me. He kept his word. However, on the day of our wedding, he told us that he had lost £2,000 the night before playing *chemin de fer* and he wished he had given us the money and stayed at home. In those days, £2,000 would have bought a house!'

His gambling associations spanned from the aristocrats and MPs such as Tom Driberg with whom he rubbed shoulders at the Barn, to the bookmakers with whom he'd gamble on greyhounds and horses like his father, through to card schools in shady *spielers*, playing with men such as Alan 'The Screamer' Trinnaman, so-called because when he began to lose he would disrupt the game by screaming or shouting until it was abandoned, Leslie Berman, Mickey Cutler and 'a chap they called Meal Ticket', as a Met Police detective of the time recalled. Whether incurred at private parties, *spielers* or the Barn, his debts grew faster than he could repay them, and where his account with the twins was concerned he began to run it like an overdraft, making sporadic small repayments that were soon cancelled by new losses. This did not amuse them. Who did he think they were, his bank managers? He was taking liberties. The debt stood at around £800, equivalent to £15,000 today, when the matter came to a head: Litvinoff braced himself and confessed that he had no means of paying it in full. Their response was unexpected and demonstrated that at that stage he retained some use for them.

Micky Fawcett had just gone on the run. He'd ratcheted up his place in the East End criminal hierarchy with a 'performance'[23] at the Hammer Club in Upton Park, during which he'd swung a knife at a rival called Freddy Skennington and slashed his cheek 'so hard it almost took his head off',[24] then responded to a punch in the head from another called Pippy Bennett by smashing a crate of beer bottles one by one on Bennett's scalp. Fawcett's mate Johnny Davies had crowned the encounter by shooting Bennett's brother Russy 'in the bollocks and, though we didn't know it at the time, only narrowly missed the crucial femoral artery'.[25] It had done the trick but they needed to lie low for a while. Fawcett 'legged it to Esmeralda's Barn to find the twins, taking my time to ensure that I was not followed',[26] he wrote in his memoir *Krayzy Days*. 'Only Ronnie was there. I told him what had happened and I knew he would understand.' For the Krays such incidents were positive PR and provided good stories to laugh and reminisce about during a drinking session. The only trouble was that he had nowhere to go: 'I've got to find somewhere safe now,' he told Ronnie.

'Well, you're in luck,' Kray replied. 'We've just taken a flat off someone over a debt.'

Soon afterwards Tim Whidborne went over to Litvinoff's flat at 4 Ashburn Place 'to find it being taken over by the Krays'. They made Litvinoff sign over the lease and told him: 'You've got to be off.' They took the furnishings, even shunting out an upright piano, but there was one possession of Litvinoff's that Ronnie especially desired. As if taking Litvinoff's flat were not enough, around this time Ronnie made a second move that reiterated his senior status: Litvinoff had also to abandon any claim on Bobby Buckley, who became Ronnie's boyfriend and a croupier at the Barn. The transfer of property wasn't an acquisition in the Krays' view: instead Whidborne heard them describe it as a 'merger', a term so far from their usual vocabulary that John Pearson suspects they acquired it from Payne. Whidborne remembered that '[Litvinoff] did not seem to mind about it, however, and it is thought that he was allowed to stay on, possibly as the court jester'.

Fawcett stayed for six months and denies that Litvinoff continued to live there, but said he would call by. We spoke at the May Fair Hotel in Stratton Street, Fawcett looking sharp in a dark jacket over a buttoned-up Fred Perry shirt. Dark glasses, no-nonsense demeanour (me: 'Can I ask you about –'; him, before I'd finished: 'Yeah go on'), seventy-six years' wear and tear on his vocal cords, puffy skin where his knuckles used to be. He had a dry wit, cultural tastes that might be surprising in an ex-con and boxing trainer (French new wave cinema, Monty Python, *Private Eye* magazine) and it was easy to see why even Metropolitan police commander Bert Wickstead found him 'very likeable'[27] and 'had a lot of respect for him',[28] albeit that the context was Fawcett's decision to assist Wickstead's prosecution of the vicious East Ham-based Tibbs gang, who believed Fawcett had tried to kill one of them and were now trying to kill him.

He said he'd come to recognise Litvinoff as a Soho face during the previous couple of years, first spying him on a street corner embroiled in an argument with a prostitute and collaring a passer-by to bring him into the conversation and defuse the situation. 'I thought, "Hello, he's a bit warm",' said Fawcett; a bit savvy in other words, knowing how to work people, work the city. Litvinoff was still writing for the Hickey column and didn't strike him as a proper underworld figure, rather someone who was 'quite naive, out of his depth compared to the characters we usually hung around with'. It was strange, too, the way that he decided to describe and extol to Fawcett the component parts of the male genitalia, 'as if he thought I'd never seen one myself', he said. 'I found it. . .' Fawcett, an articulate and analytical man, sought the right word: ' . . .distasteful.' Litvinoff also struck him as unusual in that 'he was completely out of the closet at a time when it was still very much illegal and while he wasn't effeminate, he didn't give a fuck who knew he was gay'.[29] Fawcett hadn't met anyone like that before and, being unworldly about such matters, he asked Litvinoff outright: so are you a homosexual? 'Yes I am,' he replied. 'No, I'm not. . .well, I'll have anything if it's in bed.'

It was an attitude he had in common with Ronnie Kray, who usually settled for a woman if he couldn't intimidate a young man into accompanying him home at the end of the night. The pair began to spend more and more time together; Buckley would later say that Litvinoff was one of Kray's most important associates of the time. Litvinoff made him laugh and seemed to know all the people Ronnie wanted to know, from dukes and lords to the rent boys and street kids who could keep them informed of underworld rivals' activities. Along with Reggie, who was also bisexual but, unlike his twin, firmly in the closet, they had for some time been in the habit of trawling the streets looking for young men, with Litvinoff taking the lead. Christopher Gibbs was once walking down Sloane Street at around 3am when he saw 'David suddenly rolling up in a car with the Kray brothers, these big chaps, and plainly what he was doing was going out looking for people for them'. They pulled to the kerb, wound down the window. 'Christopher,' he said, 'I'd like to introduce you to Ronald and Reginald Kray.' The introduction was made and they went their separate ways, Gibbs on his own nocturnal adventure, Litvinoff and the Krays prowling onwards into the dark, Ronnie's salacious mumbles of 'Here's a prospect' a lewd refrain through the long drunken ballad of the night. Litvinoff's taste was for 'little boys, particularly naughty, runaway Borstal boys',[30] in Mim Scala's words.* Sex had become an obsession, whether as conquest or communion, perhaps as a distraction from inner torments in multiple respects: the ego-boost of domination, of turning a rough boy pliant, the pursuit of which lent purpose in a life bereft of professional direction; the thrill of the chase, the promise of release and the momentary anaesthesia of orgasm, the blank divine flash before the melancholy world rushed in again.

He began to operate as an informal agent on the twins' behalf, his duties spanning public relations to property acquisition. Neil Oram ran a beatnik cafe on the corner of Berwick Street and D'Arblay Street called the

---

* A phrase from Scala's book that has led online conspiracy theorists investigating historic child sexual abuse to accuse Litvinoff of procuring children for VIP paedophiles, which was not Scala's intention at all, as he clarified to me in an email: 'I did not mean to imply paedophilia . . . I was referring to young men who could be found hanging out in Soho. Definitely not children. I hope this is clear.'

House of Sam Widges, and became accustomed to seeing Litvinoff
loitering on the opposite corner with a set of half a dozen obscure Soho
characters who shared his sexuality and penchant for violence. If anyone
crossed them, Oram recalled, their idea of fun was to lie the offender down
in the street and drive a car over his ankles, or haul him off to the launder-
ette and shove a pipe billowing boiling steam up his backside. Litvinoff
knew how to deploy even Soho's most quotidian fabric as an armoury in his
life's battleground: cars and laundry pipes became weapons; George Melly
recalled how he 'walked with me once through Soho and kept reaching up
to sills and flat surfaces to feel if a metal bar was still in place for emergen-
cies'.[31] Oram always felt unsettled when Litvinoff entered the cafe, not
least on the day when he bustled in and announced he was there on behalf
of the Kray brothers, whom he said wished to acquire the club in the basement. Oram refused to sell but believes that they got their hands on it later,
after he'd finished working there. He had the sense, too, that Litvinoff was
chaperoning people from Chelsea around Soho, laying on a subterranean
safari where they could feel a frisson of London's underbelly before
retreating to the safety of SW3. Gibbs observed that 'Chelsea was very
much removed from the rest of London' at that time. 'There were people
who hung out in Chelsea who might not go east of Sloane Square for
months. West of Sloane Square was a kind of dark land.'[32] Litvinoff was
moving squares of the map like tiles on a sliding puzzle: bring Chelsea over
to Soho, Soho to the East End, the East End across to Chelsea and a new
picture emerges, a surreal rearrangement charged with fresh energies from
the clashes and fusions that he catalysed. When he headed back over to
Chelsea of an evening he'd function as the twins' personal propagandist.
Fear was their lifeblood: the more they instilled in people the breadth of
London, the stronger they were. Litvinoff's reports of their activities to his
affluent Chelsea friends, coupled with his uncanny impression of Ronnie's
strange lisping mumble, served to establish the Kray mythology well
beyond the twins' natural habitat. The tales he could tell: of how Ronnie
burned Lennie Hamilton's face in the Barn's kitchen with a white-hot steel
more traditionally used for sharpening knives; how businessmen who
refused to pay 'protection' were tried at a kangaroo court in a pub's back
room, found guilty and slashed across the buttocks by Ronnie 'so every
time the bastards sit down they'll remember me'; how they set trained
attack dogs on people, cut their fingers off, and in the aftermath of the
suicide of their barman at the Double R club, hunted down his Greek

boyfriend and imprisoned him naked in a cupboard for three days, returning now and then to punch him, hose him down and chuck pieces of bread at him before locking him up again. While he conjured the Krays' legend over dinner to friends such as Deborah Dixon and Donald Cammell, the latter of whom could never hear enough about the twins' activities, Litvinoff's own reputation began to spread until he became known as the most outrageous man in London. Acquaintances told strangers stories of his disturbing humour, citing an incident at a Chelsea party where a well-known drunk collapsed in the bathroom and lay unconscious in the bath. After spotting him Litvinoff dashed to the kitchen to retrieve some fresh chicken livers he'd noticed in the fridge and proceeded to pour them on to the man's chest before giving him a shake. 'For God's sake, wake up, wake up!' Litvinoff urged him. 'Someone call a doctor. You've sicked up your lungs!'

His ubiquity heightened his menace. As his acquaintance Antony Sharples observed,* if you wished to steer clear of the Krays you could go to the ICA or the British Museum, but nowhere were you guaranteed to avoid Litvinoff. Rumours of his familiarity with violence strengthened the unease his name began to evoke. His sturdy, muscular frame bristled with a simmering energy in need of regular release; and in such moments, with his strangely large fists he could punch like a boxer. Anthony Haden-Guest called him 'one of the most physically formidable people I have ever met'.[33] Christopher Gibbs remembered once asking him to carry a Romanesque marble antique that 'weighed a ton', and Litvinoff 'walking about with it as if it was wooden'. His association with the increasingly notorious twins only strengthened the unnerving air that surrounded him. But to those close to the Krays it was plain that the relationship was unbalanced: Litvinoff would do anything to be around them, and needed them far more than they needed him. They required him as a procurer but ultimately Emanuel Litvinoff was correct. His indiscretion meant that he would never occupy their inner circle. Discretion is everything to the professional criminal: if information must be exchanged with a competitor from a rival 'firm' then its precise value must be equalled in the transaction. Business is business, no need to brag about it, to get 'flash'. The straight world is a discrete realm to be avoided as far as possible. You don't step through the looking glass. Those who transgress the invisible thresholds are beneath contempt, their hypocrisy and pathetic lack of self-control making them worse than

---

* In a reminiscence contributed to Litvinoff's Wikipedia entry.

the police. Rule number one in the criminal code is that you don't grass, and indeed one of Ronnie Kray's most excruciating delusions during his 1958 spell at Long Grove psychiatric hospital was that people thought he'd become an informer; worse still were the dark flashes in which he wondered whether their suspicions were correct, that he had inadvertently blown someone's cover. Litvinoff's personal code was not so rigid; some say he didn't even have the morality of thieves. 'He was amoral,' reckoned Nigel Waymouth. He had a head bursting with his own secrets, so to relieve the tension by proxy he was cavalier with other people's. He talked and talked, his mind and mouth perpetually absorbed and relayed information, and what others would call gossip, he considered a sign of his interest in how humans function. His friend Juno Gemes, whom he met in Chelsea a few years later, said: 'David was the one who explained to me that gossip is important, that it isn't frivolous or something to be ashamed of, but is how the world goes round – it is about being interested in other people. That's the first lesson he taught me. He would go on and on about this person or that person, going to great detail, and he saw my interest wane and I looked bored, and he said: "You're so wrong about this. You think gossip is trivial? Gossip is the means by which you get to know much more about the people you are interacting with and sharing your life with – don't ever do that again. And when I gossip, listen! And similarly remember that what you know about yourself and others is valuable information."'

The twins didn't see the world that way, however. His attitudes were troubling, as was his disrespect. In their argot he took 'diabolical liberties': truer than they knew, for he was determined to be devilish and free. He'd call at Ashburn Place and ask if Ronnie was about, except he didn't call him Ronnie. His preferred moniker for the man who had been certified insane and would later be diagnosed with paranoid schizophrenia was 'boot-nose,'* referring to the shape of Kray's broken nose. Though Ronnie persisted in styling himself 'the Colonel', Litvinoff declared to him and Fawcett that he didn't much care for it: 'I don't think "the Colonel" really suits him, do you, Micky? I think we should call him "boot-nose". Don't you think that suits him better?' Ronnie just scowled and muttered. Fawcett watched their rivalry escalate: 'As it started heating up, Litvinoff started taking the piss out of Ronnie Kray to his face, which nobody ever did. Ever. He was like a mad

---

*   Not Litvinoff's invention but a term that he knew annoyed Ronnie: see *Running with the Krays*, by Billy Webb (Mainstream Publishing, 1993), p. 54.

gorilla, Ronnie Kray, and he was upset. They say a madman's got the strength of ten men, and Ronnie used to lose it in a second and had the strength of ten men, he was really strong. It was always this friction between David Litvinoff and Ronnie Kray over Bobby Buckley.' Litvinoff pushed at the boundaries of Kray's patience by continuing to make passes at Buckley despite having been usurped. 'And Ronnie, when Litvinoff was out of earshot and he was really in his worst black moods, he'd growl to me: "I'll deal with that bastard, I'll teach him to go around seducing young boys." Which was Ronnie's strong suit anyway! "He won't get away with that. . ."'

Litvinoff was undeterred by Ronnie's threats. He would use the name behind his back too: 'Boot-nose been in today?' he'd ask, on dropping in at the Barn. 'No? Well, tell him I called by.' He was obsessed by Buckley but also engrossed in trying to understand Kray's psychology, to unpick the knot of terrors and grievances that comprised his personality and in doing so better understand his attitude towards younger men. 'I can't work out what role Ronnie plays in this,' he told Fawcett in the crisp, beautifully pronounced English he'd cultivated by then. 'He certainly doesn't father them.'[34] By the next time Litvinoff visited Ashburn Place he'd worked it out. 'He takes the woman's role!' he told Fawcett with an air of triumph. 'He likes to *mother* them!'

Litvinoff in turn seems to have assumed a parental role towards Ronnie, comforting him during his depressions. 'People go on about how rough and violent the Krays were,' he told Julian Lloyd a few years later, 'but I remember Ron getting so upset and I'd get into bed with him and just hug him and try and make him feel all right. He didn't seem such a tough, violent man on those occasions.'

But his concern didn't prevent Litvinoff from chasing Buckley, nor from procuring girls for him despite Kray's disapproval, behaviour that caused William Feaver to label him as 'either fearless or reckless or pathologically tactless'. As Nigel Waymouth put it, 'David was a sexual predator, and he also liked to feed his friends.' He was obsessed and would do whatever he could to curry favour with the younger man. He couldn't help himself. Perhaps he didn't want to help himself. Eventually, as ever, he went too far.

With Ronnie Kray in control of Esmeralda's Barn, his underlings had to obey his diktats. If he felt like bestowing his favour on chosen punters, extending their credit even though their losses far exceeded what they could repay, then he would do so, while enjoying the public demonstration of his power, like the Roman emperor who determined a prone gladiator's fate by opening or closing his hand. 'It didn't matter if this guy lost £20,000,' wrote the twins' henchman Albert Donoghue, 'Ronnie would still be saying, "Give him some credit. It's down to me."'[35]

But running the Barn according to Ronnie Kray's whims did not make for a sustainable business plan, and what should have been a lucrative operation became, in Donoghue's phrase, a 'financial disaster'[36] that wound to a close in late 1963. Besides, for many of the aristocrats the allure of attending a casino run by gangsters had begun to fade when their hosts began behaving like gangsters. No one wanted to glance up from the roulette wheel to see Ronnie smashing a chair over Reggie's head for having looked at him the wrong way, and the contrast with London's top casinos grew starker still one hot summer's night when the twins held a boxing match on the dancefloor between Bobby Buckley and Tommy Cholmondeley; while respectable casinos such as Crockfords retained their elegant, hushed sophistication, when the pair entered the ring at 2am this smart corner of Knightsbridge was imbued with sweat and testosterone as its walls echoed the aggressive, alcohol-fuelled roars of the Kray brothers' closest friends, from Lord Boothby to David Litvinoff.*

'I suppose the Knightsbridge set found it amusing to start with, seeing all these scarred faces and pug uglies roaming around,' the south London criminal Freddie Foreman observed, 'sitting down with an East End cab driver and Lord and Lady Somebody sitting the other side, then of course when a few cheques were made out and they were a bit late being honoured two or three weeks would go by and they would be round putting pickaxes through Rolls-Royces and things like that.'[37]

He had been eating alone at a cafe near Earls Court Underground station one day in the autumn of 1963. As he walked out on to the crowded

---

*   Maintaining a long London tradition of impromptu displays of pugilism: the original William Hickey once recorded an early-nineteenth-century visit to a Little Russell Street drinking den called Wetherby's where 'the whole room was in an uproar, men and women promiscuously mounted upon chairs, tables, and benches, in order to see a sort of general conflict carrying on upon the floor. Two she-devils, for they scarce had human appearance were engaged in a scratching and boxing match, their faces entirely covered with blood, bosoms bare, and the clothes nearly torn from their bodies.' *London: The Biography*, by Peter Ackroyd (Vintage Books, 2001), p. 483. Litvinoff was truly a William Hickey of the mid-twentieth century.

pavement and began pulling on his overcoat, his arms halfway down the sleeves, a man strode up to him with a cut-throat razor concealed in his hand that he jabbed into Litvinoff's mouth, sliced into his left cheek and jerked across the other cheek before turning away with the words 'Ronnie says hello'. He disappeared before Litvinoff knew what had happened: he felt surprised but unhurt, then when he tried to talk his lips wouldn't move as he wished, just flapped uselessly, and he noticed a wetness trickling down his coat. After trying to patch himself up he headed over to see Donald Cammell, who was by now mainly living in Paris's rue Delambre but had taken a flat in nearby Hogarth Place while he completed a portrait commission. 'He'd been in a washroom and put a huge band-aid over it, but he was like an animal – he didn't care,' said Cammell. He and Deborah Dixon 'took him to hospital, got him stitched up, and he looked terrible. He slept on my floor for two or three days, doped up, and I saw this wound just heal up, as if he'd willed it.' At the couple's suggestion he soon joined them back in Paris, where he had cosmetic surgery; David Cammell recalls Litvinoff contemplating whether to ask the surgeon to straighten his nose while he was at it. 'And two months later it was just a rather elegant scar,' said Donald. 'And he looked fabulous.'[38]

The fine lines – one jutting out from the left of his mouth, the other across his right cheek – left him depressed at first, only strengthening the self-loathing that he often felt on looking in the mirror, but later he would make light of them and even wear them as a badge of honour. Tim Whidborne told him he looked like Gwynplaine, the hero of Victor Hugo's novel *L'Homme qui rit*, whose mouth is carved into a perpetual grin. Hugo likens it to the Greek mask of comedy: 'All parody which borders on folly, all irony which borders on wisdom, were condensed and amalgamated in that face,' he writes. 'One corner of the mouth was raised, in mockery of the human race; the other side, in blasphemy of the gods. . . One might almost have said that Gwynplaine was that dark, dead mask of ancient comedy adjusted to the body of a living man. . . What a weight for the shoulders of a man – an everlasting laugh!'[39] Later Litvinoff would proclaim it one of his favourite novels. Certainly few readers would ever identify with its hero quite as he did. Juno Gemes asked him a few years later how he came to look that way. His answer: 'Just a little present from the Kray twins.'

Perhaps by now he was accustomed to such treatment, for it came on top of another instance of severe violence meted out by underworld enforcers. The Campaign for Nuclear Disarmament began its four-day-long marches between the Ministry of Defence's Atomic Weapons Establishment at Aldermaston and central London at Easter 1958, and repeated them annually into the 1960s, attracting thousands of people who would walk down Kensington High Street towards Trafalgar Square. On this Easter in the early 1960s he was still living at number 219a, in a tall, slender, five-storey brick building with stone parapets running either side of an ornate top-floor gable window; though he told several friends that on the night in question he was staying along the road at Adam and Eve Mews, which has a railinged roof garden.

So the bang on the door, the punch in the face, the stripping naked and tying to a chair, the head-shaving, the rough carriage to the vertiginous balcony where he was left strapped to the railings until he regained consciousness.

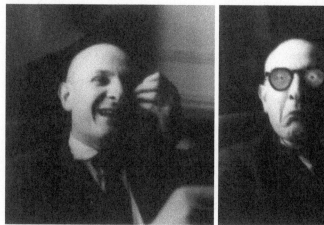

Litvinoff after having his head shaved.

It did the Krays' reputation no harm that word got around that they were to blame. But if they had a hand in the matter, they were not solely responsible, at least according to Litvinoff. He told people close to him that the instigator was another figure who flitted between the worlds of art and crime, one who knew the twins well. Several books have alluded to this. As well as Colin MacCabe's reference to the incident involving 'too many living performers for me to desire to achieve achieve complete accuracy',[40] John Pearson described the incident in *The Cult of Violence*, a sequel to his definitive account of the Krays' career, *The Profession of Violence*. 'The

Krays were blamed,' he wrote, 'particularly as Ron had fallen out with the accident-prone Litvinoff by then and in a previous encounter had smashed his nose in a club in Earls Court. But the shaving. . .incident had in fact been ordered and paid for by an influential former Chelsea friend of Litvinoff's whom he had seriously offended – so seriously that he wanted him taught a lesson he would not forget.'[41]

Rebecca and Sam Umland, in their biography of Donald Cammell, concur that 'publicly, Litvinoff attributed the event to the Krays, but in private he confided to some, such as Donald and David Cammell, that he thought the perpetrator was a certain sinister London figure, still living, whose name we shall not mention'.[42] In 1990 a *Vanity Fair* article cast Litvinoff as 'a well-known figure in both the monde and the demimonde and a fast and dangerous talker, [who] fell afoul of a close friend of the Twins'.[43]

They were referring to Lucian Freud, who by the early 1960s had established himself as one of the more malevolent inhabitants of the city's art world. Stories abound of his sexual sadism towards girlfriends whom he wished to dominate, of him posting excrement through the letter box of a gallery that he felt had slighted him, brawling in the street, and habitually driving his car in such a manner that a magistrate recommended he visit a psychiatrist. That he frequently settled disagreements by violent means is beyond dispute, though his friend William Feaver defended him against the suggestion he was behind this affair. 'I suspect the balcony scene was arranged by the Krays,' he said. 'Lucian was quite proud of his louche associates and could kick and punch when riled but it was the Krays who threatened to cut Litvinoff's tongue out when he wouldn't stop talking.

'Lucian did get into fights and he did have violent likes and dislikes but I've found him pretty accurate with his stories and explanations; certainly not given to covering up.'*

Others remain adamant that he was involved. The precise details of an underworld incident more than half a century ago in which all concerned are now dead will always be nigh-on impossible to determine. What can be said is that such behaviour would not have been uncharacteristic of Freud at this time in his life. It is known he had gangsters' henchmen at his disposal

---

* In the BBC documentary film *Lucian Freud: Painted Life*, Sir John Richardson recalls Freud mentioning knowing a man who was left tied to a balcony while an Aldermaston march passed by, but his comments shed no further light on the affair.

and that, as he put it himself, he enjoyed people treating him 'in a very delicate and careful way'[44] through fear of his underworld associations, a fact
that led to a police warning when his activities 'got rather out of hand'.[45*]
The claim is that he paid for a criminal firm – whether the Krays, which
their associate Micky Fawcett doubts, or, as John Pearson suspects is more
likely, old contacts from Paddington – to dispatch a pair of enforcers to
Kensington High Street to teach Litvinoff a lesson. Geordie Greig's account
of Freud's life corroborates that he thought little of deploying such connections to put the frighteners on his enemies. 'Sometimes he was not averse to
less orthodox means of persuasion, such as calling in a few gangland favours,'
Greig writes. 'Once over breakfast, Lucian asked me if I needed any help
from his "friends in Paddington" when I was involved in a quarrel with
someone.'[46] Greig also experienced Freud's readiness to threaten violence
first-hand. 'I rang the bell and after the clunking of several locks the door
opened a few inches and a voice menacingly asked, "What do you want?" A
ten-inch knife with a serrated edge was pointed at me. "Lucian. It's me,
Geordie. Put the knife down," I urged. And then I laughed, and when he
saw I was laughing, he laughed too.'[47]

The rumours regarding Freud's treatment of Litvinoff took root
and strengthened his mythology as a man with the power to summon the
city's most malign operators when he felt it necessary, and whose aura
disturbed even hardened members of the underworld. At Esmeralda's
Barn Freud was the only character who disconcerted Fawcett, who found
him 'sinister'. This effect was wholly intended. 'My idea was always to be
feared,' he told the art critic Martin Gayford in 2004 while painting his
portrait. 'How do you mean?' Gayford replied. 'Well, obviously, not to
have people taking cover when I approached, but being thought to be a
bit formidable.'[48]

Whether or not Freud wished his name to be attached to this
particular affair, he had by then cultivated and attained a reputation as a
dangerous character. The story became an integral part of his folklore,
helping to spread around the city his desired reputation as a man never to
be crossed.

*　*　*

---

*   This incident? Impossible to know as the police papers relating to Freud in the 1960s seem
to have disappeared; at least, they were not traceable via Freedom of Information Act requests.

I knew nothing of any such public persona when I first encountered Lucian Freud's art. From a vague interest my feelings crystallised on visiting Tate Britain in summer 2002. No paintings I'd seen before had been so impressively disturbing, and by comparison the surrealists I'd admired as a teenager, Dalí and Magritte et al., seemed self-indulgent: not a charge one could ever level at Freud, who would plainly indulge neither his own fantasies nor his sitters' vanity. It seemed at first that these were not paintings to be liked so much as admired, uncompromising creations whose company conjured unease as they proffered brutal truths; but later, despite their sitters' apparent alienation and palpable sadness, a genuine humanity seemed to emerge from the work of this self-proclaimed 'Jewish atheist' in a sense that tallied with Bertrand Russell's lines on his own atheism: that 'human comradeship seems to grow more intimate and more tender from the sense that we are all exiles on an inhospitable shore'.[49]

Writers who knew Freud well – Gayford, Feaver, Marina Warner, Greig towards the end – emphasise the appealing side of his personality. He had the most determined curiosity (in John Russell's words, 'He liked to gut a city as a fishmonger guts fish – so energetic were his explorations of Paris that his bicycle broke in half beneath him'[50]) and comes over as the most exciting man one could meet, someone who made those around him feel more alive, as if a little of his preternatural engagement with the world's fabric rubbed off on them. Funny, indiscreet, interested in everything from Ingres to boxing, a stimulating conversationalist who could reel off poems verbatim from Belloc to Larkin. At first Litvinoff was similarly reverent, telling friends of his wit, his style, his good looks, desperate to feel and convey some sense of association, just as he did with the twins. It's not accurate to say that this appeal masked Freud's darker side; rather that the mask he presented to the world bore darkness commingled with light in a manner as beguilingly complex as the skin tones in his portraits.

What could have caused Freud to take such measures? Nigel Waymouth understood that it arose from a barroom argument between him and Litvinoff over who had the more powerful underworld connections. Oliver Musker heard that Litvinoff had insulted him and caused serious offence: 'I don't know exactly how it started but I know how it ended,' he said. Tim Whidborne knew that Freud had grown particularly annoyed with Litvinoff, though he did not know why. David Cammell pointed to Litvinoff's threat to sue Freud over the portrait's title.

'He recited it to me,' said Cammell, detailing how Litvinoff extricated himself from his precarious position and found his flat 'completely wrecked', and 'he said that Freud was behind it all, because [Litvinoff] was suing him for having changed the name of the picture. . .to *The Procurer.*' However, the incident occurred some years after the short-lived legal dispute following the Marlborough Fine Arts show. It seems probable that that represented the beginning of the feud, which then escalated by degrees, Freud having in any case found Litvinoff despicable from the moment back in 1954 when he caught him impersonating him in Esmeralda's Barn. The climax seems to mark the confluence of several arguments, another relating to Freud's married girlfriend of the time, Lady Belinda Lambton, with whom he had a fifteen-year affair. A few years later her daughter Anne Lambton heard a version from Litvinoff that implicated Freud as having engineered a situation in which the gangsters would attack him; as before he used the Krays' name, probably because it was safer than revealing the real perpetrators. Anne was a wild fifteen-year-old, had just run away from home, and met him at Nigel Waymouth's home in Glebe Place. Waymouth introduced her to him and Litvinoff exclaimed: 'Lambton!'

'I said: "Yes, Lambton," and he said: "You're the reason I was hung upside down from a chair from a building by the Kray brothers."

'I said: "What do you mean?" and he said: "Has your mother got a butterfly-patterned sink and lavatory?"'

'Bindy' Lambton was obsessed by butterflies, Anne explained. She confirmed to Litvinoff that she did indeed, at the family estate in County Durham. It transpired that they were a gift from Freud, who had asked Litvinoff to lend him the money to buy them. Litvinoff in turn supposedly borrowed the necessary funds from the Krays; and knowing this, Freud refused to repay Litvinoff, leaving him dangerously in their debt.

Whether it was the Krays or other gangland contacts, whether he actively paid them or manoeuvred Litvinoff into a situation where it would happen, it seems Freud had very plausible reasons to contrive this culmination to their feud. Litvinoff's friends Shura Shihwarg and Joan Wyndham were writers and restaurateurs and bohemian *bon viveurs*; together they hosted riotous parties at their home in Wellington Square, off the King's Road, which welcomed all manner of curious figures across its threshold. As soon as Litvinoff had freed himself, it was to their tall Regency terrace house that he went, appearing at their doorstep spattered with blood.

'He trusted us because we had no *parti pris*, we weren't judgmental,' said the Russian Shihwarg. 'We had a seriously open house; I don't think I've been inhospitable to anyone. And one day he arrived and he was covered in blood. Both his shirt and his head. . .it was really horrendous, his face. I said: "David, what's happened?" and he told me the story. And the first place he went was our house. So I took him to the bathroom, he washed up, I gave him a clean shirt, and I said: "Who could have done this?" And all he said was: "I think Lucian's behind it." Freud had friends in the underworld, no doubt about that. What I heard from others was that David made a pass at the son of a friend of Lucian's, who complained to him. And Lucian took his revenge. If Lucian was behind it, to do a drastic thing like that required some cause. He wouldn't have had him trussed up and had his head shaved if he'd owed £50. And this is what I'd heard – he'd taken liberties he shouldn't have, almost provocatively, and this was the payback.'

I'd double-checked in advance with his carers and been assured that Albert Donoghue remembered Litvinoff. I drove for two and a half hours to the old people's home in Dagenham where he'd lived for nine years, was ushered through the standard communal television room – visitors' small talk competing with daytime TV blasting from the speakers, institutional furniture lining the walls, blank wizened faces gazing towards the glare – and out into the garden where one of the Krays' toughest enforcers sat alone in his wheelchair, taking in the spring sunshine. Donoghue joined the firm in 1964, a few years after the balcony affair, having impressed the twins with his reaction to being shot by Reggie. Word had got back to them that he'd said they should be shot for what they'd done to Lennie Hamilton, though in truth Donoghue didn't know Ronnie was responsible for branding Hamilton's face and was speaking in general terms of what he'd do to people who did such things. In October 1964 he heard the twins wanted to see him, an invitation that did not augur well but could not be ignored. He confronted the matter by walking into their local, the Crown and Anchor in Cheshire Street. His suspicions were confirmed when the pub promptly emptied; then Reggie blasted a bullet into his left leg. But he didn't grass, didn't run to the police or spill the details to the medical staff at St Andrew's Hospital who stitched up his wound. He kept matters discreet. The twins approved. He became one of the most feared figures in their circle, a tall, muscular, taciturn man known to be capable of extreme acts of violence, though later he would perpetrate an act that to his underworld peers was more appalling than any shooting or stabbing.

Old age had been unkind to him. He'd grown obese since suffering an incapacitating stroke some years earlier. I introduced myself and reminded him that I'd driven down to discuss his memories of David Litvinoff. Nothing. Litvinoff? Friend of Ronnie Kray's? I'm told you remember him. . .? 'Nah, don't ring any bells. What was he, Jewish fella?' Yes. . .born in Bethnal Green, grew up in Hackney. I could show you a photo if that would help? 'Wouldn't be able to see it. This eye's kaput,' he said, pointing at the expressionless left side of his face, 'and this one ain't much better.'

We got talking and the seventy-seven-year-old began to warm up. The twelve-pack of Guinness I'd been advised to bring helped. There weren't many of his circle still alive; he said most had succumbed to 'heart attacks and council tax', making the phrases rhyme. Sometimes his children came to visit. He was glad his sons hadn't taken the same route as him: the game had changed, there were too many casual shootings over nothing. He reeled out tales of men he'd done over forty to fifty years ago, those he'd punched and cut up and half strangled. Ronnie mixed with a lot of 'high-class queers', he said, and had an eye for young men: 'prospects', Kray called them, transferring into his sexual milieu the East End term for promising boxers. If Ronnie spied such a man he'd put out a 'warrant', abbreviated to a 'W', and there'd be a cash reward for anyone who came up with the goods. That was another way that Litvinoff could earn a few quid. How about this incident where Litvinoff ended up hanging from his balcony – did that ring any bells? 'Sounds like something Frankie Fraser was involved in,' he said. 'Bloke left dangling from his balcony with blood dripping on the pavement, and they had to cut him down and take him to hospital. I remember hearing about that.'

Another day, another trip to a care home in a rugged patch of London to interrogate a superannuated sociopath about something that he might have heard about half a century earlier. Frankie Fraser was living in Nunhead when I paid him a call, overseen by his sons David and Patrick. Fraser senior had been imprisoned for around forty-two of his ninety years, his offences spanning thefts, bank robberies, innumerable assaults and most infamously the unsolicited extraction of men's teeth with pliers on behalf of the Richardson brothers, which earned him one of his nicknames, 'the Dentist'. His other, 'Mad Frankie', he owed to having twice been certified insane, which led to spells at Cane Hill and Broadmoor psychiatric hospitals. Today he sat enveloped in his comfy chair, wooden walking stick resting against its arm, cracking jokes now and then. His face was a lattice of folds, wrinkles, old scars. Hooded eyes beneath bushy grey brows, a down-turned mouth, a formerly sharp nose whose bridge took a circuitous route down to its flattened tip. What had always made it unusual among London criminals was the discernible hint of Native Canadian: 'My father's mother was a Red Indian,' he said, whereas his mother's side of the family were Irish. Fraser was born in Lambeth in 1923 and, after being sent to Borstal and deserting from military service, was operating in Soho by the 1940s; the latter part of that decade saw him interned at Cane Hill, but by the 1950s he was at large again to serve as Billy Hill's most intimidating enforcer. After his final release from prison in the 1980s he established himself in a new career as a celebrity gangster, author of the autobiography *Mad Frank*, host of guided tours of the London underworld, guest on comedy shows such as *Shooting Stars*. In 1998 he fielded *Independent* readers' questions: 'Which is easier, being an author or being a gangster?' enquired one, to which he replied: 'Author or gangster – I'm a performer in both spheres.'[51]

Fraser thought he might have known Litvinoff as a face around town, but could recall nothing more. Gambling was the one thing he never got into, he said, because he could see that if it offered the possibility of making you rich, a far likelier outcome was that it would leave you poor. Successful criminals don't work to those kind of odds. Instead he and the Richardsons made money through other people's urge to gamble, a far steadier and more profitable source of income. In the wake of the Betting and Gaming Act they set up Atlantic Machines, a fruit machine business, and watched the money flow in. He explained why he'd helped bring about Jack 'Spot' Comer's downfall: 'Fucking grass he was. Well, he got his wife to do the grassing. They put eight or nine men wrongly in jail.' Fraser swung the conversation back to me: 'How about you, son? You ever had any trouble?' Would mentioning my magistrates' court appearance in 2008 for speeding on the A140 near Stowmarket place me somewhere in their world? 'No, no not really.'

Fraser said he'd known nothing of Ronnie's homosexuality. Like Donoghue, he could never reconcile the toughness of young men like Bobby Buckley with their sexual orientation. Well, Litvinoff was at the heart of that situation, I said, mentioning how he and Kray fell out over Buckley, and over Litvinoff's fondness for making jibes at Ronnie. Taking the piss out of Ronnie Kray? He laughed. Not many people did that and got away with it. Litvinoff didn't exactly get away with it, I said. Ronnie had him cut across the mouth. I showed him a photo in which Litvinoff's scars were visible. It didn't jog any memories: these things happened all the time. How about when Litvinoff had his head shaved and was tied to his balcony? Fraser looked blank. His son David said that, again, I had to understand that such things occurred so often it was unlikely his dad would remember a precise incident from so long ago. Patrick added that it was a funny one, though: 'It don't sound like the Krays. Not their M.O. They preferred to cut people.'

I'd discussed the affair with almost everyone I'd met, read more criminals' memoirs than is healthy for one lifetime, and followed Litvinoff's ghost to a dead end in an unfamiliar patch of south London. David Fraser dropped me off at Herne Hill station and I took the train back up to Victoria, peering through the scratched window at row upon row of brown-bricked terrace backs, box room over bathroom jutting into L-shaped backyard in diminishing replications that stretched out into London's vast ragged grey patchwork of merged villages, in which somewhere there must have been an individual who knew more about what had happened, but whose identity lay beyond the constraints of my time, finance and sanity.

We can say three things of the incident: that numerous sensible and reliable people believe Freud instigated it, that Freud and Litvinoff had a serious disagreement, and that Freud turned his underworld associates on people with whom he had serious disagreements. The suggestion of Freud's involvement resonated with his self-created mythology and took on an energy that neither he nor Litvinoff could control: but rather than react passively to what life inflicted on him, Litvinoff tried his best to control it by turning it into a story. It was one that he would exaggerate over dinner and fictionalise on the cinema screen, but first he would rehearse it in brutal reality.

Act One, Scene Four.

JIG: I tell you what I did some years ago was *Desert Island Discs*. . . And the point is this you see—

DL: About *Desert Island Discs*, if I can interject briefly - sorry to monopolise the conversation - for example impromptu and straight off the cuff I said to you (you know they never change the format): 'Good afternoon, ladies and gentlemen, this is Roy Plomley, and on *Desert Island Discs* this afternoon, we have the distinguished Welsh entrepreneurist Mr John Ivor Golding, and Mr John Ivor Golding will say a few words to you. May I call you John?'

JIG: Good gracious yes!

DL: 'Well, John, what would you do if you were cast on a desert island?'

JIG: My first feeling would be the same ecstasy as the rippling waters that hit the shimmering sands on the island with its coral trees and its coconuts and the alcoves and the caves. I would think to myself, I would not feel lonely because internally I would face my nature feeling now I can really be on the threshold of maturing my Madonna. You understand what I mean, don't you?

DL: Yes. You're in communication with nature and a higher order. In complete communion. I saw the light burn in your eyes after closing time when we saw you at Victoria. I thought you really had an inner light that activated and pulsed.

JIG: In 99.9 per cent of the masses the first thing they would want in a depressed situation is a phenobarbital or a Mandrax.

DL: What are they?

JIG: That eases loneliness of the subconscious, because they've got nobody to talk to on this desert island.

DL: So you'd give them lots of anthrax?

JIG: Well, they want something more or less to soothe the melancholy and the depression and the circumstances to which explicitly they have been placed. Just like Dreyfus was in the cells of Devil's Island in the Victorian age.

DL: By Esterhazy, the arch anti-Jew. Though Captain Dreyfus himself also had a monocle; he was a member of the monocled classes. Then he was subsequently manacled.

JIG: And don't forget too Queen Victoria. He got reinstated and the Legion of Honour and his full back pay and everything from Devil's Island was given back to him, and his rank.

DL: His rank? A pretty rank affair, yes.*

JIG: Knowing that I can go to the feelings of Dreyfus, you understand why a lot of people call me Methuselah.

DL: I thought of you in terms of Methuselaic connotation when I saw you. Because midst all the people hying and scurrying around Victoria on their way home to their little suburban rooms, I thought you alone had the dignity of the Third Eye. And all eyes were staring: your eyes were a magnificent sight, even allowing for the various bloodshot bits in various parts. They really were a magnificent sight. . . By the way, John, you looked in extremely good health and fairly expectorative and splenetic when I saw you – you haven't any infectious diseases such as anthrax, or anything like that, have you?

JIG: No, no. . . What made you say that?

DL: Well, I just wondered because you yourself said you're a gentleman of the road and if you wanted to go to a doctor, we'd get you all kitted out and equipped with the local commissar.

---

* As the poetry critic Jeremy Noel-Tod points out, it is in such exchanges that Litvinoff sounds particularly reminiscent 'of the Shakespearean fool, especially, perhaps, the dangerously impudent and suddenly vanishing Fool in Lear'.

Chapter 4

I Always Use a Cut-throat Razor

'People used to ask me why I was so unpredictable, so volatile. I didn't know then, but I think now it was my mental illness, my paranoia. I just couldn't stop myself from hurting people, especially if I thought they were slighting me or plotting against me. Also, I liked the feeling of guns. Usually, though, I was happier with my fists or a knife.'

Ron Kray, *My Story*

London's energy was rising. The central players in the familiar narrative of 'The Sixties' began to assume their positions. A young art dealer named Robert Fraser returned home from New York in 1962 and opened a gallery at 69 Duke Street, off Oxford Street. A guitarist from Cheltenham named Brian Jones, who led an up-and-coming rhythm and blues band and wore his blond hair in a daring bowl-cut, moved into Powis Square and thus into Litvinoff's orbit. Having gained a taste for living as a bachelor, Ronnie Kray rented a first-floor flat in Cedra Court, Stamford Hill; Reggie had always lived at 'Fort Vallance', the Kray family home on Vallance Road, other than nine months detained at Her Majesty's Pleasure but soon acquired the flat below his brother's. By 1963 Tim Whidborne had moved from a flat in Adam and Eve Mews and taken a spacious studio at the Pheasantry. On the other side of the world an art student named Martin Sharp met Richard Neville and Richard Walsh, who were respectively the editors of the student papers at the University of New South Wales and Sydney University. Out of the meeting came an irreverent new magazine: the first *Oz* was published on April Fools' Day that year. The Beatles left Liverpool for the capital in summer 1963, having scored their first number one with 'Please Please Me', and after a spell in a Bloomsbury hotel moved into a flat together in Green Street, Mayfair; their manager, Brian Epstein, moved into Whaddon House in Knightsbridge and developed an addiction to gambling, spending his evenings losing such sums that the Curzon House didn't charge him for the lavish meals and fine wines he consumed in the process. Epstein's experience of being Jewish and gay sets Litvinoff's attitude into sharp relief, emphasising the latter's fearlessness concerning subjects that were usually tiptoed around or the source of abuse, and must at times have made both men feel doubly marginalised. When in 1964 Epstein announced in the band's dressing room that he intended to write his autobiography and needed a title, John Lennon sneered: 'How about *Queer Jew?*' After he opted instead for *A Cellarful of Noise*, Lennon suggested a more apt one would be *A Cellarful of Boys*. That August saw them get stoned with Bob Dylan at the Delmonico Hotel in New York, a seismic moment in musical history but also within the development of the Beatles' and Epstein's relationship. Epstein looked into a mirror and pointed at his reflection. 'JEW!' he yelled, provoking much laughter. It was 'the first time Brian would point at himself and say "Jew",' said Paul McCartney. 'It may not seem the least bit significant to anyone else, but in our circle, it was very liberating.'[1] Around the Beatles, at least, Epstein's Jewishness had hitherto been almost as closeted as his homosexuality, which he 'spent most of his life concealing', 'something that caused him a lot of pain'.[2]

As was ever the case, the privileged classes had the capital at their disposal, its emerging characters arrayed for their delectation. A second wave of residents of the smarter SW postal areas – not Litvinoff's Chelsea Set so much as a generation contemporary with his younger friend Christopher Gibbs – found that of all the new beat groups that were snarling and gyrating their way around the nation (expedited by the growing network of motorways, which also expanded the criminal class's worldview), it was not the polished, besuited Beatles they found most thrilling but the animalistic Rolling Stones. At a time when this upper-class generation were doing their best to discard their titles and distinguish themselves from their parents, they were drawn to a band that seemed to threaten the social order; though if the Stones sought to reshape fusty post-war England it was not into an economically egalitarian society, more a sexual meritocracy in which lower-middle-class boys from Kent faced no social barriers excluding them from weekend parties at country estates where they could sleep with the daughters of the nobility. 'They were announced as bait by ambitious hostesses, courted by the bored scions of ancient houses,' George Melly proclaimed.[3] Robert Fraser introduced Jagger to Gibbs, at one of whose dinner parties the singer informed the fashion designer Michael Fish: 'I'm here to learn how to be a gentleman.'[4]

While the Stones carried an appealing air of danger for the rebellious young aristocrats, such social ties in turn connected the group to a source of far more authentic risk in the form of David Litvinoff. Amid the violent flow of humanity into this new social space, he represented the whirling eddy at the collision of two currents. London was changing at dizzying speed now. The city's nocturnal landscape began to mutate as the pop phenomenon took hold. Jazz revival and cabaret-style clubs began to make way for those playing the new music: Cy Laurie's became the mods' Scene Club, and Raymond Nash and Douglas Villiers turned the former Le Condor into La Discotheque. Upstairs Nash opened a gaming room with chemmy tables and a roulette wheel. Litvinoff could often be seen there or in the new *spielers* cropping up around the West End; and in one of them, among the troupe of young men with whom he surrounded himself, he picked up an East End boy named Gerry Goldstein and took him under his wing.

When John F. Kennedy was killed the Scene Club closed in homage, so on Friday, 22nd November 1963 a gaggle of kids buzzing on pills found themselves loitering outside in Ham Yard with nothing to do. John Pearse was there. He noticed Litvinoff cruising for trade, 'hook nose sniffing the air like a truffle pig, camel coat cape-style over the shoulders and facial scar still fresh from his East End gangster dealings'. Pearse would later co-found Granny Takes a Trip with Nigel Waymouth and Sheila Cohen and is today a well-known tailor based on Meard Street. Litvinoff had with him two French boys – 'bouffant hair, mascara, *trés* camp and druggy' – who were 'on for anything: " 'Ee haz ze black bombers. We go party weez 'im in Earls Court."'

Pearse's friends weren't interested. There was Richard Cole, soon to road-manage the Who and later Led Zeppelin; Bernard Rhodes, who would form the Clash; the Scene's DJ Guy Stevens, whose diverse musical credits would include producing that band's album *London Calling*; Mickey Finn, later the percussionist with T. Rex; a man named Denzil who'd just been named 'King of the Mods' by the *Sunday Times* magazine; and Goldstein, in Pearse's phrase 'a Litvinoff acolyte'. Litvinoff reappeared with 'Mad' Reg King, a 'bleach blond hunk, chauffeur to [Andrew] Loog Oldham', wanting 'to score weed. I propose the Flamingo, he blanks it. I tell him of our Kilburn shebean and Jamaican George: "Bound to have some." And so four of us pile in the back of the flash Yank convertible parked on Windmill Street, Reg at the wheel, Litvinoff up front wearing shades and jovial. There was an antique shop on Edgware Road with a suit of armour in the window. Litvinoff instructs Reg to slow down. "That was me inside the armour. I was a Crusader in another life. What were you, Reg?" "Dunno, David."' They reached their destination, a boarded-up shop on Willesden Lane. 'George sits on a box and bestows his customary greetings: "Come in, dey all 'ere." Not a soul inside. A silent jukebox, tiny bar and boxes to sit upon. No weed for Litvinoff to score. "What a fucking bringdown. Hey, the Stones live near here.* You wanna go meet the boys?" Negative from us. Litvinoff turns to Reg. "Too much, let's split."'

So they did. Once Litvinoff had left, George said: 'I don't dig this cat. Uncool. Maybe he with the fuzz,' then produced a huge joint which they smoked while dancing to Prince Buster's 'Madness'.

For two years Goldstein lay on the other side of a locked door. His name had been there from the outset: in one of my first interviews I'd been counselled that 'someone who must be approached, but you have to do it very carefully, is Gerry Goldstein'. The name began to echo through the conversations. 'I knew David quite well but of course it was Gerry who knew him best.' 'Litvinoff had this friend Gerry, but they called him Joey – or Joey-Gerry – you need to talk to him if you can.'

Here he was in *The Cardinal and the Corpse*, Iain Sinclair and Chris Petit's short film from 1992 that circles a book-dealer's pursuit of the 'Journals of David Litvinov'. Gerry and his wife Pat are shown riffling through pulp paperbacks at a bookstall, sitting in a cafe at a wood-effect table, remembering David Litvinoff. 'There was a whole crowd of people in Chelsea,' Pat explained. 'David Litvinoff was one of the main characters down there. Sort of rebellious aristocrats, you know. . . Lord Lambton's daughters.' Pat looked fondly at Gerry as he described the affair in which Litvinoff was left tied to a balcony. Something to do with gambling debts, they thought. She wore her long dark hair tied back, her pretty, intelligent face beginning to weary under the weight of her habits. The pair were posited as the most direct route into Litvinoff's story. Some said that Gerry's life echoed Litvinoff's: another garrulous, book-obsessed Jewish autodidact who headed west in search of some action. But here Gerry

---

*   Mick Jagger and Keith Richards had that year moved into a cheap top-floor flat at 33 Mapesbury Road, Kilburn.

seemed gentle, dilatory. He'd 'never had the breaks', in one friend's view. He grew up in Stoke Newington, the son of Maurice (aka Pip) and Tilly. Pip was a charming rogue of the old Jewish East End, the world of Jack 'Spot' Comer, street fights with fascists, lightning-witted market-traders who always had the first and last word, a man born in a Goulston Street tenement and familiar with the old Brick Lane synagogue ('vast and imposing', he told Rachel Lichtenstein[5]).

By the time he encountered Litvinoff Gerry was doing whatever it took to fund his heroin habit. Litvinoff looked after him, gave him a home. Whether their relationship was sexual is a moot point. It probably was at first but they remained living together when Gerry began a relationship with Clare Peake. She remembered the three of them spending hours in hysterics, making puns and silly little wordplays. Litvinoff was around twenty years older than Goldstein. Friends say the relationship was touching: Litvinoff introduced him as his 'little brother', fictionalising his family into his own preferred form. In the 1990s and early 2000s Gerry spoke freely and fondly of his old friend. Patrick Kennedy filmed him laughing as he recalled a favourite Litvinoff phrase: 'What are you, a steamer?' A steamer-tug, a mug. Sinclair walked with him, filmed him, tweaked him into his novels. 'He won't talk? I couldn't get him to stop,' Sinclair told me.

But Goldstein's world had turned darker since those times. He and Pat were trying to wean themselves off heroin (and in her case alcohol) when his mind collapsed into paranoia. Friends opened their email in the mornings to find venomous screeds fired their way in the small hours. Everyone wanted a part of him but where was the payback? They were leeches, closet anti-Semites, parasites the like of which he'd seen a thousand times over. He and Pat separated; she met someone else in rehab who ripped her off. She began drinking more. In 2011 she committed suicide by leaping from a friend's flat in the tower block in Shepherd's Bush where she and Gerry had lived.

Early 2013 found Gerry in psychiatric care and considering the possibility of moving into a Jewish old people's home. For the time being he was installed in an institution in Mitcham. Friends of his I'd interviewed visited and asked if he'd discuss Litvinoff. The answer was no, twice over. To console myself I constructed clever-sounding justifications about the benefits of circumventing a memory gatekeeper who appeared to have hidden or lost the key. Find a hundred narrower routes into the story rather than the well-trodden thoroughfare. Then I heard he'd changed his mind.

I took the Tube to the bottom of the Northern Line, then a bus further into the southern fringes, then walked to the psychiatric home, where I met Clare Peake, now Clare Peñate, who remained close to Gerry and would serve as my chaperone.

The conversation is not worth repeating. There was no conversation. We sat at a fold-out metal-legged table in the cafe area and tried to cajole a few memories. I gave Gerry an old book about the painter Sir William Rothenstein that contained monochrome plates of orthodox, *tallis*-clad men *daven*-ing at the Brick Lane synagogue in the early 1900s, which raised a flicker of a smile. The buoyant, gabbling scuffler of friends' recollections had been dosed out of existence and replaced by a gaunt, shuffling character who said little other than that he felt unwell. The awkward silences were interrupted now and again by other residents' outbursts, and by one man who appeared at our table and began to recite his life story. The clink of a cheap tea service, Gerry's murmurs, his demeanour of stifled geniality and general terror, his confused query about whether I'd managed to meet Litvinoff myself and in response to Clare's gentle reminder that they'd attended his funeral together in 1975, an insistence that they couldn't have because Gerry had heard Litvinoff's voice on the King's Road only a couple of years ago. What did he say to you, Gerry. . .? 'He was going to kill me.' 'Why would he want to do that?' asked Clare. 'He loved you.'

I clicked the home's front door closed behind me. I walked out through drumming rain to the busy London Road and deep into a thresh of sirens and horns and motors, the combined effect more soothing than the look in Gerry Goldstein's eyes.

In December 1964 Hew McCowan opened the Hideaway Club at expensively refurbished premises in Gerrard Street that had previously been run by Frankie Fraser, Albert Dimes and Gilbert France as the Bon Soir. Micky Fawcett recalls that McCowan made the mistake of offering the Krays a stake in the venture, then reneging in public a couple of days later, which left Ronnie furious at his disrespect. The twins' firm were instructed to ostracise and intimidate McCowan, but he took his revenge via one of Ronnie's friends: 'Mad' Teddy Smith,* whose blend of violence, homosexuality and

---

*   Not to be confused with 'Mad' Frankie Fraser, 'Mad' Freddie Rondel, Frank 'the Mad Axeman' Mitchell, 'Mad' Reg King, Mad Cyril or Ronnie Kray, whom no one sane ever called mad to his face.

literary aspiration lent him a Litvinoff-esque quality, and indeed the blue-serge-suited Smith and Litvinoff often drank together at a club in Gerrard Street. McCowan ejected Smith from the Hideaway for being drunk and subsequently told a television crew, who were scouring Soho for people who'd been threatened by gangsters, that Ronnie had sent Smith in to frighten him into handing over part of the business. The TV crew passed this fabrication to the police, who seized upon the chance to pin something on the twins. The man given the challenge of bringing them to justice was one of the force's rising stars, Leonard 'Nipper' Read, but even he found his efforts thwarted. A charge of demanding money with menaces led to their being remanded at HMP Brixton for a trial beginning on 28th February. At that time juries had to reach a unanimous guilty verdict and the Krays had managed to advise at least one juror of the likely repercussions of a conviction. The case went to retrial but in the meantime the twins' private detective had managed to unearth information on McCowan that was perceived to weaken his credibility, not least that he had spent time in psychiatric care. After the trial was abandoned they celebrated in suitably ostentatious fashion by holding an enormous party in McCowan's club, which they'd obtained and renamed El Morocco.* They emerged from the affair with an even stronger belief that they were beyond reach. Their career was at its apogee. David Bailey sealed their place in pop culture with black-and-white images as sharp as the knives in their office: including them in his *Box of Pin-Ups* conferred a fleeting equivalence with Mick Jagger, Terence Stamp and Michael Caine, and his crisp silver gelatin prints exuded a coldness that only heightened their aura of unreachability. So confident were they after the case that they agreed to give a television interview to the BBC. Sitting beside their barrister, Ronnie and Reggie both wear dark suits, white shirts and dark ties, but by now the identical twins are easy to distinguish. Ronnie is bordering on obese, slouched forward, lachrymose in his bearing and delivery, whereas Reggie inclines his head back a touch to exude a cocky menace, a curl playing on his lip and an eyebrow almost raised, his face manipulated into a silent 'Oh yeah?': the characteristic expression that during the past decade had faced dozens of

---

* Micky Fawcett: it was 'claimed by those who bought into the Krays' myths that they bought the place' whereas actually 'no money had changed hands'; it was handed to them by the property's owner Gilbert France, who had grown irritated with McCowan (*Krayzy Days*, Chapter Seven, 'A Search for the Body at the Glenrae Hotel').

men in the split-second before they were punched. Ronnie says that the trial has cost them roughly £8,000. The interviewer asks how they feel about that and Reggie replies: 'I don't suppose anyone likes the idea of spending that money for no reason at all.' Does it leave them broke? Ronnie: 'It doesn't leave us broke but at the same time it's a lot of money to have to pay out when one is innocent.' They're asked about the impression the trial has conveyed that clubland is a violent realm. Reggie counters that: 'I don't suppose it can be that bad or else people wouldn't go to them really, would they?' When prompted Ronnie mumbles a priceless reply: 'Well, I think most clubs are very respectable, you know, and I don't think there's any trouble at all in them. Except occasionally.'

On being quizzed as to why they refused to give evidence in the trial, the pair look as one to their right, whereupon their legal adviser delivers in the tone of pompous faux-self-deprecation favoured by a certain cast of barrister the explanation that 'the law of this country is well established: the onus is on the prosecution to prove its case, counsel for these two men and the third defendant were quite satisfied in their own mind, as I in my own humble way was as well, that the prosecution had not proved their case and there was no obligation on these men to make any answer to any of the allegations against them'.

Finally the interviewer asks what they intend to do now that the trial is behind them. Reggie wants to have 'a bit of family life now' and intends 'to get married in the near future' as he had been planning to do before this unfair intrusion put his romantic plans on hold. The interviewer turns to his brother: 'Ronald, what are you going to do now?' The answer again paints the twins as the wronged party suffering unjustified police attention, sounding more like something Greta Garbo would say than the 'Colonel' of the London underworld. 'Well,' he replies, 'I would like to go abroad for a short while. . .and then I would like to be left alone.'

Reggie succeeded a month later, on 20th April 1965, when he and his fiancée, Frances Shea, were wed at the great red-brick church of St James the Great in Bethnal Green Road. It was a day that set the tone for their marriage: the publicity-hungry twins invited a legion of journalists, fellow celebrity East Ender David Bailey was the wedding photographer, and Ronnie coaxed the congregation into a suitably enthusiastic rendition of the hymns by striding between the pews shouting: 'Sing, fuck you! Sing!'

*   *   *

Shadows grow vaguer the further one travels from the objects that cast them. There was someone called Ricky. Like Gerry, the name kept recurring: the essential facts were that this boy Ricky had taken an overdose and ended up brain-damaged, wheelchair-bound, unable to speak, and Litvinoff seemed to feel some obligation towards him. The chance of someone in such a condition being alive almost fifty years on seemed minimal.

Richard Levesley found my email address while searching online for photographs of Litvinoff, and then waited for months before writing. His wife, Mary, told me that. He wasn't sure whether doing so would stir up painful memories or resolve them. 'Hi! My name is Richarde [*sic*] Levesley and I knew David Litvinoff from 1963 until he died,' he wrote. 'You may want to check out my book *Into My Veins*, but I intimately knew him and would like to give you any information. Yours sincerely, Richard Levesley.'

So I bought his book. The shadows appeared to clarify. That said, its narrative leaps, decontextualised fragments, weird elisions and constant misspelling of Litvinoff's name seemed to bespeak a damaged mind, while there were various minor inaccuracies and mistaken photo captions; but the narrative's central claim was less easily dismissed.

Levesley was a Wandsworth boy, raised in a block of flats. He had a talent for drawing and considered a career in art but by his late teens he'd taken a more feckless route. He hustled a few quid by helping passengers at Victoria station carry their suitcases, did some modelling, helped a girlfriend design Harrods' window-dressing, played snooker for money at halls from Chelsea back to Wandsworth. He got to know Gerry Goldstein, and Marc Bolan back when he was Marc Feld. Once he took a black Jaguar E-Type for a test drive, picked up a pretty young woman on the King's Road and drove her out into the countryside, abandoning the car once the petrol had run out. He liked men too, though he didn't appreciate the attentions of the older pop mogul Larry Parnes. Somehow he found himself a job as a wine waiter at the Carlton Club for six months. While serving Tory MPs such as Alec Douglas-Home he'd eavesdrop on their conversations about White Papers and jot down shorthand notes on his order pad. In such clubs and restaurants he would also scan the cloakroom for fur or leather coats, then casually walk out the door wearing one and sprint to Soho to sell it to 'Spanish Tony' Sanchez. One night in the early 1960s he was at the Flamingo, 33–37 Wardour Street, where he 'dipped' a fiver from a girl's handbag and exchanged some of it for two wraps of heroin from a pair of Greek dealers. As he tried to leave he was almost knocked over by a burly figure wearing a pin-striped suit and an expensive, paisley-patterned pair of shoes, though his most distinguishing feature was his mouth, Levesley wrote. 'It was heavily scarred. One of his entourage was driving a Rolls-Royce, which stopped at a set of traffic lights. He was ambushed by a single punch to the mouth with a fistful of razors as he always had his window open (as I was to find out later). He was a notorious villain by the name of David Littvinof [sic].'[6]

Did Litvinoff give him that fabricated version of how he acquired his scars, or was Levesley's memory playing tricks? The memoir revealed nothing more of that episode. Much of it records a jaunt around Europe in 1963 with a pair of accomplices known as Andy and Scruffy Pete. The trio perceived themselves as the Three Musketeers, Athos, Aramis and Porthos, each with a particular talent: Pete was a pickpocket, Andy was a charmer and Levesley, by his own account, was a winning combination of the two. Their ability to purloin other people's money propelled them around the Continent, leaving a trail of dupes and stooges in their wake. Once they got home to their relieved parents Levesley soon hit the town, where he spied a passing Mini out of the corner of his eye. 'It had four of the gangsters inside,' he wrote, 'and one of them was David Littvinof and I knew what this meant.'[7] What it meant, he implied, is that Litvinoff had him in his sights as a sexual prospect. Levesley tried to retreat into a cobbler's shop but found it closed, so while Litvinoff was looking away he ducked into the chemist's next door, his heart thudding. He loitered there for a few minutes and asked the shopkeeper for a glass of water, which he sipped very slowly; then just when it seemed safe to leave the shop the Mini crawled by again. 'I ought to have known what he would have done,' Levesley wrote. 'I fell to the floor on my knees in the chemist, as I saw the car pass by. That was one of several escapes to come.'[8]

Somehow Litvinoff drew him in. Levesley wrote that he 'wanted a toy boy, and [as] a handsome young male, I suited all the categories'. The temptation is understandable: Levesley dined in fine restaurants, wore handmade suits and shirts, met 'all the so-called famous people'. He claimed to have bought a wrap of cocaine on Mick Jagger's behalf, brought it back and watched as Jagger sampled it and just said: 'Thanks, man!' without repaying the fiver he owed, at which Levesley punched him on the side of the head: this, he said, 'was the beginning of Littvinof's influence on me'.[9]

Like Ronnie Kray, Levesley knew Litvinoff as 'Litz'. They went flat-hunting together. Levesley liked one on the Victoria Embankment but he 'could tell by Litz' face that it was not up to his expectations. So, with a shove with his arm we were out of that area and heading towards Knightsbridge.'[10] With his usual nous and fine taste Litvinoff found a perfect home for them, with a discreet entrance set back from the street. It had a lift that took them directly into the flat, which was exquisitely furnished. Levesley found it breathtaking. Litvinoff had brought him a long way from the block in Wandsworth.

If Litvinoff felt betrayed or humiliated by Bobby Buckley choosing Ronnie Kray over him, he was determined not to feel that way again. One morning he was shaving when he called Levesley into the bathroom. 'I always use a cut-throat razor,' he said, and in the next instant he had his young boyfriend in a stranglehold. Litvinoff held the blade by Levesley's face and told him: 'If you ever betray me I will make your face look like mine!'

Levesley did betray him. The details are hazy but it seems to have to do with Litvinoff's gangland dealings. He had significant sums of money stashed in the flat, hidden from Levesley, who 'wasn't supposed to know where it was, let alone touch it'. One day in the early summer of 1965, Levesley found a wad of banknotes secreted in the oven's grill. First he touched it, then he began to take it out. He removed some notes and found a German Luger. 'This was similar to the safe in Hamburg,' from which Levesley had stolen money and where he had found a gun during his European adventure, 'except this gun belonged to someone who would use it. So, what to do? I did not want my head blown off so I took two ton [£200] and I slipped the gun into my belt. I took one last look around the flat, then took the elevator down. I knew that if I got caught I would surely have been killed. I was coming out of the flat when I walked straight into David Littvinof.'[11]

Nothing happened immediately but Litvinoff knew what Levesley had done. He brooded, bided his time. He was thirty-seven, Levesley was nineteen; Litvinoff seems to have exerted complete control over him. They moved flat again, this time to a basement in Kensington Gardens. Levesley suspected it would be his 'final resting place. It had a peculiar smell; one of dampness and one of death.'[12] They walked into the 'House of Horror', as he termed it, and then Litvinoff punched him hard between the shoulders, sending him reeling across the room. It wasn't meant to injure him, just

forewarn him. The real punishment was to follow. The description makes
it sound as if Litvinoff were preparing a life model for Francis Bacon; but
if we take Levesley at his word this was all too real.

He said that Litvinoff stripped him to his underpants and punched
and slapped him for half an hour, then grabbed him by the neck and took
him into a room that was empty apart from a light bulb with a long cord.
He threw Levesley to the floor and went to get a wooden chair. 'He picked
me up as if I was a piece of rag, sat me on the chair, smashed the light bulb
and ripped off the cord and, with force, he tied my arms and feet behind
the chair.'[13] Levesley said that Litvinoff left him tied to the chair for two
nights, akin to the incident in which the Krays left their late barman's
Greek boyfriend locked in a cupboard. Levesley was weak with thirst and
hunger and had wet himself by the time Litvinoff finally returned. The
sound of his keys in the door prompted a blend of relief and terror.

'He walked straight up to me and gave me one punch on my chin,
and threw water in my face, which made me semi-conscious. He took out
his cutthroat and held it across my mouth and said: "How would you like
to look like me?" as he slid the blade across my mouth without actually
cutting. Then after a few more slaps he took the blade and, piece by piece,
started cutting my hair with the razor.'[14]

In visiting upon Levesley the experience he'd suffered himself,
Litvinoff displayed his cruel talent for identifying someone's fundamental
weakness, in this case Levesley's vanity. It took an agonisingly long time
before he'd rendered him entirely bald, at which point he cut him loose.
Levesley collapsed to the floor. 'What happened next is beyond my comprehension,' he wrote. 'He got a bucket of ice and threw it on my body and
shouted at me to get dressed. "I am not finished with you yet!"'[15]

Levesley claimed that they then moved to a different flat, this time
in Chelsea. He didn't specify where, but Litvinoff is known to have had a
flat at that time at the Fulham Road end of Beaufort Street. He said he was
given barbiturates and then 'a pure dose of heroin': harsh justice for a junkie.
Levesley believed that the intention was to kill him. Aside from the
betrayal, Litvinoff knew that he kept a journal documenting all their
underworld encounters together, their visits to the Krays and 'people of
higher ranks and influential contacts'. In *Into My Veins* he recalled meeting
a gangster at the Hilton Hotel to discuss a possible illicit deal in gold jewellery, plying the man with whisky and recording his self-incriminating
comments with a microphone disguised as a pen that connected to a

reel-to-reel player hidden in a suitcase; perhaps the germ of Litvinoff's later covert taping lay in such blackmailing activities. 'I was among the few people who knew where David got some of his wealth,' he wrote. 'In fact, he was a professional gangster.'[16]

The new flat was close to St Stephen's Hospital on the Fulham Road. Litvinoff waited 'to make sure I was dead before he called an ambulance', but Levesley wasn't dead, not quite. He was blind, couldn't speak or move, and 'could only scream silently with pain'. While awaiting the outcome, a restless Litvinoff loitered over the road in Finch's pub, getting drunk and telling the barman and an acquaintance* that he'd found Levesley unconscious from a self-administered overdose. Later at the hospital they told Levesley he'd been 'dead for six minutes' and then in a coma. He spent four years in hospital, he said, during which time his sister attempted to bring a prosecution. As he was under twenty-one he was made a ward of court, with Litvinoff barred from approaching him. According to Levesley, his sister's efforts came to nothing because his mother wouldn't relinquish critical evidence for fear of repercussions. 'I could have had the finest barrister in the land except my mother wouldn't let my diary out of her possession. So, I was given a barrister who knew nothing about my case because the key to the downfall of Litz was in my diary. . .the names and dates and businesses would surely have shopped a world of criminals.'[17] So Levesley languished in a succession of hospitals and care homes, gradually recovering some of his faculties. Then the old world seeped back in and there was nothing he could do. One of Litvinoff's friends managed to infiltrate the ward by pretending to be an orderly and took photographs. 'I couldn't talk,' Levesley wrote. 'All I was doing was screaming. So, I couldn't converse with anyone to tell the CID officer what went on.'[18]

When he reached the age of twenty-one Levesley was no longer a ward of court. Litvinoff managed to procure the kind of goods and contacts that would regain his favour. 'He brought me all the things that he knew I liked,' he said. 'For example, a drawing of a figure by Annigoni, books like Marcel Proust, and valium. This was only the beginning as I was introduced to some friends like Martin Sharp, Lucian Freud and Robert Fraser.'[19]

Levesley could do nothing to stop Litvinoff from associating with him. His eyesight began to return but remained poor, his motor

---

*   Who does not wish to be named.

functions were devastated, his memory almost blank. Only years later did the flashes of recollection start to float up from his unconscious. Had his memory returned earlier, it might have strengthened the case for Litvinoff's prosecution; but it didn't. 'So, David Littvinof walked out a free man,' he wrote, 'except as the saying goes: "What goes around comes around."'

The Ad Lib club, four floors up in Leicester Place, played the best new American soul records for a discerning and exclusive crowd. Paul McCartney described it as 'just a great club: great dance, pull birds, chat with unusual people'.[20] John Pearse saw Litvinoff on the dancefloor 'vogueing to Fontella Bass's "Rescue Me"' in autumn 1965, sublimating himself into the music, relinquishing control to its battering rhythm, 'eyes closed, ecstatic, oblivious'.

Given Levesley's pitiful state according to those who remembered him forty years ago, the fact he could string sentences together at all was a pleasant surprise. His condition must have improved. I meandered down the Roman Road towards his and Mary's modern flat on the Hertford Union Canal edge of Victoria Park, that grand green space dividing the East End proper from Hackney where seventy years earlier the Levy boys' calls and splashes echoed around the lido, and where the teenaged Kray twins and their friends such as Bobby Ramsey fought in the boxing booth, earning a pound for every round they stayed on their feet. It was mid-June 2012: rising summer, simmering heat in the air. Mary met me at the door.
     'Richard's through here,' she said, ushering me into a cool sitting room with a pine floor, a chrome and cream leather suite and, between the sofa and armchair, a man twisted into a wheelchair. His head lay ricked to one side. His clawed and deformed hands rested uselessly on the chair's arms. He had short curly brown hair and a brown goatee beard, and wore a T-shirt and jeans. In repose his face looked aghast. He acknowledged me with a moan. I attempted to shake his right hand but ended up giving it a kind of awkward stroke, at which he moaned again. Mary and I sat down either side of him. I looked at the long list of questions I'd prepared and mentally crossed most of them out. I realised how long it must have taken him to write that short email, let alone his book.
     In trying to give answers his top lip tended to get stuck in a grimace that exposed his gums. Now and then Mary very gently moved it back

down again. She exuded kindness, patience, a manifest love for a man who had been seriously disabled for years by the time they met. Often she coaxed the words out of him, sometimes letter by letter. Gerry Goldstein had taken him to visit Litvinoff in Wales at the end of the 1960s, she said. Why was Litvinoff there? I asked. 'E. . .N. . .O. . .C. . .'

Why did he continue associating with Litvinoff if he was guilty of what you say? 'I've asked Richard the same question,' said Mary.

'He felt a remorse,' said Levesley, taking about ten seconds to articulate the sounds.

'Richard's sister and mum went to Litvinoff's flat in Chelsea and were terrified,' said Mary. The sister was still alive, in New Zealand, and did not want to talk. 'The incident is just before his twentieth birthday. Richard, you were nineteen,' she said, turning to her husband. Levesley was born on 1st July 1945. 'Once Richard was twenty-one there was no more police guard. People had access to you again. Your sister said that at one time you were thrown from a car and that was to do with the Krays. There was another incident as well which you didn't put in your book. Something about the theft of a stereo?'

'It was a frame-up,' said Levesley.

'For you?' she asked.

'I was taken to West End Central about the theft of a stereo. But the police didn't press charges.'

'You were walking down the King's Road once with David,' she prompted him, 'and someone attacked him, he pushed you out of the way and he laid him flat with one punch.'

Mary's daughter and toddler grandson careered into the room, the little boy chuckling as he skidded on the floor. There seemed little more to say.

'He told you he loved you, didn't he?' Mary asked her husband. She passed me a selection of documents they'd looked out. A birthday telegram card, its front decorated with an Edward Ardizzone illustration, sent to him at Ward 7c, St Stephen's Hospital, Fulham Road SW10.

THINKING OF YOU ON YOUR NATIVITY AND WISHING YOU THE GROOVIEST TIME*
WE VERY MUCH LOOK FORWARD TO SEEING YOU AND HAVING A RAVE*
LOVE DONALD CAMMELL DEBORAH DIXON MICK JAGGER AND MARIANNE FAITHFULL AND ROBERT FRASER*

A small book about Albrecht Dürer given to him by Philip Laski, from an 'art-lover to an artist'. A copy of Martin Sharp's *Art Book*, which contains collages combining famous painters' work, such as Magritte's leather boots merging into human toes set against Van Gogh's cornfields and cypresses. A Woody Guthrie LP inscribed by Litvinoff ('For Ricky, love Dave'); he'd had many more of Litvinoff's records until his flat was burgled a few years ago. Another birthday telegram, this one from 1974, to Servite House, Queens Walk, W5:

ON THIS BEAUTIFUL DAY WE RAISE OUR GLASSES TO YOU AND ALAYS [*sic*] LOVE PAT GERR [*sic*] AND DAVID.

Mary mentioned that Gerry and Pat Goldstein hadn't been in touch in the last few years. In the book Levesley gave Goldstein a curt dismissal: 'I must admit that Gerry was my shadow from the first time I met him and still is.' I'd never known Pat but I heard myself telling them of her recent death. Richard's eyes bulged and he moaned again. I'd intruded long enough already.

'He's a survivor,' said Mary as she walked me out towards the park. 'Did you realise how severely disabled he is?' No, I said. I had no idea. I promised I'd email some photos of Litvinoff. Then we went our own ways, she to the shade of their flat and I to Victoria Park, where people lounged on the grass and ducks shuddered on the lake. It was midday now and the park shimmered in an insistent, pervading warmth. All the world's solidity seemed to have melted a little and its materials grown absorbent, such that sounds that in winter would have echoed from cold hard surfaces now came back softened, muted, too lethargic to travel far. Even time itself seemed susceptible to the general languor as I sat by the Burdett-Coutts fountain, reconciling myself to the apparent lasting effects of this long-dead man whose life I'd decided to record. In 1862 the philanthropist Angela Burdett-Coutts funded the tall Gothic-arched octagonal structure, which once gushed clean drinking water for cockneys and their dogs: Victorian aristocratic paternalism rendered in marble and stone, topped with an ornate cupola. Four of the facades' niches enclose an array of stone cherubs that transfixed me when I was very young, as did the fearsome Dogs of Alcibiades that guard the park's Sewardstone Road gateway; and though that childhood innocence seemed distant now, to gaze on this glowing day at the pale fountain against the endless rich blue sky created an image so simultaneously hyper-real yet intangible that, at the moment of its occurrence, it felt already like a memory.

When I got home I began to ask some of Litvinoff's friends what they thought of Levesley's claims and the shadows grew hazy again. Martin Sharp read his book and considered it 'a large piece of the puzzle of David's life', but more were sceptical. The film producer Sandy Lieberson said Litvinoff always maintained it was a self-administered overdose, Nigel Waymouth too, adding that Litvinoff described finding Levesley unconscious with Billy Stewart's self-pitying soul ballad 'Sitting in the Park' playing on the stereo. Tim Whidborne was in Surrey on 'the night Richard had the overdose', when 'David telephoned me in a very emotional state, asking me to come to his flat'. He drove up to London 'to find him very distraught. Richard was presumably taken to hospital. I gathered he had taken some pills, perhaps Purple Hearts, and had overdosed.'

Was Litvinoff lying to them? Richard seemed sincere and had no apparent reason to concoct such an elaborate claim, but could his damaged mind have confected false memories that he believed were true? The fact he couldn't recall which court heard this allegedly aborted trial hindered my search for archival records, which if they ever existed could in any case have been destroyed years ago. Freedom of Information Act requests and an article soliciting retired officers' memories in the *London Police Pensioner* magazine yielded nothing.

I sent Richard and Mary a selection of photographs, some from when Richard knew him, and one of a ten-year-old David Levy looking impish but innocent. I never heard back and concluded that, quite reasonably, he had found it too traumatic to reopen his memories of the man whom he said destroyed his life. Over the coming months I thought of them often, picturing Richard spending his days slumped in his chair, his time passing by, his present fixed by an incident that occurred forty-seven years earlier. Mary wrote to me five months later to tell me that her 'beloved Richard' had died six weeks after we met. They'd been on their way to Lourdes when he was taken ill. At Richard's funeral their parish priest, Father Michael, to whom he was very close, mentioned Litvinoff and Richard's book. He told the mourners that this final journey of Richard's was *Into my Veins. . .the Sequel.* Writing the book had laid something to rest, and now he was ready to go where he believed Litvinoff had tried to send him almost half a century earlier.

Act One, Scene Five.

DL: I must tell you in advance, though, and obviously
we're going to have a certain amount to do with one
another. . . I ought to say I'm slightly - not exactly
addicted - you won't tell anyone, will you, John? Now
this is important. I'm trusting you like a brother. I
can rely on you implicitly?

JIG: My dear, believe me - better than the inanimation
of these four walls I'm looking at now and this telephone and where you're speaking from now.

DL: Oh splendid. Well, I'm afraid that I'm rather keen
on the grape. I like to drink wine. I'm afraid I drank
rather a lot of wine you see. Four bottles.

JIG: Why worry about that? You did not enjoy it because
of my absence. I'm going to be quite frank: when I
waited that hour, I thought to myself 'This *deliberate affront* by Gerry', because I did look right
round the bar many times, and I thought to myself
'There's no point hanging about with the fuzz about',
you know what I mean?

DL: What are the fuzz?

JIG: That's a common name given to the P-O-L-I-C-E.

DL: Oh the *police*. I'm afraid I can't have much time for
the police.

JIG: So therefore I didn't hang about.

DL: You see, Gerry is having this nervous breakdown. You
presumably gathered.

JIG: If he'd only turned up and I'd have come back with
you, you'd have enjoyed those four bottles, because
one of the most unsavoury reactions when you deliberately turn a personal friend down - I can give an
example of this at Llanwellyn with Sir Robert McAlpine
(I was a timekeeper cashier for three and a half
years) - I actually paid the rates which him and his

wife wanted, and I said I'll be waiting at the Royal
Oak, which is off Commercial Road, Newport, and I
shall be in the saloon bar waiting. This is many years
ago - this is 1953 - I paid his rates, it amounted to
twenty-six guineas, and I waited from quarter to six
'til closing time at eleven o'clock.

**DL: Good heavens. While not touching a drink yourself.
Just idly playing with an orange juice in front of you
for five hours. Monstrous.**

JIG: David. . .what is your address now?

**DL: My address at the moment is c/o the Basil Street
Hotel, Basil Street, Knightsbridge. Of course I am
involved in a rather extraordinary synagogual church
syndrome. But my own flat, which is in Brompton
Road, Knightsbridge, is being decorated out for me
again. . .**

JIG: And what is your telephone number there?

**DL: I have an extension there. My telephone number there
is the same as I gave you: 2546. And you can also get
me at Flaxman* - I don't know if you have a pencil
handy? You can write my brother, Flaxman, Flaxmania[†]
8830.**

JIG: That's your brother - has he got children?

**DL: Oh no no, he's got a huge place, lots of rooms and
he's an artist. Martin he's called.**

JIG: How old is he?

**DL: He's twenty-six. He's awfully nice. I told him about
you and he would love to meet you. . .**

JIG: Where is Martin's address now?

---

*   The FLA in Flaxman equates on a telephone dial to the numbers 352, which remains the
Chelsea area code.
†   Term referring to the great popularity of the sculptor John Flaxman (1755–1826) during
the Romantic generation. His works included the poet Thomas Chatterton's grave monument
and a statue of Lord Nelson.

DL: I'll give it to you, it's an artists' studios. Studio Five, a place called the Pheasantry –

JIG: The Pleasantry?

DL: No, not the Pleasantry, the Pheasantry – 152 King's Road (apostrophise the King's would you please, between g and s), SW3. The telephone number, as I said, is Flaxman 8830. It's next door to the Classic Cinema. An old building.

Chapter 5

Gaily Coloured Posters and Gaily Coloured People

'In 1958 I wrote the following: "There are no hard distinctions between what is real and what is unreal, nor between what is true and what is false. A thing is not necessarily either true or false; it can be both true and false." I believe that these assertions still make sense and do still apply to the exploration of reality through art. So as a writer I stand by them. But as a citizen I cannot.'
Harold Pinter, Nobel Prize for Literature acceptance speech

The city's blood flowed thinner and faster than today. The arteries hadn't furred to the point of morbid congestion, Oxford Circus wasn't yet the atrophied heart squeezing pulses of tourists down Oxford Street's clogged aorta. There was always somewhere to park the car, no one needed as much money, and now the 1950s' invisible blockages – between places, between social classes – dissolved too, accelerating the rush of ideas and connections around London's veins. The temporary freedoms Litvinoff had relished in the Blitz re-established themselves; around now he met his friend Martin Wilkinson who sensed he had been awaiting the 1960s since the 1940s. A subliminal energy that had been gathering for the past decade became palpable in the King's Road, which shifted into an acknowledged place to be seen: paradoxically the new freedom created its own obstructions, a harbinger of the city's future. In the wake of *Time* magazine's Swinging London issue of 15th April 1966, longstanding residents of Chelsea and Fulham began to find their progress down the road hindered. Seven months later Godfrey Hodgson wrote in *Town* magazine that 'The only impact this whole swinging London thing has had on me is that I can't get up the King's Road on a Saturday lunchtime to buy a piece of steak. It's too choked with Americans hurrying on down for a piece of the action. Never mind. We ought to be proud of them. Because now, they say, this great grey gloomy water-colour city of ours, that used to be the nub of the empire and the blue-nose capital of the universe, has been transformed by the wand of the Bad Fairy. . .into Babylon 1966.'[1]

The road was created for King Charles II to make his way between his palaces at Whitehall and Hampton Court. Until 1830 it remained a gravelled path restricted to royalty and those to whom they granted the copper tokens required for passage through the gates. In 1769 a mansion was built on the northern side that by 1864 had become the premises of Samuel Baker, a 'dealer in ornamental poultry', thus becoming known locally as the Pheasantry. In 1881 it had a drastic renovation under the ownership of an artist and interior decorator named Amédée Joubert, which produced a facade that remains unlike anything else in London. In granting the building a Grade II listing, English Heritage described the Pheasantry as 'a curiosity'. The upper part of the red-brick frontage features three pedimented windows, which stand between four metal panels advertising the Joubert family's diverse upholstery and decorative services, inset into one of which is a blue plaque to the Russian princess Madame Seraphine Astafieva, who founded a dance academy here in 1916 attended by Alicia Markova and Margot Fonteyn.* The ground floor has a grand central doorway, but to reach it from the King's Road you pass first through an entrance arch and a walled courtyard. Opinions vary on its collective architectural merit – Nikolaus Pevsner's *The Buildings of England* offers only a terse single-sentence dismissal of the archway, 'an odd extremely heavy display of Grecian enthusiasm'.[2] Between the mid-1950s and late 1960s Litvinoff sloped hundreds of times through this threshold, beneath a wild charioteer borne by four rampant horses, between black caryatids and ominous eagles, across the small paved yard and through the front doorway supported by a pair of white telamons, who look away as you pass between them.

The building had, by then, long been known for its bohemian quality: in 1932 the ground floor and basement became the Pheasantry Club, whose habitués over the next three decades would include Dylan Thomas, Marc Chagall, Aneurin Bevan and Jennie Lee, Virginia McKenna, Francis Bacon, Lucian Freud, Peter Ustinov, Pietro Annigoni, Timothy Whidborne and David Litvinoff. According to a local historian who visited in those days, 'one experienced a little frisson of fear as one held one's head high' and crossed the courtyard, for doing so 'heralded entry into a private world, exciting to visit, but which hinted darkly that if it didn't like you, you could be kept out'.[3] Within gathered a waspish crowd who traded news

---

* The Greater London Council erected this plaque in 1968 at the suggestion of Tim Whidborne.

and gossip and insults by the light of candles in Chianti bottles, feasting on roasted pheasant or flaming shashlik kebab brought to the table not on a skewer but a sword.

Advertisement for the Pheasantry Club from 1933.

The club closed in 1966 with the death of its owner, Mario Cazzini. Whidborne's studio was upstairs and now, as the building was divided into studios and flats, he opened a printmaking business on the ground floor and paid Litvinoff to help oversee its running. What is today a spacious interior was then a warren of rooms and corridors. Julian Lloyd first encountered Litvinoff there that year.

'As you came into the Pheasantry studios you came into a long hallway,' he said, 'which led right out to the back of the studios, and David had a little cubbyhole, a funny little office just in that hallway. There were a lot of shelves in it with a lot of signed prints of Annigoni's portrait of the Queen. Tim Whidborne. . .used to make prints and sell them, and David seemed to be in charge of this business.

'So it was a strange paradox: this small urgent figure used to pop out of this cubbyhole every time you walked down the hall and arrest people with chat and banter, selling these incredibly square pictures, which, even by standards of portraits of the Queen, were pretty stiff and formal. Sometimes he used to use them as kind of currency. I remember there was a very good hi-fi store in Chelsea and a guy called Si who ran it had a very resigned look every time David came in, and then David would barter probably yet another signed Annigoni portrait of the Queen, in exchange for some bit of Leak or Quad valve gear.'

Litvinoff had use of a flat in the Pheasantry where he would stay at times, and combined selling prints for Whidborne and Annigoni with a bit of dealing himself. Dora Holzhandler's *Lady with a Daffodil* and Edward Wadsworth's *Vorticist Composition* both cite him in their provenance. He continued to handle books, too, using his command of the market to procure valuable rare editions and on occasion, in Martin Sharp's words, 'sell them to the firm who had originally published them because they would be something they didn't have any more'.

After their satirical but far from obscene work in *Oz* magazine led to their imprisonment in Sydney for printing an obscene publication, Sharp and Richard Neville left Australia and trekked through Asia, parting company at Kathmandu and then making their way independently to London. On arriving, Sharp stayed with Neville's sister Jill, during which time he spent a night out at a newly opened club on Margaret Street favoured by musicians, the Speakeasy. There he joined a table with his friend Charlotte Martin and her guitarist boyfriend and told them of a poem he'd just written, a surrealistic recasting of ancient Greek myths. The musician needed a lyric for a tune he had in mind that manipulated the descending riff from the Lovin' Spoonful's 'Summer in the City', so Sharp scribbled the words on to a serviette along with his address and handed them to his new acquaintance, who turned out to be Eric Clapton. The two men's words and music combined to become 'Tales of Brave Ulysses' on Cream's second album, *Disraeli Gears*, which would bear a more obvious sign of their friendship in the form of Sharp's dayglo psychedelic cover. Sharp's collage included photographs of Clapton, Jack Bruce and Ginger Baker taken by Robert Whitaker, with whom he had begun sharing a flat in Joubert Studios, just next to the Pheasantry. Whitaker was English but had Australian ancestry and had recently completed a three-year spell at the University of Melbourne, where he had contributed to *Oz* and made connections in the city's artistic circles, not least with the Mora family: Mirka, a French artist, her German-born husband Georges, an art dealer, and their three sons including Philippe, who was now making a name for himself as a teenage film-maker. When the

Beatles toured Australasia in June 1964 Whitaker accompanied a friend who interviewed Brian Epstein for Melbourne's *Jewish News*; Whitaker took Epstein's picture and it was used alongside the article, which led eventually to his becoming Epstein's staff photographer.

So Whitaker and Sharp arrived already set on their artistic paths and quickly found that London's tighter, wider, higher-charged networks would enable them to ascend to a new level of creativity and influence. At first they were fettered by their living conditions at Joubert Studios but, with characteristic timing, Litvinoff appeared and opened a door that would grant them the space they needed.

'It was a wonderful studio there that I shared with Bob Whitaker, but it was really suitable for one person rather than two,' said Sharp. 'I remember very vividly David knocking on the door; he sort of just arrived there, possibly with Michael Rainey,' who was married to Jane Ormsby Gore and ran the fashion boutique Hung On You,* 'and that's when I first met David. He was just curious about what I was doing and having a look around, I'm sure. And then when the apartment in the Pheasantry became available David suggested to me that I could move there, so that led on to lots of other things. So he was very instrumental in my life, David.'

Sharp's exile from Australia arose from more acute circumstances than most, but formed part of a broader trend in which the country's brightest young people felt compelled to escape to England if they were to achieve their potential. Their home country, gripped as it was by a censorship culture that not only persecuted them but even saw the American ambassador's gift of a copy of J. D. Salinger's *The Catcher in the Rye* rejected as an obscene publication, felt a stale and repressive place. There remained a sense of deference towards the mother country, the 'cultural cringe' that at that time still bedevilled Australia's self-esteem. London offered the prospect of unmediated excitement and intellectual stimulation, a contrast to their passive position at home where they worked as well as they could while awaiting dispatches from the front. Philippe Mora arrived at the Pheasantry from Melbourne in 1967 as a seventeen-year-old and found it 'a pleasant shock to read magazines where the date on the magazine was the date you bought the magazine'.[4] Sharp and Neville launched a British version of *Oz*; now Mora began painting and collaborated with them on the spectacular 'Magic Theatre' edition. Germaine Greer took a room downstairs and began

---

*   Opened in 1965 in Chelsea Green and moved to the King's Road in 1967.

to write *The Female Eunuch*, and another flat went to the young English art journalist Anthony Haden-Guest (dubbed Unwanted-Guest by Litvinoff).

Eric Clapton and Philippe Mora at the Pheasantry.

The effect of this rapid coalescence of artists, musicians, photographers and writers was to convert the Pheasantry into a somewhat poky, in places dilapidated, but always invigorating hive of creativity and spontaneity. Today it is a branch of Pizza Express. I asked the manager if I could put up an A4 notice bearing a photograph of Litvinoff taken there. . .

Litvinoff at the Pheasantry c.1968.

. . .and asking people who remembered him to contact me, but she said I needed to make an application to the marketing department at head office. The restaurant's decor references the building's former cultural significance by way of a glass case of books and memorabilia and, more obviously, a vast psychedelic painting combining pheasants, a floral-shirted Eric Clapton and a list of other notable residents, the lower ones' first names part-obscured by a piece of collage: Martin Sharp, Lindsay Kemp, Robert Whitaker, -avid Litvinoff, -nthony Haden-Guest; Litvinoff marginalised, an acknowledgement of his presence that at the same time edges him from view.

Nowhere embodied Swinging London more than Sibylla's, a nightclub on Vine Street that opened in June 1966. All the scene's most significant constituents had a stake in the venture. George Harrison's involvement lent a gleam of Beatle glamour; its co-owners included the young millionaire baronet Sir William Pigott-Brown and Kevin MacDonald, a relative of Viscount Rothermere; its manager, Laurie O'Leary, represented the Charles Kray Entertainment Agency, run by the twins' older brother. The new working-class pop aristocracy, the old English aristocracy, the kings of the underworld: all embraced in a moment that captured the era's dynamic, and with it the brittleness and self-regard that evolved as the city's brightest young people noticed the world watching them and began to play to the gallery, believe their own publicity. As the scene's hitherto fluid self-conception became fixed by repeated representation in the media, so at the same time it began to calcify. Carnaby Street was already becoming a theme park: miniskirts became defined as the moment's icon and flogged to tourists, liberation commoditised. A few weeks after the *Time* magazine piece, another journalist writing about the new London took a trip to Mayfair and called in for a chat with MacDonald, who laid on him this jaw-dropping *spiel* about Sibylla's sophistication and exclusivity.

'This club exists for people who can communicate with each other. A lot of people ring me up and say, "How do you become a member of Sibylla's?" Well, of course, anyone who had to ask how to get into Sibylla's wouldn't be a member. I mean, it's logical. If you were going to be a member here, you'd know how to be one. It's all communications. Someone said to me the other night, "All cigars and motor cars." I came back at once with "Better than all marines and flying machines." I can see you don't understand, but in fact without having to mention it we were having a political discussion about Cuba.

'This is Psychedelphia, man. It's all happening. Can you read me? No, well, I'll try to explain. You see, it's a dreamland, and to enjoy it you have to be dreaming. Everyone here's in touch. Sibylla's is the meeting ground for the new aristocracy, and by the new aristocracy I mean the current young meritocracy of style, taste and sensitivity. We've got everyone here, the top creative people [he clicks his fingers], the top exporters [click], the top artists [click], the top social people [click], and the best of the PYPs [Pretty Young People]. We're completely classless. We're completely integrated. We dig the spades, man. Relationships here go off like firecrackers. Everyone here's got the message [click]. Can you read it, man? Sibylla's is the message. We've married up the hairy brigade – that's the East End kids like photographers and artists – with the smooth brigade, the debs, the aristos, the Guards officers. The result is just fantastic. It's the greatest, happiest, most swinging ball of the century, and I started it!'[5]

It was an astonishing display of what Litvinoff would call the scenesters' 'frozen attitudes of hip' and as such very easy to mock, but hindsight makes it more poignant than amusing. MacDonald's performance indicated the fragility behind the city's swagger. On October 15 of that year, having been diagnosed with schizophrenia and twice discharged himself from psychiatric hospital, he took himself up to a Chelsea rooftop and jumped off. The coroner would be far from the last to weigh up the final moments of an integral figure from Swinging London and return a verdict of suicide.

Through a black door on an old street off the Chelsea Embankment and up a staircase: to the right, a glimpse through a doorway of an office wall bearing Martin Sharp's *Mr Tambourine Man* poster (the curls of Dylan's Jewfro abstracted into a hundred circles, one lens of his dark glasses bearing the legend 'BLOWIN IN THE MIND'); to the left, a tastefully furnished sitting room where I perched on a creamy soft sofa and kept sipping at a tongue-scalding coffee between treble-checking my Dictaphone. Then a familiar rasping voice from down the corridor, the accent located just where rural Surrey starts glancing towards south-west London, growing louder until he was in the room. Eric Clapton looked smaller without a guitar; bestubbled, greying, dressed casually in a marl T-shirt and hooded top. There was nothing starry about him, no aura to penetrate, just a gruff cheeriness that dispelled my anxiety in a moment. He'd always had an easy-going manner but forty-five years ago an internal unease propelled him from one fixation to the next: once he had what he wanted, it began to lose its appeal, be it a woman, a band, a sports car. Having driven John Mayall's Bluesbreakers to greater prominence he began secretly rehearsing a new group; when the news got out Mayall was 'pretty angry' and 'upset . . .that I was jumping off the train just as it was beginning to gather speed',[6] he wrote in his autobiography. Cream made their debut in summer 1966, their name reflecting Clapton, Jack Bruce and Ginger Baker's awareness of their positions within the London music scene's hierarchies. The ten tracks on *Fresh Cream* set their sound – band membership reduced to a spare trio, volume increased into overload to fill the space – but it was the following year's tours and releases that fixed their reputation. Summer 1967 saw them play the Fillmore West in San Francisco, where they found an acid-fired hippie audience who would willingly lose themselves in twenty-minute interpretations of blues numbers such as Willie Dixon's 'Spoonful' and Skip James' 'I'm So Glad' punctuated by the wild-eyed Baker's pummelling drum solos and Clapton's wah-wah-flavoured pentatonic peregrinations. In November 1967 *Disraeli Gears* consolidated this new musical vista, its amped-up psychedelic blues creating a weirder, drum-tight but thematically looser British R&B that combined with Sharp's irresistible cover to create an album that merits the over-used label 'iconic'.

After the album's release – overshadowed at first by Jimi Hendrix's *Are You Experienced?*, to Clapton's dismay – he and Charlotte Martin moved into the Pheasantry at Sharp's suggestion. The studio had a large kitchen and an even bigger living room with wooden floors and dormer windows from which one could survey grand views over vibrant Chelsea at the height of Swinging London. Clapton decorated his room in 'bright red and gilt, a reflection of the times'.[7]

'It was a massive, beautifully lit studio and there was a flat on the top, which we divided up into three tenants,' he said. 'There was Martin, myself and a chap called Philippe Mora. I moved in with these guys, I didn't really know them very well, and it just seemed like, in the space of about two years, Litvinoff was in our lives. I don't remember how; it could have been that he just started talking to us. We used to go to the Picasso across the road for breakfast, lunch and dinner, or just stay in there all day sometimes. David would kind of comb the King's Road.

'He completely fascinated me on every level because he was so outrageous. It was quite normal for him to take on an entire restaurant if the whim took him, and this would be to entertain whoever he was with. Often it would just be me and him. Or he'd take on the street too, stop people and object to the way they were dressed, or just harangue them. I fell in love with it, I just thought he was fantastic.'

Litvinoff soon assumed the self-appointed propagandist role that a few years earlier he'd performed for the Krays; he didn't write the famous 'Clapton is God' graffito that appeared in 1965 on Arvon Road in Islington, but according to one of Clapton's biographers it was Litvinoff who now ensured that the phrase 'was scrawled all over London, including on the wall of the Pheasantry'.[8] He continued to create bizarre cultural collisions: he even became acquainted with the Queen Mother owing to her occasional visits to Pietro Annigoni's studio there, and on one occasion introduced her to a very stoned Clapton. Often the two men would leave the Pheasantry for a walk up to Granny Takes a Trip, the boutique at 488 King's Road (the World's End end, which was more fashionable than during Litvinoff and Whidborne's mid-1950s spell there). On one of these regular trawls along the King's Road and homewards again they were 'coming from the World's End walking back up' when Clapton passed an admiring comment on Litvinoff's shirt and asked him where he bought it. 'Oh, this fucking thing?' Litvinoff replied. 'And he undid the tie a bit, and hooked it over the top of the shirt; he had a jacket on but he ripped the shirt to pieces. It was almost like a circus act, a woman taking her bra off without taking her outer clothes off. He got the whole shirt off and threw it on the floor, then he had the tie, naked chest and jacket on, and it was without skipping a beat, you know. It was so creative. He was really a street guy, and an incredibly important part of the machine – he was really in everyone's lives.'

Often these emergences in people's lives were quite unsolicited. Clapton witnessed a quality in Litvinoff that others often mention: his uncanny ability to unsettle complete strangers by seeming to read their mind, deconstruct their performance, penetrate their appearance as if the mask they presented to the world were transparent. 'He'd go up to people he'd never met before,' he wrote in his autobiography, 'and launch into a diatribe about them, pointing a finger in their face and telling them what they did, where they'd come from and where they were going wrong. Then somehow he'd turn the whole thing back on himself, as if to redeem the person he'd been attacking.'[9]*

Waymouth added that 'because he was so bright and quick, he was actually frightening sometimes, because he was almost like a mind-reader. He could sometimes sit with somebody and tell them their life story, and he'd only just met them. He had that very quick, street-smart instinct, intuition, whatever you like to call it. He had the intelligence to place – he knew who he was, and he knew who everybody else was.'

Like any 'mind-reader', what might seem telepathic owed more to a shrewd ability to read people: their accent, dialect, mannerisms, posture, sartorial taste, all the little 'tells' that make the most guarded of us legible to a practised decipherer of human beings. Whether by diction or bearing Litvinoff could pick out the product of a minor public school in seconds and despite his own origins give them a snobbish dismissal; like aristocrats and criminals he saved his greatest vitriol for the timid conservative middle classes. His ear for dialogue betrayed his intimacy with street life across the breadth of the capital. Sharp was especially struck by this: Litvinoff would 'hear someone's voice and he'd tell them where they came from, pretty much the street they lived in,' he said. 'He had an amazing ear. I think he was totally fascinated by people. He might have been like one of those Hasidic rabbis in a way, without the context.'

After several people had attested to this ability I decided to ground it in proper context by contacting an expert in the field. Tony Thorne is a linguist and lexicographer at King's College London with a particular interest in slang and cultural history. He'd heard of Litvinoff and while he suspected that time and memory had amplified his powers a tad, the general premise seemed plausible.

'I doubt the claim that he could distinguish street from street, but I can believe that he could identify certain features that would tie someone to an area of inner London such as Smithfield (all the trade groups like the meat porters, flower sellers, market stallholders, tailors, etc., had their own jargon, nicknames and peculiarities of pronunciation), Petticoat Lane and Chapel Market, Bermondsey.

* Litvinoff's love of Bob Dylan might in part have involved a recognition of an identical trait, apparent in vituperative songs from 'Ballad in Plain D' to 'Idiot Wind'.

'Telling south London from west, north or east London used to be easy: my own grandmother could do this from accent. The word "south" itself might be pronounced "souf", "sarth" or "sahf" in each of these. In east London "r" would often be "w", whereas in some districts it was in the throat like the French "r", or a sort of mixed "wr", otherwise just swallowed or muffled.

'The famous glottal stop – the swallowed consonant(s) adopted by Mockney as in "bu'er" instead of "butter" – could actually vary from place to place. In some places it was not only used for "t" but for "p" or "k" or "d", too.'

The important point was that local dialect is not just accent, which is unlikely to vary from street to street, but also the use of slang terms, nicknames, catchphrases and other idiosyncrasies that might echo back and forth between neighbours and friends within a small community. Knowing this was one reason why a safe blower named Jimmy Evans, of whom more later, grew to suspect his wife was having an affair with someone close to the Richardson brothers. One day she casually used the sarcastic phrase 'Oh you're lovely, ain't'cha?', which rang alarm bells in the ever-wary Evans' head: he had only ever heard Charlie Richardson say it before, and he knew it was associated only with their pocket of south London. Children had their own lingo too, Thorne explained.

'Kids in Notting Hill in the late 1950s used to taunt one another with the cry "Bivvard!" This meant "Hard luck, mate!" and was derived from "Bit of hard cheese". As far as I know it was limited to a few square miles. In south-west London in the early 1960s "Brian" was used as a mocking or challenging term of address for a male, just as "John" was used across much of London, as in " 'Oo you lookin' at, John?"

'If Litvinoff was talking about the East End or Soho there were groups of Jews, Indians, Sikhs, Maltese [and] Italians who would have particular accents [and] ways of combining their languages with English and interspersing their own key words ("*Goy*", "*basta!*") with London English. "White Anglo-Saxon" Londoners might use back-slang (still very much alive in those days in the meat markets for example) and theatrical types, sailors and gays would use Polari. These would also help identify where, or at least from what social subgroup, people came.'

One example that would have been familiar to Litvinoff was the lingo used among groups of shoplifters as they worked through large stores such as Harrods.* Regular customers would hear people mutter to one another 'nitto', 'sweet' or 'on your daily' without having any idea that they were thieves' code for 'don't go ahead', 'all clear' and 'don't touch it' (because a store detective was watching).

'If you were familiar with the combination of pronunciation peculiarities plus real local place-names, slang terms and nicknames for places and people, you might be able to pin someone down to a smallish area of London back in a time when people still generally stayed put in their extended families and communities of neighbours,' Thorne said. 'I can readily believe that Litvinoff could do this.'

While the ability seemed striking to his artistic and bohemian friends, most of whom had not grown up in the city, those who shared his background often also developed a finely attuned ear for the nuances of different districts' speech. Micky Fawcett recalled a time at Esmeralda's Barn when Ronnie Kray overheard a man at the bar and muttered: 'Look at him. It's one of that Canning Town mob,' and then, in Fawcett's words, proceeded to 'do a contemptuous nasal imitation of the Canning Town accent – our part of London was so tribal that there were real differences between them and Ronnie's neighbourhood, which wasn't really that far away in Bethnal Green'.[10]

It was a trait that impressed Clapton as much as it did Litvinoff's other younger artistic friends, but he appreciated Litvinoff as far more than a streetwise savant or entertainer. Their relationship developed a genuine substance and affection, forged in a common love for music and, related to this, an awareness of Litvinoff's pivotal influence on Clapton's career.

'Deeper down, he understood a lot of things. I hadn't met anybody who had such a wide grasp of the arts – music and painting and literature and film – and we could talk about anything. For me, the big hook was his knowledge of music and the blues. He could talk about that like nobody I'd ever met. He loved all the old stuff, he loved Bessie Smith – he talked about it and it was the *Grand Guignol* to

---

* A rich hunting ground: Diana Melly remembered him arriving at her and George's house in 1964 and giving them a fine embossed black cigarette case that he'd just lifted from Knightsbridge's premier department store; similarly his friend David Gittleman remembered Litvinoff sharing a one-litre, £100 jar of caviar acquired from Fortnum and Mason.

him.* It was incredibly theatrical to him. Early blues, he loved. So that was our meeting point.'

The *Grand Guignol*, the Parisian theatre where frenzied audiences lusted for grotesque melodramas that conveyed a rude truth missing from the more refined theatrical tradition. Clapton put his finger on it. The blues contains all human life and every known emotion; while its greatest performers were alive to myriad nuances of sadness, it is far more than the depressive music of cliché: it can be as joyous as it is heartbreaking, and as such compellingly paradoxical. Singers such as Blind Willie McTell squeezed an exquisite beauty from their sadness that elicits a rare pleasure, then on the 78's flipside barrelled out a rollicking up-tempo burst of Saturday-night sexual braggadocio that contains a poignancy born of the singer and listener's shared apprehension that it will soon be Sunday morning. And the early jazzy female singers gave it something extra, a blend of melodrama and defiant self-reliance that lent their performances and personae a quality more associated with black American divas of forty years later: camp.† Litvinoff, the gay son of an extraordinary matriarch, revered strong women who didn't let affliction grind them down. Seen this way, Bessie Smith's rendition of 'T'aint Nobody's Business If I Do' – with its uncompromising opening lines:

---

*   Litvinoff in a note accompanying an exhaustive Smith compilation he made for Nigel Waymouth: 'With Bessie, she follows the Alexandrian principle of poetry, and thus the titles are only loosely buried in the interstatement, usually within 25/35 seconds of the song, though occasionally in the penultimate or last line. . . I know this Bessie tape is a long haul, man, but she is after all is said, the world's greatest soul artist. Right? Right.'

†   While Litvinoff was not camp in its casually used sense of 'appearing effeminate' his outlook accords with the sensibility that Susan Sontag essays in her 'Notes on Camp': indeed in the following excerpts she might have been describing him. Note 10: 'Camp sees everything in quotation marks. It's not a lamp, but a "lamp"; not a woman, but a "woman". To perceive Camp in objects and persons is to understand Being-as-Playing-a-Role. It is the farthest extension, in sensibility, of the metaphor of life as theater.' Note 53: '. . .its metaphor of life as theater is peculiarly suited as a justification and projection of a certain aspect of the situation of homosexuals'. Note 51: 'Jews and homosexuals are the outstanding creative minorities in contemporary urban culture. Creative, that is, in the truest sense: they are creators of sensibilities. The two pioneering forces of modern sensibility are Jewish moral seriousness and homosexual aestheticism and irony.' Note 55: 'Camp is generous. It wants to enjoy. It only seems like malice, cynicism.' Note 56: 'Camp taste is a kind of love, love for human nature. It relishes, rather than judges, the little triumphs and awkward intensities of "character".' 'Notes on Camp', first published in *Partisan Review* (1964), accessed at http://www9.georgetown.edu/faculty/irvinem/theory/sontag-notesoncamp-1964.html.

There ain't nothing I can do, or nothing I can say
That folks don't criticise me
But I'm goin' to do just as I want to anyway
And don't care if they all despise me

– becomes a natural precursor to Gloria Gaynor's 'I Am What I Am' or 'I Will Survive'.* Along with Ma Rainey, Smith vied for contention as Litvinoff's single favourite singer: he loved to play their blues at full blast, and found something deeply moving in their music. Listening to Smith it's easy to see why: James P. Johnson's stately andante piano, distanced yet intimate, her moaned vocals teetering on the cusp between orgasm and sorrow, the sheer independence of it all. The blues also offered a fictionaliser such as Litvinoff his preferred variety of truth: the kind that is, in the poet George Szirtes' words, 'true in the way that poetry is true, and not in the way that evidence is true'.[11] In the folk tradition songs are whittled over time into perfectly formed vessels of emotional truth, which held a particular appeal at a time of hollow posturing of the kind performed by the unfortunate Kevin MacDonald. 'Floating verses' recur and resonate across the canon. Hype can make a hit but not a song that endures over decades or centuries; in the long run, humanity has better taste than that. History's filter sifts out the chaff, retains the pure stuff; the only trouble is that too much good stuff also slips through the mesh. As W. H. Auden said of books, some songs 'are undeservedly forgotten; none are undeservedly remembered'.[12]

Clapton, Sharp, Litvinoff and Waymouth shared an obsession with the pre-war American music and each cultivated substantial collections of obscure tracks culled from old singles, early 1960s reissue LPs, Library of Congress albums, Alan Lomax's field recordings, tapes of work songs and laments made in Southern state penitentiaries. The appeal had many more strands besides; sure, there was the kudos of digging up something others hadn't heard and developing a reputation around Chelsea, but

---

* She and the collar-and-tie-wearing Ma Rainey also foreshadowed the 1960s and 1970s by virtue of their proud lesbianism. Angela Davis wrote that Rainey's 1928 recording 'Prove It On Me Blues' precursed 'the lesbian cultural movement of the 1970s, which began to crystallise around the performance and recording of lesbian-affirming songs'. *Blues Legacies and Black Feminism: Gertrude 'Ma' Rainey, Bessie Smith, and Billie Holiday*, by Angela Y. Davis (Vintage, 1999), p. 40.

in playing these crackly old numbers there was also the more intimate sensation of kindling a faint line between the singer and the listener, that in setting the needle to the groove you created a tin-can telephone with the other end in the Mississippi of 1931. As such the poor recording quality becomes not an obstacle but a virtue. A chill frisson derives from the music's very faintness: listen to Cousins and DeMoss's banjo-backed vaudeville number 'Poor Mourner', recorded for the Berliner Gramophone Company in 1897, and the tingle is voyeuristic, as if a pair of ghosts are having a party next door and you're eavesdropping through the wall. Litvinoff's collection spanned a thousand radiations from the idiosyncratic survey of working-class America's musical landscape collected in Harry Smith's *Anthology of American Folk Music*: zydeco, bluegrass, Cajun, ragtime piano rolls. Since the Soho days he'd been mad for Jelly Roll Morton's brand of New Orleans jazz; perhaps, like many Jews, he felt something in its blue-tinged energy that stirred genetic memories of the jiving melancholia of klezmer, the dance music that articulated the wistful hopes of pre-Holocaust *ostjuden*.* But while some call it 'old timey music', to listen to the sound of pre-war America was no nostalgic retreat; it was the antithesis of nostalgia, laden with a recognition that life wasn't simpler then and that it's eerily miraculous that even a simulacrum of a voice from such times should carry to the present. Doing so cultivates new memories of the near-forgotten and a sense of keeping something endangered alive; at its heart Litvinoff's pursuit of obscure records was therefore humane, though to the underachieving egotist in him there was a certain psychological withdrawal in preferring a generation who were not his contemporaries and whose veneration constituted no reminder of his own relative lack of

---

* More generally, Litvinoff embodied a tendency within secularised second- or third-generation Jewish music-lovers to feel (or hope) that their own history confers a degree of legitimacy in empathising with or performing African American blues. This sense was reinforced by both cultures' having a tradition of expressing their sorrows in song. 'Many of the Jews participating in the production of popular music were sons of cantors... The melancholy of the cantor's art displayed a striking resemblance, for many, to the pathos of African American music, which suggested that because centuries of suffering had instituted lamentation as a dominant expressive form in Jewish culture, individual Jews were particularly able to give musical voice to affliction. African American music...was commonly understood to express primarily pathos and humor, and Jews, as a result of their own religious history, appeared well equipped to handle the pathos.' *A Right to Sing the Blues: African Americans, Jews, and American Popular Song*, by Jeffrey Melnick (Harvard University Press, 1999), p. 169.

success. The old music became his fundamental obsession and formed the substantial tether in several of his most significant friendships. A Finnish artist named Axel Sutinen got to know Litvinoff and Sharp a few years later and felt that this bond had become exclusive. 'Blues music and vaudeville songs were always echoing around like they had a bubble around them and I felt it impenetrable,' he said. 'I was aware that I was an observer to a theatrical event or performance of a very high intellectual standard.'

Clapton's and Litvinoff's mutual reverence for this music would create a similarly tight attachment. As ever Litvinoff would try to impress with his knowledge and connections; where the blues were concerned, however, in Clapton he met his match. Did Litvinoff manage to introduce him to any old blues he didn't know?

'He was always trying but he couldn't do it! Because I knew as much as he did. And I think he liked that, that we could fence around that stuff; he would try to impress me and it wouldn't work, or I'd shoot him down: "Well, actually that guy didn't come from Atlanta, he came from Texas, David. Get your facts right!"'

In another musical field, however, Litvinoff managed to produce something that would surprise Clapton. During the course of their friendship he grew dissatisfied with life as part of Cream, and it wasn't just his relentless need for a new toy that was to blame. Bruce and Baker's fractious relationship required the diplomatic Clapton to broker an uneasy peace time and again, but this was a small factor in a broader malaise. The band's official debut gig had been at the sixth Windsor Jazz Festival in August 1966; when they played the festival again a year later 'it did not escape our attention how little we had progressed', Clapton wrote.[13] The band's sales remained below those of the Beatles, the Rolling Stones and the Jimi Hendrix Experience. Gigging night after night across America had left little time for the creative process, and Clapton also felt a degree of complacency within himself, born of the audiences' apparent adulation however well the band played. He was more than ready for a change; in fact he required one if he were to shed a creeping sense of shame at being part of a band that felt like 'a con'. What he needed was to rediscover something vital, organic, real.

One day in late 1967 or early 1968 Litvinoff played Clapton a recording of Bob Dylan's *Basement Tapes*. In the aftermath of the gruelling 1966 tour in which the electrified Dylan and his backing band the Hawks received nightly abuse from erstwhile fans who deemed him to have betrayed his position as a folk-singing spokesman for a generation, the near-broken singer-songwriter learned that his manager Albert Grossman had just agreed a new schedule of more than sixty dates. On top of this his publisher, Macmillan, was leaning on him for delivery of his promised but unfinished novel, to be titled *Tarantula*. On 29th July Dylan's wired, ever-accelerating 'thin wild mercury' years culminated when he straddled his motorcycle and took to the roads near his home in Woodstock, upstate New York. However serious his crash was, it removed him from the spotlight in the way that his nervous system demanded. But during his recovery he continued to create music; in fact, living in rural peace with his wife Sara and their baby Jesse, he was more prolific than ever. Down in the basement of the house known as Big Pink in nearby West Saugerties, which had become home to members of his touring band, he concocted a batch of songs that retained his oblique humour while issuing a greater wisdom, something deep and true and devoid of affectation. The uptight outlaw had morphed into a laconic cowboy. There was a new warmth in his weirdness. 'Million Dollar Bash' was as funny as anything he would ever record; 'Tears of Rage' revealed a dramatically broadened vista of sadness; 'This Wheel's on Fire' seemed to recast his motorcycle accident, or the one that had recently killed his friend Richard Fariña, or both, in a strange and mournful slow motion. He'd come back from the edge, embracing the sincere emotions of father-hood after years of sharp-witted posturing and shape-shifting: from faux-Woody Guthrie, to finger-pointing civil rights agitator, to brittle hipper-than-thou surrealist, to a deeper-voiced emotionally resonant Dylan who seemed suddenly to have reached manhood. Something of that, entwined with the astonishing instrumentation provided by Robbie Robertson, Rick Danko, Garth Hudson and Richard Manuel, who along with Levon Helm* were now calling themselves the Band, accorded precisely with Clapton's needs.

The tracks that became known as the *Basement Tapes* wouldn't be released officially until 1975 (and not in full until 2014) and Clapton had no idea how Litvinoff had laid hands on them so soon after their recording. Presumably he never asked: Nigel Waymouth did and received an answer that emphasised Litvinoff's knowledge of how to work the city. 'David

---

* Helm was absent from the sessions involving Dylan but features in the basement record-ings in which members of the Band take lead vocals.

said: "It's simple, man. All I did was go to the music pushers in Denmark Street and they had all the demos, because they wanted bands like Manfred Mann to record them.'" (Witness that group's cover of 'Quinn the Eskimo', or Julie Driscoll and Brian Auger's 'This Wheel's on Fire'.) 'It's subsequently come out that these were like demo tapes,' Waymouth added. 'Albert Grossman was very shrewd; Dylan would write these songs and Grossman would give them straightaway to Peter, Paul and Mary. David was quick and he understood that. And of course it was a badge he could show off around Chelsea: "You think you're hip? Dig this."'

Litvinoff's conjuring act in producing these recordings certainly had the desired effect on Clapton.

'At that time, I was struggling to really get into Dylan,' he said. 'I had been so interested in black music that I really didn't like any white music at all, including myself. It was very difficult to figure out how I fit into the scheme of things. Martin Sharp made me work very hard to get me to like *Blonde on Blonde* and I could hear some music in that that was familiar to me; there were some great players on that album. It was just the whole idea of taking a musical form and using it as a backdrop for poetry. It annoyed me at that point in time.'

But then it clicked. 'And then Litvinoff showed up with this stuff, and man! It was like a time bomb went off. He actually was the first guy that I knew who had the Dylan *Basement Tapes*. He had the acetate. That was extraordinary.

'And the next person I saw, I think he might have been instrumental in this too, was Mick Jagger. Mick came down to see me just after I'd moved out of London, right after these *Basement Tapes* became available, talking about "I Shall Be Released" and these songs, and how profound it seemed to be now: that Dylan had had a near-death experience and was now writing on some level of a different point of view; it wasn't so cynical any more, it had some depth to it. He grew into himself. I suppose he fully matured. And what I learned later was this was a band I was going to become very fond of too, that were playing on the *Basement Tapes*.

'So that was a bonding experience for me and Litvinoff: it was a keystone part of our relationship that he knew that he had turned me on to one of the finest things I'd ever heard, and that I held him accountable for that. How would I have heard it otherwise? I probably would eventually, but he was on the money.'

Litvinoff playing him the acetate was a moment that prepared Clapton for a new musical direction. In summer 1968 Clapton heard more of the Band when his friend Alan Pariser, a Los Angeles-based entrepreneur, played him *Music from Big Pink*, their debut album. Clapton had told Cream's manager, Robert Stigwood, numerous times in pained transatlantic phonecalls during US tours that he couldn't go on for much longer. Now his growing immersion in the Band's music catalysed a new phase of his career. Within weeks he'd agreed that Cream would play a farewell concert at the Royal Albert Hall in November 1968, and had begun feeling around for a new way forward. It took time, and many jam sessions with the keyboardist and singer Steve Winwood, but when he materialised again from his self-described 'vacuum' it was as a member of Blind Faith, a short-lived group whose softer, humbler and more spiritual tone indicated the direction his music would pursue. Whether in his subsequent stint as a sideman with the American country rock duo Delaney and Bonnie, or his return to centre stage with Derek and the Dominos, Clapton continued to draw from the rootsy Americana explored by Dylan and the Band in those fabled recordings. Litvinoff's role here and the formative nature of their relationship lent him a significance that became plain in the way Clapton spoke of him forty-five years on.

'I thought the world of him, he was a very compelling man. I think I've met seminal people like that throughout my life. . . There've been very powerful magnetic men in my life and they've been like stepping stones, I spent a lot of time with and learned from [them].'

So did you learn anything from him? 'I think I did, I learned a lot about courage. He was a very brave man. That's the thing, it seemed like he was incredibly confident. And I was lost for words most of the time back then, I was happy just to bask in his glory. Watch him entertain people just in himself. He seemed to know himself incredibly well. The sad part was I could tell that he had also quite a lot of self-disgust going on; that was part of his whole thing. He could make it funny, he was very self-deprecating, he could tease about himself without it being embarrassing. But I knew he would suffer. He was capable of great suffering.'

In his autobiography Clapton describes Litvinoff as 'a fast-talking East End Jew, with a stupendous intellect, who appeared not to give a shit what anyone thought of him, even though I know he really did, and sometimes painfully so'.[14] Julian Lloyd saw that vulnerable, tender side too. 'There were times when David was very quiet and very low and not exactly crushed, but very humble,' said Lloyd. 'For all these gangster associations and everything, he was just a kind and funny man, with this extraordinary insight as if he knew how people were feeling and could very quickly join in and express it. I remember him feeling low one night and his face was rather crumpled, and he said, "You know, man, I'm just like anyone else – if they like me, I like them."'

Both men detected in Litvinoff a self-esteem linked to his perception of other people's perception of him, which is no programme for mental stability. Clapton also connected the source of that 'great suffering' to Litvinoff's acute awareness that his flaws would prevent him from attaining his intellect's potential. While 1967 saw the decriminalisation of homosexual acts in private between consenting men, a decade on from the Lord Montagu affair and the Wolfenden Report, Litvinoff also seemed at this moment rather reserved about his relationships, at least in Clapton's company. The latter also intuited that the regular disappearances that in some people's eyes lent Litvinoff a furtive mystique probably had a sadder, more banal causation.

'We didn't know, there may have been some chemical imbalance. Because he would disappear, then he would come back. He'd be full on, then he'd disappear again. He could be what they call bipolar now. But it baffled me too. . . I don't think he had any problem with his sexuality, but he didn't want to broadcast it. He would talk about Joey-Gerry,' referring to Gerry Goldstein; 'he would always be his "friend" but it was quite clear that it was more than that. But I think. . .I just felt that he felt he ought to be able to do more. That's why he would run himself down, but only in a general way.'

Clapton tried to tell him that it didn't matter. Not everyone had to place their achievement on record, submit to the egoistic urge to leave a mark on the world that would survive beyond their death; everything washes away sooner or later, all is ephemeral to a varying degree. Better to burn bright within the moment, to occupy one's character entirely and enact the ultimate performance than strive for futile acclaim from posterity. 'I loved people who could just be like that in life, without it having to go on to a canvas or into a book – that you could just, like you say, be a performance artist, your actual life is your art. And I wanted to try to impress that on him whenever I could: that he was just a great man to be around.'

As the new chapter in Clapton's career developed, his connection with the Pheasantry began to fray, and with it his and Litvinoff's friendship. There was no falling out, only a drifting apart through circumstance after a 'very short intense period of time'. Clapton had mentioned that Harold Pinter's *The Caretaker* was his favourite play; he'd watched the film version starring Alan Bates, Donald Pleasence and Robert Shaw 'hundreds of times'.[15]

'What brought the end to the Pheasantry really was [that] he swore he knew the guy that Pinter had based *The Caretaker* on,' Clapton said. 'John Ivor Golding. And we all had to meet John Ivor Golding,' he sighed.

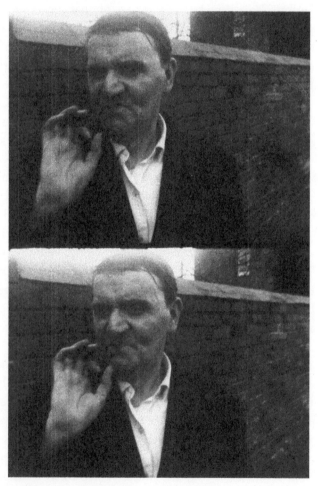

Images of John Ivor Golding taken from 'J. G.', a short film about him.

Act One, Scene Six.

JIG: The point is this, you see, I've been to all these countries with coloured people but this island *cannot afford to have them here.*

DL: **No - you're just conscious of the financial debt under which this country is straining. It must worry you all the time while you're on the bottle.**

JIG: And they get far more assistance than what I do.

DL: **Good heavens. It's *most* unfair.**

JIG: And they've got them in these outrageous hospitals, because they are outrageous - you read *The Caretaker*, didn't you? You understand me? I can enlighten you on anything like that.

DL: **What's your sign of the zodiac?**

JIG: That's a Scorpio.

DL: **Does it have much influence on you, that?**

JIG: Well, I do read them all every day: sometimes I take notice, other times I think 'Ah, this is artificial'.

DL: **If it says you're going to meet a tall, dark man, you keep out of the way of every copper.**

JIG: Not only that, the point is this you see, the law knows I don't really trust them, because when they don't send letters of apology. . .

DL: **Which they rarely do.**

JIG: . . .especially when you get this confrontation, and it's only carrier bags, with my shaving gear in inside, and papers.

DL: **They never want to know what's inside; they only want to know what's called 'the contents'.**

JIG: The point is this, I don't know nothing, I escalate like an Iron Curtain towards them -

DL: Do you know what you've just done? Are you aware of the import of what you have done? You have just, in the past thirty seconds - you'll forgive me saying this - you've used two negatives. 'I don't know nothing,' you said.

JIG: True. Why do you say that?

DL: Well, you've used two negatives. And the two negatives make the double negative, don't they?

JIG: Of course they do, yes. On the plural and the predicate.

DL: Yes. You use the predatory tense quite a lot?

JIG: It all depends what frame of mind I'm in, David. Sometimes, with a prayer or personal experience I can go better than the scriptwriter. In fact I have done work with a scriptwriter.

DL: Yes, I know about that: for the *Caretaker* play.

JIG: The point is this, you see, I did that *in camera* you see, and I did that with complete philanthropy and I've never seen the person since. But nevertheless I don't let things like that worry me.

DL: Were you not paid?

JIG: Not at the time and I haven't been to this very day. But I don't worry about that.

DL: Mr Pinter, wasn't it?

JIG: Quite.

By now the reader will be familiar with the attitudes of John Ivor Golding. If he had a claim to fame, it is that he was the likely inspiration for Harold Pinter's character Mac Davies, not that Pinter would confirm as much. Louis Waymouth, the son of Litvinoff's friend Nigel, found himself seated beside Pinter at a dinner party some years ago. 'I asked him whether it was true that he used Golding as a model,' Louis said, 'and Pinter just turned his back to me and ignored me for half an hour.'

The closest Pinter came to discussing the matter on the record was in an interview where he was asked: 'Have your plays usually been drawn from situations you've been in? *The Caretaker*, for example.' He replied: 'I'd met a few, quite a few, tramps – you know, just in the normal course of events, and I think there was one particular one. . . I didn't know him very well, he did most of the talking when I saw him. I bumped into him a few times, and about a year or so afterward he sparked this thing off. . .'[16]

Golding shared Davies' hint of a military past, his obsession with the whereabouts of his papers, and his racism, being one of those who try to order the unorderable world via a dull taxonomy of ethnicity. Litvinoff skewers his views with bitter sarcasm. At times he seems to be taking the roles of Pinter's characters Mick and Aston and appropriating lines from Pinter's script: compare the offers of money and accommodation, the questions about Golding's references, the flattering suggestion that 'You're a man of the world', his description of the Gestapo as 'fibbers', the intimation towards the end that he's 'very worried about Gerry', which echoes Mick's 'I'm very worried about my brother'. If Litvinoff's attitude towards Golding seems cruel at times, Martin Sharp remembered that he was genuinely intrigued by him as a curious specimen of humanity.

'John Ivor was a fascinating character, very difficult to cope with. [Litvinoff] could communicate with him; he was fascinated with people and he realised there was a great character there, an example of the human mind that had gone off the rails but had its own brilliance. I think he was busted for something or other, one imagines some sexual misdemeanour. . . He was on Largactil.* He gave me one once and I was paralysed, it was the tranquilliser he was on.

'He was a star in his way, John Ivor, and David appreciated that he was a star. A "gentleman of the road", David described him as. He used John Ivor like a sort of secret weapon. He'd send him over to people and places. He sounded very lucid when you got him on the buzzer on the door but when you let him in there was this sort of mad tramp.'

In Iain Sinclair's words, Golding 'was inducted by Litvinoff into the play of the city'. The Pinter connection piqued Litvinoff's initial interest, though the itinerant Welsh philosopher had left it behind, insofar as he ever left his past behind. Mac Davies had assumed a life of his own while Golding played out his final years. 'He is unconcerned that his

---

* A drug to treat schizophrenia.

surrogate has moved on to such fame in the world,' wrote Sinclair, 'while he is left out in the cold at the mercy of a sadistic constabulary. Litvinoff is his last hope. He doesn't know that his conversation is being recorded and he probably doesn't care. He is being directed. In Litvinoff's parallel universe, Golding *is* the caretaker. He precedes Pinter's theatrical creation. He's full of chat, rant, theories, memories of an Arcadian past peopled with vipers.'[17]

One day Ginger Baker came to the Pheasantry and warned Clapton that he'd heard from a police source he was next on Sergeant Norman Pilcher's list. Pilcher was making a name for himself in his pursuit of drug-taking young rock stars, and in the process had picked up the nickname 'the Gardener' because he was so good at 'planting'. Clapton fled Chelsea for the safety of Robert Stigwood's home in Stanmore, assuming that without him to arrest Pilcher would lose interest. That night Pilcher buzzed at the Pheasantry's intercom and yelled 'Postman, special delivery!' before bursting in, whereupon he found Sharp and Mora and arrested them for drugs offences. Clapton would never forgive himself for not having thought to warn them. Before the case came to court, Sharp was advised that he would probably be let off lightly if he gave a grovelling apology and promised to respect the law; when the day came, he informed the judge that he really ought to try smoking hashish and received a £50 fine. Clapton's Chelsea period came to an end as he moved back to his familiar Surrey, into a large villa called Hurtwood Edge near his friends George and Patty Harrison, becoming another character whose intersection with Litvinoff's life would prove vivid and formative but all too brief. 'I only knew him for a short period of time,' he said. 'He kind of disappeared, and I moved out of London.'

Chapter 6

A Diabolical Liberty

'I am just too old and too tired to care for Fame. The real fun, which I enjoy, is moving others. I infinitely prefer the background for my own performances. There is more room there for real gymnastics than on the top where youngsters sweat and struggle for public applause.'

Frederick Rolfe, in *The Quest for Corvo*, by A. J. Symons

If the Kray twins felt themselves untouchable after the Hew McCowan case collapsed, so it seemed to the establishment that the most prominent pop stars also imagined they could do whatever they desired. Eric Clapton's near-arrest came in the context of a determined campaign by Pilcher and his colleagues in the Metropolitan Police to cut these *jeunesse dorée* down to size. Then, as now, the police and the tabloid press had a close working relationship, and as Mick Jagger lay in bed on the morning of 19th February 1967 and read that morning's *News of the World*, the fact became inescapable: sue the nation's favourite purveyor of sleaze and it would find someone, anyone, to taint your reputation and undermine your case.

Someone had betrayed them, that much was clear. Eighteen police officers don't pitch up at an isolated Sussex farmhouse on a whim. Lurid journalese drew the newspaper's readers into a scene of bohemian debauchery. 'A strong, sweet smell of incense' filled a room decorated in a style that was part-Olde England, part Marrakech bazaar: rich Moroccan drapes hung on the walls, tapestried cushions lay underfoot, and here and there were assorted fey young drug-fiends in languid repose, one of them a woman clad only in a fur rug. Bob Dylan sneered from the speakers, a film flickered mute on the television. Readers learned no names, only the fact that two of those present were nationally known pop stars (Jagger, Keith Richards) and another anonymous star (George Harrison) had departed before the police arrived.

Jagger had threatened legal action after the paper's 5th February edition quoted him admitting that he'd taken LSD and Benzedrine;* the hapless hack who thought he'd interviewed him in a nightclub had actually been talking with Brian Jones. Jagger hadn't taken hallucinogens at that point – he was too cautious, too keen on retaining control. When the police raided Redlands, Richards' estate outside West Wittering, and found the Rolling Stones' lead singer in possession of amphetamine sulphate, his claim for defamation didn't look good. The police didn't even realise that Jagger had been persuaded to take his first acid trip that day. Life was already getting too heavy for his liking; a week before the bust, he'd left Redlands muttering to Donald Cammell: 'This is all getting out of hand. I don't know where it's all going to end.'[1]

The denouement unfolded as follows: at 10pm on Saturday 11th February someone telephoned the *News of the World*'s news desk to let them know that the Stones and their circle would be using illegal substances at Richards' place in the country that weekend. It was agreed that this informant would meet senior reporter Trevor Kempson in St James's Park on Sunday morning for a proper conversation. After that meeting the paper informed Chief Inspector John Lynch of the Metropolitan Police, expecting in return full details of the raid; but despite the conventional wisdom that the establishment were engaged in a concerted, draconian campaign, it seems that Lynch had no desire to get involved. The cannabis legalisation campaigner Steve Abrams said that Lynch told him he 'was not expected to stamp out cannabis, but to keep its use under control. If he arrested Mick Jagger every lad in the country would want to try some pot.'[2]

So the Met deemed it a parochial matter and batted it back, at which point the *News of the World* passed the tip-off instead to West Sussex Police, whose chief constable, Thomas Williams, had, only the previous week, told the local press of his 'deep concern on drugs' and his fear over whether 'society contains sufficient safeguards for people to have a fair chance of being resistant to the contagion of less moral neighbours and workmates'.[3] Redlands farmhouse was far enough from the neighbouring properties for all but the most delicate souls to withstand the moral decay emanating through its old stone walls that weekend, though they could

---

*   The second article in a three-part series titled 'Pop Stars and Drugs: Facts That Will Shock You'.

probably hear the music that was playing so loudly that no one within heard the police make their way up the drive.

After the force's mob-handed arrival just after 8pm on Sunday 12th February and the subsequent charges, Jagger switched from pursuing libel damages to facing criminal prosecution for drugs charges, along with Richards and their friend Robert Fraser, aka 'Groovy Bob'. So who was the informant? Most of those who'd been at Redlands that weekend seemed beyond reproach. Fraser's Moroccan manservant Ali, Christopher Gibbs and the photographer Michael Cooper were trusted friends. There was David Schneiderman, nicknamed 'The Acid King', the Canadian who'd floated into town only weeks earlier and walked straight into the midst of the Rolling Stones' lives on account of his ability to procure the very finest LSD – on this occasion a variety named California Sunshine, concocted in a San Francisco laboratory and ingested in bright orange pellets. They'd spent the day tripping courtesy of Schneiderman and were riding the final waves when the police came calling.

Who else? Nicky Cramer, a King's Road flower-child who was clad in velvet and wearing make-up according to the policewoman who searched him, and who was often to be seen reclining in his finery while blowing bubbles into the air. Cramer was somewhat deranged but hardly dangerous, other than to his pets. Barry Miles, the co-founder of the *International Times* and the Indica Gallery, remembered him as 'one of those typical King's Road freaks, with his hair completely frizzed out. At one point he had a rabbit that he dyed bright green, that committed suicide by leaping off the roof [of the Pheasantry]. I think he used to give it acid. He was a fucking mad idiot. I mean, there were a lot of people like that, particularly at the Pheasantry, it was really filled with them.'[4]

Cramer had tagged along for the weekend in Sussex because Keith Richards didn't have the heart to stop him. When the case came to court and Richards stood in the dock, he told the judge of Cramer: 'I can only say that in my profession there are people who are hangers-on who you have to tolerate.'[5] He wasn't in their inner circle, so in the paranoid atmosphere of the bust's aftermath he fell under suspicion. A few of the Stones' favourite inhabitants of the underworld applied pressure. There was 'Spanish Tony' Sanchez for instance, Richards' dealer. He'd come up in 1950s Soho as a protégé of Albert Dimes, he of the Frith Street fight with Jack 'Spot' Comer, worked as a bouncer and croupier and moved into the Stones' orbit as a general fixer; someone who, in his own words, 'knew exactly where to go for anything from a bag of grass to a Thompson submachine gun'.[6] Earlier he had proved his clout and ingenuity by saving one of their closest friends from severe trouble.

Robert Fraser enjoyed mingling with gangsters, as Keith Richards wrote in his autobiography; Richards attributed this to a combination of the Old Etonian's repressed sexuality and rebellion against his background. This drew him towards Litvinoff, Richards noted, and in turn to Tony Sanchez, who used his wiles to rescue Fraser when he had dangerous gambling debts.

In the early 1960s Fraser worked up debts to Esmeralda's Barn to the tune of £20,000 and wrote the casino a series of duff cheques. He received daily threatening telephone calls, then the twins' enforcers turned up at his gallery. One night, over a whisky in Berwick Street with Sanchez, he slammed his glass down and declared: 'I'm being destroyed, Tony.'[7] He had no means of paying and feared for his life. Sanchez intervened directly, turning up at the Barn and demanding to see the twins. It helped that he was known as Albert Dimes' man, for they respected Dimes. Sanchez sat in Reggie's tiny office and explained Fraser's situation.

'It's a bad business,' said Reggie, 'when a gentleman like him has no honour – look at all these.' Kray spread a sheaf of bounced cheques totalling more than £5,000 on the desk before him. 'I'll tell you what I'll do. Because Albert is a friend of mine, I'll cut my losses on this guy if he pays me three grand by this time tomorrow. I can't say fairer than that.'[8]

That night Fraser played chemmy at Le Chat Noir, a gaming room where Sanchez worked as a croupier, and Sanchez rigged the game so that he won enough to clear the debt.

Sanchez formed part of the post-Redlands inquisition team, and so did his old Soho associate David Litvinoff. There was a simple way to find out what Nicky Cramer knew. He was invited to 53 St George's Court, Litvinoff's new flat on Brompton Road, where Paul Simon had previously stayed during his mid-1960s spell in London, according to Nigel Waymouth. Litvinoff and a notorious young tough guy from Fulham, John Bindon, lay waiting. Christopher Gibbs and Gerry Goldstein were there too, and they watched aghast as Litvinoff and Bindon took the liberty of subjecting Cramer to a trial by ordeal. They smacked him around, fractured his ribs and interrogated him in the hope of extracting information. 'It was absolutely awful,' said Gibbs. 'Horrible, vicious, cruel . . . Nicky Cramer was a sweet, fey creature and David was terribly cruel to him. It was a very unpleasant side to him.'

Finally Litvinoff and Bindon dangled Cramer out of a window by the ankles, but still he refused to confess. The two-man jury returned its verdict to an appalled Jagger, who'd known nothing of the torture: not guilty.

Later the spotlight swung on to Schneiderman, whom it was claimed had been caught trying to bring drugs into the UK and was only allowed to enter after agreeing to engineer the Stones' bust. Cooper and Richards had stumbled on his suitcase at Redlands and found it to contain multiple passports and identities, but at the time Schneiderman told them it was because he was on a worldwide mission to turn people on to LSD. They couldn't raise the matter with him after the event, as he immediately disappeared without trace.

But Richards gave his final conclusion in his autobiography by revealing that his very well-paid Belgian chauffeur, whom he named only as Patrick, had alerted the *News of the World*, for which he heard he received a punishment that left him with permanent leg injuries.

In the weeks following the bust, Robert Fraser continued his usual business as best he could – he had begun to champion Andy Warhol's work and in May 1967 hosted a screening of Warhol and Paul Morrissey's film *Chelsea Girls* for around fifty people who squeezed into his flat at 23 Mount Street. Whether Litvinoff was among them is unclear but it seems he grew acquainted with Warhol and his crowd at this time. On 29th June Jagger, Fraser and Richards received respective prison sentences of three months for possession of amphetamines, six months for possession of heroin and one year for allowing cannabis to be smoked at his home. Though the *Times*'s intervention helped to see Jagger and Richards freed on appeal, Fraser spent the next four months in HMP Wormwood Scrubs, his imprisonment representing a brutal encapsulation of the 1960s' symbiotic relationship between bohemia and the underworld. 'Groovy Bob' was never quite the same again, but his sacrificial experience sparked a new criminal connection that would catalyse one of British cinema's greatest films.

Act One, Scene Seven.

DL: I must get straight this financial question with you
    on the telephone, because I don't want you to be
    embarrassed.

JIG: Good gracious no - I accept it with open arms!

DL: It's only sterling?

JIG: Very much indeed. I have an amnesia for it you see!

DL: And not a penny of it will go on drink?

JIG: Good gracious no, I'm more of a Jew-baiter in holding on to it than anything.

DL: Indeed. I must say one thing about these sheenies, they do hold on to their money, don't they? The devil's work. Speaking as a good democrat I must say that I do feel sometimes that they are emissaries of the devil.*

JIG: Well, I have been to these Arundel Castle witch-craft parties—

DL: Well, Lord Norfolk's a Jew, isn't he? He's posing as a somdomite† head of the laity, the Catholic laity.

JIG: And I can assure you, David, that everyone is a brother and sister irrespective of what it says on their birth certificate. You understand?

DL: Yes. Everyone is a brother or sister irrespective of race, creed and colour with the exception of yids and niggers.

JIG: That's true. Wait! Now wait! There is a difference between a yid and a nigger, please. Now don't say that. Because I have a lot of good friends - I have a very good friend who actually comes from Israel and I've told you yesterday, he's a qualified man—

---

*   Referencing the historical tradition of likening Jews to the devil: from medieval beliefs that Jews were devils liable to seduce and corrupt gentile women – their devilish quality seemingly reinforced by their facial resemblance to Satan, though such a 'resemblance' arose only because medieval illustrations of Satan often mimicked Jews – through to Dickens' Fagin, the corrupter of children, the 'merry old gentleman' who even sports a satanic red beard. Such ideas run deep: even Litvinoff's friends often unthinkingly reached for Dickens' anti-Semitic carica-ture when trying to describe his character.
†   Referring to the calling card that Alfred 'Bosie' Douglas' father, the Marquess of Queensberry, gave Oscar Wilde, accusing him of 'posing as somdomite'.

DL: He's qualified as a man?

JIG: He's qualified in medicine.

DL: Oh. Yes. A medicine man.

JIG: And I have been to his synagogue in Cathedral Road, Cardiff. You know the big synagogue they've got there?

DL: Oh I'm very familiar with that. [A beat.] Is there a synagogue in Cathedral Road? The affrontery of them putting it there. That beautiful road. . .*

JIG: So there's a vast difference because with a yid he's got intellect, with a nigger he hasn't.

DL: I understand. Now because you're so perceptive, I'm very worried about Gerry. He doesn't seem to know whether he prefers the company of boys or girls. He seems to think that boys have a more considerable physical aesthetic than girls. . .

JIG: Nonetheless, as I say, you ring Martin and let him know that I'm coming on down. . .

DL: Yes, John. Would you mind holding on there for a few moments? I'll ring you back. Goodbye.

On 3rd April 1967, in his St George's Court flat, Litvinoff tore out page 41 of the previous day's *Sunday Times* and kept it to hand as he connected his telephone to a tape player, pressed 'record' and, while the analogue dial whirred, murmured into the handset: 'I'm now ringing a fantastic crook called Laski, who's just been exposed by the *Sunday Times*. . .'

The newspaper's Weekly Review had led with an investigation by its Insight desk, which since its inception four years earlier had exposed the Profumo affair and the extent of Peter Rachman's activities. This time the story concerned a painting by Joan Miró – or rather one that Christie's had billed as a Miró in an auction of 'Important Impressionist and Modern

---

* An example of his perception that a certain pious Christianity sees its purity as susceptible to sullying by Jewish vulgarity, and Jewishness as a general taint: the kink in the hair, the tint to the skin, the bump in the nose, the blind spots in the moral vision. . .it was a resigned, self-poisoning humour, in which sarcastic jabs won tiny Pyrrhic victories in what he felt to be a doomed battle.

Works' on 24th June 1966, when it sold to the Findlay Gallery in New York for £4,725, but which had been an unsigned, unattributed little abstract valued at 30 shillings when it was acquired by Laski six years earlier. In early 1961 the painting featured in the spring exhibition at the Obelisk Gallery in Crawford Street: its provenance was 'The Philip Laski Collection', its title 'Mother and Child', the artist Miró. As the *Sunday Times*'s journalist wryly put it, 'This attribution was largely based on a fine, dated signature which must have escaped both Sotheby's and Phillips'.[9]

Laski answered the telephone in his effete, crisply enunciated manner. 'Hello, Philip?' said Litvinoff. 'It's David here.'* Some say that Litvinoff was amoral. The following forty-five minutes suggest otherwise, though what he displayed was the most twisted, 'through the looking glass' brand of morality imaginable. How to subvert the defence of an art fraud-ster? Litvinoff would never have assisted a prosecution; instead he perpetrated an off-radar justice by giving his old adversary a blend of plau-sible guidance mingled with acid drops of disinformation. This was Litvinoff in his element, negotiating the fields of influence below the surface of London life: reeling off the contents of his dossier on the press barons (revealing Lord Thomson's address in Kensington Palace Gardens, noting that his clubs were White's and the International Press Club), goading Laski by professing sympathy and then in the next breath insinu-ating that he'd forged the signature, displaying his art world knowledge by namedropping Miró's agent and gallery in Paris, and toying with the fact that he was secretly recording the entire conversation, under the guise of advising Laski how to deal with journalists. 'You've got to be very careful, Philip, when you speak on the telephone because they tape-record you, did you know that?. . . Anyway I don't trust even this telephone we're on now. How do you *know*?'

They agreed to speak the next day. Litvinoff replaced the handset and pressed 'stop' on the tape recorder. Later he would copy it on to another reel-to-reel tape, recording over much of *Sgt. Pepper's Lonely Hearts Club Band*, which was released two months later, play the recording for the amuse-ment of his friends, then circulate copies among them that they continue to listen to when they feel like reminding themselves of the days when they

---

* Or rather, as Litvinoff had elected to adopt a clipped upper-class accent for this perform-ance, 'David *h'yah*'.

knew David Litvinoff, in doing so resurrecting this strange conversation between two rogueish eccentrics in 1960s London, Litvinoff's unique take on justice serving to perpetuate Laski's humiliation to the present day.

On the tape Litvinoff and Laski make way for the final strains of 'A Day in the Life' but after a time, as the long E major piano chord fades to silence, the listener has a disturbing surprise when Litvinoff's voice returns. He is reading a poem, perhaps of his own composition; no one seems able to identify it as another writer's work. It certainly has his qualities: it is crepuscular, haunted, preoccupied with memory, violence, loneliness and loss, reading like Rudyard Kipling rewritten by Jean Genet.

If you remember the east wind alone on a street corner,
A footstep lost, a word found, night spreading its dark banner
*   over battalions of roofs and, being only sixteen, the sound of*
*   symbolic hoofs, the dark hunter's horn [?],**
Also passion breaking wave after wave, onslaught of blood and
*   angry limbs grown smooth and violent with manhood[?], and,*
*   faltering, remember even a lost moon and futility,*
A frail dream strung on seven stars in the miraculous sky;
If you remember death, remote as a faint cry in the heart,
A shadow in the empty street of fear,
First casualty of doubt and, remembering no easy escape into
*   some commonplace of sin,*
The spring's sap rising up into summer of early greenery[?],
*   transforms this bitter scene of blood and winter,*
Blends into thoughts of flesh and bone to flower in your
*   dreamy hand[?].*

* * *

Competing for headlines with the Rolling Stones' predicament in June 1967 was the crisis in the Middle East. That month saw Israel emerge victorious from the Six Day War, during which time Litvinoff and Julian Lloyd shared a cab across London. 'Obviously a lot of London taxi drivers are Jewish,' said Lloyd, 'and he could see this one was, and [he was] talking about it and being very proud' of Israel standing up to Egyptian, Syrian and

---

*   The recording is poor quality and I have inserted question marks after words that are hard to hear.

Jordanian aggression, his views being far from uncommon at a time when British progressives still broadly approved of Zionism and saw its *kibbutz* movement as a laudable exercise in socialist living. That summer, Litvinoff's old friend Andy Garnett married Polly Devlin, a young Irish writer for *Vogue* magazine who would go on to an acclaimed career as an author and journalist. Litvinoff was not invited to the ceremony. In writing to him Garnett evidently struck an apologetic note, which prompted Litvinoff to borrow some headed paper from Whidborne's Pheasantry Studios on 8th August, and tap out a letter to the newly-weds' holiday home in Italy explaining that he quite understood, and that on their return they should call to pick up his 'modest present' to them, 'which is now at the studio awaiting your pleasure – it's a very modern clock in black vinyl or something (see John Vaughan Environment feature, *Queen*, this week, I believe, for illustration). Sale Goods cannot be exchanged, its dial practically faceless and untrammelled by rococo details such as hands or numerals.' Meanwhile, 'now that London can breathe again' he looked forward 'with awe and wonderment to the swift emergence of a brilliant new duality where heretofore there were two single bright sparks', apropos of which he tendered a little marital advice: 'Remember, my children, exactly who and what you are, try not to get constipated, beware of red-headed Jewish dwarfs, take dope if you must but never join the Flower Children and support the International Jewish Conspiracy in Israel and elsewhere as she bestrides the Middle East like a tiny colossus – the old firm, still going strong after 2,000 years. Till the end of time my dears, David (Litvinoff) xx.'

Act Two.

David Litvinoff: Hello, is that you, Martin?

Martin Sharp: Yes, yes it is.

DL: How are you?

MS: Okay.

DL: Did I wake you up?

MS: Yeah.

DL: Ah. . .I thought of taking you out for lunch, if that's cool, and having a little chat with you. . .

MS: Okay. . .

DL: I asked this friend of mine (I think I mentioned him to you, did I not - John Ivor Golding? This Welsh philosopher. He holds the chair of philosophy at Swansea) to meet me for lunch. He's just come up to town. I said I'm going to take him out for lunch, shall I meet him at your place? So what's the time now, quarter past one - shall we say at two?

MS: Is it quarter past one?

DL: Mmm. Shall we say at two? He's awfully - *by God* he's interesting, and he's seen a couple of your posters in various places, and of course he's been on that symposium at Brandeis University with Dylan and Sartre and all that sort of thing. And he's got a lot of very interesting stories. I thought we might all have lunch. So I'll meet you at your place at two o'clock. If he gets there before me, would you just hold on until I get there? John Golding. You're Studio Five, aren't you? Super. See you later, bye, Martin.

When he wasn't at the Pheasantry, Litvinoff haunted the lozenge of well-to-do London between Brompton Road and the King's Road, foraying out from St George's Court, an imposing 1930s red-brick block with neo-Georgian white-framed windows: his fifth-floor flat looked eastwards over Chelsea, down to the Hourglass pub opposite and over the rooftops towards Lennox Gardens, Sloane Street, the distant Cadogan Square. He seemed to have little money, but none was required for his preferred method of shopping. Julian Lloyd witnessed a startling demonstration of his brazen streak during a wander along the King's Road. 'There was a clothes shop that had various racks outside, a lot of clothing imported from America, so we looked and I remember saying: "Oh look, that's a nice shirt." And all round the shop were signs saying "No Thieving", "Shoplifters will be Prosecuted", a lot of these very threatening signs everywhere. He said: "Do you want it, man? Do you like it?"

'"Well yes, it's lovely, a very nice shirt. . ."

'"You want it, man? I'll get it for you." And he very flagrantly, in front of the counter, took this shirt off the hanger, stuck it under his jacket so that at least nine inches of it was hanging out, walked up to the guy behind the counter, engaged him in conversation about this, that and the other for about three minutes with this thing just hanging right out, and then said: "Okay, man, let's go," and walked out on to the street, took about four paces and took it out, shook it and handed it to me and said: "There you are, man." He had an extraordinary bravado.'

But as Litvinoff approached forty, Lloyd also saw his growing sense of isolation. Few people around him by now heard much of his family, other than when he spoke with admiration of Emanuel or Barnet's latest books or introduced them to nieces and nephews whose youthful outlook and appreciation he enjoyed, but whom he would never have expected to provide the support that he desired. For their part, his siblings wanted to help but felt he had moved beyond their reach; they'd see him now and again at weddings, where his younger brother Phil recalled he would 'turn up looking completely different from anyone else, with no shoes on'. They tried hard, 'but they didn't realise, as I didn't – nobody did – that the guy needed a psychiatrist'. Litvinoff even hinted at his alienation to John Ivor Golding, who cited an aphorism he attributed to Confucius: 'If you want advice go to a friend, if you want help go to a stranger, if you want nothing at all go to your relations.'

'Good heavens,' Litvinoff replied. 'He was so right, wasn't he? He had the *mishpacha** well sussed out.'[10]

This sense of detachment developed in tandem with a growing ambivalence about his Jewishness. It defined him, gave him a simultaneous sense of pride (what a thing, to be part of the tribe that spawned so many contemporary geniuses from Lenny Bruce to Bob Dylan) and despair: his physiognomy, his perception that an atavistic anti-Semitism lurked in the English DNA, his sense that the supposed tradition of kinship between Jews rang hollow where he was concerned.

'I remember David coming to me,' said Lloyd, 'and he said: "Hey, man, you know I'm a Jew?"

'"Well, of course, David. . ."

'"You know how Jews always look after each other?"

'"Yes, David."

'"Well, do you know any Jews, man?"

'"Why?"

'"Well, I need some Jews to look after *me*."'

---

*   Hebrew for 'family'.

The radical psychiatrist R. D. Laing took to visiting the Pheasantry: he observed Sharp and Mora for prolonged periods, then told them that they were normal and it was the rest of society who were mad. On one occasion John Dunbar, who was married to Marianne Faithfull and co-founded the Indica Gallery with Barry Miles and Peter Asher, was on an acid trip with Sharp when Litvinoff cornered him and began talking at great length about the Kray twins and how they had dangled him from a window.

'I think it was a test,' said Dunbar. 'He was seeing if he could weird me out, but he couldn't.' Dunbar was steely enough to shrug it off, but what more delicate souls might have made of the combination of LSD and David Litvinoff in their face can only be imagined. Over in the East End the Krays were succumbing to their own variety of hallucination. By 1967 Ronnie and Reggie's existing personality disorders had expanded and distorted to new extremes of paranoia in a fog of alcohol and, in Ronnie's case, heavy anti-psychotic medication. On 6th June Reggie's fragile twenty-three-year-old wife, Frances, committed suicide* after enduring a marriage that would have driven any but the strongest woman to despair. She saw little of her husband, who slept with a flick knife under the pillow of their marital bed, a gun and a sword by the bedside, and dressed quickly in the morning before disappearing for the day, only to return home drunk late every night. When they were together he told her she was ill, and he wouldn't speak to her at all in his brother's presence.† Ronnie's loathing for almost any woman but his mother Violet, for whom they had just bought the Carpenter's Arms on Cheshire Street, expressed itself in a campaign of vitriolic hostility towards Frances and towards his brother for distracting himself from the serious business of maintaining their reputation and making money. Since 1966 there had been another strand to Ronnie's taunting. On 9th March of that year he strode into the Blind Beggar on Whitechapel Road and shot the Richardson brothers' associate George

---

* In all likelihood, though some people, including a former cellmate of Reggie Kray's, insist that Ronnie murdered her by means of a forced overdose.

† '[He] came back night time. By the side of bed gun, sword, knife, chopper, flick-knife. . .' she wrote in her diary. 'Went to his house – his brother walked in bedroom in underwear, swore at me.' Frances's papers also record that Reggie wrote to her that she was a 'spiteful little tormentor' after she 'humiliated' him by going out dancing with friends. http://www.independent. co.uk/news/people/reggie-krays-wife-frances-sheas-diaries-drunken-abuse-weapons-and-constant-isolation-9369440.html.

Cornell in the head, before calmly walking out again while the jukebox continued to play the Walker Brothers' 'The Sun Ain't Gonna Shine Anymore'. It was a measure of the twins' sense of untouchability that Ronnie felt he could act with impunity in enacting Cornell's public execution, and sure enough no one in the Blind Beggar that night would talk. At the inquest in November 1966 the coroner's jury returned a verdict that Cornell, of New Church Road in Lambeth, was 'murdered by persons unknown'. Now there was a disparity between the identical twins, an imbalance between two unbalanced men. The psychologically dominant Ronnie pestered and taunted his brother for his supposed cowardice: 'I've done mine, about time you did yours.'[11]

They had always been distrustful of everyone around them but now they saw betrayers at every turn. Leslie Payne, the firm's business master-mind, had recently severed his ties with them and rumours that he was talking to the police prompted Ronnie to place him 'on the list', a tally of people who needed to be killed that he'd been compiling in his head for the past two years. They delegated the duty to a pill-popping, perennially drunk and unreliable minor member of the firm named John McVitie, better known as Jack the Hat, whose vanity about his baldness meant he was rarely seen without his trilby. McVitie took £1,500 and a large gun. His abject failure to carry out the deed – he and fellow Kray associate Billy Exley ventured to Payne's address, where his wife answered the door and told them he was out, so they went away again – along with his public boasts that he wouldn't return the advance payment and the feeling he was a dangerous liability gave Reggie all the excuses he needed. On 28th October 1967 McVitie was lured to the basement of 97 Evering Road in Stoke Newington where, after initially trying to shoot him with a gun that misfired, Reggie stabbed him repeatedly while Ronnie held him in a bear hug. McVitie was 'uncouth' and 'a vexation to the spirit',[12] the unrepentant Reggie said on his deathbed, thirty-three years later. That made them responsible for three confirmed murders within nineteen months, including the death of their old friend Frank 'the Mad Axeman' Mitchell soon after they sprang him from Dartmoor prison. Mitchell won his nickname and a life sentence for escaping Broadmoor in July 1958 and holding a married couple hostage in their home while wielding an axe. After being sent to HMP Dartmoor in 1962, he grew frustrated by the prospect of a future of indefinite detention, which he and the twins felt was inhumane. He was, however, trusted with a certain amount of freedom to roam the moors and feed the ponies, which made springing him from prison far easier than it would have been elsewhere. Albert Donoghue and 'Mad' Teddy Smith were sent to Devon to scoop Mitchell up during one such outing and drive him back to London, where he would be contained in a flat in Barking. A series of letters penned by Smith on Mitchell's behalf to MPs such as Tom Driberg, whom the twins had known since his days gambling at Esmeralda's Barn, failed to advance his case. Within a couple of weeks the twins realised they didn't know what to do with this phenomenally strong and increasingly violent man, who was also growing angry at their failure to visit him, which they deemed disrespectful given how grateful he should have been for his freedom. Freddie Foreman and his accomplices Gerry Callaghan and Alfie Gerrard provided the solution, shooting Mitchell in the back of a van on their orders on 24th December 1966.

At New Scotland Yard the police's success in breaking up the Richardson gang – the series of 'torture trials' in 1967 addressing charges of fraud, extortion and grievous bodily harm saw Charlie Richardson receive a twenty-five-year sentence and his brother Eddie and Frankie Fraser ten years apiece – produced a new resolve to free London from organised crime. 'Nipper' Read, the detective behind the twins' failed prosecution for demanding money with menaces from Hew McCowan, was elated after hearing that he had been selected to lead a mysterious secret inquiry. A few days later his mood deflated in an instant when he received his brief from the Assistant Commissioner (Crime), Peter Brodie. 'Mr Read,' he announced, 'you're going to get the Krays.' The dazed Read could hardly take in what his senior was saying: 'We've got rid of the Richardsons and it's time we cleaned up the rest of London. The Krays have been a thorn in our sides long enough. Now you can do it any way you like, but I'm looking to you to get the right result.'[13]

The twins seemed beyond his grasp but Read had no option but to start afresh. He insisted on selecting his own team of trusted officers and operating from his own premises. Working from a specially established office at Tintagel House on the Albert Embankment, Scotland Yard being too leaky for a case where secrecy was so important, Read began to draw up what he sardonically termed his 'delightful index' of underworld characters whose evidence would propel the force towards at last securing a conviction. High on his list of people to interview was David Litvinoff, whose treatment for stalling on his debts at the Barn and whose mouth-cutting for insulting Ronnie had merged into the stuff of London legend.

'The story as I heard it was that first of all Litvinoff was put under some pressure, and then when he was unable to pay he was called to the club,' Read recalled. 'A sword was placed in his mouth and pushed, with the result that he received a terrible gash which split his cheeks.

'I saw him by appointment in the Carlton Tower's Bar in Chelsea. Looking closely at him it was possible to see faint scars across his cheeks.' Litvinoff told Read how he had fled London after the incident and gone to Paris for cosmetic surgery. Finally, Read thought as Litvinoff chattered on, a breakthrough. 'I thought that, at last, I had found a victim who would be co-operative. Wrong. Litvinoff said he had no intention of making any written statement or assisting in any prosecution, maintaining that although he had been attacked he could not identify his attackers.'[14]

It appeared that Litvinoff had belatedly learned the value of discretion in underworld matters; it may technically have been true that he couldn't identify the man who cut his mouth in the street, but he knew well that Ronnie Kray had ordered the attack. Read wasn't alone in attributing his scars to a sword. The story illustrates how Litvinoff became a repository for London myth, someone on whom to pin tales that would otherwise float away, assisting in the city's self-understanding through the stories its inhabitants told themselves. His face was slashed at Ronnie Kray's behest. Kray was obsessed by blades of any kind, from flick-knives to swords. The facts meld and create a new fiction: Kray pushed a sword through Litvinoff's face. This fate is applied to a character in the 1990 film *The Krays*, hauled backstage at one of their clubs for allegedly laughing at Ronnie, who informs him: 'I'm gonna make you laugh for the rest of your fucking life.' Litvinoff's status becomes reinforced as the source of the scene. Putative authorities bolster the myth by retelling it to new audiences who'd never before heard of him: 'Ex-*Mirror* journalist Lynn Lewis recalls the shocking sword punishment meted out to David Litvinoff virtually splitting his face in two from ear to ear', promises the blurb for a documentary about the twins,* in which Lewis, whose account is made more plausible by the fact that he met Litvinoff while researching the twins' connection with Peter Rachman, states that 'I understand Ronnie had held it in two hands and done that [miming pushing a sword horizontally forward] while somebody was holding him still and widened his mouth.' The cycle of myth-making spins on and Litvinoff's ghost appears to consolidate just as the facts grow ever fainter.

---

* *The Krays: The Final Word* (BBC, 2001); it also includes the deathbed interview with Reggie Kray in which he revealed his lack of remorse for McVitie's killing and admitted the murder of another unnamed person.

As the Krays' and 'Nipper' Read's paths locked into convergence in the shadowy background of the luminous 'Summer of Love', another significant moment was emerging across town in SW3. After seven years living in Italy and France, the latter months immersed in developing a new film treatment with Anita Pallenberg and his girlfriend Deborah Dixon (now Roberts), Donald Cammell felt that London finally looked exciting enough to merit returning home. Soon after his arrival at the exact moment the party hit its peak, and in order to ensure that the script had the precise atmosphere he desired, one blending the homoeroticism he detected in gangster life and an authentic flavour of the underworld, he moved into 53 St George's Court with David Litvinoff.

<u>Act Three, Scene One.</u>

John Ivor Golding: Hello?

David Litvinoff: Is that you, John?

JIG: Mmm.

DL: Oh hello, it's David here again.

JIG: Mmm.

DL: That doesn't sound like you. . .

JIG: AH, OF COURSE, DAVID, IT'S JOHN!

DL: Ah, now it does. I'm so sorry, man, that I kept you waiting a couple of moments. I spoke to Martin who's looking forward very much to seeing you.

JIG: What did he say when you told him?

DL: He said 'That's wonderful', because he's a young man, a very successful artist—

JIG: Yes, and did you tell him that as soon as he opened the door John wanted a double brandy waiting for him?

DL: He's got all sorts of drinks and wines there—

JIG: IS HE GOING TO RING ME NOW OR WHAT?

DL: No, he's expecting you around there and I'm going to meet you around there. We're all going out to eat. I thought if you can get round there for about two o'clock.

JIG: Now, I put a challenge to Fyfe Robertson,* I did mention *Picture Post* to you just the other day—

DL: You did, yes, just *en passant*—

JIG: Well now, I put a challenge to him—

DL: Now if I may interrupt just for a moment, but regarding joining our common ménage, there's not a great deal but a certain amount of travelling involved. I take it you're proficient in Uzbekhistani and Kurdistani, aren't you?

JIG: Yes, yes.

DL: Oh excellent. Carry on with Fyfe Robertson.

JIG: Well—

DL: You speak the lowland dialects of course?

JIG: True. I put a challenge to him. You know, I said when I was given the chance in my younger days. . .I could have been a licensed surrogate in Llanelli in Carmarthen, you see.

DL: What a beautiful part of the world. . . Who are your heroes, would you say? Amongst men of letters, of music. You've got a way with the young, with young men?

JIG: You mean like Somerset Maugham, Montaigne, and I do like Voltaire.

DL: He's an awfully nice chap. You never get a cross word out of *him*. What about younger people like John Osborne, Anthony Burgess, Anthony Haden-Guest, Anthony Hopkins, Mick Jagger?

JIG: I know, but what's the matter with all these people is, David, they don't know the subversiveness of the Dark Ages.

DL: They *don't*, do they?

---

* James Fyfe Robertson (1902–87), Scottish journalist, picture editor and feature writer at the *Picture Post* in the 1940s and 1950s.

JIG: Now that is a weakness in them all, you see. An oral articulation in a violent manner can be more effective than physical violence or anything else. . . I do like something like *Ein Reich, Ein Volk—*

DL: *Ein Führer*. And what do you think about Christopher Gibbs and his attitudes?

JIG: Not too bad, I do get a sense of proportion there. . .

DL: Indeed. Philip Laski, does he turn you on?

JIG: Yes, yes, very good.

DL: And what about someone like. . .that well-known philanthropist, what's he called? Donald Cammell.

Chapter 7

How to Lose Friends and Influence People: the Making of *Performance*

'Then it was also possible that from this bright diurnal world, which was all he had known hitherto, there was a door leading into another world, where all was muffled, seething, passionate, naked, and loaded with destruction – and that between those people whose lives moved in an orderly way between the office and the family. . .and the others, the outcasts, the blood-stained, the debauched and filthy, those who wandered labyrinthine passages full of roaring voices, there was some bridge – and not only that, but that the frontiers of their lives secretly marched together and the line could be crossed at any moment. . .

'And the only other question that remained was: how is it possible? What happens at such a moment? What then shoots screaming up into the air and is suddenly extinguished?'

Robert Musil, *Young Törless*, trans. Eithne Wilkins and Ernst Kaiser

A man sits tied to a chair with a gag in his mouth while three others shave his head. To pass the time this sharply dressed trio make small talk saturated in a strange mixture of irony and menace. 'Your old man was a barber, wasn't he, Rosey?' says a sturdy, implacable young fellow who is holding the customer's head in place by clenching his nose and ear. 'No. No he wasn't,' replies his stern-looking older colleague, as he lathers the shaving foam with a brush. The third man hacks his hair with scissors, scrapes a cut-throat razor over his scalp, breaks off to release a moment of pent-up scornful fury when the first man quips 'Hair today and gone tomorrow!' then continues unperturbed until nothing remains but a few bristles and trickles of blood. He whips out a pocket mirror so the seated man can approve their handiwork and tells him to explain what has happened to his 'owner', a word brimming with sadomasochistic sexual connotations emphasised by his situation, gagged and bound and slumped forward on to the backrest of his chair. The three men stroll out of view.

Left to right: James Fox, Stanley Meadows, John Sterland (seated) and John Bindon in *Performance*.

This time the scene plays out on screen rather than in Litvinoff's flat and the audience is rather larger, and ever-increasing: not a gathering of peace activists marching down Kensington High Street, nor a private performance starring only Litvinoff and Ricky Levesley, but the millions of people who have watched one of British cinema's most disturbing and brilliant creations between its release in 1970 and the present moment. These rogue freelance barbers are Rosebloom, Moody and Chas Devlin, the last being the one with the razor. Their victim is a chauffeur, the location his lock-up garage, the car he drives a navy Rolls-Royce of the sort that once ferried Peter Rachman around Notting Hill (in which connection his stance astride a chair seems a grotesque parody of Lewis Morley's famous photograph taken five years earlier of Christine Keeler), and his owner a lawyer by the name of Harley-Brown, who has been representing a bow-tied businessman named Fraser in a legal dispute with the man whom the trio represent, Harry Flowers. The garage is at 35 Queen's Gate Mews, tucked away off Queen's Gate between Kensington Road and Cromwell Road. Harry Flowers is a businessman in the Ronnie Kray mould: keen to acquire rival firms at 'competitive' rates, ever willing to apply pressure through a team of enthusiastic representatives, never happier than in the company of an athletic younger man. His voice is rough and rasping but he operates from a smart address in Mayfair. The company names on the office door read South African Development Ltd, Presto Repossessions Ltd, Sportsmen's Management Assoc., Daisy May Toy and Shoe Factors Ltd, which more than echo the business activities – the failed Nigerian construction scam, the long firm frauds that lay behind ostensibly benign manufacturers – perpetrated by those 'well known sporting brothers', as the press euphemistically tagged the twins in the days when it seemed risky to say anything more explicit.* When a bookmaker in the Fulham Road, Joey Maddocks, rejects his overtures, Flowers sends over a few of his boys – Rosebloom, Moody, a chap known only as Mad Cyril – to help him reconsider. Devlin wants a piece of this action too, is desperate to be involved, but Flowers bars him from participating and alludes to his and Maddocks' history – it's 'double-personal' between them, he says. But Devlin disobeys his orders. Back at his flat in Shepherds Bush he selects from his fastidiously arranged cufflinks, enters the spotless bathroom and washes his already clean hands, admires himself in the mirror, tweaks his hair, removes a loose tile by the floor and reaches inside for his Smith and Wesson revolver and ammunition. He loads the gun and tucks it in the waist of his trousers. He arrives at the betting shop in the aftermath of his colleagues' visit, gloating as he surveys the carnage – the smashed front window, telephone lines ripped from their sockets, white paint spattered all over the yellow and blue walls, papers strewn across the floor, more broken glass. He foists Maddocks' Burberry overcoat on him and escorts him from the building to serve him up to the awaiting Flowers. When they arrive at the firm's headquarters, however, and adjourn to the adjoining club, a displaced pocket of brash working-class London in Mayfair,† Chas's boss is far from impressed. Flowers reassures

---

* The reference to South Africa connects more closely still with the Richardsons, who had mining interests there.

† Referred to in the script as the Hayloft Club: this obvious reference to Esmeralda's Barn isn't made explicit on screen, though the decor is plainly modelled on the Krays' club and

Maddocks he hasn't been 'taken over': 'No, Joey, the word is. . .merged. You was *merged*, my son.'* Devlin has taken liberties and shown that he's not to be trusted, working for no one's interests but his own. He slips away from the club after Flowers has torn into him, but when he arrives home at 4.30am he steps through the door to take an immediate punch in the face. We see that his flat has undergone the same treatment as Maddocks' betting shop (and as Litvinoff's flat in Kensington High Street). His smart suits have been cut to tatters, feathers from slashed pillows mingle on the floor with dozens of his precious cufflinks and a scattering of magazines and crumpled photographs of himself: throwing a punch in a boxing ring, lifting dumb-bells, tenderly cuddling a terrier (a dog being his only safe outlet for affection).† Pictures have been pulled from the walls, which instead are decorated by sloshes of red paint into which someone has scrawled the word 'POOF'. Joey Maddocks and his mates Steve and O'Brien grapple with Chas and haul him through the chaos they have created, punching and kicking him until he's barely conscious, knocking his revolver to the floor and out of reach. They throw him face down on his bed and rip off his shirt so that Maddocks can whip his back with a dog-lead and force Chas to admit what he really is. . .but just as it seems that their violence has broken this uptight man to the point where he will confess his closeted homosexuality, he loses consciousness.

Then he's back again. He winks at Maddocks before tussling with him and Steve, whom he hurls into the bathroom: Steve knocks the tap as he falls into the bath, then lies there semi-conscious with the shower soaking him. Chas scrabbles on his stomach across the floor, retrieves another gun from beneath his laundry basket and swings around to face Maddocks. In an instant the dynamic has reversed.

Maddocks pleads and stutters, then raises a sheet in front of his face, which offers no protection and can only be to spare himself from seeing his old enemy's grim exultancy on pulling the trigger. 'I am a bullet,'

---

features a mural reminiscent of Annigoni and Whidborne's.

*   Reiterating a theme central to the film, one that at the very beginning we've seen mirrored in the 'straight' world by Harley-Brown's supercilious barrister's remarks to court, when he describes an 'admittedly bold but in no way unethical merger – I said "*merger*", gentlemen, not "takeover". Words still have meanings, even in our days of the computer.'

†   Reggie Kray never loved any human being as much as he loved his Pekinese, Mitzi.

declares Chas, identifying himself with the gun's conquest by penetration, which climaxes and concludes whatever previous couplings the pair have experienced.*

And so in a twitch of his right index finger he moves from being an enforcer to a murderer. He needs to escape: from Maddocks' associates but also, though he doesn't yet realise it, from Harry Flowers', as they have concluded that he is a mad dog and, as Moody tells his boss's sidekick Dennis, there's only one way of dealing with a mad dog. It's the same way as the Krays had Freddie Foreman deal with Frank 'the Mad Axeman' Mitchell. 'I'd put him to sleep, Dennis.'

Chas calls his mother, an anxious Irish woman who, you sense, has spent a good part of her life worrying about her errant son. She agrees that he should hide at her sister's in Barnstaple. Then fate intervenes. While waiting for his train at Paddington he eavesdrops on a conversation. A musician has just left his digs with some reclusive washed-up rock star despite owing £41 back rent. The address is 81 Powis Square. Chas is there within minutes, armed with the cash and a concocted story about being a juggler who's just had a car crash. He's met by the gorgeous, bewitching Pherber, who senses, whether or not she actually believes him, that his electricity could jump-start her boyfriend Turner's dormant mojo, and so Chas manoeuvres his way across the threshold.

Thus ends the first 'half' of *Performance*; actually closer to the first third of its one hour and forty-one minutes, but it is always described as a film of two distinct halves that pivot on this moment. The second part exudes a very different tone – as decadent and surreally bohemian as the first half is sharp and queasily virile – and portrays Turner and Pherber's gradual success where Maddocks failed, in breaking Chas to the point where his guard finally drops and a tender side emerges. Their tool for achieving this is not physical force but a more insidious violation: playing

---

* *Performance*, and in particular Chas's final dominion of Joey Maddocks, illustrates George Melly's observation that Litvinoff was a man who 'understood entirely the excitement of violence' ('Lights, camera. . .decadence', by Mick Brown, *Telegraph Magazine*, 3rd June 1995, p. 27), and moreover the sexual excitement of violence, a fact also well known to the Kray twins. Albert Donoghue wrote of their time in an army jail circa 1953 for assault and desertion during National Service: 'they kidded the corporal on guard into the communal cell and beat the shit out of him. Then they all held him down, while Ronnie masturbated him. So that is weird, yeah?' *The Krays' Lieutenant: Their Chief Henchman and Final Betrayer*, by Albert Donoghue and Martin Short (Smith Gryphon, 1995), p. 83.

with his mind and spiking him with a hefty dose of psilocybin, then dressing him as a woman, Pherber placing a mirror on his chest that reflects her bare breast. Mirrors, mergers. The 1960s' most potent performers broke down barriers by every means imaginable, from violence to hallucinogens to love. Once this reconfiguration of Chas' personality is achieved, and with it such a revival in Turner's powers that he feels his life's purpose fulfilled, the merger is complete; at which point Rosebloom and some of 'the chaps' arrive at 81 Powis Square. Chas satisfies Turner's death-wish by shooting him in the head before being led to his own fate; as the white Rolls-Royce pulls away the betrayed Chas turns to look out the window, but it is Turner's face that we see. *I'll make your face look like mine.* A full analysis of the plot, its subtexts and the myriad rumours attending the shoot can be found in entire books on the film;* instead we will focus on the elements germane to this story, which are plenty. On its American release in 1970 it was roundly panned, notably by Richard Schickel in *Life* magazine, who called it 'the most disgusting, the most completely worthless film I have seen since I began reviewing'.[1] During a test screening a Warner Bros. executive's wife was so upset by the violence that she vomited. It fared better on its UK release in 1971, with *Time Out* devoting a special issue to its release, and it is now acknowledged as one of the high points of British cinema. Marianne Faithfull provided as elegant a summation of its tone and significance as any: '*Performance* was truly our *Picture of Dorian Gray*,' she wrote. 'An allegory of libertine Chelsea life in the late sixties, with its baronial rock stars, wayward *jeunesse dorée*, drugs, sex and decadence – it preserves a whole era under glass.'[2] The credited authors were Donald Cammell and Anita Pallenberg, both intellectually gifted artists whose imprint here is unmistakable; but as Colin MacCabe argues in his book for the British Film Institute (BFI), if one accepts that what 'makes *Performance* the greatest British film ever made' is its unfathomably deep inhabitation of the late-1960s moment when the underground and underworld lay briefly entwined, 'it is even possible to make a perverse argument that the real author of the film was David Litvinoff. Even more than his great friend Christopher Gibbs. . .it was Litvinoff who provided the bridge between the world of the Kray twins and the Rolling Stones. It was

---

* *Performance: a Biography of the Classic Sixties Film*, by Paul Buck (Omnibus, 2012); *Performance: BFI Film Classics*, by Colin MacCabe (BFI, 1998); *Mick Brown on Performance*, by Mick Brown (Bloomsbury, 1999).

Litvinoff who ensured that the range the film covered; that the intersections of class and sex that it explored; the complicities of violence and society that it revealed, were much greater than any predecessor or successor.'[3]

One day in 1967 as Litvinoff held court on the Picasso cafe's terrace, his audience comprised Granny Takes a Trip's co-owner John Pearse, Martin Sharp and Eija Vehka Aho, Sharp's silent Finnish 'ice maiden girlfriend', as Pearse remembered.

'I know all there's to know about surrealism,' declared Litvinoff. 'Buñuel is the man. The rest of you are *schlemiels.*' Here came Charlie Thomas, an 'art spiv' sporting the 'same grey DB flannel suit as his friend Lucian Freud', the tailor noticed. 'See this guy,' said Litvinoff, 'he knows the price of everything from a Hotpoint to a Tintoretto. . . There's gonna be a film about my life as a glamour boy,' he told Thomas.

'You fucking poof!' came the reply.

'Straight up, I'm writing it with Cammell.'

By late 1967 the number of names 'on the list' kept by Ronnie Kray was expanding. While George Cornell and Jack McVitie had been ticked off, Leslie Payne remained there and in growing company: a guy in Poplar called Bobby Cannon who'd supposedly been heard criticising the twins, for instance, and Cornell's grieving brother Eddie, who had been drunkenly threatening reprisals. Some, such as Cannon, were lucky and fell off again when Ronnie's mood changed, but one addition whose name was widely deemed to be inscribed in indelible ink was George James Evans. Jimmy Evans was a highly charged character, handsome and self-regarding with a hair-trigger temper, a former protégé of Albert Dimes now known to the Krays, Freddie Foreman and the Richardsons but unaffiliated to any firm, preferring to operate as his own boss. He was known for his expertise as a safe-blower and for his arsenal of revolvers and rifles, at least one of which could almost always be found about his person. Since the end of 1964 he had been in a feud with Freddie Foreman's gang that began when he bugged his wife's car and discovered she was having an affair with Foreman's brother George. Evans' method of terminating the liaison unfolded on the evening of 17th December 1964 when, after an altercation during the daytime, he headed over to George Foreman's flat in Lambeth. The Foremans were expecting him and had left the door open while they and half a dozen colleagues waited in the dark upstairs. When Evans had climbed the flight of steps, breathing through the high tang of urine that hung in the dirty stairwell, he called out for George, who emerged and asked Evans in for a chat. Evans told him that 'the only thing that's going to do any talking around here is this', at which he drew a sawn-off double-barrelled shotgun from his raincoat and, with a cry of 'Happy Christmas, you cunt!', fired it into George Foreman's groin – 'Wallop, and he shot him in the orchestra stalls',[4] as Frankie Fraser later put it. Foreman was almost castrated, which Albert Donoghue recalled left him 'very upset'.[5]

Freddie Foreman was very upset too. On the evening of 2nd January 1965, Evans and his friend Tommy 'Ginger' Marks were out on a safe-blowing mission. They passed Fuller Street,* and were by the Repton Boys' Club in Cheshire Street when a car pulled up containing Freddie Foreman, Frankie Fraser and Alfie Gerrard. Foreman yelled, 'Ginger! Come here a minute!' and when Marks stopped, Foreman discharged a volley of .38 bullets. Several hit Marks and brought him crashing to the ground. Evans was wearing a bulletproof vest and ran away with his head down. They caught him with a single bullet to the back, which hit the vest like a hammer-blow, but he staggered into Wood Close and rolled under a parked car to hide. He heard one more shot before the car roared away again. When the injured Evans wriggled back out, Marks was nowhere to be seen. Fraser later said that he 'made good incinerating material':[6] the firm had a south London crematorium at their disposal. Freddie Foreman claimed that Marks' crime had been to assist Evans in the attack on his brother; Evans responds in his memoir that Marks had no involvement and the real reason was that Marks had revealed Freddie Foreman's assistance in the police's pursuit of the Great Train Robbers (a suggestion that Foreman strongly denies). Either way, Evans remained a target and Freddie Foreman remained determined to hunt him down. He claims to have spent an entire night with his rifle on a roof opposite Evans' house, waiting for him to appear, only reluctantly leaving the scene at dawn, although Evans says this never happened. While he accuses Foreman of being a police informer, when I mentioned Evans' name in passing to Frankie, Patrick and David Fraser, they interrupted in unison with a shout

---

*   Which, to its residents' anger, had just been condemned to demolition in the London County Council's programme of slum clearances.

of: 'Grass!' This isn't the place to attempt to resolve inconsistencies between the score-settling efforts of two equally dubious characters: Evans' book is a relentlessly self-promoting and abrasive affair, and his unremorseful account of the punishment beating he gave his unfaithful wife is shocking, even by the standards of the criminal memoir genre. What is indisputable is that the Krays owed Foreman's firm a favour after his involvement in murdering and disposing of Frank Mitchell. They offered to take on the job of tracking Evans down and killing him, then delegated the task to a new associate whose abilities they needed to test, an American called Alan Bruce Cooper, also known as Mr ABC. Charlie Kray brought Cooper to the Crown and Anchor in Cheshire Street to meet Reggie and Ronnie, who told him that they needed someone who could carry out a hit in an unusual way – not with a gun or a knife, not in a manner that would be identified as the *modus operandi* of the Kray firm. In due course he took delivery of a briefcase that had a ring-pull beneath the handle connected to a concealed spring-loaded hypodermic syringe of cyanide, which would shoot out through a small hole at the bottom of one side of the case and inject into the victim's leg, causing death within eight seconds. Reggie Kray was impressed. But despite having ample opportunity to carry out the act, for some reason Cooper and his chosen hit man, a courier and pirate radio engineer named Paul Elvey, never managed to do so. One likely reason is that Cooper was an *agent provocateur* working with the police; another possibility, Evans' belief at least, is that the twins were kidding Foreman, making it seem they were repaying a favour while actually having no intention of killing him. He points out that they had many better opportunities to do so as he often socialised with them, and also that Charlie Kray warned him to keep a low profile. But if he were correct, to their closest associates they maintained the charade: Albert Donoghue records that the 'plot to kill Jim Evans was never called off. We were still meant to be looking to do him right till the end.'[7]

Evans survived, though his book claims he was instead persecuted over the coming decade by Foreman's friends in the Metropolitan Police. He was charged with shooting George Foreman with intent to cause grievous bodily harm but was cleared in court owing to a lack of evidence; the Foremans' determination to nail him did not extend to assisting a prosecution. He was less fortunate in July 1967 when he was (in his view) framed for armed robbery with violence and sent to Wormwood Scrubs, which coincided with Robert Fraser's time there. Evans took to Fraser because he felt he'd taken a fall for the Rolling Stones, though he soon spotted that he was not a man to trust. He noticed Fraser cheating while playing chess with other prisoners, which did not faze the equally unscrupulous Evans, but more worrying was the trait that had landed Fraser in trouble with the Krays: his inability to honour his debts. Here he had engineered a situation in which a Scottish murderer nicknamed Chick would steal him steaks, eggs and milk from the prison kitchen in return for Fraser sending money to Chick's family, who were struggling while he served his life sentence. In Evans' words Fraser 'was living in the lap of luxury, even though he was in jail, and for the next couple of months he had an easy life'[8]. Then Chick had a visit from his relatives and learned that no money had materialised. He returned in a rage, telling Evans that he would kill Fraser as he had nothing to lose, but Evans told him that he did have something to lose: 'If you have a crack at him, I'll have a crack at you. Leave him alone.'[9]

Fraser escaped unharmed, having been advised by Chick that it was only Evans' protection that had saved him, and would always value Evans' role in looking out for him during his imprisonment. Soon after Evans' release in spring 1968 he was sitting outside a King's Road cafe drinking a cappuccino when a grey Alfa-Romeo convertible drew up at the kerb and the driver called out: 'Jimmy! Jimmy! Come here a minute!' Fraser 'hailed [him] like a long-lost brother' and had a proposition: how would Evans like to make £5,000? He got in the car and Fraser continued his *spiel*: 'I want to introduce you to some people. They're making a film called *Performance*. Mick Jagger's gonna be in it, it's gonna be his debut, there's a girl called Anita Pallenberg, and James Fox is going to play the leading part. It's a gangster film and perhaps you could help them.'[10]

Evans agreed to come and find out more, so Fraser drove over to St George's Court and they headed up to flat number 53. Litvinoff was introduced to him as a writer. They telephoned Donald Cammell and he arrived, then James Fox turned up too. Evans had spent much of his time in jail working out in the gym; he 'couldn't keep still for a moment and in no time. . .was lying on the floor doing press-ups with James Fox'.[11] Fraser had previously described to them all how Evans had helped him. They began to question him: where do you keep a gun? How would you hide one in your house? Litvinoff could have answered these queries himself but in honing Chas Devlin they had in mind a very different breed of criminal, a handsome, narcissistic, taciturn, intensely driven creature operating for higher stakes on a higher criminal echelon, one who had made crime his career, rather than an unreliable, unplaceable, hyper-talkative scuffler prone to debilitating bouts of melancholy. Evans showed them the little chamois leather holsters he'd sewn inside his suit jackets, and told them that he usually secreted a gun in the bathroom laundry basket among the towels. He lent Fox some suits and shared stories of his exploits that turned Fox and Cammell's faces pale. 'A lot of it was modelled on. . .Evans,' Cammell later said, adding that he 'was known as a man who enjoyed the mayhem. He was a highly adrenalized character. Very good looking. He walked like that, he talked like that, he was a real East End hood. I was a bit frightened of him. I disapproved of some of the things he told me, very strongly, and I would get all huffy about it and say: "Listen, this is going *too far*, Jimmy." And he would have a good laugh about this.'[12]

The only sticking point came when Cammell mentioned that they wanted Chas to be bisexual, because 'a lot of gangsters are bisexual; Ronnie Kray's bisexual'. Evans wasn't having it. 'Name another one! Name one more! Because I know everybody who's at it. I know all the bank robbers, all the safe-blowers, I know all the cranks – and there's only Ronnie that I can say is like that.'[13]

Albert Donoghue, on the other hand, reckoned he could name 'half a dozen villains. . .who were queer, and they weren't shy about letting anybody know about it'.[14] In any case, via Litvinoff Cammell knew well that there was a particular gay milieu within the underworld, and Evans' views were immaterial: they took from him what they needed in creating Chas and disregarded the rest.

'I didn't mean it in any way to be mocking,' Cammell said. 'I mean – it was a mark of respect for that gay world, that they had, in a sense, so much influence and control in the underworld. And my access to that world was through Freud, Bacon and so on, and that was a world of great, great artists, a number of whom happened to be gay. And the overlap between the underworld and the artistic world was what I was showing in *Performance*.'[15]

Evans helped them for a few weeks and ultimately refused any payment. Instead Litvinoff and Fox took him to the Pheasantry, where they introduced him to the wildlife painter Basil Ede, whom Fox described as 'one of the Queen's artists'. The connection was Tim Whidborne, who had become another of the Queen's artists: over the course of four one-hour sittings at Buckingham Palace, Whidborne was engaged in painting Her

Majesty's portrait, depicting her in regalia as Colonel-in-Chief of the Irish Guards, mounted on a grey police horse during the Trooping of the Colour. Fox asked Ede to give Evans 'a nice watercolour' and he departed with one depicting a pair of jays. That concluded Evans' involvement with *Performance*, but the process of creating his cinematic doppelganger was only beginning.

While Evans' character and his need to lie low to evade Foreman and the Krays echoed Chas' personality and situation, the plot concerning a fugitive gangster needing a hiding place was established before he became involved, forming part of *The Liars*, a predecessor script to *Performance* that was to star Marlon Brando as an American hitman on the run. If it had a seed in reality, it is more likely this amalgamated Frank Mitchell's fate – holed up in a flat in Barking then driven away to be shot – with the stories Litvinoff told Donald Cammell about his home at Ashburn Place, which Ronnie Kray took over (or rather 'merged') in lieu of gambling debts, and was where Micky Fawcett and Johnny Davies hid after the fight at the Hammer Club. Litvinoff's contribution to *Performance* is hard to quantify: while it is possible to attribute specific instances of his input here and there, it is better to take the co-author and co-director's word for the way that he informed its general atmosphere. 'I used to go around with David Litvinoff as a teenager,' remembered Donald Cammell. 'We hung around Soho together when I was still going to school. David was, apart from me, the most important person involved in the movie.'[16]

Donald Seton Cammell was born on 17th January 1934 in the Outlook Tower by Edinburgh Castle to Iona MacDonald and Charles Richard Cammell, the heir to the once prosperous Cammell Laird ship-building company, and a friend and biographer of Aleister Crowley. Three years later his brother David was born in Richmond, Surrey, and a third boy, Diarmid, was born in London in 1945. By the time of David's birth Donald was already being coached as an art prodigy. After winning the school prizes and studying under Annigoni, he painted what was hailed in 1953 as the society portrait of the year, showing the young Marquess of Dufferin and Ava dressed as a pageboy at the coronation. But by the late 1950s his enthusiasm for painting had begun to ebb, though his appetite for sex and narcotics remained undimmed. The actress Barbara Steele had come to know Cammell through attending the Chelsea School of Art and looked on as he departed in late 1959 for a spell in New York, followed by Italy and then France.

'I don't believe that he had a driving conviction or passion to be a painter,' she said. 'His father wanted him to be a painter, you know. When he moved to Paris he kind of dropped his painterly life. He felt that painting had basically died with the Impressionists, even though he was an ardent admirer of Picasso and Bacon. . .but he felt that, God is dead, you know? Painting was over. Now film was the new medium.'[17]

This sense that painting was a moribund discipline must have been allied with the fact that he was simply tired of it, having been schooled as a precocious talent from such a young age, though he continued to paint to some extent in Paris. During those seven years he lived a cosmopolitan, intellectually and sexually adventurous life in mainland Europe while watching his home city's ascent from afar.

'London was absolutely at the height of the Swinging Sixties at the point when he returned,' said David Cammell. 'He could see this strange mixture of aristocrats and gangsters, politicians, creative people, destructive people, all in a kind of exciting melange.'[18]

By then he had written two films, both of which were flawed efforts mixing an insipid brew of criminality and pop culture. *The Touchables* was rewritten by Ian La Frenais and directed by Robert Freeman. *Duffy* was a cringe-inducing Swinging London caper directed by Robert Parrish and starring James Coburn alongside Cammell's friend James Fox. Cammell wanted little association with the completed version of either. The next film would be different, though. He brought home with him the script for *The Liars*, which he and the Italian-born actress Anita Pallenberg had been developing in France, and redrafted it into a version he titled *The Performers*. He began talks with his agent, Sanford Lieberson, who hailed from Los Angeles but had settled in London while working for the Creative Management Agency, and who also represented Mick Jagger and the Rolling Stones. Lieberson knew that Jagger had an eye on a movie career and had little trouble in agreeing a deal with Warner Bros., who were keen on the idea of a commercial Rolling Stones equivalent of *Help!*, something to capitalise on the marketable Swinging London cool that they'd read about in *Time* magazine. He was so struck by Cammell that he found himself telling him that the only way to avoid this new project going the way of *Duffy* and *The Touchables* was to take complete control: that is, to direct it himself. Any fears on Warner Bros.' part about his inexperience were assuaged by the arrival of co-director Nicolas Roeg, whom Cammell had known for years; it was also Roeg's debut directing gig but his work as a cinematographer had garnered him a substantial reputation as a technician. They needed a producer, so Lieberson formed his own production company, Goodtimes Enterprises, and raised the necessary money. Cammell's brother David came in as associate producer: again he was a novice in his role, better known as a partner in a successful advertising agency, Cammell Hudson and Brownjohn. He brought *Performance* in on time and on budget, a fact that counters the legend of chaos surrounding the shoot. If there was chaos, it was conjured and controlled by Donald Cammell, a practised manipulator of people whom Keith Richards never forgave for encouraging Jagger and Pallenberg to make their characters' sex scene as authentic as possible while Roeg filmed them under the sheets with a 16mm camera. When I met David Cammell at his garden flat in Glebe Place, among his first words were a pre-emptive piece of advice: 'You have to remember that my brother Donald was a genius.' And genius brought with it a degree of latitude in terms of permissible behaviour, at least in Donald's view. Eric Clapton remembered Litvinoff bringing him over to the Pheasantry: Cammell 'managed to stage a power cut in the flat, and then tried to grope my girlfriend Charlotte in the dark,' he wrote. 'A peculiar chap.'[19] In the film, Turner's situation as a man living with two girlfriends, Pherber and the androgynous Lucy (played by Pallenberg and Michèle Breton), paralleled Cammell's own preference for threesomes. Before Pallenberg the American actress Tuesday Weld was in line for Pherber's role, as Cammell's then-girlfriend Deborah Dixon recalled. 'He sent her around to me to see what I thought and David Litvinoff and James Fox were there as well,' she said. 'She seemed extremely nervous and, having just learned a new technique for relaxing which involved linking elbows, back to back and then lifting the other person on to one's back and slowly shaking the verte-brae one by one, I tried this with Tuesday. She was so tense she immediately catapulted over my head and hit a bookshelf, breaking her ankle as it turned out. She was obviously in pain and David sprang into action and got us all to the emergency room of St George's Hospital (since become a hotel I believe),* where they put her in a cast. She returned to LA the next day and we both escorted her in a wheelchair to her plane. She was not pleased.'

I met Sandy Lieberson at a Russian tearoom near his home in Primrose Hill. He was grey-haired and bearded and his stature recalled the miniature

---

* The Lanesborough Hotel on Hyde Park Corner.

cast of elderly Jewish relatives who populated my childhood. (Was Litvinoff quite diminutive? 'No, no. . .5'7", 5' 8".') He'd answer questions with questions. 'Do you think he had a Jewish melancholy?' 'Do *you* get melancholy?' A fair response; later I came to see the idea of a particular Jewish melancholy as a romantic cliché. Elsewhere he was quoted as having called Litvinoff the greatest scriptwriter he'd ever met. He felt he'd been misunderstood. . .how could he have said that when Litvinoff never completed a script? 'I would say he probably *could* have been a brilliant scriptwriter,' he said. 'If he wasn't David Litvinoff.'

With the kind of generosity that Lieberson displayed in later loaning me a sheaf of letters and putting in a good word with Litvinoff's other friends, he did his best to help him achieve his potential. First there was a possibility that Litvinoff would write the film's official novelisation. In one of the letters, dated 22nd May 1968, the forty-year-old would-be author addresses this idea with an eagerness that is heartrending in retrospect. 'I am. . .grateful for your interest in my writing a book based upon the film,' he wrote,

and I have thought the matter out, and could let you and Donald have a draft at any time about how I see the form that this book might take. I feel confident that I could produce a finished work which would not let you, Donald, or anyone associated with the picture down; and would complement, without compromise of quality of writing, the promotional impact and commercial distribution of the film. Since speaking to me the other day, I have as you know, talked with Donald, as to his thoughts on this book. He feels that the most propitious time to commence in earnest work on the book, would be after the full finished screenplay, based largely on the treatment, has been written; and that the book would be described as being 'based on the screenplay by Donald Cammell' . . . I know that I can turn out a successful product which would be exciting and meaningful and would balance the essential ingredients for its successful reception.

Nothing more came of it. The novelisation job went instead to a writer named William Hughes who was provided by Warner Bros. But Litvinoff agreed a deal in which he would be paid $4,000 for his work as Dialogue Consultant and Technical Advisor, and with the film's production deal in place and the principal stars on board he would prove fundamental to the next stage, the preparations that would infuse Cammell and Roeg's evolving creation with its noted intimacy and authenticity. The set builder, John Clark, considered Litvinoff 'very good on details' such as 'All the things for Chas's apartment: the colours, ashtrays, phones.'[20] Locations were David Cammell's responsibility and he drew on Litvinoff's ideas on a couple of occasions. 'One was the interior of the flat of Harry Flowers. He suggested getting a suite in the Royal Garden Hotel in Kensington Gardens, and I went up and that was absolutely bang-on.' The gay pornography and copy of the *Jewish Chronicle* scattered on Flowers' bed in the film indicate Litvinoff's influence. 'Then for the exterior he suggested driving up the Edgware Road where there were some Mock Tudor blocks of flats on the right.'

David Cammell knew well his feeling for the city's geography and its historical textures; as an impressionable teenager he'd accompanied Litvinoff on long walks around east London, where his guide would point out the Krays' house on Vallance Road, the docklands where great ships sailed between the streets; here the likely location of the steps where Magwitch set sail, there the opium-den-riddled Limehouse Chinatown of Fu Manchu. He seemed to know everyone: the *schmatter* merchants on Petticoat Lane, the flower sellers on Columbia Road, the dealers in forlorn rabbits and parrots in the pet market on Club Row, where it was said you could lose your dog amid the crowds at one end and later buy it back from a stall at the other. The pair would roam Chelsea too; once they were strolling down the King's Road in friendly conversation when Litvinoff spotted a police car approaching and flagged it down. 'Constable! Constable!' he cried. 'Arrest this man! He's harassing me.' The policeman drove on again. Christopher Gibbs, who designed the interior of Turner's home just as he had Brian Jones' mansion at 1 Courtfield Road, remembered similar perambulations departing from his antiques shop. 'He would come and see me in Bond Street, start talking and he would continue while we walked back to Chelsea, stopping off here and there, talking to flower sellers and newspaper sellers. . . He had this breadth of acquaintance that was quite remarkable, and it always had this Jewish overtone to it, knowing all these people who were Jewish and brilliant. . .he invested all these people with this mystery and glamour and foreignness.'

This familiarity with a vast swathe of day-to-day city life enabled Litvinoff to tease out the strange demotic flavour that is *Performance*'s signal quality: the brusque dialogue and the immediacy of the selected actors whose comportment and delivery were honed not in drama school but in the pubs and streets of south London. A significant element of his role as Dialogue Consultant and Technical Advisor was to improve the script. When Donald Cammell stayed with him at St George's Court, Litvinoff would stride the room talking, chattering out lines of dialogue which Cammell wrote in longhand before passing to his secretary to type. James Fox noted 'the line where Chas goes to the pornographer in Soho and says, "You know, I don't think I'm going to let you stay in the film business" – that's very David, isn't it? That throwaway combination of wit with threat.* He was just in love with that.' Others see his imprint in the dialogue prompted by Moody's comment 'Your old man was a barber. . .' and the prescient jibe to Turner that 'You'll look funny when you're fifty'. But the tone soaks into the film's entirety. Paul Buck, in his book *Performance: The Biography*, notes that while the violence is graphic, the language achieves its unsettling quality in a contrasting manner: as he writes, 'Only once does Jagger say "fucking", and yet all the way one feels that the language is overbearingly crude. That is because the very fabric of the language has been penetrated. They've gone right inside and rooted around for the violence within language itself. And that is Litvinoff, and that is Pinter.' Here and throughout his life it was the muscularity of Litvinoff's language that so disturbed, the sense in his interrogations that he could reverse a conversation's momentum at will, that he understood syntax as a mechanism he could wrench tighter whenever necessary. It seems Litvinoff had no illusions about the extent to which his influence on the script would be credited beyond the vague term 'Dialogue Consultant', however. 'I would see him a lot during the making of that film and he was bitching on about the fact that he was writing it and he knew very well he wasn't going to get any credit,' said Eric Clapton. 'He said, "I'm writing this", and he would tell me what scenes he'd composed. I'd see him in the evening and he'd tell

* Donald Cammell once commented that he 'always saw *Performance* as a comedy', which brings to mind Max Brod's description of listening to Franz Kafka reading from his work: 'We friends of his laughed quite immoderately when he first let us hear the first chapter of *The Trial*. And he himself laughed so much that there were moments when he couldn't read any further.' *The Biography of Franz Kafka*, by Max Brod, translated by G. Humphreys Roberts (Secker and Warburg, 1947), p. 139.

me what he'd done during the day and say, "I know very well that they're not going to put my name on it.'"

Aside from working on the script, set dressing and locations, he recruited some of the actors and helped James Fox assume his character. Johnny Bindon, who played Moody, he'd known for at least a couple of years, the pair having collaborated in the meeting with Nicky Cramer after the Redlands bust. Bindon had already appeared in Ken Loach's *Poor Cow* as a thief who beats his girlfriend: not a great stretch for the twenty-four-year-old, who was notorious for his violence towards both men and women. When we meet Moody he is criticising the previous night's television, as he'd been unimpressed by seeing some bloodshed at 8pm when 'kiddies are still viewing'. His line 'there's claret all over the screen, a geezer's got half his ear hanging off' was, depending on one's stance, made funnier or more appalling by the knowledge that Bindon himself had bitten a man's ear off in a fight. He was also renowned for being the very proud possessor of a one-foot-long penis, which was a familiar sight to almost anyone who associated with him for more than a few minutes. He'd flop it into someone else's pint of beer – 'Look, he's thirsty!' – ask a woman for her phone number and then whip it out and write the number down crossways, or thread it erect through the handles of three half-pint mugs and leave them hanging there as his party trick. Just the sort of character, then, to impart to the film a certain rough-and-ready quality.

Johnny Shannon, who played Flowers, was a former print worker and fruit stallholder who in 1968 combined running a betting shop in Pimlico with training boxers. He'd been in Henry Cooper's corner two years earlier for the world title fight with Muhammad Ali. Lambeth-born Shannon was no criminal but he mingled with a good number of the 'chaps' at the Thomas a Becket pub on the Old Kent Road. On the ground floor was the bar, upstairs was a boxing gym in which Shannon had trained Cooper. Adrenaline, sweat, alcohol fumes, perfume and cigarette smoke all blended into a fug that lent the Becket a potent atmosphere: and yet at the same time it had its own glamour. It was a place that working-class south Londoners would dress up for on a Saturday night. Much of its allure had to do with the charisma of the landlord and landlady, Tommy and Beryl Gibbons, whose lively pub was also frequented by Jimmy Evans and the Foremans. Litvinoff knew Tommy Gibbons and sought his help with moulding Fox into Chas, and Gibbons in turn spoke to his good friend Shannon, who agreed to introduce Fox to a few of the characters – boxers, boozers, dapper fellows who 'never hurt their own' – who inhabited this stratum of south London life. The Harrow-educated actor arrived at the Becket flamboyantly dressed in a big hat and floral scarf but soon adjusted to the local dress code. Upstairs in the ring where Shannon had coached Cooper he now taught Fox how to jab and hook. He was impressed by his new pupil's focus: 'He came up there a number of times and trained with the boxers. . . He sparred with them and did all right, he held his own with them. He caused blood to come from one of their noses, and he was so proud of it that he was doing well. He was a guy, Jimmy Fox, that if you told him to do something, the educated person that he was, if you told him in boxing a good punch was a straight left hand – "Punch it out straight, Jim!" – he would be perfectly straight and was catching the guy with good shots, good punches straight to the face. And he worked very, very well.'

Then Shannon's involvement in the film deepened. Fox suggested to him that there was a part for which he'd be perfect: the bald-headed Shannon initially assumed he meant the chauffeur, but he was referring to Harry Flowers. Not long after he had a call from Litvinoff to come see him at St George's Court.

'I think he just wanted to have a chat with me, see what sort of fellow I was and see whether I would fit into the character of Harry Flowers in the movie,' said Shannon. 'It was sort of ninety per cent cast. They hadn't completely agreed, I didn't know if I was going to get it. I went to his flat, having not met David before that, and wondering what sort of chap he was. I felt a bit wary [of] what sort of guy he was. The funny thing was, to a person in my walk of life, I got to his flat and saw this little scruffy guy, very pleasant but very scruffy sort of guy, and he offered me a drink, and I said no, I didn't want a drink. He said, "Have a gin, whisky, whatever, or have a cup of tea," and just to keep him quiet I said I'd have a cup of tea. And after a while the cup of tea came out in a chipped mug with a broken top, and it was a terrible, terrible cup of tea, and then he started playing me Mick Jagger records and telling me all about Mick Jagger and asking what sort of music do I like, and played me records for over two hours. And I'm thinking, "What's happening here?" And then he suddenly said, "Would you like a drink now?" and I said, "No," and he said, "Would you like another cup of tea?" so to keep him quiet I said, "Go on, I'll have another." He poured a cup of tea from the same pot that had been stood on the table for two and a half hours. Which to me at the time was a very strange thing to do.'

Litvinoff's decision to contact Tommy Gibbons had opened up a new pool for the film to draw from and indirectly spurred the recruitment of a man whose role as Flowers would add significant vitality and realism to the production. It also unlocked a successful new career for Shannon, whose future as an actor would include roles in television shows from *Dixon of Dock Green*, *The Sweeney* and *Fawlty Towers* through to playing Peter Rachman in *Scandal*.

As *Performance* began to roll towards production Litvinoff received another letter from his old friend Andy Garnett, who enclosed a clipping that set his mind running. The result was a reply to Garnett that displayed both poles of his personality. The opening fusillade shifts from a knowing nod to his own sensitivity about anti-Semitism into an archetypal Litvinoff ironic fantasia, in which the most *goy*-ish of writers are closeted Jews, an absurdist satire on the anti-Semitic belief that Jews hide their identities to better exert a malign covert influence. Then he hits the brakes and shudders down a couple of gears: the tone lilts into melancholy, his sentences weighted in a way that displays the poignancy he could imbue into his writing, despite the fact that here and there his mind evidently worked faster than his fingers could tap the typewriter's punctuation keys. Here was the self-deprecation that Clapton recalled as his saving grace, and here too a hint of the obsession with another electrifying Jewish satirist that would come to grip him over the next couple of years.

```
From: 'Dun' Roamin'        53, St George's Court,
      The Rockery             Brompton Road
      'Rolling Acres'         London, S.W.3.
                              Kensington 8021.


                         23rd February, 1968.


Dear Andy,
   Thanks for your letter. You realise I take it as a
typical anti-semolinic diatribe on both racial and
chemical grounds. The original is of course now in the
hands of my lawyers, messrs William Hickey, Waterfield,
```

Robert Jacobs et Fils* and their successors. They are all out on bail at present, but you may rest assured you will be arraigned through their bad offices when they find some. As they say in the elegant jargon of the property-improver's world - Letter now - Writ follows. As for the contents of the clipping which you sent. . . Every well informed member of the B'nai Brith Anti-Defamation League knows that most of the leading figures of the Irish literary renaissance between 1910 and 1937 were really just young Yiddisher boys living in the Auld Country pseudonymously owing to a brush with the British tax authorities, surely? W. B. Yeats (real name Wally Barney Yalovsky) J. M. Synge (Judah Monty Schmenckelbaum) Remember his 'Playboy of the Western World'?† This was all about anti-Jewish business practices in Turco-Ruthenian taxi-cab circles between 1920/24. A fascinating literary device he employed was in using the sub-plot pre-frontally as if it was the Celtic-Maverick-Deirdre of the Sorrows-Mother-Myth-fixated usual Abbey Theatre‡ offering of its time. Clever, Nu! Its real title (the Irish Press, notably the *Cork County Examiner*, obviously couldn't review the play in its real title which was an elegant euphemism in itself - 'Why don't you give a Yiddishe boy a chance?'). . .

Well, man, how are you getting on. I wish our paths had crossed more often over the last few years. I am glad that you are making it with your lovely lady by your side, you took a stand. As for me, I was 40 years old last week. I own a plastic night school type

* That is, the Georgian rake who gave his name to Litvinoff's *Daily Express* column, 'Dandy Kim' and the property developer who bought numerous ex-Rachman properties after Rachman's death.

† John Millington Synge's play might have resonated with Litvinoff: it concerns a man who appears in an Irish pub and tells the locals that he has killed his father, but his audience are more interested in his mesmeric storytelling than the facts of the crime that may have occurred.

‡ The Irish National Theatre in Dublin, founded by W. B. Yeats and Lady Augusta Gregory in 1904, which would stage Synge's play in 1907.

briefcase, stuffed with 8 writs summonses, and a repos-
session order or two. My count-up at midnight on the
3rd February, the actual date of my nativity, revealed
4/6d - devalued. Even failure has to be profession-
ally worked at before it becomes pristine, elegant and
complete. I am still learning. When are either or both
of you coming back over here. Soon, I hope. Tim has
nearly finished his equestrian portrait of H.M. It's
being done both at the Palace and the Pheasantry.
It's an amazing old dinosaur of a conception as a
picture, and it says much for Tim's gargantuan appetite for his own brand of surreal living that he could
conceive in 1967/8 this lovely thing. Can you please
send me two copies of a paperback book, published in
December, 1967, in New York? I have tried most places,
but I can't get it over in U.K. It's published at 95
cents by Ballantyne Books Inc. 101, Fifth Avenue, New
York, N.Y. 10008. I would be really grateful, man, if
you could do this thing and lay these little volumes
on me. It's called 'the Essential Lennie Bruce'.* I can
let you have my album of 1895 Tavern Ragtime melodies
of the West Country, all transcribed from piano rolls.
Very lovely they are, too. Would it be a drag, Andy,
about the Lennie Bruce books, if it isn't, can you send
them to me at this address on this letter by Airmail
Bookpost. Is there anything you want me to send you
or Polly from England. Let me know, and I'll do it as
required.

Well, man, thanks for your letter etcetera. I forgot
to mention that Tim was going to sell his studio to
Mick Jagger and his lady love Miss Faithfull, and is
hoping to recover all his bread which he has spent
there over the past few years, in this transaction.
He doesn't really dig the place so much now, as the
Pheasantry Club has been taken over by the Speakeasy

---

* Or, to correct Litvinoff's misspellings, *The Essential Lenny Bruce*, edited by John Cohen,
Ballantine Books, New York, 1967.

club people, and this means he will have about a thousand hippies hovering around his door each night, so
he wants to cool his own scene there. He may try to
get a small place in Italy. It would be a gas and it
would be nice for you to have Tim as a neighbour whenever you are in Castellina-in-Chianti.

My everlasting fond love to you both.

David (Litvinoff).

* * *

On 17th March 1968 an angry crowd of 25,000 people crammed into
Grosvenor Square to protest against the Vietnam War. As Litvinoff stood
on the fringes by a line of police with interlocked arms, he spied an opportunity: 'I've always wanted to see a policeman's cock,' he announced to his
friend Victoria Ormsby Gore before unzipping the nearest officer's flies.
Mick Jagger stood further back, surveying an increasingly violent scene
from the steps of a house on the square, and later went home to write
'Streetfighting Man'.

Jagger took his role as Turner extremely seriously. 'The character was much
discussed by Donald and myself about how he was supposed to be,' he said.
'This very reclusive person. You know, you make these roles up of yourself
and an amalgam of other people you know. Bit of Brian Jones in it, but it's
not really Brian Jones.'[21] His relations with his bandmates grew fraught
during the shoot and began to hinder a substantial element of the production in that the promised Rolling Stones song that had helped entice
Warner Bros. showed no sign of materialising. Cammell kept asking Jagger
if he'd written it yet and Jagger kept stalling, the unspoken difficulty being
that Richards had withdrawn his collaboration after hearing unfounded
rumours that Jagger and Pallenberg had slept together. Pallenberg was
renting a room at Robert Fraser's flat during the shoot; during the day
Fraser would kindle Richards' paranoia, and when she returned at night the
pair would greet her with a sarcastic interrogation about what she'd been up
to at work. (The answer to which, aside from acting, could have included
her new hobby of toying with Fox by teasing him for being 'straight' and
telling him that she had spiked his drink with acid.)

Eventually Jagger broke down in tears and explained to Cammell
the pressures he was facing, after which Cammell, and perhaps Litvinoff,

helped him to write the song. The finished work melded Ry Cooder's dazzling bottleneck guitar with lyrics that combine needling surrealist inquisition, homoerotic sadomasochism, references to Jews, to corporate corruption, to William Burroughs' *The Soft Machine* ('Fun and games, what?').[22] Burroughs lived in London in the mid-1960s and was often seen at Christopher Gibbs' home at 100 Cheyne Walk, where Litvinoff met him at least once. Jagger also had to cope with the devastating effects on Faithfull of her miscarriage of their baby, something to which he would allude in the song's final line. 'Memo from Turner' became a riveting musical centrepiece in which a hallucinating Chas imagines Turner and Flowers as a single merged performing entity, and which concludes with one of the film's defining images, Flowers' firm lying naked on their office floor in an arrangement suggesting a Francis Bacon painting. Close examination suggests how Litvinoff's preoccupations and stock phrases coloured Jagger's creation of the song; Litvinoff's letter to Andy Garnett a year previous had included the advice to 'Remember, my children, who and what you are' and he'd often greet younger men as 'faggy boys' to get a reaction. 'The whole lyric is that dark film noir imagery that David would have written,' said Nigel Waymouth. 'As talented and as brilliant as Mick is, it's not his scene. But he understood it because David was a very powerful influence on him.' He and Jagger were as close as they would ever be by now. Jagger loved Litvinoff's language and came to see him as something of a mentor, a useful source of energy and genuine danger in comparison with which his establishment-shaking pop group seemed merely dilettante middle-class outlaws; a channel to London's murkier recesses, a peculiar worldly-wise survivor whose formative years were conducted in the shade before the world's spotlight swung on to the city, an authority on the blues and R&B on which his band had launched their career and which remained their music's backbone. For his part Litvinoff drew energy from vibrant younger people and enjoyed the intelligence of Jagger's company, the sensual, androgynous way he discarded the stale old ideas about gender, his strange compelling countenance with its blend of the innocent and the bestial; in those days there was something at once bashful and lascivious in the gradual unfolding of his smile.

That said, at times Litvinoff found his younger friends' posturing intolerable. Jagger, Pallenberg, Donald Cammell: all had a certain hauteur that was guaranteed to antagonise him. On one evening he returned to the Pheasantry from a day's shooting and exclaimed: 'Oh man, man, *man*, I can't stand those people and their frozen attitudes of hip.' 'The phrase always stuck in my mind,' said a friend who was there. 'Anything and anybody overtly cool, putting on attitudes, he couldn't wait to pull the rug from under them.' Litvinoff's references to Jagger in his letters tend to come with a tone of wry amusement. The closeness that the two men enjoyed for a spell was apparent to Litvinoff's niece Sarah, Emanuel's younger daughter, when her uncle gave her an opportunity that would have been beyond most teenage girls' dreams. 'He told my father that he was working on a film with Mick Jagger and that he had written it all,' she said, betraying Litvinoff's tendency to blur the truth to impress his older half-brother. 'I know that he's credited as the dialogue coach. He was saying that it was his script. Obviously as a fourteen-year-old girl I was a great Stones fan and not really because the music meant anything but more in the boy band sort of way, and Mick Jagger was God. So my mother could not veto me going to meet Mick Jagger! She was very, very reluctant. . . Anyway, he took us to tea at Cheyne Walk and it was exciting for me that there was Mick Jagger, and I remember Marianne Faithfull walking down the stairs and striking a pose and coming to chat with us for a bit. Afterwards I remember her saying to David that she thought my father had a wonderful "vibe". Nobody used that word in those days; it seemed a very glamorous word. David took over the whole occasion, he was talking nineteen to the dozen and then he got to Mick Jagger's record collection and said: "Oh, you must give Sarah this! Look, you've got lots of copies, give Sarah that." He pulled out lots of Stones records and said: "You want to give them to my niece, don't you?" So Jagger said "Yes, okay", and he signed about four albums and then David pulled out an early pressing of *Beggars Banquet*, it had little pictures in the middle, and he signed it. Then we went back to my father's for tea with David's boyfriend, and the thing that stands out for me about the whole occasion was that, yes, it was very exciting meeting Mick Jagger, but I was totally bedazzled by David. He was by far the most inter-esting thing about it. And he just told story after story after story – my eyes were getting bigger and bigger – one of the things he said was that Mick Jagger had written "Jumpin' Jack Flash" about him. And I knew it wasn't true because the young boyfriend kept trying to put the record straight and was saying: "Well not quite, David. . .it's not *quite* like that, David."'

It wasn't true, of course; the song's spark of inspiration lay in his and Richards' hearing the crunch of Richards' gardener's feet on gravel at Redlands, though the title reflected Litvinoff's dynamism, while Richards' relentless propulsive riff drove forward with the same urgency with which

Litvinoff energised time, sparked successions of events and created collisions between worlds. It was no wonder that the phrase attached itself to him. The literal truth didn't matter to her, said Sarah, just as it didn't matter to most of his friends. What mattered was the quality of the stories, not their accuracy. He made people laugh, gasp, think harder, always feel *something* whether or not the sensation was enjoyable. She was desperate to meet him again but her mother forbade it, for fear that he might exert the same malign influence he had on Vida. 'She wasn't going to allow another of her daughters to get sucked into his murky world,' said Sarah. 'And I never saw him again.'

The episode illustrated how distant he had grown from most of his siblings while assuming a role as conduit to a more exciting London for their bored suburban children: take Vida, who considered him 'a sort of genius' but 'a genius with a fatal flaw',[23] or Pinchus' Rosa, then a frustrated adolescent in Golders Green, to whom he seemed 'so exotic'. Her abiding memory of him is his scent and the tactile affection he showed her and her father, who by this time was suffering with multiple sclerosis. He wore 'this incredible perfume', she said. 'It was a sweet, musky smell. I don't think it was an aftershave, more a perfume, like patchouli, but sweeter. I wear something similar today, and perhaps that's why.'

At St George's Court he continued to live with Gerry Goldstein, who was presumably the 'boyfriend' whom Sarah Litvinoff met, though it was around this time that Gerry fell in love with Clare Peake, who helped him in the first of his recoveries from heroin addiction. Goldstein's psychiatric condition was already precarious: he'd ensconce himself in her kitchen, 'him too frightened to set foot outside and me trying to help him find a balance between paranoia and manic gregariousness',[22] as she writes in her memoir. Through Gerry she met Litvinoff, whom she recalled despaired of his heroin use and warned Clare, in a caring way, that if she were ever to begin using the drug herself he'd be furious. Her initiation into Litvinoff's world could hardly have been stranger or more sudden. The first time they met, he invited her and Gerry to join him at a dinner party being thrown by two new friends he'd acquired, and on accepting Peake found herself immersed in a Mad Hatter's tea party transposed to 1960s Chelsea. The hosts were a pair of octogenarian spinster sisters who were 'Janeites', devoted admirers of Jane Austen's works. 'The cheery old ladies scuttled around the room, giggling and clutching their individual tin openers, which they brandished with all the pride of a Samurai warrior clutching his sword,' she wrote.

Pilchards served straight from the tin were carefully placed on our plates, arranged as if they were a gourmet meal they had been preparing for hours. For pudding, we each had a cornet with a scoop of strawberry ice cream and an artistically placed chocolate flake poking out at a slant.

The dinner was spent in mad conversation that went to and fro between the sisters, David, and John Crittle, a tailor who owned Dandy Fashions.* Gerry contributed a spattering, and, from me, utter petrified silence. The banter that went back and forth was abstruse and disjointed. Nobody's answers bore any resemblance to the question, but everyone nodded sagely as if they did. Although I had never been subjected to much in the way of ordinariness, this evening won first prize for the most peculiar dinner party I had ever been to.[25]

But for all the bizarre nights out, there were long nights in, during which Clare grew to overcome her reticence and adore Litvinoff's company while enjoying meeting his circle of friends. Eric Clapton would come over and give Gerry lessons on the Martin acoustic guitar Gerry bought from him after winning £1,000 on the Premium Bonds. While she was well aware of Litvinoff's savage wit – she recalled seeing 'confident men cut to shreds within a second by a sentence from David, and it wasn't a pretty sight'[26] – she never faced his wrath herself. The three of them smoked and talked and laughed until she ached. Yes, there were times when she and Gerry retired to bed and a little later sensed a presence at the keyhole, followed by the receding sound of scampering tiptoed footsteps; but within the relaxed sexual mores of the time it didn't trouble them. He spoke 'at an extraordinary speed, his repartee skipping from one subject to another with the speed of a jaguar', she wrote. 'It could be some juicy gossip of the day, an obscure Nietzsche quote, an unrecorded Mississippi Delta singer once heard and never forgotten, or the less obscure hierarchy of the English nobility. In other words, he knew a lot.'[27]

---

* Crittle was Australian and had come to London in the early 1960s. By 1965 he was working at Michael Rainey's boutique, Hung On You, then opened his own shop at 161 King's Road which later became Apple Tailoring. He would drive through Chelsea in his Rolls-Royce with his young daughter Marnie in the back seat. She later found fame as the ballerina Darcey Bussell, by which time she and her father were estranged. He died back in Australia in 2000.

On one occasion he was discussing the film's problems and mentioned that he wasn't satisfied with its working title, *The Performers*. 'I suggested, instead of *Performers* what about *Performance*, and he liked that idea,'[28] she said. He wrote to Clare and Gerry while they were staying in the countryside, alluding to his loneliness in the wake of an unexplained falling-out and discussing his work with Fox. 'Gerry said that you were fantastically isolated, that's me and 53 the buildings. Just now Mr Fraser, Mr Gibbs, Mr Richards and Miss Faithfull were here on Saturday night/ Sunday morning, and as a result of some peculiar lie, an enormously unpleasant situation has arisen, devolving around a story which is obviously going the rounds in these ere parts. Hateful and strange.' This might have been the suspicion, put forward by the Stones' driver Tom Keylock and briefly entertained by Richards but later dismissed, that Litvinoff himself had tipped off the *News of the World* before the Redlands bust and beaten Nicky Cramer as a decoy tactic.

'The film drags wearily and hysterically on,' he continued. 'I am working a lot with James Fox at his and this place, and though he's very charming, once we get down to the real grass roots of the character he's to play, and the frightening areas of the psychotic, he gets very uneasy. I tell him that Devlin would almost certainly have used a razor and dagger on his victims when younger, and describing the intrinsics of where this is at frightens and nauseates James, so there is a distinct air of chimera on the "authenticity" of this XXX picture.'[29]

Half a century on Fox had lost none of his charm. We spoke first on the telephone and later with the actor and film-maker Patrick Kennedy at a flat in Powis Terrace opposite Hedgegate Court, Peter Rachman's first major acquisition in the area. Meeting him emphasised the dedication he applied to transforming himself into Chas Devlin, for in person he could hardly have been more different from his character: thoughtful, considered, self-deprecating, flattering and quite visibly carrying an endearing touch of self-doubt. In the summer of 1968, however, on and off screen he could be terrifying. He stormed into the production office in Chelsea on one occasion, smacking his fists down on a table and frightening the secretaries, angry that he felt Shannon wasn't going to be paid well enough. Shannon recalled a night out when they finished drinking in the early hours and found that for a joke the 'chaps' had parked a car in front of Fox's, blocking his way. No matter, he just roared on to the pavement and around the car, dispersing his newfound friends, who saluted in amused admiration as he drove off. Nigel Waymouth saw him and Litvinoff out one night at the Baghdad House, a venue that Waymouth feels is overlooked in the cultural histories. 'It was opposite the cinema in the Fulham Road at the end of Drayton Gardens. It was on the corner and it was run by this man called Abbas. He had this red-headed Scottish girl, Valerie, who used to serve the tables. We all used to go downstairs to the basement, where it was quiet and we were allowed to smoke and bring out the hookah and the hummus and everything. And then he used to get these guys in from Baghdad who used to play the *oud*, and Valerie used to do her belly dancing. Meanwhile upstairs were the local fuzz! One night I went down to the Baghdad House and David was sitting there with James Fox, and James was dressed like he was in the film. He had this John Smedley thing, kind of mod, very dapper. And then: "Oh Nigel man, have you met James Fox?"'

Fox looked up and greeted Waymouth: "Allo, mate, 'ow are yer?'

'And this was the English public schoolboy who was in *King Rat*. . .he was now method, fully. "I'm just taking James to meet Reggie and Ronnie. . ." He was getting him psyched up for the part.'

Litvinoff had at one point floated the idea that he could bring the twins themselves on board as consultants,* while the letter written on 22nd May 1968 to Sandy Lieberson has a marginal note saying 'Jack Spot – £800 – expenses', which hints that they subsequently considered bringing in the forcibly retired 'King of the Underworld'. In any case, as Donald Cammell put it, 'There was some suggestion that the Krays would be hired for technical assistance – an idea which was aborted due to their unavoidable absence.'[30]

At dawn on 8th May, after assiduously compiling an immense dossier of evidence from former accomplices who had been persuaded to talk, 'Nipper' Read and his team swooped and arrested Reggie, Ronnie and Charlie Kray, Albert Donoghue and Freddie Foreman on charges relating to the killings of George Cornell, Jack McVitie and Frank Mitchell. Chief among the prosecution witnesses was Paul Elvey, the dynamite-runner whom the twins wanted to kill Jimmy Evans. 'They knew the police were going to get them by fair means or otherwise,' he recalled in 2015. He'd heard from people close to them that 'the Krays intended to go out in a blaze of glory, literally. They were going to attack

---

* Johnny Shannon said at the time of the film's UK release: 'I understand they helped Litvinoff with some ideas' – quoted in the *Guardian*, 23rd January 1971.

a few of their most hated police stations in the East End of London. Their most hated police station was Leman Street; this was high on the list for retribution. Number two was a police station in or near Bethnal Green. They had machine guns and hand grenades etcetera. It would have been carnage. The police just had to act.' Others arrested among their associates included Bobby Buckley and Micky Fawcett, indicted on 'conspiracy to defraud' charges relating to long firm frauds that were later thrown out.* Only Donoghue would plead guilty: after the twins informed him that he would take the blame for Mitchell's murder, despite his only involvement being to drive the van in which Foreman carried out the shooting, he decided to assist the prosecution instead. He would be tried separately, having the murder charge rescinded and receiving a token two-year sentence for serving as an accessory to McVitie's murder. 'Hell of a lot better than thirty years!' he said when we spoke, but the hidden tariff was the lifelong burden he'd carry as a perceived grass. Litvinoff arranged for Fox to meet Ronnie, but by now the location had to be HMP Brixton, where he was in custody charged with murder.

'It was obviously to do Ronnie a favour or pay back a favour that David owed,' said Fox. 'He was just quite scared of them, I think. I think David terribly wanted to be loved, and to please people. That was a deep need. But what was so refreshing was that with him it was so obvious; it was something he was natural about, but he did need acceptance. And I think he was quite scared of Ronnie and probably needed to do him some favours to try to do anything he could to connect Ronnie or Reggie with so-called normal, respectable, outside life.

'He certainly wanted to be back in favour with the gang, so he put me on to Ronnie, which didn't help me as much as actually meeting Tommy Gibbons and people in the Becket. . . What's amazing about him is that, unlike people today, he didn't seem to want to gain any great personal credit from it. It was enough to live on the stories, and to dazzle people with his wit and connections and his company. That was enough for David, it seemed to me.'

Fox remembered Litvinoff conducting a long tape-recorded interview with an anonymous hitman that they used in creating Chas. 'There

---

*   Also among the long firm indictments is a David Levy. Members of David Litvinoff's family thought this referred to him but it turned out to be a false lead: this David Levy was two years older and from a large criminal family in Bow.

was a big gangland scene in London and he must have been close enough to it, so when the film was being prepared, David must have been the key resource I would say. He wasn't just a researcher, he was a resource. And I bet you he was a creative resource as well for Donald – he must have supplied Donald with many scenes and characters. He definitely would have nudged me in the direction of where to get an authentic accent, and I love the whole idea of him being a dialogue coach. . .he would be so far from what we would call a dialogue coach today; he wouldn't know what that was and would be bored by it very quickly. It was all to do with the stimulation of his connections and his vitality and his personality. This is what rubbed off.'

Where Litvinoff couldn't help Fox was with the business of acting. If he confided to Clare Peake that he felt Fox was falling short of confronting the requisite darkness – well, Litvinoff was not an actor and, ironically for a compulsive self-fictionaliser, he did not appreciate that acting is fundamentally an imaginative rather than a factual business. Just as in 1963 Fox preoccupied himself twenty-four hours a day with the psycho-sexual sadomasochistic manipulations perpetrated by Dirk Bogarde's Hugo in *The Servant* (directed by Joseph Losey, scripted by Harold Pinter),* now the month he spent steeped in south London life gave him much of the material he needed to craft Chas. What ultimately produced his convincing portrayal on-screen was not a matter of copying but creating.

'All I can say is that it was an immersion into the culture, and I would say David was influential on where I went to for the wardrobe, which was very important. That was a shop called Cecil Gee in Shaftesbury Avenue. So that whole wardrobe was influenced by David and the choice of look and haircut. . . What so helped was to go to the Becket, to go to the boxing performances, to train in the gym myself – and what's remarkable about *Performance* is that in some ways it's ahead of *Taxi Driver* in terms of its depiction of street life, a very authentic London street life. And all of

---

* Fox's then-girlfriend Sarah Miles, who co-starred in *The Servant*: 'After shooting all day, Willy [his first name is William] would either go missing or arrive home wrapped so tightly in his character that I couldn't find him. I'd offer to help him unwrap the part and hang it up for the evening, but he'd get defensive and start clinging to it all night as well. . . We all put a great deal of hard work into that project, as well as risky soul-searching, but for [Fox and Bogarde's] two characters the delving inward had to go even deeper, and it paid off a thousand-fold in the finished film, the only place where it matters.' Quoted in *Performance*, by Paul Buck (Omnibus Press, 2012), p. 92.

that was what I was immersed in, and it was through Johnny Shannon, who became my mentor, so I became a friend of Johnny and his wife and his family, with the Gibbonses, and a little bit with some of the lads. We'd go to some of the clubs in the suburban areas where the boys were, and we'd drive around in cars together, and we'd drink together. . . It was an exposure that was completely invaluable.

'I was completely [in character]. What was great about them was that they basically never looked upon me as anything but Chas. So when I was in that world, I simply was one of them. And it was a marvellous example of *their* imaginative connection, in that they obviously privately had their own opinion of me and my background. Johnny Shannon was very aware of the world I came from, and I remember him having dinner with my mum and dad when my dad had a flat in Eaton Square. Johnny very well knew the amazing contrast of where I apparently was coming from. . .but had this imaginative connection which was full of acceptance and full of positive spirit, that this was doable, and enjoyable.'

Rumours attached to the film have suggested that Fox ended up accompanying some of his newfound friends in their criminal activities, for instance being shown how to break into a house. 'I don't remember, as they commonly say in inquiries! But I genuinely don't remember. I should think I probably got up to a bit of mischief. I've either wiped that or it didn't happen, because I don't. . .I seem to remember everything was in connection with the *fiction* of Chas, rather than the reality. And I don't believe that the reality would have added much to my imaginative process. It's as if the imaginative process is more important sometimes than the reality. And that was in no small measure due to the fact that during the preparation there was not a switch-off. It worked, and this is David Litvinoff: he must have been a chameleon, in many ways, he must have been one thing in one environment, and with Christopher Gibbs and the artistic crowd in another. A completely adaptable person.'

It was not a double life but at least a triple life. Litvinoff spent nights in Stoke Newington at the Imperial Sports Club or the Farleigh pub, where the Krays' friend Bobby Ramsey once beat him senseless in the toilets; then dinner in Chelsea with Quentin Crisp, whom he proclaimed offered 'the best conversation in London';[31] then at home he was the diligent auto-didact, reading until the small hours, coursing through Jean Genet, who had long been something of a role model, or Henri Bergson's theories concerning the social purpose of laughter, or Mark Twain, or the modern 'beat, hip Jewish writers: Norman Mailer, Bob Dylan' as Nigel Waymouth recalled. Waymouth touched on a pertinent connection: *Performance* illustrates how Litvinoff had by now become a London beat figure parallel to Neal Cassady in his role, influence, energy, verbal invention and insatiable sexual omnivory. Both men arose from a tough, lawless youth to mesmerise gentler creative associates with their philosophies and dangerous stories, both told these stories with their whole body, their muscular gesticulations complementing their torrenting speech, both nursed unrealised creative ambitions while watching shrewder friends draw profitable inspiration from their tales, both would 'burn, burn, burn', as Jack Kerouac had it,* until they burned out in their forties.†

Waymouth was right in describing Dylan as one of Litvinoff's favourite writers; while the world awaited the possible arrival of his novel *Tarantula*, Litvinoff would play Dylan's latest album over and over again and rhapsodise over the lyrics, read too much into them, tear into them, but always engage with them as literature that merited sustained study. Dylan's own reinvention post-motorcycle crash – chemical-fuelled hipster goes to ground and re-emerges in the countryside wiser and gentler, crop-haired, bespectacled and bearded like some kind of young rabbinical paterfamilias – seemed a model for hippiedom Litvinoff could emulate. These years saw him try to move towards a new truthfulness in his life. His preference shifted from pills and alcohol to hash (at times almost chain-smoking joints from when he awoke in the morning) and, a little later, acid. The result was a marked softening in his demeanour, for a time at least. He began to describe himself as 'an old Jewish hippy', no doubt with a degree of irony, but you sense too that he held out hope that the movement might achieve its aspiration of a fairer, freer, less uptight and hypocritical society and that he was willing to give it a shot. His letters speak often of love and honesty. He maintained few possessions: 53 St George's Court was sparsely furnished; a

---

* 'The only people for me are the mad ones, the ones who are mad to live, mad to talk, mad to be saved, desirous of everything at the same time, the ones that never yawn or say a common-place thing, but burn, burn, burn like fabulous yellow roman candles exploding like spiders across the stars.' *On the Road*, by Jack Kerouac (Penguin, 1991), p. 8.

† Researching Litvinoff also brought to mind a sad reminiscence I heard from Carolyn Cassady, Neal's widow, at her Berkshire home in 2007: 'What everybody was so amazed [by] with Neal was the energy and the risk-taking and hedonism. They didn't care much about his mind, which is so sad, because he had such a brilliant mind.'

bicycle, his books and music, a mattress on the floor and a hi-fi system. He developed the habit of arriving home, removing all his clothes and dancing naked around the flat, or lying on his mattress smoking joints while listening to tapes with his eyes closed, the volume turned to maximum. One night he opened his eyes from his stoned reverie to find himself surrounded by several policemen who, after knocking politely for some time, had eventually grown frustrated and broken the door down in order to tell him the music was annoying his neighbours.

After the endless rewrites, negotiations and research, by July 1968 it was time to commit the collective conception of the Cammell brothers, Litvinoff, Pallenberg and Roeg to celluloid. 'Suddenly we were in this void,' Roeg recalled, 'and had a freedom that nobody was checking up on. How often could that happen? Now you have eighteen people on the set questioning whether someone raises their fork or not.'[32] Litvinoff was rarely on set, though the lighting cameraman, Mike Molloy, had one distinct memory of him making an appearance: he recalled Litvinoff 'grabbing me, fixing me with a manic glare and saying: "What this film needs is a kind of visual Esperanto!"', a cinematic language restrained by no borders. The exterior shots of Turner's mansion were of course filmed in Powis Square, Notting Hill, a territory well known to Litvinoff and the Cammells since the days a decade earlier when it stood at the heart of Rachman's property empire. Most of the interior scenes, however, were shot in the far more affluent Lowndes Square in Belgravia, which witnessed a sudden disruption to its usual gentility when the film crew appeared without warning: noisy people milling about at all hours, catering vans parked in the road. Soon a neighbour complained about the disturbance and announced her intention to halt the production, informing David Cammell and Sandy Lieberson that there were 'more titled people living in Lowndes Square than in any other square except Eaton Square'.[33] (Although Eaton Square was where James Fox's parents lived, 'we were not typical Eaton Square type people,' he said. 'It was just because [my father Robin] was making some money as an agent at the time'; still, it emphasises the contrast between his background and the world he entered in preparation for the film.) The neighbour argued that the shoot contravened the terms of the landlord's lease; it went to court and eventually Cammell and Lieberson paid for her to go on holiday while the film was being made. The owner of 15 Lowndes Square was a Captain Leonard Plugge, an eccentric MP, scientist and entrepreneur who was now living in nearby Dolphin Square. The house was already familiar to David Cammell as the source of a painful memory: earlier in the decade he had lost a substantial sum of money there at a gambling party. The Captain kept there a large number of paintings known as 'the Plugge Collection', apparently comprising works by Rembrandt, Rubens and Velásquez, and while he allowed the flat to be used for filming he insisted that the collection remain on the walls and be insured for $2 million. David Cammell remembered asking the resident caretaker to keep an eye on the paintings: 'He said: "Don't worry, guvnor," pulled out a Luger pistol and said, "They'll all be safe."' Perhaps alarm bells should have rung at that stage. 'One morning, very early,' he recalled, 'I had probably been working late and was still in bed, and the telephone rang. This voice said: "Mr Cammell? This is Inspector Hector Vector of the South-Eastern Sector, and I'm ringing about the missing Plugge Collection." And I said: "What on earth are you talking about?" and it turned out to be David Litvinoff. But he wasn't having a joke, he had just heard that the Plugge Collection had gone missing.'

Someone realised that the caretaker had just bought himself a new car and hadn't been seen for a few days. He was on the run for a fortnight before being caught at Paddington station, unwittingly playing out a mirror-version of *Performance*'s plot. It emerged that he'd sold the paintings for a paltry £3,800, as they all turned out to be forgeries. Via his solicitor he then asked David Cammell to stand his bail; Cammell understandably refused. 'I said: "Are you completely mad? I've had more trouble from that man than anyone else in my life!"'

While Litvinoff spent little time around the shoot, he was a regular presence in the film's production offices in Shawfield House, Shawfield Street, Chelsea. Caroline Upcher was aged eighteen and staying with the Cammell brothers' parents. She gained herself a job as secretary, typing the handwritten script and assisting Donald, and as a wide-eyed, impressionable teenager she found him and Litvinoff dazzling, overwhelming personalities. Litvinoff was kind and approachable, even if his sense of humour was disturbing; some time later, when Donald was developing his next script, *Ishtar*, they all returned to a flat he and David Cammell shared in Old Church Street and hung out in Donald's bedroom. After a time Litvinoff slipped away for a few moments; then he returned and proceeded to perform a striptease, removing his clothes until he was naked but for a bra, knickers, a suspender belt and stockings, an image that seared itself on to her memory. Still, he was reliably friendly and during *Performance*'s production he always made conversation with her at the office. Then one day he walked past her desk by the door and she looked up to see his face swollen and covered with blue-tinged bruises. 'Oh David,' she said, 'have you had a bad time at the dentist?'

He looked at her oddly without saying a word and then walked away. After he'd gone one of Upcher's colleagues turned to her and in a hushed voice said: 'For God's sake, we have to tell you what's happened. You cannot talk to David like that.'

Upcher was told that Litvinoff had been taken to an old-fashioned block of flats with an atrium in which there was a well surrounded by railings. He had been beaten up by persons unknown and tied to the inside of these railings with his feet dangling over the well, so he could have fallen to his death. They hung a sheet over him and kept him there for an entire weekend, and whenever he came to they knocked him senseless again. That was the story, in any case. It sounds so similar to the incident at his flat on Kensington High Street that one wonders whether the teller stirred in some details from the already extant mythology surrounding him. Others around London heard different explanations around the same time, among them Neil Oram, the former owner of the jazz cafe in Soho called the House of Sam Widges, who in the early 1960s had fended off Litvinoff's overtures on behalf of the twins. 'I was told from two or three different sources that at one point the Krays had tarred and feathered him, and that would be in about 1968,' he said. 'Literally – you'd get tarred and they'd break a bolster for the feathers. It was a particular thing for somebody who double-crosses you. It would be something to do with a deal where he didn't come up with the amount of money that they thought he should have done. He was involved in all sorts of deals.'

If Johnny Shannon was right that the twins willingly gave Litvinoff some ideas for the film, they doubtless felt that he should have paid them a cut of his consultancy fee; if he didn't, that would fit with Oram's theory. Though much later 'Nipper' Read wrote that Litvinoff refused to comment, at the time of their meeting at the Carlton Tower Hotel rumours abounded that he had chosen to assist the police; Francis Ormsby Gore, for instance, later heard that he'd given a statement detailing their connection with Lucian Freud.

It's also suggested that in the late 1960s he ran a gambling club for the twins on the King's Road, in which case he would have been expected to filter through regular payments. Litvinoff himself would later tell people that even after their arrest they had hounded him for his involvement in

Performance, accusing him of taking liberties by putting so much of their world on film: Harry Flowers* obviously being modelled on Ronnie, the 'gangster on the run' theme echoing Frank Mitchell and Micky Fawcett's experiences, Joey Maddocks' business undergoing the same type of 'merger' as Ashburn Place. And whoever shaved Litvinoff's head and wrecked his flat was probably equally unamused to learn that the incident would be recreated on screen. It's plausible: the Krays had killed people for less, as had many of 1960s London's more obscure gangsters with all the twins' viciousness but none of their lust for publicity. Whatever the nature of the punishment or the reason, Litvinoff responded as anyone else would. By now John Pearson had begun his research into the Krays' official biography in earnest and was following up leads he'd been given. Bobby Buckley told Pearson that he needed to talk to Litvinoff and gave him his telephone number at St George's Court, but whenever he called there was no reply. Litvinoff had disappeared, leaving the long-suffering Tim Whidborne to foot a hefty bill from the landlord for redecorating his flat.

If *Performance* captured an era under glass, as Faithfull put it, it documented a moment in which the decade's gathering heat turned London into a crucible in which characters were forged into steel or burned out. After *Performance* Fox retreated from acting to join the Navigators, a group of Christian evangelists, his need for a drastic change precipitated by a combination of his drug intake, his father's cancer diagnosis, his sense of spiritual emptiness, and the conflict of his personal frailty with a cast of domineering characters. Mick Brown tracked down Michèle Breton, who played Lucy, in Berlin in 1995. She recalled the cold hostility on set: 'There was no love there, no understanding between the people. Everybody was on a heavy ego-trip. James Fox was the only person who had some human communication. . .he was very gentle to me.'[34] Brown discovered that she had drifted for years, developed a heroin habit, experienced on watching *Performance* again in 1987 'a feeling of death'. She told him she had done nothing with her life.

Jagger emerged harder than ever. Faithfull noted that he graduated from *Performance* with his public persona fixed: 'In the same way that some actors get to keep their wardrobe, Mick came away from *Performance* with

---

* His name also summons another shady connection: Harry Towers (1920–2009), a film producer and screenwriter, supplier of prostitutes and possible Soviet agent whom Litvinoff may have known through his acquaintance with his girlfriend, Mariella Novotny.

his *character*. This persona was so perfectly tailored to his needs that he'd never have to take it off again. This *is* Mick Jagger as far as most of the world is concerned and by this point probably to himself as well. He came out of *Performance* with two new characters, actually. The one we know and feel whatever it is we feel about it – *that* Mick – and another, more sinister one: the gangster figure, heart-of-stone type.'[35]

By the time of its half-hearted release in January 1971* by a disgusted Warner Bros., *Performance* already seemed a missive from a bygone age. The post-production was bedevilled by studio interference and the fact that the chief protagonists had other projects to pursue. Roeg had had to begin filming *Walkabout* in Australia so Cammell and an editor named Frank Mazzola completed the final edit in Los Angeles without him. Litvinoff was far from the project by then but what emerged still bore his fingerprints. Even the film's grammar offered an uncanny echo of his personality: the jump cuts, intersections between seemingly discrete matters faster than most people could detect the connection, the occasional fade. Deborah Dixon recalled that Litvinoff was 'just a whirlwind coming into the room, six simultaneous conversations on six different levels. His energy and his violence were just incredible, as if his mind didn't fit his body.' The film critic David Thomson noted this parallel in an appraisal of *Performance*: Donald Cammell, he wrote, 'had this friend, David Litvinoff, the most brilliant nutter anyone had ever met. He would talk a blue streak about the most amazing stuff, always jumping from this to that. When *Performance* came out, there were critics who said, "Aha! Note the leaping editorial style, the self-interruption, the cross-streaming of consciousness" – and before I'd sniffed the film, I said, "That is your David Litvinoff." Well, David was the whole film: he knew all your books and authors, but he knew the Krays, too – Reggie and Ronnie – very naughty boys who'd cut you up with a sword. And so David was the catalyst – he just brought the whole thing together.'[36] It appeared from his tone that Thomson knew Litvinoff himself; but when I wrote to ask for his memories he replied that he'd assumed the fictionalised persona of a gangster to write the piece and in truth they'd never met.

'I give the name violence to a boldness lying idle and hankering for danger,' wrote Jean Genet in *The Thief's Journal*. 'It can be seen in a look, a walk, a

---

*   In Britain, that is – in the USA it was released in August 1970.

smile, and it is in you that it creates an eddying. It unnerves you. This violence is a calm that disturbs you. One sometimes says: "A guy with class!"[37]

'A tasty finish, a man of taste.' Chas channels his energy into running a fingertip along the chauffeur's Rolls-Royce. All good art is to some degree violent: it demolishes a previously held conception of the world, then smuggles other people's thoughts into our heads and stimulates ideas that we come to think of as our own, though they are spawned by the intercourse of two minds. Creative and destructive violence, sex and art feed off one another in *Performance* to devastating effect. The film examines the merger of personalities, of social milieus, in a way never achieved before or since. Merger: from the Latin '*mergere*', to dip or plunge, an immersion from which one must emerge, resurface, or else drown. The moment couldn't last.

It's often said that Litvinoff achieved nothing, left nothing behind. True to his life, his contribution to *Performance* is undefinable: no one can agree on its extent, and some of it is contested and political; to play up his input is not to play down that of Donald Cammell, who suffered in his lifetime from seeing the critics and public pay more attention to Nic Roeg's half of their joint-directorship. Rather it is to emphasise the degree to which Litvinoff's brutal experiences, acute observations and creative energy melded with Cammell's own undoubted talents as a writer and artist to create a masterpiece. Just as identities merge in the film, so creatively *Performance* was a collective effort: Cammell and Roeg thought and operated as one on set, Cammell drew deep from Litvinoff's outpourings when the two men were shut in the room with their minds, the pen and the page. A firm consensus emerges that Litvinoff was fundamental to *Performance* becoming what it was: a film that reordered people's thinking, preserved a strange and pivotal moment in which the old barriers had melted away, applied a rare intelligence to analysing the shared impulses between artistic and criminal performers, exposed the parallels of legitimate and illegitimate business, manipulated language to dangerous effect. Achievement has many varieties, and most issue more credit than Litvinoff ever attained, but surely this is an achievement all the same.

Act Three, Scene Two.

JIG: Have you got a Sunday paper with you?

DL: Yes, I have them all.

JIG: Well, if you have a look at the greyhounds you see—

DL: Oh, I haven't got that one.

JIG: Well, it's in all the papers.

DL: I've got the *Jewish Chronicle* and *Our Feathered Friend*, the *New Leader*, the *New Scientist*, the *Atomic Monthly*, and the *Nuclear and Biological and Chemical Warfare Review*.

JIG: Well, there you are. . .

DL: I've been the victim of equestrian unpredictability when I've had a wager or two. Perhaps we could discuss those sort of things because they basically relate to philosophy, don't they?

JIG: They do, yes, very much so, yes. Very much so. Especially with the Roman Legions.

DL: Yes. Seven Tortoiseshells of the Apocalypse.

JIG: That's true, yes.

DL: Is there a subject one mentions that you don't have opinions on. . .?

JIG: Very discreet, I keep them very discreet. . . because I'm very Grecian-minded regarding that. And also very Persian-minded.

DL: Yes. Greasy-minded and Persian-minded. Perhaps in a previous existence you were a Persian.

JIG: Well, there you are, there you are. . .

DL: Your attitude towards work and being industrialised is unyielding as the law of the greasy Persians. And unchanging.

JIG: It is. Now, not to waste too much time, I've got to make my way down there.

DL: Indeed. . . I suppose the best way to do it, John, is to - it's in the King's Road, Chelsea - is to get to Sloane Square by Tube, direct, and then just to walk up. Next door to the Classic. Studio Five. You'll love the place. It's full of gaily coloured posters and gaily coloured people.

JIG: Is there a bell there? How many rings shall I give?

DL: **You walk straight into the building and there's a sort of hallway, and then you go to Studio Five, which is a yellow door, and you speak into it and just say: 'John Ivor Golding, David's friend, and we're all having lunch.'**

JIG: Okay, and have you told Martin I'm coming over?

DL: **Oh yes, he expects you.**

JIG: Okay, well, I'm on my way now.

DL: **Be there about two o'clock.**

JIG: Okay then.

DL: **See you later.**

JIG: Bye bye, Dave.

Part Two

Chapter 8

Celticlimboland

'Llan Ddewi Brefi is a small village situated at the entrance of a gorge leading up to some lofty hills which rise to the east and belong to the same mountain range as those near Tregaron. . . The place wears a remarkable air of solitude, but presents nothing of gloom and horror, and seems just the kind of spot in which some quiet pensive man, fatigued but not soured by the turmoil of the world, might settle down, enjoy a few innocent pleasures, make his peace with God, and then compose himself to his long sleep.'

George Borrow, *Wild Wales*

'When all else fails
Try Wales.'
Christopher Logue, 'To a Friend in Search of Rural Seclusion'

As you drive deep into Ceredigion in midsummer it's hard to keep your eyes on the road. Clouds' khaki shadows creep across steep hillsides flecked with sheep, beaded with drystone walls, crowned with dark copses. You rush down into enveloping woodland, the tree trunks whirring by in a zoetrope flicker, sunlight and shadow strobing through as if beamed by a Morse code signaller on Benzedrine. Blurred green banks of nettles and hedgerows, a glimpse of churning weir, seagulls hanging jauntily on a thermal and pigeons tracing grey waves across the blue sky, dilapidated farm buildings in ashen stone that is more usually blackened by rain. When at last you reach Llanddewi Brefi, you drive further. Narrow winding lanes weave out to the west of the village into farmland divided by the River Teifi, which flows beneath the five-arched, eighteenth-century Pont Gogoyan before twisting twice and broadening into a southward course that runs beside an old stone cottage with a slate roof and whitewashed walls. Between the cottage and the river is a meadow of long grasses riddled with ox-eye daisies and buttercups, and here and there demoiselle damselflies skim by the water's edge. In the sunlit shallow by the bank you peer down to see a shoal of minnows doubled by their shadows, and on the far side hawthorns cast impressionistic reflections on the fretted water. It is the kind of scene that might lazily be labelled 'timeless', though it contains more indicants of time's passage than any urban scape: the damselflies' palpable mortality, the flowers that wilt away in autumn, the tree leaves' future transition from waxen green to mulch on the ground, the thin perpetual white noise of water gushing over river cobbles, downstream and out of view.

The tail end of the 1960s saw a bohemian exodus to the countryside, to reconnect with the land and collect their thoughts after the previous years' intensity. The Rolling Stones' friend Sir Mark Palmer left behind his English Boy model agency, which he'd established above Ossie Clark's boutique Quorum in the King's Road in 1967, to travel the old ways in a horse-drawn gypsy wagon. Much of the period's music reflected this feeling: from Paul McCartney's 'Mother Nature's Son' and John Lennon's unreleased 'Child of Nature', which turned up on *Imagine* in 1971 adapted into 'Jealous Guy', to Ray Davies' winsome laments in *The Kinks are the Village Green Preservation Society*, to Led Zeppelin's 'Bron-y-Aur Stomp', named for the cottage in Snowdonia to which Jimmy Page and Robert Plant retreated in 1970. In the USA Canned Heat caught the spirit with 'Going Up the Country', which conjured the liberating delight of an impromptu flight from the city for a simpler rural life, and Bob Dylan had of course anticipated the trend by recuperating in Byrdcliffe, New York, after his motorcycle crash.

Accompanying this urge towards the pastoral, in Britain at least, came a nostalgic twinge to the parental generation – a retreat into the comfort of the familiar that pastiched the sounds of their childhood (especially the dance bands of the 1940s) while often also invoking the literature that fed their young imaginations. Lennon tweaked the melody from the crooners' standard 'Stay as Sweet as You Are' into the 'White Album' track 'Bungalow Bill'; McCartney nonchalantly knocked off his own take on the tradition in the same record's 'Honey Pie'. English psychedelia, as Ian MacDonald observed in *Revolution in the Head*, drew deeply from the daydream-like, enchanting but faintly disturbing bucolic surrealism of Victorian and Edwardian children's books: Lennon alluded to Lewis Carroll's *Through the Looking Glass* in 'I Am the Walrus' and 'Lucy in the Sky with Diamonds'; Syd Barrett was inspired to name Pink Floyd's debut album by Kenneth Grahame's hallucinatory vision of the Piper at the Gates of Dawn, in which the Rat and the Mole's heightened receptivity in the presence of the divine seemed redolent of the psychedelic experience: 'Never had they noticed the roses so vivid, the willow-herb so riotous, the meadow-sweet so odorous and pervading.'[1] To trade the city for a rural existence seemed to offer bohemian exiles from London a temporal and psychological as well as geographical shift from their pressured urban adult lives.

Few had quite such an imperative to get out of town as David Litvinoff, though. For one, the beating he'd received necessitated leaving London and finding a secret address far from where any underworld performers would be able to find him. Two, he had a book to write. After the *Performance* novelisation had eluded him, his friend Sandy Lieberson had prepared an entrée for a possible book deal for which Litvinoff would write about their mutual comedic hero, the recently deceased Lenny Bruce. Bruce was one of the great Litvinoff obsessions, and one can see why he might relate to a fast-talking Jewish satirist whose 'sick' humour only drew out the sickness of the society that sought to crush him. A small, primitive cottage in west Wales might seem the least likely place to write such a work but Litvinoff had his collection of Bruce's live recordings, a head crammed full of ideas and the book that Andy Garnett had posted him from New York. He acknowledged its receipt in a letter on 20th December 1968:

```
A thousand thanks for your trouble and kindness. . .
HOW HOW HOW HOWL can I repay this debt? Love and
peace, but plenty of lively controversy,
    David
    Last of the Chelsea Meatcutters' Society,
    alive and well and Jewish and constipated in London/
Wales.
```

He would return to London now and again during his time in Llanddewi Brefi, but he had no fixed residence in the capital whereas the riverside cottage known as Cefn-Bedd became his home (the name means 'beyond the grave'; there were old tombstones in the back garden). In an unusual move for a man seeking obscurity, he allowed himself to be listed in the telephone directory: in the 1970 edition for Swansea and South-West Wales there is a 'Litvinoff D, Cefn-y-bedd, Llandewi [*sic*] Brefi, Llangybi 346', the name looking conspicuously alien beside the run of local institutions: Llanarth post office, Llandeilo service station, Llandovery borough council, Llandybie rugby club and so on. While Litvinoff was at heart a metropolitan creature whose horizon usually traced rooftops and chimney pots rather than a sweep of distant pasture, he was probably playing up for comic effect when he told George Melly that he couldn't understand the countryside's appeal. 'David can only breathe in London,' Melly wrote in *Owning Up*, his first volume of autobiography published in 1965. 'We once went to the country to deliver some furniture to somebody's* mother. He was appalled at the waste, at the lack of human activity. "All that grass. All those trees. . ." he speculated irritably. "They must be worth something to somebody." His hatred of nature is so intense that he refuses to acknowledge that there are any separate species of bird. He calls them all – even sparrows – ducks.'

Whether or not he sincerely felt that way back in the 1950s, by the late 1960s Litvinoff loved the countryside, finding it magical. It provided space to think and gain perspective on his life, safety from those who were harassing him and seclusion in which to write the book. The only possible obstacle could be himself.

The first that the villagers of Llanddewi Brefi knew of this stranger's arrival in their midst was when he presented himself one evening in late 1968 at the village shop and post office, which is little changed today, occupying a squat building near the looming grey bulk of the twelfth-century church tower. He explained to the shopkeeper, Gwilym Pugh, that he'd only just arrived in the village, he had no cash and needed provisions, promising to pay him back if he would help. Pugh trusted him and Litvinoff soon repaid the debt. Word spread quickly that there was a newcomer at large, a strange, scar-faced, puckish little man who was staying at the old cottage next to John Griffiths' dairy farm.

Cefn-Bedd, Llanddewi Brefi, as it appears today.

---

*   Andy Garnett's.

Griffiths was a character himself, a London Welshman who could swing his accent between deepest Wales and perfect cockney, and a keen musician too. He and his wife Mair soon bonded with their new neighbour. Goronwy Evans is now a Unitarian minister well established as a prominent community figure in nearby Lampeter, and as a trainee minister in the late 1960s he spent much of his time in Llanddewi Brefi. He encountered Litvinoff for the first time when he walked into the Griffiths' farmhouse to find John playing trumpet, Mair on piano and Litvinoff on typewriter, providing enthusiastic percussion by hammering his hands up and down on the keys.

The family gave him a golden Labrador puppy which he named Jack, after a reference in Rick Danko's verse from 'The Weight' on one of his favourite albums of the time, the Band's *Music from Big Pink*. The dog provided much-needed company. Litvinoff had arrived in Wales in time for winter, when the skies grew dark and the clouds redoubled their year-round efforts to keep the hills and valleys green. The facilities in the cold, damp cottage were primitive: electricity had been installed but no heating, the only sources of warmth being coal fires and a variety of paraffin-burning contraptions. The property belonged to a young man named Andrew Powell, who was working in Edinburgh so his father, the London-based Brigadier Patrick Powell, looked after the letting. 'Whether David answered one of the small ads my father put out or came to know of the place because of its rather tenuous music-industry connection I don't remember,' said Andrew. Previously they had let it to young musicians who needed an occasional discreet hideaway. Litvinoff was 'a fairly difficult tenant, though through a mixture of threats and wheedling I usually got belated payment of the very modest rent,' he said. Litvinoff began to tell any friends who visited that the Brigadier was the elder brother of Enoch Powell, whose infamous anti-immigration 'Rivers of Blood' speech of April 1968 was fresh in the memory. He informed Nicky Samuel that when he first set foot in the cottage he found the bookshelves empty but for a single small volume, and that was a copy of *Little Black Sambo*. Was there any family connection? I asked Andrew. 'No relation!'

As basic as the cottage was, with its doors and windows closed and a log fire burning there should have been little to distract him from writing. The typewriter. The blank page. Lenny's *spiel*. Litvinoff's mind. All he needed was to amalgamate the four components into one brilliant whole. He could write, he knew that. He wrote letters, journalism, poems. He'd written parts of *Performance*; well, dictated them at least. People told him he ought to be a writer, Martin Sharp recalled, though to an extent their comments were platitudinous: 'You know how when someone talks a lot, people say "Why don't you write a book?" Just to. . .well, it's a put-off in a way.' But Litvinoff agreed with them, and had no aversion to describing himself as a writer. He'd pitched for the *Performance* novel, talked (and talked) about writing the libretto for a musical about Antony Armstrong-Jones (slated title: '*Tony!*'). He knew how good he was, or could be: often the cogs in his mind ground so fast he couldn't even catch all the sparks. People with a tenth of his intellect topped the bestseller lists for weeks. So write! But something lay blocked. The energy that should have flowed through his fingertips just short-circuited within his brain. Anything he committed to paper immediately seemed stale, banal: slow and dated compared with the velocity of his ever-moving mind. If he turned the music down he might better hear the voice within his head: but that was precisely why he kept it blasting, echoing back and forth such that Cefn-Bedd's dense stone walls enclosed a cuboid space full of noise. Jack the dog grew so accustomed to the high volume that he could fall asleep with his head resting against a speaker. Litvinoff roared, sobbed, ripped drafts from the typewriter and screwed them up. In mid-Wales no one can hear you scream. As the land darkened the surrounding silence grew louder. Night, the mind's own territory, the object world's analogue for the unconscious. By virtue of two decades' effort he'd syncopated his circadian rhythm to the point where his clearest thoughts emerged in the small hours of the morning. Sometimes he'd walk out with Jack, try to draw clarity from the dark silent stillness. The Welsh night brought a pure multidimensional blackness through which one might move as if in a void, devoid of stimuli, forced to contemplate the half-ignored doubts and fears that lurk within, but also the better to view the faint coloured projections of the imagination. As the cinema lights fade to enable the audience to watch a movie, so nightfall ushers a darkness that brightens the flickering images within the mind. The city's joy lies in its distractions, the countryside's in its lack of them. Or so he hoped. 'Haven't come up with a single damn answer yet, after a year by myself,' he wrote to Sandy Lieberson in January 1970. 'Except maybe some of the questions are a bit more muffled/irrelevant?? Dig?'

Inevitably, in his case, rural relocation also had a Jewish context. For one, he would have known that early Zionist idealism dreamed of a return to agriculture, a reaction to the laws prohibiting *shtetl* Jews from owning land. Two, Dylan's withdrawal to upstate New York had provided a model of a new rustic Jew, a reminder that the common cliché of the Jew as effete, neurotic, urban intellectual had a short history. Litvinoff soon went to the local market in Tregaron, where he bought a dozen farmer's smocks, and took to coupling them with a gypsy-style knotted red necker-chief. While he would never break a sweat here labouring on the fields, he would have been well aware of the traditions that he simultaneously embodied and parodied. It was a camp revival of the Eastern European Jewish character whose decline the Belorussian-born Hebrew author Zalman Shneour lamented in the 1930s when he wrote:

Where are you now, you Jews fashioned like sturdy oaks, with your broad-toed high boots and fleshy, sunburned noses like those of lions? Where are you now, you teamsters, butchers, hod carriers, plasterers, carpenters? Your voices used to roar in rolling echoes, and virility gleamed in your gentle eyes. . . You were the source of supply of the healthy blood and earthly passions of the Jewish people. Had it not been for the boundless energy in your sturdy limbs and the antediluvian fire in your veins, today's Jewry would consist merely of weaklings, of the pointy-nosed idlers, of twisted pates, of windbags, of shrivelled zealots, of gaunt neurasthenics. You rekindled the embers of love and song. In your bodies smouldered the delight and zest of toil. From your simplicity came the nostalgia for field and forest.[2]

In exile Litvinoff also took to describing himself as a 'wandering Jew', likening his own rootlessness and flight from enemies to that of the peripatetic, supranational figure that so haunted the anti-Semitic imagin-ation, compelled to roam the globe owing to his inability to recognise the Messiah or assimilate wholly into any nation but his own people's mysterious worldwide fraternity. He did so with irony while acknowledging its literal truth: and knowing that he embodied an anti-Semitic archetype he'd ramp it up further for dramatic effect as a retort to society. You want a wandering Jew? I'll give you a wandering Jew. Now try to pin me down.

There were many ways to avoid writing the book. He grew obsessed by making music compilations on reel-to-reel tapes. He filled around thirty such tapes for Nigel Waymouth, each containing at least three hours of recordings, each accompanied by neatly typed pages of notes. The content was beyond diverse: reams of pre-war Cajun and zydeco, Django Reinhardt, Jimmy

Witherspoon, Sleepy John Estes' endearingly lyrical blues, sermons by the dubious American evangelist Aimee Semple McPherson (there for amusement value), Art Tatum, Randy Newman, the grand, cracked late recordings of the near-broken Billie Holiday, ragas by Ustad Vilayat Khan and Ravi Shankar, the touching ethereal piety of Washington Phillips, Harold Pinter plays including *The Caretaker*, Miles Davis with his tone as chill as a ghost's breath, John Lomax's recordings of Angola prison work songs, Bach piano compositions riddled with arpeggios that at once ascend and descend like an Escher staircase, ska and rocksteady singles that had been making their way from Jamaica to London's sharper clubs in the previous five years. One featured ska singer, still alive today, had had a run-in with Litvinoff a few years earlier: 'This is a spade singer-ponce from Wardour Street circa '65 who put an iron bar across my head at that time,' he explains in the notes, using a racial epithet more common then even among people such as Litvinoff with no sympathy for racism. 'All good clean fun and I put him in here for historical interest.' Then a sublime comic monologue from Lord Buckley, whose jive-poetic cadences ring through at times in Litvinoff's letters, a burst of Tijuana Brass, drag artist Lee Sutton's live album *A Near 'Miss'?*, singles by Manfred Mann, an excerpt from Gandhi's funeral service (note to Waymouth: 'Got the full five hours, more if you want?'), Frank Sinatra, Stravinsky's *The Rite of Spring*, Albert Ammons and more in such vein.

Then there was the lingering post-production of *Performance*. He had a telex machine in the cottage through which he communicated with the office in London. Stills from the shoot lay strewn around the furniture, along with a typed sheet of the lyrics to 'Memo from Turner', which he presented to visitors as evidence that he'd written the song. His friends began to beat a path between London and this remote patch of Wales. When Gerry Goldstein came to stay, the pair exploited Goldstein's passing resemblance to Bob Dylan to fool the locals into believing that Litvinoff had Dylan living there under the pseudonym 'Gerry'. When *Nashville Skyline* was released in April 1969 and Litvinoff showed them the cover, the villagers remarked in surprise: 'Look, Gerry's got a record out!'*

---

*   Some remain adamant that Dylan stayed there. I emailed his manager Jeff Rosen, which prompted an amicable occasional correspondence over the first half of 2015, at the outset of which he said he would ask Mr Dylan when he had time; but at the time of this book's publication, resolving the matter had inexplicably failed to ascend to the top of Mr Dylan's 'to do' list, and so the mystery remains.

Goldstein brought Ricky Levesley over for a while, to give him a refreshing change from his institutionalised life in London. Their old friend Marc Bolan was another who made the trek out to Cefn-Bedd along with his bandmate Mickey Finn. The fourteen-year-old Rob Parrett, an aspiring guitarist growing up nearby, would tell his parents he was going fishing and then slip down the road to the cottage. There were occasions when he carried on to the river, having clocked that it wasn't a good moment, such as the time when he spotted Litvinoff naked up a tree and clutching an axe, but more often than not Parrett called by and was received with great kindness. It was an eye-opening experience for a teenage boy: on one occasion he was promptly given a glass of champagne which he was instructed to take through to the bathroom for Bolan's girlfriend, a beautiful woman whom he found luxuriating naked in the bath. Also present was a menacing character known only as the Jester and dressed as such, who was there as her minder. Parrett was at the cottage with his brother on the afternoon of 2nd July 1969. 'We were there and the phone rang and it was Brian Jones,' he said. Jones had been sacked from the Rolling Stones less than a month earlier. Litvinoff spoke with him for half an hour, pressing the record button on his tape player as he sat down to listen to a confused and rambling Jones telling him what a nice man he was, explaining that he had taken Mandrax, moaning about Mick Jagger, continuing in this vein and growing increasingly hard to comprehend. Litvinoff came off the phone looking troubled and told Parrett: 'That was Brian Jones. . . I'm very worried about him.' That night Jones drowned in his swimming pool. In the weeks that followed Litvinoff played the tape recording (which has long since vanished) to various guests, one of whom said: 'Shouldn't you submit this to the coroner for the inquest?' He just laughed.

It is hard to reconcile the tranquillity surrounding Cefn-Bedd now with the scene that visitors describe from those times. Daimlers, Jaguars and Rolls-Royces became a familiar sight squeezing down the lanes and parking by the cottage. The Rolling Stones came to say hello: in the village post office Litvinoff told an excited throng of schoolgirls that he had Cliff Richard waiting in the car outside, but when he ushered them out they were crest-fallen only to find a bemused Keith Richards. Mick Jagger watched John Griffiths flattening molehills on his field and expressed concern for the moles' welfare, at which Griffiths quipped back: 'You give me your Roller and I'll give you mine.'[3] Sir Mark Palmer and Nigel Waymouth floated into the village in their finery. Jimi Hendrix apparently called by. The recently married John Lennon and Yoko Ono stayed at a bed and breakfast in the nearby village of Pontrhydfendigaid and seem to have paid Litvinoff a call, as he wrote to Lieberson that they'd given him some of their acorns which he was using to massage his aching feet: 'I use them rather a lot for one of my tender years.' On sunny days Litvinoff would hoist his stereo's speakers up into the branches of the trees by the cottage and blast music out across the fields while he and his friends went skinny-dipping in the river or lounged naked on sofas in the meadow, smoking hash. When he left the cottage he'd lock the door and then hang the key in plain view over a twig of the rosebush that grew around the entrance arch, which was endearingly trustful but not a habit likely to keep his landlord happy. Before long the stories of the scene gathering around Cefn-Bedd reached Andrew Powell via his father, the Brigadier. 'He certainly inspired a number of spectacular rumours and I did once go down there to investigate,' Powell said. 'He had installed a reel-to-reel tape recorder and several enormous speakers in the tiny sitting room and since he played music at full volume almost all the time conversation was difficult. I dimly remember smoking some insipid dope while he spoke (so he claimed) to Mick Jagger on the phone. He was entertaining if eccentric company and we got on rather well. When I left he presented me with a square of hardboard covered in painted squiggles that he claimed was an unsigned Patrick Caulfield. To the surprise of absolutely no one, it wasn't.'

The stories also led a local newspaper reporter to turn up at the cottage with a brief to write an article about this man who was bringing Swinging London to rural Wales. The journalist was a humourless, strait-laced character with an antagonising air of self-importance. When he shooed Litvinoff's recently acquired cat off a chair before sitting down, Litvinoff barked: 'Don't do that – he fucking lives here, you fucking don't.' He goaded the journalist that he'd missed a major scoop: he should have dropped by last week when God came to visit. Litvinoff was referring to Eric Clapton. His guest soon made his excuses and no story appeared in the press.

But to most others at this stage he proved a welcome addition to their world. Goronwy Evans loved his 'croeso', his hospitable attitude, and was cheered when Litvinoff and Jack led the way in a charity fundraising walk around the country lanes that he organised. Residents of a nearby caravan park were grateful, if somewhat perplexed, when he turned up unannounced one day to give them each a new frying pan that he'd bought at Tregaron market. Raymond Daniel, a young photographer, lived nearby and became intrigued by this man who was drawing so many new faces into the village. He got friendly with Litvinoff and tried to take his picture, but Litvinoff didn't want to be photographed; it was at such moments that he remembered he was meant to be in hiding. Whenever Daniel looked through the viewfinder Litvinoff would pull down his trousers and underpants and stand there exposing himself until Daniel put the camera away. The photographer hatched a plan. He grew to know Litvinoff's daily routine, and that he would visit the village store and post office at a certain time: so he placed his camera on a wall and used a remote trigger to take a photo without his subject noticing.

Outside Llanddewi Brefi post office and general stores.

I wondered at first whether I'd ever locate a photograph, whether I'd be able to gauge his existence only through its impact on others – James Fox's acting, Lucian Freud's portrait, associates' contradictory recollections. ('With Litvinoff, what is there apart from lots of people talking about him?' said Iain Sinclair.) Why the hell would anyone have a photo of a man who lived between worlds and feared being pinned down? Then I bought Lyn Ebenezer's book *Operation Julie*, published in summer 2010, which features Daniel's picture. His face was just too distant to discern the detail …where were these scars everyone mentioned? I also found it in the book's publicity pack on the internet and, like a twenty-first-century version of David Hemmings in *Blow-Up*, zoomed in on the image in search of evidence. Litvinoff's face revealed nothing, only retreated into pixellated abstraction, and I found myself gazing with discontent at a chequered screen of varyingly grey squares; the closer I looked, the less I could see.

The book describes the world's biggest LSD bust, which took place in Llanddewi Brefi in 1977. In the 1970s the village assumed metropolitan proportions on the secret map of countercultural Britain. Alston 'Smiles' Hughes and his acid-dealing cohort lined up bottles of champagne on the bar of the local inn, lit their cigars with five-pound notes. A pretty policewoman named Julie Taylor went undercover. Six million tabs of LSD were recovered and £800,000 discovered in Swiss bank accounts; seventeen defendants got 130 years between them. 'Julie's Been Working For The Drug Squad,' sang Joe Strummer the following year, fixing the hippies' fate in punk folklore. Ebenezer places Litvinoff as the vanguard for the psychedelic army.

'Llanddewi Brefi, long before Little Britain*. . .and even before an LSD ring was operating locally, was well known to the London in-crowd and its beautiful people,' he writes. 'The visits by Keith Richards, Hendrix and Clapton. . .all add up to more than coincidence. So, eight years before Operation Julie, the area was known as a secluded drugs paradise. David Litvinoff, like John the Baptist, may have been the man who led the way that others would follow.'[4]

Around Llanddewi Brefi the weather veers from volatile to melancholic. You can watch a glowing sunset on a summer night then step out the next morning into a crisp valley cloaked in mist, each further hillside a paler shade of mint, criss-crossed hedgerows and old oaks pencil-sketched in the haze; silhouettes, leaden sky, sharpened air, softened forms. Sometimes the day rouses itself and dissipates the moisture, but more often the gloom sets in to stay. Growls and gusts of wind, drum rolls of rain against the window ad nauseam, trickles latticing the glass. It didn't help his temper. 'It's been raining torrents for five days now and I'm feeling liquefied,' he wrote to Sandy Lieberson; in another letter to Lieberson he spoke of being 'back here. Alone. Feeling low and mean. Not even a bloody passing stranger to come upon the scene.' He reminded Lieberson

---

*   Matt Lucas and David Walliams filmed the television comedy's 'Only Gay in the Village' sketch there.

of his 'standing invitation for this godforsaken rain-drenched hole'. As 1969 rolled towards the new decade he got away when he could. In August he travelled down to Redlands to join a party of Keith Richards' friends that included John Dunbar, Donald Cammell, Michael Cooper, Tony Sanchez and Robert Fraser as they sailed overnight by yacht to the Isle of Wight Festival, where Bob Dylan would make his comeback appearance. He headed back to the Pheasantry, where Philippe Mora was making a film financed by Eric Clapton and the Australian painter Arthur Boyd, and shot on the 'short ends' of unused film stock from *Performance*, provided by Lieberson. Mora pulled together as many of his Australian friends in London as he could for *Trouble in Molopolis*, a 'Brechtian fable' and tribute to vintage Hollywood (the *Threepenny Opera* meets the Marx Brothers, in Mora's words) in which a mayor bans milk and then has to contend with 'milkeasies' popping up all over his city. Germaine Greer played a cabaret singer, Martin Sharp a mime artist, Richard Neville a public relations man – and with typical *chutzpah* he cast Litvinoff in a cameo as a man being harassed by a pair of gangsters, who force a gun into his mouth.

Litvinoff in *Trouble in Molopolis*.

As for his lead role, the mayor of Molopolis, he needed someone who could give a convincing portrayal of a man with psychiatric difficulties. 'I said to David, "Can you find me a lunatic?"' Mora said. 'He said, "No problem, I'll find you a lunatic."' He produced John Ivor Golding. Golding had arrived for lunch with Martin Sharp on that rainy Sunday, Litvinoff didn't. His joke at Sharp's expense was Golding's entrée to the Pheasantry. Once he was in, like Mac Davies he proved hard to shift. While Clapton withdrew, Mora embraced him, temporarily at least, as the star of his movie. Sharp and Neville granted him a page to present his views in *Oz* number 24, the 'Beautiful Freaks' issue of October–November 1969. He's introduced with a brief biography: 'John Ivor Golding: Welsh genius drop-out, lateral talking drifter. When in town resides at a men's hostel near Drury Lane. Lives off disability pension of less than £4 a week. One time: photographer for *Picture Post*. Gunner in Singapore. Dancer in BBC chorus line. Recently discovered by prodigy Chelsea film maker [i.e. Mora]. Mr Golding ("call me J.G.") is renowned for his unscheduled guest appearances at such social high-spots as the Ritz – for the christening of Lord Harlech's grand-daughter – and George Harrison's home – where the new-cool pop celebrities were not amused.'[5] Golding gained a brief notoriety for such intrusions into exclusive events, these absurd Dadaist situations often engineered by Litvinoff. At the premiere of Mora's film he passed out in an alcoholic stupor, wetting himself as he sat collapsed in his front-row seat. Soon he would be taken into psychiatric care again and would return to Wales, where in 1973 a student film-maker named Neil White shot a short film about him titled simply *J. G.*, a portrait of Golding as a voluntary day patient at Whitchurch Psychiatric Hospital, Cardiff. A couple of years later Golding died.

If Litvinoff's time in Wales felt bleak, back in the city the fading, souring decade left him increasingly alienated. Neither location satisfied. He had been trying to reconfigure his personality in Wales, to connect with something deep and organic in the country as opposed to the brittle hip posturing that surrounded him in London, trying to eschew the tinny jaundiced pleasures of irony and cultivate a new truthfulness, seeking at last to secure himself a role that had some basis in reality. If he succeeded to any extent, he felt no better. Even in the depths of depression, though, finding himself in the numbness that lies beyond sadness, he managed to summon a typically self-lacerating strain of humour. He wrote Lieberson a letter in which he laid himself bare. It is presumably from Cefn-Bedd around this time, though he gave no date and only an address that riffed on the long Welsh place names that surround Llanddewi Brefi.

```
Fromdavidincelticlimbolandwherenothingisthenormand
                                      quiterightlyso.
```

```
Dear Sandy. . .,
    Thanks a lot for your groovy p.c. Almost my major
event of the month, certainly the nicest.
    I had a simple address once: 2302179 Levy David. H.
M. Prison, Sparkhill, Birmingham 8. One day I may
oblige you by patronising the same ever welcoming
Property Management Company.
    When am I coming to London? Ain't got no plans. Why
be crushed, miserable and pointless in London, when I
can [be] blue, manic and depressed in Wales. You do
get my point I hope.
    I don't seem to have emotions just now, but if I
did, I would love you all too. I feel very honest
these days (quote from Robert Maxwell/Joe Hyman* et
al).
    A groove that 'what I need is available in London'
etcetera. 'Tis a thousand pities, Ladye mine, that I
languish in the fields and bridle paths'. Felt quite
high just thinking about it!
    Forward into the Seventies with Harold Wilson!
    Again, my love to you all down there.
    David.
```

The prison reference, if it were not a pure invention,[†] may have referred to a spell in custody ahead of the aborted Ricky Levesley trial. The snippet of Romantic-style poetry seems to have been his own. Sceptical references to Harold Wilson's premiership litter his other letters from the time,

---

[*]   Ruthless chairman of the textile company Viyella International, and one of the 1960s' most prominent businessmen.
[†]   It must be at least partly fabricated, as HMP Birmingham is not in Sparkhill.

suggesting that the reference here was sarcastic and his former enthusiasm for socialism had waned into something more despairing. At the same time, his weariness with the hardening attitudes prevailing in the Rolling Stones–Robert Fraser–Donald Cammell set became ever more apparent. 'Robert Fraser I hear sold to Rory McEwen* for 1,350 quid the sounds I left for him by having tapes made for them,' he wrote in another letter to Lieberson. 'Baby, we're beginners at this game, yes? Have you ever tried to get blood out of a stone? That's been my experience lately with the cowboys of Cheyne County.† Mick asked me to make him a number of tapes of old stuff I've scored down here in return for a demo of their Alabama stuff. Now he says he's lost it.' He reported having heard the 'Alabama stuff' in January 1970, in a letter that also describes his first – and, by comparison with his young friends, belated – experience with LSD. He went on his 'virgin trip (can you believe it?), in London,' he said. 'Groovy at Mick/Marianne's, bummed badly when back Chez Donaldos.‡ Locked up in room in empty house, whilst he and his Coptic entourage dined out.'§ He preferred to dwell on his time with Jagger and Faithfull: 'Heard beautiful sounds at Mick's for *Ned Kelly*, from Dylan and Johnny Cash. Sample. He sings this as a funereal lament. Very beautiful too.' He goes on to quote the lyrics from 'Wild Horses', which the Stones had recorded the previous month at Muscle Shoals and would release in April 1971 on *Sticky Fingers*. 'Never heard Mick into this mature kind of bag,' he observed. 'First time to me he sounds like a man and not an English Goy kid.'

Acid became a serious enthusiasm. Christopher Gibbs described him as evangelical on the subject. It had already reshaped many of their friends' outlooks, fostering the era's ethos of collectivity, their discrete individual minds partaking of, or at least aspiring towards, a universal consciousness, the perceived psychic boundaries falling away. 'Acid changed his life a lot,' said one close friend of the Stones who often saw him in Wales. 'It changed all our lives. It can't not open your mind. He stopped being a criminal really when he took acid, because that's what it does, it's

---

* Scottish folksinger and artist, in the latter respect best known for his botanical paintings.
† Playing on Jagger and Richards' London address and a reference to Chaynee County in the Dylan song 'John Wesley Harding'.
‡ Donald Cammell.
§ Probably referring to friends such as Kenneth Anger, who cast Cammell as Osiris in his film *Lucifer Rising*.

the truth drug. It makes you look at yourself and see things, and lies after acid are a bit pointless. But then he used lies in a different way, to tell the truth, so he probably carried on! He told outrageous lies but they always contained the truth in some weird way: he used lies to tell the truth.' He kept a container of tabs in the freezer and revelled in turning people on when he had company, at other times tripping alone: once he spent a night in the garden during a thunderstorm, directing the lightning.

In another letter he pursues a conversation he and Lieberson had had about the Lenny Bruce book being published by Calder and Boyars, although he muses first on a since-forgotten proposal that Mick Jagger (or 'Mick the Knife' in Litvinoff's sardonic assessment) might follow his acting debut in *Performance* by playing Jelly Roll Morton, the great New Orleans jazz pianist and bandleader.

```
Jelly Roll was a big man, A FUCKING BIG MAN INDEED,
one of the heavies of all time. Can our young friend
agreeably impersonate such a one. Only time and the
river will tell. Don't shoot until you see the small
print of their eyes contracts. Enclosed is a letter
to Marion Boyars* (was there ever a Boyars plot).† I
did behave PROFESSIONALLY! As you put it so discreetly
dear, I waited a minute or so before asking her if she
was a dyke or was there room for an old Jewish hippy
in her crowded literary life. She seemed taken aback,
apart or afront (affront, get it?). Look here she
said. Where I said. Here she said. Oh there I said.
That's right she said. It's dark in there I said.
Don't worry she said. I'm not I said. I just haven't
done this thing before. And on the telephone too. And
to music too as Mae West (Mike Sarne's‡ discovery)
said. Send me a letter she said. I will I said. What
```

---

*   Former independent publisher who in 1963 joined Calder to form Calder and Boyars.

†   *Ivan the Terrible Part Two: the Boyars' Plot*, a 1946 film by Sergei Eisenstein, disapproved of by Joseph Stalin for its depiction of state terrorism and later confiscated and probably destroyed.

‡   Actor and briefly pop star, in which incarnation best known for his 1962 hit 'Come Outside', with Wendy Richard.

shall I put in it. What you fucking like she said.
Will you read the poxy thing I said. No she said
(demurely) I fucking won't. O.K. then I said (I
concluded too) I'll write it then.

Actually Sandy, it's all quite cool. We talked about
and around the project and directly on to it, and
achieved some kind of understanding I feel. She was
obviously (as you'll have gathered) not too wildly
optimistic about [the book] in its existing format. I
can see her point. It would probably need a deal of
promotion which Calder and B don't give their stuff.
I know for a fact that their books have to 'do their
own graft' in a manner of speaking. Get me? So she
suggested I put a few ideas in a letter to her and we'd
meet when I got to London. It was all nice and cool
and friendly and rational etcetera, but I've got this
fucking dog case, which I'm defending myself here at
the local quarter sessions. I don't want my dogs
destroyed. Apart from you and yours, my dog Jack is
my only true friend and I love and respect him. Did
you know you can have respect for a dog. <u>Boundless</u>
respect too. (We're just good friends.) Anyway, Sandy,
I've attached the letter to Marion Boyars (see how
cautious/cool I can be). If it's not too mad, get your
secretary to lick the flap and put it in one of H.M.'s
red pillar boxes. Otherwise chuck it away. (I threw it
all away said Bob).* So did I. But he's still got a bit
left. What have I got. I only have eyes for you. . .

Money, you postscripted. Vot's dat. A balm you say.
To ease away the pain you say. Sounds O.K. by me. (By
me's alright Hyman Kaplan†). I'm not working and
living in 'a society like ours' - your quote - I think
maybe I'm dying in it. Dying by the hour. There's a

---

*   'I Threw It All Away', from *Nashville Skyline*, Bob Dylan, 1969.
†   Hyman Kaplan, or rather in his preferred styling H*Y*M*A*N K*A*P*L*A*N, is the hero
of Leo Rosten's (writing as Leonard Q Ross) comic stories about an Eastern European-born
Jewish New Yorker's endearing but ill-fated attempts to master the English language.

lovely line of the great Bessie Smith. She says: *I
woke up this morning. I had the blues five different
ways.* Now that's great stuff Sandy. Later in the
bridge of the song she comes on with this: *If the
blues don't* <u>*kill*</u> *me, they will* <u>*thrill*</u> *me through and
through.*

Love to All of You Dave.

The potential for sadness was always present. If all the strands concurrent
in his mind were musical notes, only one needed to descend a semitone to
turn the chord minor. The weather, his isolation and his uncertainty over
the book were more than enough to plunge him into a trough, and the 'dog
case' was a distraction he could have done without. As he'd told Lieberson,
Jack had become his great source of comfort and consistent company
during his exile. While Litvinoff didn't keep Jack on a lead he usually stayed
at heel. Sometimes, though, people would find him roaming the village or
the fields. Usually they would drive him back to the cottage but on one
such occasion on 10th January 1970, there were repercussions. Over the
winter John Griffiths had another farmer's sheep 'in tack', kept safe in his
lowland field rather than in the more exposed conditions of the farmer's
hillside holding. The teenage Cledwyn Davies was working on the fields
when he saw Jack savaging and killing one of the sheep. He had to report
what he had seen, so Litvinoff found himself facing three criminal charges:
of being the owner of a dog found worrying sheep on 10th January, the
same charge relating to another date in which a sheep had been attacked,
and failing to keep a dog under control during the hours of darkness, to all
of which he pleaded not guilty. The next quarter sessions were to be held in
May before Tregaron Magistrates, who sat at the town's Memorial Hall.
The night before the case Raymond Daniel passed by the field to hear a
strange yowling sound, and on investigating further he found Litvinoff had
procured a bitch for Jack in order to give him one final night of pleasure
before his likely death sentence. Davies was summoned to give evidence
and, shaking with nerves, he read a statement saying that he had witnessed
the dog covered with sheep's blood. Then it was Litvinoff's turn to provide
his defence. He left the witness box and began to stride around the court
remonstrating and gesticulating while he made an impassioned case for
Jack not to be destroyed. The court records and brief report in the *Cambrian*

News give only the bare facts, but reading between the lines one imagines that the bench had no idea what had hit them and swiftly resolved to draw a line under the affair. He was found guilty of the offence that Davies had witnessed, acquitted of the second, and they withdrew the third, while, most importantly, Jack's life was spared. Under the headline 'DOG OWNER FINED' the newspaper reported that 'David Litvinoff, a 36-year-old writer of Cefn Bedd, Llanddewi Brefi, was fined £2 by Tregaron Magistrates'.[6] He was also ordered to pay £8, 14s, 6d in costs. But while the report lacks detail, on closer scrutiny that opening sentence alone is revealing. None of the first three 'facts' about him was true: he was David Levy, aged forty-two and he was incapable of committing words to a manuscript.

He returned to Cefn-Bedd but something had changed. He wasn't seen out so often. In the village he would blank people who said hello, and he no longer acknowledged Davies' existence. He had leaned on the young Rob Parrett to vouch for him in court; Parrett didn't want to commit perjury and Litvinoff grew intimidating, causing him to stop visiting. In September 1970 Litvinoff travelled down to Somerset for the first Pilton Pop Festival, later to become the Glastonbury Festival. Soon after arriving he broke an ankle but remained there without getting treatment, and returned to Wales in agony, his mood worse still. Soon afterwards, Lyn Ebenezer was introduced by a mutual friend and invited to call by on the proviso that he did not publicise their meeting; Ebenezer was a young journalist at the time. He knocked on the door at 10am to be greeted with a yell from the upstairs window – 'Who the fuck is that at this time of the morning?' – but when he explained Litvinoff perked up and invited him in. He played Ebenezer his recordings of Brian Jones and of John Ivor Golding, including an excerpt where Golding speaks with Sandy Lieberson, whose voice Litvinoff claimed was that of Bob Dylan. Ebenezer noticed on the mantelpiece an invitation to the funeral of Jimi Hendrix, who had died on 18th September. It was due to be held on 1st October in Seattle. Attached to the invitation was a sweet laced with LSD, which anyone who couldn't attend was instructed to take at the same time as the funeral.

Goronwy Evans visited soon after that. 'Would you like a sweet?' his host enquired. Evans declined, deciding that he didn't fancy one. Not long afterward Litvinoff had another visitor, a local policeman. This time his guest accepted the offer. He lay tripping on the sofa for hours, his walkie-talkie emitting increasingly frantic blasts from his headquarters as they tried to determine his whereabouts, before finally Litvinoff enlisted a villager to drive him back to the police station.

Even after they had been jailed for murder, even despite their apparent anger before he fled London, the Kray twins exerted a hold on him. He remained fascinated by their dark charisma and conflicted in his feelings. Following their imprisonment he took a trip back to London during which he bumped into their associate Micky Fawcett after a gap of several years. Fawcett and a friend were walking down Oxford Street when he hailed them: 'Hello, hello! You all right? I thought you two would be at the bottom of the Thames by now with fruit machines round your legs.' Fawcett took the joke. It was the first time he'd seen Litvinoff since Ronnie had had him 'dealt with'. 'We didn't comment on the fact he had these marks, like this,' he said, running his fingers outward from the sides of his lips. 'The guy I was with said afterwards it looked like cat's whiskers. I said to Litvinoff, "What about the 'other two',* eh?" because they were doing thirty years each by then. And he says, "You know, I don't know if I'm sorry to see them go or not." There's no reply to that is there, when he's standing there with these scars on his face?'

At this time his letters suddenly began to sound buoyant again. He'd broken through and the words were flowing at last. Naturally he was keen to know whether the publisher had given Lieberson any indication of their interest. 'Everything here very quiet,' he wrote. 'Though the insistent click of this machine is heard throughout the land on Lennie project. My mind is really starting to loosen up on the book now. It's as if I were sort of constipated about it before. Maybe it's just diarrhoea now. Only time and possibly a publisher's reaction will tell... Sandy. That talk we had (or was it a soliloquy/ monologue): please treat as cancelled. From now on it's all systems go baby! (God! What crap I write. Lord have mercy!).'

His mood must have been boosted by a characteristically canny piece of dealing that had landed him a copy of Dylan's experimental novel *Tarantula*, which was written in 1965–6 and available on the black market for the next five years until its publication in 1971. 'Sandy, by devious (and I do mean devious baby) means I've scored the manuscript of Dylan's

---

* As the twins were often known to their friends.

unpublished novel,' he wrote. 'He junked it a couple of years back. Believe me it's insane. Fantastic. The imagery is wild. He's really been there in this book. And come back to tell the tale. His statement on Humpty Dumpty is a masterpiece of Bergsonian compression. Shall we be naughty and mimeograph a hundred thousand bootleg copies at forty shillings per?? Shall we be that naughty? It would sell the odd copy or two I feel.'

He received the book from a friend identified only as Arnold, and in writing to thank him he noted that Dylan bore parallels with Lenny Bruce in his character and total commitment to his art. In writing about Bruce, Litvinoff could only try to reconstruct the man from his words, a maddening business: he found himself pursuing a ghost, tantalised by the hints of his presence, haunted by what had vanished beyond recovery. 'Fact of it is that both Lennie and Dylan are always "on",' he wrote. 'In the sense I mean that they are always flowing. Fuck only knows what pearls of Lennie's have been lost. Sunk without trace.'

But he kept pushing ahead and three weeks later he remained on a high. His continued effervescence is apparent from his next letter to Lieberson, which came laden with references he knew the Jewish-American film producer would unpack.

```
LLANGYBI 346                              Cefn Bedd.
                                    Llanddewi Brefi,
                                       near Tregaron,
                                      Cardiganshire.
                               September 29th, 1970.


Dear Sandy,


    WHY NOT a film about the great contraceptive wars
of the Lower East Side? It would be better than one
about the loves of a tennis pro, surely?
    A lovely envelope containing g—ss. From you obvi-
ously??? Gee, that was swell 'f ya, real swell (As
Anne Sheridan used to say to Jimmy Cagney, back in the
Oomph Girl* days). . .(see 'The Life and Loves of a
```

---

*   Sheridan's nickname in her time as a 1940s Hollywood pin-up.

Catholic Pederast' by Albert Z. Zugsmith,[*] pub. by the
Yale University Press for the Breen Office[†] in 1949 at
25 cents (mailed in plain wrapper). I refer to the
Hyman Kaplan[§] translation naturally.). . .

Is no news good news where the Lenny Bruce book is
concerned? I've been deluged with silence where this
is concerned? I am now really into the feeel [*sic*] of
the thing, Sandy. After much listening to the feed-
back I get from Lenny, I know I've finally broken
through to the clear plateau of understanding what he
was really all about. You know this could represent
the Last Stand of the Printed Word As We Know It.

Seriously though, man, is anything concrete
happening? I'd love to know if it is.

Summer. . .

You old Indian Summer[‡]. . .

Love (How much we all need it)!!

Dave.

Friends continued to visit now and then. Lieberson and his young
family spent a week there, Michael and Jane Rainey (née Ormsby Gore) and
their children stayed a while too. In London the artist Caroline Coon arranged
for a blues collector named Jim Vyse and his friend Derek Cattell to visit for
a weekend and sell him some reel-to-reel tapes. When Vyse spoke to him in
advance on the telephone Litvinoff veered between excitement about the
music and sudden bursts of crying as he reminisced about the poverty of his
childhood. When the pair visited they listened to music and the Brian Jones
tape, and discussed politics. They were both Trotskyists but found themselves
floored by his clipped retort to their vision of a new world: 'So what would you
do about the Mafia?' He made another comment that lodged in Cattell's
mind. 'After playing us some us out-takes of Stones tracks that would soon
appear on the *Sticky Fingers* album, he heaped praise on Keith Richards,

---

[*] American director and producer of 'exploitation' movies whose credits included *Sex Kittens Go to College* and *Female on the Beach*.

[†] The Hollywood movie censorship office while under the stewardship of Joseph Breen, a Catholic layman and venomous anti-Semite.

[‡] A phrase from 'Indian Summer', the crooner's standard performed by Frank Sinatra et al.

saying that he was really concentrating on becoming a world-class guitarist,' Cattell recalled. 'Then he turned to me and quietly said: "These people are only really interested in me as I'm a forty-year-old oddity."'

That afternoon they drove into Lampeter in a Mini, with Litvinoff 'clinging on to his huge dog in the back'. There they bumped into his new friend Julian Cayo Evans, the leader of the Free Wales Army, who had recently left jail after being convicted for 'conspiracy to cause explosions' in English property in Wales. Litvinoff introduced them: 'Jim and Derek, Trotskyists, meet Cayo Evans, terrorist.' When they returned to the cottage an excited Litvinoff announced that he'd had an idea: 'I thought we'd all take an acid trip,' he said. He took a matchbox from the fridge and removed 'what looked like the cut-off heads of matches', but 'turned out to be the strongest and purest LSD. Litvinoff cut the acid tab with a razor blade and we picked up small fragments on our licked fingers.'

It took about twenty minutes for the acid to take effect. 'As I sat on the lawn of Cefn-Bedd that summer's day in 1970, the blades of grass gradually appeared as a mass of struggling tiny people,' Cattell said. 'I remember the vivid colours, strange perspectives and extended time. I felt I could step into the music coming from the speakers set up in the garden. That afternoon the mercurial David Litvinoff had introduced me to a world of drugs that would become an intricate part of my life for the next few years. I was just seventeen years old.'

He made a daisy chain for Litvinoff – the response, a barbed 'I see you're making yourself useful then' – and as the light faded and the insects flew up from the River Teifi they retreated into the house. When they left the next morning Litvinoff gave him a clutch of gifts, among them recordings of the Stones' Muscle Shoals demos and the newly published hippie book, *Playpower* by Richard Neville, editor of *Oz* magazine. Litvinoff had previously planned to return it to the author, who wouldn't much have enjoyed the message he'd scrawled inside: 'This book is a downer – a fake – A pile inducing darksome diorama by a self-promoting born non-entity – It holds out no hope. None at all. Thank you Neville but no thanks.' Neville's *Oz* collaborator Martin Sharp made the journey up from London later that year.

He remembered walking by the river when a huge salmon leapt out of the water, causing him and Litvinoff to look at each other in shock for an instant. But the presiding emotion he detected was sadness again. Litvinoff seemed very alone. 'I could tell he was getting very depressed then,' Sharp said, 'and I wanted to offer him an alternative of some kind, which he took.'

* * *

He had been in Llanddewi Brefi almost two years. He'd left an indelible mark on the village, to the point where people speak of him now as if he were there yesterday. But the anonymity he'd half-heartedly tried to assume had failed, not least owing to his constant need for human contact and the consequent stream of friends who'd come to stay. By the spring of 1970 he had already written to Gerry Goldstein about a less welcome appearance on his doorstep: a little-known criminal associate from Soho whom he hadn't seen for three years, one of those who in the early 1960s loitered with him opposite the House of Sam Widges on the corner of Berwick Street and D'Arblay Street. His visitor banged on the door at 2am having been 'on the run from Stafford Nick* for about 7 weeks or so,' Litvinoff said. 'Filthy dirty, without a penny to his name, starving, living rough, he had tramped and hitched his way from the North to the West country (Cornwall) looking for me he said, and someone told him I was in Wales. He'd got to North Wales worked his way to the West of Wales and people at the newspaper office of the *Cambrian Times* said they thought I lived near Aberystwyth. He asked people there and he found me. So much for a secret address eh. He is a bloody insane nightmare and I've just got rid of him at slight cost to my pocket and nerves.'

Worse was to come, though. Later in the autumn, after he'd told Lieberson that the book was at last coming together, he had a tip-off from Raymond Daniel, who told him that he had seen policemen sitting in their car and surveying the cottage. Dosing a visiting copper with an acid-impregnated sweet will tend to have that effect. The next day Daniel called to see him but he had disappeared. Litvinoff was never seen in Llanddewi Brefi again.

Back in London he spent time with relatives in Wealdstone, keeping his head down while he prepared for his next move. With the turn of the decade London was changing. For years Litvinoff had transferred his energies into the city and fed from it in turn, but now it no longer seemed willing to reciprocate. Friends had got married, started families, moved out of town. The Pheasantry faced the threat of demolition. Brian Jones and Jimi Hendrix were gone. The Beatles had split, the Rolling Stones were pushing ahead after the horror of Altamont and preparing for a major European tour. The optimism of 1967 had exhausted itself. Fervour settled into torpor. The scene had established a self-conception and thus stopped

---

*   He means the prison, rather than a man named Nick from Stafford.

becoming: 'They're selling hippie wigs in Woolworth's, man,' to quote Danny the dealer from Bruce Robinson's *Withnail and I*. The buzz of Swinging London had slumped into something more redolent of the opiates in which the rock musicians were increasingly finding solace. It wasn't peer pressure that facilitated the spread of heroin, more that they saw that friends had found a method of distancing themselves from the intense pressure of fame and decided to try it too. The jazz pianist Hampton Hawes experienced this back in the 1950s and in his hip oblique way nailed the attitude in his autobiography, *Raise Up Off Me*.

> You come out of the haven of the church humble and unsure, turning the other cheek, trying to find some balance in your life and life slapping you down every day – you either cave or you get mad. I didn't do either; I went through center, thought I'd make a touchdown. I reasoned, if I can't get anywhere playing by the rules, let's turn things around, see what the other end looks like; can't be much worse, might be a shade better. Balance tips funny to one side, weigh it down on the other; take your destiny out of other people's hands; fucked up on land, jump in the sea. But *try something different*. And that something different was what a lot of cats were into and they all seemed to be grooving – confident, sophisticated, independent, not hurting or not much anyway, hostility slipping away, new lease on life. . . What is this shit?. . . Now at a young and impressionable age you're standing on the curb and see seventeen cats swing by in seventeen green Buicks, would you start to wonder, What's with the green Buick?[7]

Eric Clapton developed a habit as he sought to cope with his obsession with Patty Boyd, who was married to his friend George Harrison. In 1968 he met the sixteen-year-old Alice Ormsby Gore and, despite his feelings for Boyd, in September 1969 they became engaged, moving in together at Hurtwood Edge, where Alice joined him in his addiction. Her family did their utmost to help them, paying for treatments that didn't work and later sending Clapton up to Brogyntyn Hall, the family estate near Oswestry, in the hope that country air and manual labour would inculcate a healthier lifestyle. The Ormsby Gores' land was being managed by Alice's younger brother Francis, or Frank, with whom Clapton became firm friends.

'I think I bumped into [Litvinoff] once at Frank Ormsby Gore's place, he used to hang out with them,' he said. 'They spent a lot of time together. He was nuts on Frank. Frank was like *The Picture of Dorian Gray*, you know, this beautiful young aristocrat. Very attractive to David obviously.'

The reception room at Brooks's Club in St James's Street sits beneath a great glass dome that casts pale daylight on red leather sofas, framed portraits of eminent former members, a black-and-bone-white tiled floor and a marble fireplace with a mantelpiece bearing a small black clock whose minute hand completed one and a half circuits while I awaited the arrival of the sixth Baron Harlech. Doing so afforded time to inspect the curious pinstriped specimens who inhabit Brooks's of a Thursday lunchtime. Elderly gentlemen stooped across the room, hands clasped behind their backs, hailing one another before milling out of view: a few up the broad red-carpeted stairs (one answering his guest's comment about the club's conservatism with the murmur 'Mmm, more Whiggish actually'), but most heading left into the bar, from where I could hear the chink of crockery and a bassy burble emanating from a few dozen male diaphragms. To my imme-diate left was a writing desk with a brass lamp, letterhead paper and a glass case of cigars, and above it a framed roll of honour of Brooks's members who had 'lost their lives in the service of their country during the Great War'. Marble busts of severe Romans sat in the alcoves overlooking the stairs. Behind me a portrait of 'Thomas William, the First Earl of Leicester' stared at the fireplace, where a few orange embers flickered in the grate. Litvinoff knew clubland well, and his passage across any such threshold must have prompted a tingle of infiltration. In its chapter on London Society, which its author styles 'the enclave', *The New London Spy* documents the attitudes prevalent among the staler sections of the upper class circa 1966. 'There are various minor attributes which may be regarded as impediments to member-ship of the enclave, though none is totally insuperable. To be Jewish is a great disadvantage. The Rothschilds are the one family said to be accepted, but it is the foreign branches who are more welcome than the indigenous variety and there are many enclave members who would prefer their daugh-ters not to marry them. Other Jews may be partially accepted but must be prepared for sly digs if they slip up in any way.'[8]

Litvinoff never had any illusions about the crustier old men he encountered during his adventures among the aristocracy; instead his response was to satirise their received ideas about Jewish clannishness.

Lucian Freud, in warmer mode, told William Feaver how he admired
Litvinoff's spirit: Feaver recalled 'stories about causing a St James's clubman
to practically have a heart attack when he responded to his thanking him for
helping him on with his coat with "Anything to help a fellow Jew"'.

    Still the minute hand crawled around the clockface. The fire
crackled. Now and again the navy-capped porter appeared, an incongruous
Yorkshireman: ' 'E'll be 'ere soon, 'e'll come rushing in, always does,' he
assured me. And so he did: here at last came Francis Ormsby Gore, aka
Frank Harlech, his face rendered sweetly simian by a pair of overgrown
black triangular sideburns, all lurking beneath a broad-brimmed black
fedora ('I'll tell you the story of that hat later,' he promised moments after
arriving). Pinstriped navy suit, royal blue shirt, navy tie with splashes of
yellow, brown waistcoat, black hair slicked back in the vampiric manner,
and a voice thick as treacle, veering into West Country yokel and comic
cockney as often as not. I'd first heard his distinctive tones on my answer-
phone a month after I wrote him a letter: 'Reference your communication
regarding David Litvinoff. . . This *extraordinary* man. . . There is much to
say. It's going to take *time*. I shall try you again. Good evening.' We spoke
for an hour the next morning, the outcomes of which were a dazed sensation and a date for meeting; now that voice was embodied before me, softly
apologising for his tardiness. He'd apparently come over from Ireland,
endured some unspecified difficulties with the Holyhead ferry, popped
home to his Glyn Cywarch estate to pick up 'the whistle and flute' and his
briefcase, and jumped on 'the old rattler' to Euston. Brooks's kitchen were
about to down utensils so we shuffled along St James's Street to Wheelers
and took a small table by the window, Harlech and I sitting at right angles.
A swift large Martini seemed to settle him, then it was time to order a good
bottle of white wine. I had no watch on. Just before I'd entered Brooks's my
erratic mobile phone had decided to switch itself off irreversibly. No clock
was visible from my seat looking into the restaurant. Moments felt like
minutes, an hour slipped past in a few seconds. Harlech's company had
a pleasant narcotic quality that tweaked my perception, edged me into a
parallel universe in which it seemed quite a logical progression to move
from his first encounter with Litvinoff in late 1960s Chelsea to an involved
account of a sojourn in China, where he said he had been summoned to
advise on improving their year-round agricultural yield, back to Llanddewi
Brefi for a spell, and thence to the Balkans, where he had travelled in the
1990s in his capacity as secretary of Parliament's British-Yugoslav Group.

Since losing his hereditary place in the House of Lords during the 1999 reforms his fortunes had wavered, though the family's course had never been straightforward. The *Daily Mail* and the *Daily Telegraph* had long extracted a sadistic joy from chronicling their travails: 'Fall of the House of Harlech' read a typical *Telegraph* headline from 2000 when he placed a £5 million price on Brogyntyn Hall, the eighteenth-century ancestral home in Oswestry, scene of many country weekends for Litvinoff and their circle.

Brogyntyn Hall, Oswestry, in 1887.

His father David, the fifth Baron Harlech, acted as Harold Macmillan's ambassador to the USA and also founded Harlech Television. On 29th April 1962 the eight-year-old Francis Ormsby Gore was photographed sitting on a carpeted step beside Macmillan at the British Embassy in Washington as they waited for John F. Kennedy to arrive for a dinner. The greying, pensive prime minister is wearing a tuxedo and black bow tie, his fingers clasped together around his knees. He peers vaguely towards the small boy, who wears a white shirt and patterned tie, dark shorts, shiny shoes and long socks pulled tight halfway up his shins. His black hair gleams under the lights of the embassy dining room. He gazes at Macmillan, his fingers entwined in just the same manner. Behind them we see the legs of white-skirted girls, and further back another floor of black and white tiles.

Five years later his mother died in a car crash. Jackie Kennedy supposedly always regretted declining the widowed ambassador's proposal of marriage a few years after her husband's assassination. Then in 1985 David Harlech died in another car crash. On assuming his title Frank had to pay more than £1 million in death duties. His older brother Julian would have succeeded their father had he not shot himself in a Fulham flat in 1974. Their younger sister Alice found his body. Unlike Eric Clapton, she never succeeded in overcoming heroin addiction; in 1995 she died of an overdose in a bedsit in Bournemouth. Recent years had brought him marital break-up and well-documented troubles. In March 2011 the *Daily Mail* gave its readers a gleeful update (the headline: 'Curse of Harlechs hits again') but one year on Harlech seemed undeterred, even ebullient. Aristocratic ex-Tory peer he might have been, but his shtick was that he was just a trucker at heart: 'Always had one leg in pinstripes, the other leg in overalls,' he chuckled. 'Litvinoff and I used to sit in the cab together. "Faackin' 'ell, Frank," he'd say, "come on, boy. . .!"'

They met via his older brother Julian in Chelsea in 1968, when he was in his early teens, he explained once we'd ordered lunch. 'David Litvinoff was very associated with the Kray twins, and Mick and Marianne. They had a flat at the time down near the Flour Mills on Chelsea Wharf. Julian had an incredibly close friend called Charlie Thomas, who was an incredibly well-connected, good East End boy. Six foot three, immaculately dressed, smoked like a chimney, not just tobacco. Which my brother never did. David on the other hand was a heavy smoker. We went round one evening, Charlie said: "We'll stop in 'ere, Frank. I want a word with this bloke and that dippy girlfriend of his. You know her bloody husband, don't you, Frank?" I said: "Oh yes. John Dunbar,"' the artist and gallerist who married Faithfull when she was eighteen. 'We walked in. He was doing *Performance* with James Fox at the time. And in this room was this very strange chap, who Charlie knew backwards, called David Litvinoff, who was working with Mick on the film. Marianne was fairly pissed off because she didn't get the role, that other girl did. Anita Pallenberg.

'So, an extremely strange man. Highly intellectual. Razor, *razor*-sharp mind. Of course Jagger and Faithfull hadn't got a clue; he seemed to be running the show. Yes, they were doing the film and he was involved in its production as we know, but what was more, the business of gangsterism. . . I haven't fully explained. . .when he first came up to live with us in Shropshire, he'd been on the run. According to the mob he betrayed them by associating himself with making this silly film, with this garish. . .*pop star*. And they knew, and he knew, what they didn't want revealed. This is the Krays.

'So, he came up to Shropshire and asked me, because he'd made arrangements to go to Australia, he asked me to look after his house in Llanddewi Brefi. So just now and again I get on my motorbike and go down there. He says: "The absolute bastard landlord is the elder brother of that ridiculous MP."

'"I know that, David. Enoch Powell." That was the landlord, who I got on quite well with! David loved playing old 78s, and remember this: he was an absolute master of music. An absolute master. And he said: "When you get to Llanddewi Brefi, Frank, don't bother bringing any records." I said: "Why not?" He had this bloody dog, Jack. He gave me this bloody dog to look after. I actually took Jack back to Oswestry. Anyway, maintaining the house, making sure it was warm and dry and the windows worked – he said: "You've got to remember, just use the spools."

'"The *what?*"

'"Just use the spools." This was a reference to the fact that it's all very well having wax and 78s and vinyl: "45s, you can go to a truck stop and put one of them on, can't you?" That's what he said. "I want you to keep these very safe. I'm going away."

'It was a bit Captain Oates. He didn't say "for some time", but he said, "I don't know when I'm coming back." And he said, "The only way to listen, either to dance or relax, is spool to spool, three hours at a time."

'I said: "Okay, David. . .why's that?"

'"Well you don't 'ave to go and put the needle on the record, do you? Come on, wise up! What's the matter with you, son?"

'"Oh I take your point, thanks very much. Right, Llanddewi Brefi, you hate the landlord, got it."

'So, the reel-to-reels. He was absolutely determined about them. And he disappeared. He legged it. And I had the bloody dog for two years.'

When Harlech got to Llanddewi Brefi he met the Brigadier, who told him that Litvinoff had cleared off without warning and owed him back rent. Harlech paid up, assuming the role that Tim Whidborne had played in the past. Over the course of the afternoon at Wheelers his conversation wove around Litvinoff's life, through the fields of British society, across the depths of time to the late-1960s moment when London hung poised between the possible future its youth had dreamed of and the one that transpired. Litvinoff seemed, in Harlech's eyes, an emblem for the era's failure to deliver on its promise. 'He didn't have any inhibitions,' he said, before clarifying: 'His inhibitions were about himself. He didn't think he'd stepped up to the bench, he didn't think he'd delivered. He thought he was intellectually much better than his peers, and no one recognised it. And what he really should have been. . .he had an absolutely encyclopaedic memory of music, and not just music.' They'd challenge each other to recognise songs. Litvinoff was hard to beat. This sparked a digression: 'Oh yeah, by the way, the story about the hat.'

It was a long story. It was George Melly's hat. He and Harlech were at the wake after Harlech's aunt's funeral. They'd had a bet: Harlech challenged him to name the singer of an old blues song, just as he and Litvinoff used to do. 'So I said: "All right, your encyclopaedic knowledge of early, mostly black, music. . . Right, the hat is the bet. That okay, George?"

'"'Course it is, Frank."

He named a song from 1926, the title 'Whip It to a Jelly'.

'He scratched his head. He said: "Litvinoff play you this? Hmm. . ." I said: "'Whip It to a Jelly'. Gardenia behind her ear. Bigger than Bessie Smith. Would lean on that grand piano and bloody near break it, the weight she was."' Melly paused, eventually gave up. She was called Clara Smith. 'And that's how I won the hat. Dear old George.'

I tried to move the conversation back to Wales at the cusp of the 1960s and 1970s. So Litvinoff remained in trouble with the twins after their conviction and imprisonment?

'The twins were in prison, that is correct. There's absolutely no doubt that he was "contracted to a cleaner". And that doesn't mean changing a Hoover bag. In fact there were two. The first cleaner was a fellow from a place called Linlithgow,' and he gave a name so common that there are probably half a dozen innocent men in Linlithgow who could be libelled by printing it. 'Not very flash,' said Harlech. 'Lived by the docks. A hit in those days – well, for David to want to leg it. . . The second one was an Eastern European.' Harlech spelled the name out on a scrap of paper. 'An Eastern European man, contracted for some sum, hired by the boys when they were in nick.'

He couldn't recall any further details. No one else had heard anything of a contract being taken out on Litvinoff, the alleged assassins' names meant nothing to anyone, and those close to the Krays dismissed the idea. What might be more accurate to say is that Litvinoff believed his life was at risk, and he intimated as much in a way that seemed plausible to the young Francis Ormsby Gore, who forty years on found himself repeating what he recalled of the conversation, but between Litvinoff's paranoia and the fallibility of memory the truth had been knocked back and forth until it became a fiction.

* * *

'The oddest profession is that of the *batlan*, the Eastern Jewish joker, a fool, a philosopher, a storyteller. Each *shtetl* has at least one *batlan*. He entertains the guests at weddings and bar mitzvahs. He sleeps in the prayerhouse, dreams up stories, listens to the men arguing, and racks his brain about all sorts of useless matters. No one takes him seriously. But he is the most serious man imaginable. He could have dealt in feathers or coral just as well as the prosperous merchant who invites him to a wedding in order to laugh at him. But he doesn't trade. To work, to marry, to have children, to become a respected member of society – all these seem beyond him. Sometimes he treks from village to village, from town to town. He doesn't starve, but he's always on the brink of starvation. He doesn't perish, he goes hungry, but he wants to go hungry. His stories would probably cause a stir in Europe if they were published.'
      Joseph Roth, *The Wandering Jews*, trans. Michael Hofmann

'Yet, the figure of the storyteller, someone who tells jokes and entertains guests at weddings, is different from that of the "batlan". The Yiddish word for this specific type of storyteller is "Badchen". It is very likely that Roth, who only knew Yiddish imperfectly. . .did not understand the difference between the two terms. Consequently, in writings about Roth, this mistake is repeated.'
      Ilse Josepha Lazaroms, *The Grace of Misery: Joseph Roth
      and the Politics of Exile, 1919–1939**

The *batlan* as Joseph Roth described it didn't exist. At least not then. Roth

---

*   My thanks to Patrick Kennedy for finding Lazaroms' correction of Roth's mistake and preventing me from repeating it.

conflated the *batlan* and *badchen* to create a tradition that had no history, a fiction that Litvinoff made a reality, becoming the writer's invention incarnate: an exemplar of the symbiotic play of truth and myth. Roth tweaked history into fiction, Litvinoff through his fabrications turned Roth's error into fact. He seemed an oddity in post-war England because his context was pre-war Galicia. Those such as Frank Harlech became ghost writers of an unreliable narrator's unwritten memoir.

I asked a waiter for the time. Somehow another two hours had passed: I was late already to meet Christopher Gibbs. I grabbed my coat, offered to settle up – to no avail, he wouldn't hear of it – and left in a hurry. As I scurried into a cab outside I thought back to the figure I left sitting at the table, and his forlorn last words before we said our goodbyes: 'But there's still so much more to say. . .'

Chapter 9

The Extraordinary David Litvinoff

'There is only what *is*. The what-*should*-be never did exist, but people keep trying to live *up* to it. There is only what *is*.'
    Lenny Bruce, *How to Talk Dirty and Influence People*

Martin Sharp's open-topped Mini Moke roared down Macleay Street and pulled up to the kerb at the junction with Challis Avenue, causing a young photographer named Jonny Lewis and his brother Tim to halt and look around. It was March 1971 and the rough, lively Sydney district of Potts Point was about to get rougher and livelier.

'This bloke leapt out of the Mini Moke,' said Jonny, 'and he accosted us: "What's two faggy boys like you looking for?" He was in close to our faces, and he was smoking a joint. It was like a whirlwind had suddenly descended in a blaze of energy, and through the aroma and smoke he continued talking impossibly fast.

'Who *is* this bloke? He wore shorts, a Balinese print shirt, sandals and sunnies, he passed the tiniest of roaches to us as if we were beyond all contempt, and quickly disappeared. What an intro! I never forgot it.'

Since the 1950s the Terry Clune Gallery at 59 Macleay Street had shown works by radical modern Australian artists, among them Martin Sharp, until it fell into disuse and faced possible demolition at the end of the 1960s. Now it was to be the venue for an artistic project conceptualised by Vincent Van Gogh almost a century earlier but never before realised. In a letter to his brother Theo, Van Gogh mentioned an aspiration to turn the 'Maison Jaune' where he lived in Arles into a residence where artists such as Paul Gauguin could live and work alongside him. Here in Australia, frustrated by the bureaucracy and constraints of exhibiting in traditional galleries, Sharp revived and expanded the idea. Ian Reid, the husband of his cousin Kate, bought the building and allowed him to fulfil the vision. Sharp was its instigator and presiding spirit; Litvinoff was there supposedly as the cleaner (someone recalled him once scrubbing the front steps with a toothbrush) but his real role was to be the in-house catalyst, a provocateur charged with ensuring that the dust would never settle. Dozens of rooms in this four-storey Queen Anne Federation Style building and an adjoining property would become home to a coterie of creative Australians who would revitalise it into a perpetually evolving work of art. Peeling walls turned vivid with murals after René Magritte; floors that had borne scorch-marks from dere-licts' campfires were cleaned and decorated, one with a likeness of Van Gogh's famous chair painting from his cohabitation with Gauguin; where cobwebs had hung from the ceiling, there were now lush red velvet drapes with golden tassels; in one room the walls, floor and a table with fruit bowl and wine bottle were all painted so as to have the appearance of stone, in another the artist Brett Whiteley created a bonsai display, a sign of his belief that Australians needed to understand themselves as part of Asia rather than displaced Europeans. Aggy Read, one of a group of underground film-makers calling themselves UBU, shot an interview in which Sharp explained its genesis: 'In Arles, Vincent Van Gogh had an idea of a Yellow House in the sun where artists would work and create and live together, and it took a long time for his idea to come true, but it has now come true. And it's not Arles, it's in Australia. But it's an artists' community in the south in the sun. And it's probably one of the greatest pieces of conceptual art ever achieved!'

His interviewer laughed back at him: 'You're so modest!'[1]

The Yellow House assembled more than a dozen of the brightest young artistic talents – sculptors, painters, performers, photographers, film-makers, musicians – around Sydney at the dawn of the 1970s. They were as struck as their London counterparts by Litvinoff's sudden disarming enquiries. At the nearby Le Cafe he happened upon Antoinette Starkiewicz, the only female painter to have a solo show at the Yellow House: 'Dreaming of your long-lost Polish lands, princess?'

'I wasn't, as it happens, dreaming of lost lands,' she recalled, 'but he was, as usual: incisive, witty and a great conversation starter. We spoke about Russia.' Bruce Goold was only a student when Sharp gathered him into the fold to help furnish the house. A successful career as an artist and printmaker lay ahead of him but at this time the seventeen-year-old had never left Australia. Sharp and Litvinoff blew into his world like 'ambas-sadors from the King's Road', he said. 'David had these things that made him luminous to us, starved as we were for the first-hand, still getting everything from magazines. He seemed to have hung out with everyone we found fascinating. It's no wonder we adopted him.'

For another of the younger artists involved, a Finnish painter named Axel Sutinen, Litvinoff would come to embody the enterprise's very spirit. Sutinen often ran into him in the corridors or the front gallery, known as the 'Cloud Room' as its walls were painted with blue skies and soft clouds, where he and Sharp always seemed to be deep in conversation impenetrable to the uninitiated. Almost everyone wanted to know Litvinoff's opinions and hung on his every utterance. To Sutinen he always cut a striking figure in 'very well-made and -cut shirts', 'blazers with psychedelic patterns and colours with different kinds of scarves' and sunglasses 'always on his head or in front of his eyes, even at night'; though as graphic a memory as any came when looking on from afar at 'his silhouette moving in the gold-painted entrance hallway of the Yellow House with artworks on the walls around him'.

The first show to be held there collected a selection of Sharp's works. He was the gentlest of men, though tough in his own way, shrewd as any career artist needs to be: he could get things done, knew which strings to pull and how to win attention when necessary. Take the decision to send Litvinoff out to face the local television station's cameras at the opening night: a masterstroke that provoked a head-on culture clash of the sort both men adored. The black-and-white news report from 31st March 1971 is a brief but remarkable piece of footage that gives a burst of Litvinoff's surreal menace, and a delicious example of a representative of the straight world colliding with the counterculture and walking away dazed and confused. The reporter begins a piece to camera rich with the kind of gentle ironies and wry wordplay familiar from local TV news today: 'It's an old saying that nobody's surprised what goes on in Kings Cross any more. But this at least might raise the occasional eyebrow. This is the street's latest art gallery. It's called the Yellow House, after a venture by Vincent Van Gogh, who set up an artists' community a century ago, a venture which, incidentally, failed.

'But that's only the beginning. The whole place seems to honour what's usually considered offbeat, strange and even downright bizarre – although to many, it's still a lot of fun. The first showing opens tonight. It's called the Incredible Shrinking Exhibition, dedicated not surprisingly to Tiny Tim. It's a collection of works by Yellow House's director, Martin Sharp, consisting of posters, collages and photographs, all scaled down to postage stamp miniatures. In fact the only thing that isn't miniature is the price, ranging from $30, but that includes a gold frame specially mounted for each.'

Cut to Litvinoff: his right arm leans taut against a wall, the other hand clutches an apple and rests on his hip, he acknowledges the interviewer with a camp toss of the jaw. He looks wired, wiry, his body one great clenched muscle. At one point he bites violently into the apple and devours it while continuing to talk. He's forty-three years old but dressed somewhat like a child, in rolled-up shirtsleeves, black shorts and a black eye-mask that lends him the look of Batman's sidekick Robin's malevolent twin.

On the Sydney television news at the Yellow House's opening.

In truth, it derived from the Yellow House artists' interest in Fantômas, the masked murderer in Marcel Allain and Pierre Souvestre's French crime novels. The reporter inclines a microphone towards him and asks his first question; subsequent ones grow increasingly hesitant in their delivery.

'David, what do you think public reaction will be to this exhibition?'

'I think it will be one of massive indifference. And I believe the public will stay away in their thousands.'

'Why?'

'Well – is that a rhetorical question? Well, there's several movies showing at the same time, I believe the Moscow Circus is arriving in Sydney. . . I'm only the cleaner to this gallery, for that you'll have to ask other people. I don't understand the Australian collective psyche 'cause I'm just a modest unassuming young Hebrew boy.'

'These, er, works, show a marked, er, if I can say, backward step only in the sense of time.'

'Oh yes, it is a great step backwards. The Great Leap Backwards. Yes – he's got a *Blue* Plastic Book.'

'What, er, do you think will be, er, the average Mr and Mrs Man Off the Street's, er, idea when they see these paintings of, er. . .?'

'This is Potts Point, Macleay Street. Mr and Mrs Average is a very, very peculiar sexual and psychiatric case here. Have you been around Macleay Street at night-time? Well, I live not far from the King's Road, Chelsea, and I've seen nothing until I came to Macleay Street. You've got 148 different sexes going here, full blast.'

He'd swapped old west Wales for New South Wales and it felt good: from isolation and rain he was swept into a gloriously sun-drenched city to explore, understand and catalyse. There were new connections to make, new stories to acquire; and also a new audience for the old stories, impressionable kids who would be bowled over by the names he could drop and the gossip he could impart. With Aussie informality they promptly dubbed him 'Litva', which he found amusing. He'd arrived via Bali, hence the shirt. Twin sisters Jane and Caroline Blunden, the daughters of naval lieutenant-commander Sir William Blunden and Pamela Purser, were aged twenty-two and travelling there with their cousin Robin. They were a tight trio, which initially irritated Litvinoff: 'What is it about you three that makes you so inscrutable a unit?' he asked. He wanted to break into their clique, Jane recalled, and they were happy to let him do so. 'In those days David was the centre of the gang in Bali,' she said. They stayed at a guest house by Kuta Beach called Dayu's, 'named after the lovely Brahman lady who owned it,' she explained. 'He held court in the evenings and we hung around listening to his endless stories, by candlelight, by campfire, in villages, at music festivals – he was there. . .he was also there in the waves, swimming without a bathing suit. We were more prudish! He was there too when I was dragged out by the waves and on one occasion he came to my rescue (fully clothed) and we ended up being pounded by water and sand, turning somersaults and finally being dumped in a heap, together, on the beach.'

He told them to catch up with him again in Sydney. They picked up where they'd left off. He introduced them to his new friends, took them to galleries, gave them a tour of the Yellow House, which 'seemed to me like the house that Jack built,' said Caroline. 'David invited us inside to wander through the rooms, each one giving a different experience. This magical place was one large art installation. We followed David through a pitch-dark passageway walking over foam flooring while ping-pong balls hanging by different lengths of thread hit you gently in the face as you felt as if you were walking on air. . . Another room was brightly lit and painted light blue with a deckchair under a large sun umbrella in the middle of the floor on a heap of sea sand, complete with a child's bucket and spade.'

It was a sign of his intention to stay for a substantial period that he had shipped out to Australia a bulky collection of around 200 reel-to-reel tapes, which proved a source of fascination. He played people his telephone conversation with Brian Jones and casually propagated the then-prevalent lie that Mick Jagger had had him murdered. As word spread that he'd fled London because he'd angered his underworld connections in making *Performance*, their fascination only grew greater; perhaps, too, some of them saw another (far inferior) British gangland movie released that spring, *Villain*, in which Richard Burton plays a sadistic gay East End gangster who slashes an informer's mouth before leaving him tied to a chair dangling from a high balcony. Litvinoff's mythology had begun to bubble up into public view. Rapidly he became one of the Yellow House's noted attractions, along with its mutating display of artists' work and regular evening performances. In May 1971, wrote Albie Thoms, 'Our Friday night soirées continued to mix the media, with *An Evening Dedicated to Tightrope Walkers Everywhere*. It featured Arthur Dignam reading Genet's *The Funambulist*,[*]

---

[*]   'Funambulist' meaning 'tightrope walker'.

and was accompanied by "The Love of Two Puppets", a combined mime and puppet show by George Gittoes, which was performed in the garden with Jewellion playing Pierrot.' There was a celebration of the late anarchist poet Harry Hooton, a night with a magician, screenings of Fritz Lang's *Metropolis* and Leni Riefenstahl's *Olympia* and a performance 'by Mikkus and Cazza, who moved through the house delivering their stirring sound poems', while an event 'billed as "An Evening with The Extraordinary David Litvinoff" had him telling stories and playing some of the sound-tapes from the vast collection he had brought from London. These included bootleg tapes of Bob Dylan and one of Kurt Schwitters reciting his "Ursonata".'

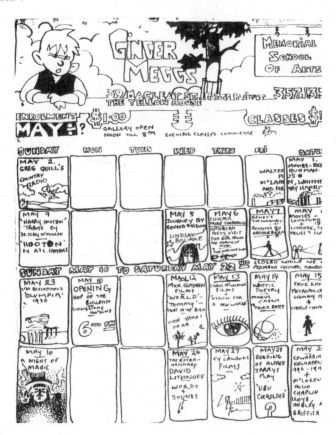

Events at the Yellow House, May 1971.

From his black-painted bedroom in the attic to the downstairs galleries and the backyard, Litvinoff pervaded the entire property.

Dickie Weight, Peter Wright, Albie Thoms and Litvinoff in the Yellow
House's backyard.

His radius of influence quickly expanded into the broader zone
of Kings Cross, an area of Sydney known for its bohemian character. It
combined bars hung with the Stars and Stripes to welcome the wild,
traumatised American troops on leave from Vietnam, the city's red light
district, theatres, old music halls, a congregation of drug dealers.
Litvinoff had it nailed within days of his arrival. 'The Cross' bore
comparison with Soho as a residence for those who shunned straight
society and an occasional destination for 'straights' who fancied a walk
on the wild side; and as in Soho a decade earlier Litvinoff attracted a
crew of street boys who gravitated around him. At the same time he
grew close to Brett Whiteley, one of the few characters wild enough to
match Litvinoff's rogue energies. Oliver Musker, an antiques dealer and
Marianne Faithfull's boyfriend of the time, remembered the two together
later in London. Whiteley was in the midst of one of his hero-worshipping
fixations, the present subject being Arthur Rimbaud. He had in mind a
piece of conceptual art that would truly do justice to his reverence for
the symbolist poet.

'There was a whole plot because what Brett Whiteley wanted to do was to get someone to go and dig up Rimbaud's skull,* and this went on and on and on,' said Musker. 'And David kept saying: "You mean, man, you really want me to get some people to go with a bucket and spade and dig up Rimbaud's skull?"

'This went on for weeks. So he said: "Okay, Brett, we can organise all this, it'll cost a little money but we can do it, it can be done. But please tell, what are you going to do with it once you've got it?"

'So he said: "I'm going to create a completely dark room, in the back of my studio, paint it black, and put the skull on a pedestal, and put a spotlight over it."

'He said: "Well, that's interesting. But then what are you going to do?"

'"I'm gonna wank over it!"

'And for once, David was silenced.'

Silence was rare when either man was around, let alone when they were together. 'Both Brett and Richard Neville could speak at 100 miles per hour,' said Albie Thoms, 'and they would get into each other's faces and be talking at the same time. David was the only person that could shut them both up. He was faster.' Litvinoff described their discussions – 'if you can call the antics that go on between Brett Whiteley and myself a discussion' – as 'a couple of old hustlers hanging on some dialectical poems', and, to those looking on, their tangential dialogues could be hard to understand. They spun one another into ever-higher planes of verbal disquisition on art and Bob Dylan and life, collaborating too in a determined enquiry into the effects of mind-altering substances on the doors of perception. Now Litvinoff set aside his earlier professed loathing for the opiates with which he had been au fait at least since meeting Ricky Levesley and Gerry Goldstein, and which had been central to Lenny Bruce's adult life. Axel Sutinen saw him again in the Yellow House around this time. 'He came towards me in the stairway with his usual entourage,' including Sutinen's close friend Sam Bienstock, a young American who had come to Sydney to avoid the draft. 'They announced that they had taken heroin. I responded with: "Isn't that dangerous?" David replied that it was just an intellectual exercise and [Sam] could certainly handle it with no effort. I looked at Sam in dismay as he said that he had now experienced everything that there is

*   Arthur Rimbaud is buried in the Charleville-Mézières cemetery in the Ardennes, France.

to know, and he might as well just die as nothing means anything any more.'*

At the Yellow House in 1971.

Nigel Waymouth maintained that heroin was never Litvinoff's kind of drug, and that if he tried it in Australia it was only in a spirit of enquiry, as he'd suggested to Sutinen. Still, he experimented with characteristic commitment. When I interviewed Dickie Weight, a painter who was also part of the Yellow House collective, at Albie Thoms' flat in

* Bienstock's memory is slightly different: he recalls the comment not so much as nihilistic as tongue-in-cheek, meaning 'only that I had then tried all the full range of drugs of recreation there were at that time available to the counterculture at large and that there was naught left to try'.

Macquarie Street he said: 'Standard fare in the Yellow House was grass, hash and LSD. I think he went on to heroin.' Thoms concurred: 'Yeah, definitely. He was all the time smoking pot and he had a little cigarette rolling machine, but after he moved out of the Yellow House and he was staying at Lavender Bay, a woman arrived from Vientiane in Laos selling pure heroin and he got some of that. And that night in the Cross someone died of an overdose because it was pure. But David was right on to it; since the first day he arrived his connections had been built up. And then Brett was on heroin and I wouldn't be surprised if they were doing it together because they were living in the same area.'*

Sam Bienstock settled in Australia to become a street photographer, with work published over the years in the *New York Times* and *Sydney Morning Herald*, and collected at institutions including the National Gallery of Australia. To a wide-eyed twenty-year-old just arrived in Sydney, Litvinoff seemed akin to a returning soldier from the rock'n'roll trenches, 'a raconteur of the highest order [who] held sway [over] an audience night after night with stories from the front'.

'David seemed to have no need to actually work,' Bienstock said. 'He seemed to have oodles of money to splash about, especially when it came to drugs of recreation.' Presumably what remained of the $4,000 he'd received for *Performance* continued to weigh heavy in his wallet. 'He was constantly surrounded by much younger boys – street kids, I would label them now. At the time nothing seemed out of the ordinary to me although his behaviour *now* might be categorised as predatory. He was constantly at the Yellow House and on several occasions raced me off under the influence of what I would come to realise later on was probably an opiate or its derivative.' Raced you off? A delicate clarification established that he did indeed mean 'masturbated'.† 'I must add here that, at the time, I did not flee those encounters but nor did I particularly want or encourage them,' Bienstock said. 'They just happened "under the influence", so to speak. I never felt violated as I felt that I could, in fact, stop it if I wanted to.'

---

*   Whiteley's biographer, Ashleigh Wilson, however, believes that Brett Whiteley began using heroin in 1973.

†   This quest involved numerous 'How the hell did I get here?' moments, but none more acute than finding myself asking a stranger on the other side of the world to expand on the suggestion that he'd been tossed off by David Litvinoff forty years earlier.

Sutinen also found himself the object of Litvinoff's flattery, increasing attention and sexual opportunism. Sutinen's bedroom was on the second floor, above the galleries. 'The room was on a halfway-landing off the stairs and had no lockable door,' he said. 'It had a white silk parachute suspended from the ceiling and it came down covering the walls and the doorway. There was just a large mattress with pillows and bedclothes on the floor that fitted in the small room. David suddenly appeared through the doorway, jumped on me and started trying to seduce me while he was talking at me intensely. As I was still very inexperienced in any sexual relationships I had to push him away. He was dismayed and taken back, so he left very quickly.'

After that rejection Litvinoff ignored him for months. Another young man he fell for was Bruce Goold, who became his guide to Sydney, walking him through its historic sites and touring him around the new Opera House during its construction. Albie Thoms' black-and-white footage from the Yellow House showed Goold performing a dance that climaxed with him writhing naked on the floor before an audience either laughing embarrassedly and averting their gaze (Martin Sharp) or paying avid attention (Litvinoff). 'We were good friends,' said Goold. 'I didn't know his age, whether he was gay, a term not used then, though he was demonstrably affectionate. He was just completely remarkable and fascinating.'

They headed out of the city too, up to the Blue Mountains where they looked out from Echo Point and saw the 'Three Sisters', rock columns that Aboriginal lore said were women turned into stone. Litvinoff had a moment's revelation and realised that one of the sisters' names, 'Gunnedoo', was probably the source of a previously incomprehensible lyric in the final verse of 'Quinn the Eskimo' from the *Basement Tapes*. He appeared to Goold a kind of 'musical instructor', someone whose purpose seemed to be the dissemination of the music he loved. He'd sit on a sofa and play Bessie Smith and Ma Rainey from a portable tape deck that he'd stop and start with his big toe, which a transfixed Goold noticed had no toenail, interspersing the recordings with explanations of the songs and biographies of the singers. Despite his connections in the London art world he didn't come across as someone interested in art; in fact quite the opposite.

'David wasn't actually very enlightening about us or our work because David wasn't into painting,' he said. 'But he could be scathing and cruel about us, which was part of his attraction. He would leave a swathe of people muttering in disbelief as he'd go cruelly through Sydney. Often David would just dismiss Brett's work, or not even talk about it. This would infuriate Brett. He'd do the same with Martin at the Yellow House. I don't think Sydney had ever seen anybody quite like him.'

Jet-lagged and inarticulate, I wandered Macleay Street towards my hotel sweating in the heavy coat I'd worn when leaving the cold English spring, finding myself transplanted into the sticky heat of an Australian autumn, feeling now and then a vertiginous, sole-tightening tingle from the knowledge that 7,900 miles of crust, mantle, core, mantle and crust lay between me and the people I love. Later I looked for the Yellow House and found it turned into a restaurant called Brass, so I took dinner there and peered around for traces of its former incarnation. The mustard-coloured facade on to Macleay Street was little changed but inside a coating of magnolia concealed the clouds, though the chipped orange gloss on its wooden window frames called up from a stranger and livelier past. The waiting staff knew nothing of its time as the Yellow House: they said I should return the next morning as the manager would be there, but when I did so I found the restaurant locked and deserted.

At last, many months into his Australian adventure, he plucked up the courage to confront the overdue task of writing to Sandy Lieberson. Though he told people in Sydney that he was a writer and that he was working on a book about Lenny Bruce, by now even Litvinoff didn't believe what he was saying. He abandoned any such pretence in writing to Lieberson's family and instead relaxed into a more natural, candid, tender tone.

> Dear Friends - you know me well enough by now to know that I'd rather rap than write. Still, there's little excuse for not doing so before. I got your lovely letters and read them several times over a period when I was feeling lonely & was working on this cattle station in the A.C.T. (Australian Capital Territory).*
>   I have thought of you all many times, with trepidation and love. The first for blowing the Lenny Bruce

---

*   Ian and Katie Reid's farm at Captains Flat, southern New South Wales (not actually in the ACT), where he stayed for several weeks in 1971.

gig, the second for the warmth and help I've always got
from you. . . I am and have been for a long time very
much into the deepest scene I've ever been into in my
life. He is a boy giant about 6'4" tall called Rowley
and he'll be coming back to England with me. I've told
him lots about you. You'll dig him because he's one of
the most beautiful people I've ever met. . .

Sandy, this Australian thing has been the freakiest.
I'll hip you to the details when I see you. . . My head
is in a curious way almost totally together and very
open to ideas. I hope I can get something together in
England to pay you back the $500 I got in front for
Lenny. Till I see you in a few months all my love. . .
David

Rowley Davidson was slender, willowy, delicate-featured with long
blond curls, and he found Litvinoff mesmerising. Litvinoff in turn had
never been so enraptured. After his bleak days in Wales he found himself
revitalised by the blend of love and sunshine and supportive company into
which he'd immersed himself in Sydney, this beautiful city full of irreverent, uninhibited artists who were engaged in a process of cultural self-
creation and cared nothing for people's social background, only for what
they were doing with their lives now. He had rarely felt so at home as he
did here on the other side of the world, and then Rowley arrived to provoke
a happiness he'd never before experienced. It was a relationship that would
rejuvenate him; then it would age him terribly.

September 1971. Aggy Read took his camera into the Yellow House,
with Litvinoff in tow. They headed for Martin Sharp's room and walked
in, Litvinoff turning interviewer. He sounds stoned and thoughtful.
Anyone who didn't know his past would be entitled to believe him when
he claims that like Sharp, he operates from the side of gentleness rather
than violence: perhaps because, by now, this was what he wanted of himself
and he was persuasive in his projection, even if at other times he fell far
short of his own aspirations. At the same time his growing intolerance for
posturing and affectation and insincerity – or bullshit, as he succinctly
puts it – is on display again, and in the same vein he refuses to flatter
Sharp about the Yellow House. There's no sign of anything but affection

for his younger friend, though, mixed with a measure of amusement at his inarticulacy.

'Oh he's here, in bed too! Hello, Martin. We're making a film, and curious enough you're part one of the film, so we thought we'd come and see you in bed. Now there's one or two questions about you, Martin, which have frequently given rise to a certain amount of puzzlement in me. Now I suppose you're some kind of aerialist: you're walking a tightrope and there's this fucking incredible drop on either side. And it's pretty long tightrope, Martin, and if one can. . .make that tremendous leap outside bullshit, in an absolute person-to-person term, can you tell me what you are trying to do for me?'

'I'll give you a good answer to your question— '

'Give me any answer, man, not a good answer but a truthful one. Good answers is the province of the lawyer.'

'Er. . .what I'm doing for you?'

'No, you tell me what you're *trying* to do for me, and I'll tell you what you're doing for me. Or to me.'

'Mmm. . .'

'Now you've got ninety seconds, take all the time you like.' Laughter from Sharp. 'Yes,' Litvinoff continues. 'Well, I thought it was a rich field we were mining. What it's doing to me? Well, to begin with it confuses me. It doesn't give me an appetite for food. It doesn't make me feel I want to jump into bed with the nearest member of the human race. But it doesn't fill me with feelings of grave disquiet either. So somewhere between those two fields it's performing a function vis-à-vis me. . . I mean "What can it do for me?" with the best will in the world, and yet I genuinely don't get the message. I genuinely don't get the thing. I haven't applied myself continuously to it, but I have applied myself intently to it at times; I genuinely don't get the message except I know we are somehow on the right side of things. We're both on the distaff side; we both see things from the point of view of gentleness as opposed to violence. And you know, Martin is not sent here as an instrument of the devil or a negative devilish idea – Martin is composed of neutrons and protons the same as anyone, in different proportion in different degree, and I feel sure he would have reached a point of impasse, of self-extinguishment, of suicide if he had got a truthful realisation somewhere inside of him that he was negative. He wouldn't have gone on doing this, right? I think it would be untenable for you.'

They're interrupted when someone knocks at the door and comes in to hand Sharp a poem, which he reads aloud. It's an accumulation of phrases – 'images of inconsequential trivia until it overloads and gives you a headache' as Litvinoff puts it – that seems now and then to concern the Puerto Rican Palm Sunday Massacre of 1937. Litvinoff dismisses it in a way that explains why he couldn't write the Lenny Bruce book. 'Okay, well it's an impressive feat of pyrotechnics but I don't feel any better now you having read that than about fifty seconds ago. So in the final feeling there's a deficiency of his feeling: in other words, bullshit. It's unnecessary. Unless it's essential to the river of life, it's bullshit. It must come into that area. But it's undoubtedly pyrotechnic and clever. And it's undoubtedly not the most pyrotechnical or the cleverest we'll ever come across. So what's the point of it?'

Litvinoff: Did I wake you up?
    Sharp: Yeah.
    Litvinoff: Ah. . . I thought of taking you out for lunch, if that's cool, and having a little chat with you. . .
    Sharp: Okay. . .
    Litvinoff: I asked this friend of mine (I think I mentioned him to you, did I not – John Ivor Golding? This Welsh philosopher. He holds the chair of philosophy at Swansea) to meet me for lunch. He's just come up to town. . .

Martin Sharp lay asleep, a breathing tube running from his nostrils and across his thin cheeks. Despite being seriously ill with emphysema, he retained his quiet charisma. He was like a silent star who pulled others into orbit. Forty-four years after Litvinoff replaced the telephone receiver and prepared to phone Golding back, his and the Welsh philosopher's voices echoed around the studio at Wirian, Bellevue Hill, while I sat by the stereo and Martin lay behind me on a couch; as the twenty-six-year-old Sharp's voice issued from the speakers, I turned to look at the seventy-year-old version of the man and saw that his eyes had closed, his chest rising and sinking to minimal degrees, and heard his breath escaping with a gentle burr.

In his youth he was so handsome that one woman I interviewed could barely look at him. His sparing speech increased his mystique. In his forties he grew a full dark beard, and now that beard had turned silver-white like his shoulder-length hair. The illness left him almost housebound; he set out once a week for a blood transfusion at St Vincent's Hospital but little else drew him outside. The effect was to turn the dashing knight of

Australian art into a wizard-like character, shuffling around the house mumbling asides that were funny once you tuned in. The breathing tube trailed from his nose to a machine, restricting his movement to a certain radius like a dog tied to a lamp post, an indignity he bore with good grace. 'They like trying to imprison me on a chain of oxygen,' he murmured as he made his way to his desk. He cut an other-worldly figure whose mind ranged through space and time while his ailing body remained tethered by gravity and infirmity to the confines of his home. A white-painted 1920s mansion named for an Aboriginal tribe, Wirian was a work of art in itself, a baroque version of the Yellow House. Moving through it swiftly was impossible: not because of the clutter but because of the arresting sights wherever one looked. Great oblong windows cast pale rhomboids that drifted across bookcases and walls, as if to spotlight a different arrangement of curios by every hour. A miniature herd of elephants sculpted from ebony and ivory; an old green-bound biography of Van Gogh beside *Idols of Perversity*, Bram Dijkstra's 1986 study of *fin-de-siècle* misogyny; a print of Albrecht Dürer's Praying Hands, a quick sketch of Sydney Opera House, posters bearing the *commedia dell'arte* mask face of Tiny Tim, an ornate art nouveau carriage clock. On a deep windowsill, the *Oxford Dictionary of Quotations* lay open at a page of lines from John Donne. 'One short sleep past, we wake eternally, / And death shall be no more; Death, thou shalt die.'

By my bed, where I awoke in the mornings to hear yawns of traffic from Bellevue Hill, was a small table bearing a pyramidal whisky bottle filled with marbles, balls of crimson, yellow, mint green and sky blue glass. On the corridor wall opposite my bedroom door was a still life of a melon and lemons; beneath it, in Sharp's cursive script,

The Sparrow has Flown, God Bless her Loving Soul
Amen.

The emphysema came after a heart attack and a stroke a few years earlier. He almost died in November 2011 but 'clambered back into existence', in his words, and by the time of my visit was experiencing a period of creativity such as he hadn't enjoyed for years. His diet of takeaway Thai food and continued cigarette habit despite the lung disease provoked exasperation among his friends, who valued his continued incarnation in this world more highly than it appeared he did, though when his health rallied in 2012 he was jubilant: 'Thank God, I'm back,' he wrote in an email to me and Patrick Kennedy. His Christian faith sustained him and informed his worldview entirely, like his great friend Tiny Tim, to whom he'd been introduced in 1968 courtesy of Eric Clapton and whose music became his abiding obsession. 'Tim's appropriation of song is very much like my appropriation of images,' he once said. 'We are both collagists taking the elements of different epochs and mixing them to discover new relationships.'[2] He spoke of Litvinoff's gambling, noted that the numbers on a roulette wheel add up to 666. Litvinoff, he observed, had no faith other than in himself. 'I think perhaps he was reliant on his own zest for life, and then he began to lose his strength,' he said when we had the first of three interviews, conducted in his studio at his desk, a great trestle table occupied by an elaborate architectural form in which paper stacks, paint pots, brushes and pot plants all seemed structurally integral. We spoke when he felt strong enough, broke off when he needed to rest. Sharp's benevolent magnetism pulled out the same quality in others, not least Litvinoff. Their mutual friend Nigel Waymouth saw the company of artists as a balm to Litvinoff's soul: 'He loved gentle, creative company. It was soothing to him. And I often think this whole obsession with the tapes and music was the same: it's the story of David playing his harp for Saul, soothing the savage breast.' ('And it came to pass, when the evil spirit from God was upon Saul, that David took a harp, and played with his hand: so Saul was refreshed, and was well, and the evil spirit departed from him.' 1 Samuel, 16:23.)

Martin ambled between the desk, the chaise longue where he rested and the easel at which he had for months been reworking a large Japanese-influenced painting of a shell diver. He'd finesse a line here, retouch the sea there; friends said he would never finish it, but finishing it did not seem to be the point. Like the Yellow House, like life, the painting was in what Dylan called 'a constant state of becoming',[3] reflecting that life has no genuine moment of arrival, other than the moment of departure. 'Martin finds it quite difficult to even have an exhibition,' said Wendy Whiteley, an artist herself and widow of Brett, 'because nothing's ever finished. And it's not going to be finished until the day he dies. And it probably still won't be finished enough.' As Leonardo da Vinci said, 'Art is never finished, only abandoned.' Sharp had worked the same way on a portrait of Litvinoff that he began in 1976.

'It was large,' he explained, 'on a board that already had a drawing on it, of a boy by Cressida Campbell when she was a young girl. I must have been thinking of David, I did just a few brush strokes, and he was there. I was amazed. But then I worked over it, and I think I sort of lost that freshness. . . And it was over the other drawing, though it would have actually worked now I think of it, because she has become a great artist. And there was the child and the man. . . It was interesting. It was him looking down. I kept working on it, but I never quite got it right. The best version that I ended up with was like a Pierrot. I did him with a red mask, that didn't work, and tried different things.

'And David Vaughan came out here to stay for a while, he was an English artist, and he painted over the top of it or something, and then I just threw it out. You know, one does.'

Face Dancer by Martin Sharp, on display before its destruction.

Since the mid-1960s Sharp's cartoon-like works had made even the boldest primary colours seem strange again. Acid laid bare the fallibility of perception. No foundations seemed certain now, nothing was 'real', though one's interior and the exterior world seemed all the more radiant and alive for this revelation. 'Mick said to me one morning it was very difficult to carry on doing the job you were doing when you've lost your ego,' said Stash Klossowski de Rola, son of the painter Balthus and close friend of the Rolling Stones. 'Psychedelics made everything seem multidimensional, and revealed consensus reality as threadbare. After it, the game of life had changed.'[4] No artist made this more apparent than Sharp, whom the Yellow House patron Ian Reid calls 'a locus for the change in consciousness at the time'. In his portrait of Litvinoff his colours were characteristically vivid: a white face modelled with mint-green shadows, with eye-mask and lips in blood-red. 'I think [the title] may have come from *Dune*: I called him a Face Dancer. He had a twinkle in his eye. He had eyes like an eagle, I felt, but I saw a great kindness in them at times. I did see that tenderness: that behind the face-dancing, if you like, there was a glimpse of this loveliness. Some people he wasn't pleased with – I saw him go at George Melly once, that he didn't have the right to sing the blues, at a party. And he was very powerful with his voice. He didn't need to be physically violent. I saw him pin someone to the wall just with his voice, and cut them to pieces with. . .a stream of words and insights. So I can see why he got himself cut: he was provocative and probably truthful as well.

'I remember when he came out here, it was great, but I asked him. I got him the ticket to come out here. . . Through Bali he came. He looked very well, fit and healthy when he arrived. And he stayed at the Yellow House. Of course he was the most interesting thing there really. . . It was amazing to get him here. I think it might have given him a few more years. And he fell in love with Rowley, and he spent time with Brett Whiteley and I think the needle might have become involved there. I think he dabbled in heroin. Brett certainly [did].'

When we met Sharp knew that he wouldn't leave Australia again. He missed London and seemed to remember Litvinoff most vividly there. 'There was a time, I'm sure I was with Christopher [Gibbs] and [Martin's girlfriend] Little Nell.* She liked David very much. One of the great nights was when we went down to the Turkish baths in Piccadilly, Nell had very short hair at the time, and got right down to the very bottom level, this inner heart of this all-male precinct and suddenly there was this beautiful girl there, like this earthquake. That was a typical David invention. He was fearless. It's hard to earn a living doing it, but he made an enormous contribution to people's lives. It's not something you can send someone a bill for. Many people do send people bills, take their percentages. . . I'm sure he was poor, David. He was like a star without a setting; a diamond rolling along, flashing.' In an interview for a later Albie Thoms film titled *Something Old, Something New, Something Borrowed, Something Blue*, Sharp described his old friend as 'someone who was always trying to break the skin of reality and usually succeeding: he was a man who could open any door'. He picked the theme

---

*   Nell Campbell, Australian actress and singer, and sister of the artist Cressida Campbell.

up again now. 'Some people, Tiny was another person, they created reality when they moved, you know? Where they walked and talked, reality was made.'

Sharp saw me to the tall metal gates and waved me on my way; as my taxi drove away I turned to see his stooped back as he shuffled into Wirian, to his increasingly urgent sift of a lifetime's accumulated possessions, to his painting of the Japanese diver. It was influenced by his love and empathy for Hokusai, the artist and printmaker who died aged eighty-nine in 1849 having used more than thirty names over his lifetime, the best known being the one that he assumed from the age of seventy: Gakyō Rōjin Manji or, as Sharp explained with a hint of a smile in his voice, 'the old man mad about drawing'.

Three observations extracted from audio recordings in the Yellow House that would appear indicative of David Litvinoff's preoccupations on an unspecified day in September 1971:

1. Everyone is on the game, everyone is fucking hustling, there's no doubt about it. And hustling is fundamentally bullshit. You are too, you're banging the drum. That's what I mean by a hustler. The means justify the ends, Martin. . . You hope not to be some time in the future but at the moment you're doing a hustling operation and you're a hustler. Thank you. But what's wrong with being a hustler, if the times call for hustlers?

2. I can never think of what people in Alaska are thinking at this precise moment. I know I ought to be tuned in that way. Maybe I am because I can vaguely, very vaguely, feel things going through every single human being going through me. I'll tell you quite frankly, at one time I used to be on fire with energy. . .but I don't get it quite so much, by far, today.

3. I think if someone takes a dagger and stabs it in your back, you're going to feel something and know it's not bullshit. . . That's going to be an area of something that comes from the guts. Now does art make that kind of statement today?. . . When a couple of thousand miles from here people *are* plunging knives into

people's backs,* and we're just commenting on it. Where the
action is, is not where the comment is. The comments are the
sidelines. You've got to change things at the core. An apple
doesn't start to grow from outside, it's got to be right into it.
Now into it is a very, very heavy place to be. I'm not into it. And I
don't know anyone I know around Sydney who is really into it . . .
There's probably more liberation of spirit here than any other part
of the world I've been in.

* * *

In October 1971 Solomon Levy died in London. Litvinoff remained in
Australia and did not attend his father's funeral. In July he'd left his room
at the Yellow House for the flat Albie Thoms mentioned in Lavender Bay,
North Sydney, near Brett and Wendy Whiteley, and near Rowley
Davidson. Thoms found himself with nowhere to live in October so
Litvinoff invited him to stay, and he slept on a mattress in the hall. The
Yellow House began to lose its momentum and Sharp decided to move
back to London to paint a mural for Keith Richards, transferring the
project's running to a classical guitarist named Sebastian Jorgensen. They
held a farewell party at which Axel Sutinen and Litvinoff finally repaired
their friendship, which had foundered after Sutinen rebuffed his advances.
'He ceremoniously handed me one of his signature neck-scarfs, a long
silky oriental-looking piece of cloth, as a gift,' said Sutinen. Like his
friends Peter Wright and Dickie Weight, Thoms withdrew too at this
time. 'My retreat from the Yellow House left me in a confused state,' he
said. 'I needed to find somewhere to live, and had to earn more money so
that I could get back to work on *Sunshine City*, but also needed a rest and
time to recover from the experience. My temporary accommodation on
Litva's floor was not the solution, since sharing space with a person who
had been dubbed "Jumpin' Jack Flash" was hardly relaxing, and though I
enjoyed his constant repartee, it was the opposite of the respite I needed.'

'*Do You Like My New Car?*' A moment's blast of Frank Zappa over a blurring image of Litvinoff: he's in a Mini Moke again, a cross between a Mini
and a beach buggy, and this time Rowley Davidson is in the driving seat.
Then the Rolling Stones' live version of 'Jumpin' Jack Flash' from *Get Yer*

---

*   In Vietnam, presumably.

Ya-Ya's Out kicks in on the soundtrack as the pair tear across the Harbour Bridge, the cameraman's car close behind, burning through the flickering city towards Bayview Road, where the shot disembarks and zooms towards a gate bearing the number 9. Litvinoff's flat. Glimpses of him talking, Rowley looking languid and Byronic and pensive, then a cut to the garden, tightly framed around Litvinoff lying on the grass.

Rowley Davidson as featured in *Sunshine City*, directed by Albie Thoms.

It is early 1972 and Thoms and a colleague are recording interviews for his avant-garde documentary *Sunshine City*, which sought to record his generation's experience of life in Sydney. Frustrated with what he felt were the misleading, prissy editing techniques of conventional journalistic and documentary interviews, Thoms opted to let his subjects speak uninhibited until his film stock ran out (though even then he would leave the audio running, in this case capturing another ten minutes of Litvinoff's speech unaccompanied by images). 'The Underground press had been publishing unedited transcripts of tape-recorded interviews for some time, with Andy Warhol even starting a magazine devoted to them, and I had been taken by the nuances they revealed, with the naked words of the transcripts seeming more truthful than those that had been sculpted into neat answers,' he wrote in an email to me. 'I preferred these rambling conversations to interviews with a tight Q&A form, and opted for the former in the five-minute conversations I shot for my film.'

Sunshine City was to be Thoms' document of his city's cultural coming of age. Other interviewees include Brett Whiteley, Germaine Greer, Mick Glasheen, Martin Sharp and Aggy Read. He knew that he needed to capture Litvinoff on film, both to preserve a singular character on record and as a significant element of a critical phase in Sydney's artistic evolution. In doing so he achieved what few others did, in that his five minutes of colour footage illustrate first-hand how Litvinoff gained his reputation. The opening moments reveal a man entirely alive to his surroundings, utterly engaged, incorporating and riffing off external stimuli as he coerces reality into his own paranoiac narrative. Thoms leans in front of the camera and mimes closing a clapper-board. Litvinoff lolls on a cushion on a lawn enclosed by bushes, his body sprawled across a palette of chlorophyll greens as bright and hazy as a memory, wearing a yellow short-sleeved shirt, sunglasses, a dark floral neckerchief and skimpy shorts, left elbow propping him up, his right hand free to gesticulate. The picture's lack of clarity reiterates the sharpness of his words.

From *Sunshine City*, directed by Albie Thoms.

A bottle of wine stands before him, a joint nestles between his fingers, a slim tabby cat brushes against his smooth girlish legs. 'I tell you this cat won't move for five minutes,' he says. The cat moves, but Litvinoff strokes it gently so that it rolls over on its back, and he continues tickling its tummy.

Thoms: 'I didn't move at all!'

Litvinoff: 'Yes you did, you set off a chain motion of paranoid noises. Now's the telephone.'

A faint ringing from somewhere indoors.

'Oh, yeah. . .'

'You'll hear something paranoid for the next thirteen seconds now. That silence is a paranoid type of silence, until it's broken. Now we'll see what breaks it.' Five seconds' quiet, the hum of distant traffic crossing the Harbour Bridge, a breeze shimmering soft shadows on the grass. 'It's throbby, isn't it?'

The cat begins to walk away, weaving past the wine bottle. 'Oh dear. I hadn't reckoned on caprice,' he says and chirrups to attract her back. Albie murmurs something off camera about movies and sets him rolling, nought to 100 miles per hour in a few seconds. There's a likeably light, camp-ish drawl in his delivery now and again, a very different diction from his performances on the Laski and Golding tapes. If he veers into the realm of stoned verbiage, more often he displays his wit and acuity. Here in this *spiel* is everything to admire and dislike about the man: his humour and tenderness, monomania and self-absorption, arrogance then redemptive self-deprecation, speech patterns that switch from staccato to glissando; his immanent violence, sad streaks of Jewish anti-Semitism that betray a creeping alienation, and at one point a quite disarming prescience, when he predicts the digital era's proliferation of portable screens and the concomitant explosion in pornography.

It is not only the speech that is compelling, it is also his physicality. While he remains prone throughout he communicates with his whole body, gesturing and emphasising with his blockish hands ('a strangler's hands,' shuddered his friend Shura Shihwarg with theatrical relish) and giving occasional ingratiating glances to camera. He's picking blades of grass, fiddling with them as he speaks, suddenly snapping them in minute expressions of violence. This is why people talk about David Litvinoff.

'Well the fundamental thing about movies, man, which I don't know how many people who don't know much about movies are not properly cognisant of, is that *movies are watched in the dark*. I've just panned on to that [rapping his knuckle on his scalp]. Now, there is no other medium whatsoever in which the sole illumination, the sole absolute, the second dynamic pragmatism of energy, comes at you purely in light waves. Otherwise you'd be totally in the dark. Because everything else has theatrical lighting or things like that. Movies don't. That itself must be an important sublimation to do with the kind of way it gets into you [miming light entering the head], its durability in you and what it does to your emotional and inter-reactive processes. . . When I was Rowley's age, the movies – I never paid, I jibbed [sharp click of his fingers] – the movies to me were a kind of strange palace of some sort of love which was both sacred and profane at the same time [twisting his fist, then a magnanimous flourish over his head]. And I would sit in the masturbating stalls and, you know, practically send my piss into the screen.* This is the way I thought of movies then. You'd see them all day long. You know, like, you'd get off a crowded East End street, wallop, straight into that fleapit, you don't come out until two o'clock the following morning. Amazing films! And those films seemed to cater for that kind of exegesis of the head. Ah they were fabulous, movies were fantastic. Nowadays I go there to just stir one's [mimes a stirring motion] critical paranoid faculties a bit. You know, take a look at what he's done there, what they've done there [jabbing at imaginary screens] – because if you've worked on a single film, all the other films creak. You realise the bullshit if you've actually worked on a film.

'I don't think movies actually are. . .' He pauses and gazes for a moment off camera. 'I was going to say either they're dead or they'll be really starting. . . No. I think the thing is movies will get smaller. The relationship between telly and the movies, the apparent delineation, is just beginning. . . Oh, absolutely. They must be so related and yet they're thought of as different. I think they're much more than brothers. I think it's just bringing movies into the house. You'll be able to get your own movies [mimes holding a miniature screen like a smartphone and looks down at it].'

Thoms comments that rather than calling them movies and television they should just be called 'video', and Litvinoff interrupts: 'Yeah, but

---

* He is plagiarising and coarsening Emanuel Litvinoff's recollections of youthful cinema-going as described in 'A View from the Seventh Floor', broadcast in the 1960s on the BBC's Third Programme and then included as a chapter of *Journey Through a Small Planet*: 'I went to the cinema as often as I could. It was the era of Mae West and, slumped in the masturbating dark, I longed hopelessly for a love that would be both sacred and profane' (*Journey Through a Small Planet*, p. 122).

I don't think of it in a paraphysical sense, I think of it more like in a Bergsonian type of sense, a pleasure. The market for pornography and movies hasn't even been started. Stag movies, just imagine. . . Look at the size! [Cups his hand and looks down at the imaginary screen, mimes frenzied masturbation.] It's just incredible. The censors, man, the censors are almost fantastic, because they are a dying breed; they've even got a Romanesque name, which is almost non-accidental [with an effete flourish of the hand]. I'm absolutely certain that the floodgates are down and pornography will have to exhaust its own energy before it can be legislated against.'

Litvinoff's image cuts out and his voice is left jabbering over a white screen, which gives way to juddering footage from within the Yellow House. 'Because I think pornography is part of the staple approved diet of the American executive middle class,' he continues. 'I mean, I'm sure that Nixon and everyone has seen pornography in various forms and relishes it whether they can privately or publicly admit it. Pornography is a necessary . . .it's a dirty joke, isn't it? A visual dirty joke. How old would you think the dirty joke is? Since comedy first became apparent in sex, I'd say.'

Thoms chips in to mention Walt Disney, and Litvinoff interrupts with the claim that Disney was 'an anti-Semitic fascist: did you know that?' before reminiscing on when he 'used to get a kick looking at the very fantastically beautiful, in obviously fascist parts of the East End, young boys and girls' and how this 'Genet trip' made him 'understand my Jewishness all the more.

'It's extremely interesting to be a Jew. That's the thing that gentiles don't understand, that it's actually *interesting*. You cannot say it's interesting to be a gentile.' Thoms protests at this provocation. 'Well, you do because you're in a turned-on area. But I think it's tedious semantics, man, to disallow the fact that I think the Jews are spreading all the paranoia in the world today, because they proclaim the god Efficiency, and I would say that efficiency is not what the world actually needs; it's very low down on the priorities. You get the greatest unhappiness where there's the greatest efficiency. Erm. . .is this thing still. . .have we started yet? Well, it must be well over. No? Well that's ridiculous. 'Cause you understand that by a cheap narcotic my time sense is *fucking deranged*!

'Mind you, I've heard three or four lots of trains. Now this is not pot open-air paranoia, those trains come at an average schedule – I've looked at the schedule, Rowley and I, we took a train yesterday, would you believe it? It was an incredible experience. We were having a fantastic argument without any words on this train, and I was picking up on all the things Rowley told me about trains. Rowley and I are planning to. . .have you ever read Mark Twain's *Idiots Abroad*?* Oh it's a fantastic book! It's a fantastic celebration of being [a] hick. That's really what we're planning: we're going to make a fool of ourselves in about seven different countries. It's going to be such a gas. . . I feel more alive now, not because I've smoked a bit of a rather good joint, having met Rowley, than I can remember for at least fifteen fucking years. And—'

Thoms: 'That must be incredible!'

Litvinoff: 'It's just totally fucking ridiculous. I'm a *dangerous* person. . . What I was trying to say was that the most intense recollected experiences that I can recall are firmly in the realms of a kind of intellectual mad Jewish paranoid nostalgia kit which is shoved somewhere in the lower part of my brain, and the kind of absolutely real and incredibly and painfully topicalised experiences I've had with this young Australian guy. . . I think that Rowley's a very spaced person. Because he understands me so totally that it fucking frightens me. And it's bypassed the cerebral to get to that. And it's not carnal any more, which is fantastic, because we have the most incredible experiences in that department but they—'

Thoms: 'Do you understand him to the same extent?'

Litvinoff: 'No. No. I'm very heavy. No, I don't. And the reason I don't is because I'm fucking selfish. Because I've got this whole Führer complex flipped about nine times. I don't know whether it's at his feet, my feet; in fact I would like to define the male and female in our relationship and I can't get that one straight. I know all the clubs and I know all the people in Europe and London and the States who are into that scene. I know the permutations, I know the level from casuistry to sexual sophistry. I know that fag scene inside out. But it defeats itself because it's art for art's sake. Now, one can therefore only go – you've got to throw all that, it's a trivialisation, it's a game, a quasi-philosophical game – one can only go therefore into – I don't like to use this word because it's a propagandist, mediumistic type word – a gut reaction. You can only go by that. Because it's the only useful barometer of how your feeling is: so accurate,

*   Or rather *The Innocents Abroad*, as Litvinoff surely knew. Published in 1869, it charts Twain's journey around Europe and the Middle East two years earlier.

it's calibrated, it hasn't had a chance to bullshit it yet, it's the only bit left of you which is not programmed properly. It was such a long time before the human gut evolved as a human gut it therefore must be a very fucking long time if it means anything and has actually got gut before it can be assimilated and controlled by technology. It can't happen in 300 years. Otherwise it's *not a gut*! And it painfully and patently IS A GUT! Because everyone's got guts and you know what they are and you feel things in your guts. It's no good anyone trying to talk to you, and use cerebral reasoning to tell you that's not your gut feeling, because your gut's telling you something a priori to that which is going to say "Bullshit to that, and this is my gut and this is the message". That's where it's at as regards you as a person.'

He calms down again. An aside about the artist 'Le Douanier' Rousseau in response to Thoms' suggestion that this stoned philosophising echoes Jean-Jacques Rousseau's ideas about the noble savage. The roar and fade of a passing train, gusts of breeze. Litvinoff offers Thoms his joint. 'You want some of this illegal stuff, man? What about some of this legal stuff?' He pours another glass of wine.

'What I'd like to say here and now, just for the record, folks, is that *I dig Rowley*. And he's one of the most fantastic people I've ever met in my life. And that's not only a declaration which is totally subjective, it also happens to manifestly contain any objectivity which I can morally and legitimately in an existential or pragmatic context be expected to contain. In other words it's also as truthful as I can get. He's one of the most amazing people – because I have been *amazed*, in the literal, linear sense. I have actually been amazed. Before amazement there comes fascination and there's also something before that: there's confusion. Then you think the next contusion of the cerebral cortex is amazement, and I went through various things – the whole rational process that I'm putting up the energy and I fantasised this guy up and blah blah blah, you know. . .and it's sort of an extraordinary kind of thing, because I'm not homosexual, curiously enough. If you look at my situation, who and what I am, and what representation and misrepresentation/alignment/normalcy/misalignment/abnormalcy – legal definitions, moral definitions, aberrations and things that are such common practice that they hardly constitute aberrations any more – anyway, my entire psyche, as far as I can recognise it, seems to me to be directed to a proper appreciation of what ladies, girls, women and grandmothers are, and are supposed to be, in a genetic historical Judaeo-family context, which is the context which you gentiles, you *goyim*, are living under in Australia. You're living under conditions made by Jews thousands of years ago. Have you picked up on that?'

He takes an abrupt leap to a prediction that the wool industry will give way to prostitution as Australia's chief industry in the 1980s, then segues into observing that the world 'does demand in the collective sexual quintessence of the psyche a Marilyn Monroe: they've got them in Singapore, they've got these Malaysian movie stars, you've heard about these fantastic Sophia Lorens of the Orient?. . . All the most amazing movie things are going on in the Orient. I tell you where they *are* going on, man, is fucking Bali.'

'Are you going back there?'

'Yep. Definitely. Only my fucking evil Jewish mind is trying to work out a fucking humdinger of a letter to the most appropriate department of all, that Rowley becomes a photographer and I'm going to write a definitive fucking bullshit "*à la livre de tourisme*" on the thing and I think I can do it, and con three first-class fares all the way. They're travelling ten per cent, man, of capacity. All airlines, they're all fucking empty. . . Qantas has just withdrawn its fucking jumbos from Perth to Singapore. They've been riding at three per cent; ninety-seven seats out of a hundred are empty . . .it's bullshit.' Almost imperceptibly he repeats himself: 'Bullshit,' as faint as a second echo. Then he rouses himself. 'Is this finished? You've definitely started it? It seems to me it's gone on a long time. . .'

'We can stop whenever you like. . .'

'Have you done the five minutes?'

'Oh certainly! It's been fantastic, we've been grooving out on it. . .'

'Oh wow.'

Chapter 10

Face Dancer

'And yet, how many of our present pleasures, were we to examine them closely, would shrink into nothing more than memories of past ones! What would there be left of many of our emotions were we able to reduce them to the exact quantum of feeling they contain, by subtracting from them all that is merely reminiscence? Indeed, it seems possible that, after a certain age, we become impervious to all fresh or novel forms of joy, and the sweetest pleasures of the middle-aged man are perhaps nothing more than a revival of the sensations of childhood, a balmy zephyr wafted in fainter and fainter breaths by a past that is ever receding.'
Henri Bergson, 'Laughter: an Essay on the Meaning of the Comic', trans. Cloudesley Brereton and Fred Rothwell

Faced with the daily deluge of Litvinoff's declarations of love, his flattery and generosity, his determination that this was the great relationship of his life, it was hard for Rowley Davidson to vocalise the doubts that nagged in his mind. He tried now and again but Litvinoff talked over him, sought to reassure him: go with it, we were meant to be together. But Rowley couldn't agree. His difficulty was a fundamental one: unlike Litvinoff's perverse claim that he wasn't homosexual, Rowley really wasn't. When Juno Gemes stayed with Litvinoff, 'Rowley was around there a lot,' she said. 'And Litva would say to me, "Oh, look how beautiful he is, he's the love of my life, I can't believe how lucky I am to have found him." His conversation was a lot about his love of Rowley. And Rowley's conversation when we'd got to know and trust each other was: "Yeah, David's wonderful, he has the most amazing mind. He's so knowledgeable, smart and funny, I really dig him. But the truth is that I'm not really gay. I'm not into it in the same way as he's into me." So I could see tragedy brewing here.'

Rowley admired Litvinoff, found him fascinating and stimulating and amusing; but not sexually attractive. How to make him understand this? It pained him, and he knew that the only solution would itself be painful.

Conversations with a Sydney taxi driver, part one. As Martin Sharp disappeared into Wirian this forty-something man – chubby sallow face with stubble, greying black hair, flitting eyes, a quick and softly spoken rasping Aussie accent – greeted me with: 'So who's that guy?'

'He's an artist—'

'Ah right, selling shit for loads of money so he can afford a house like that.'

'No, I believe he inherited it from his family.'

'So what are you doing here?'

I told him. He'd got one hand on the wheel and one eye on the road, the other hand behind the passenger seat's headrest so he could more easily twist round and glance over his left shoulder towards me in the back.

'So you want to make a lot of money?'

'No, not really. . .just enough to keep going.'

'You wanna be famous then?'

'No. . .'

'Sounds like you're wasting your time, mate. I've never heard of him, why do I want to read about him? Just 'cause he was mates with some artists and rock stars? Probably had sex with them all, didn't he? Debasing their bodies. Doing drugs. What'd he die of, AIDS? Sounds like a frickin' loser. Why you putting a loser up on a pedestal? I don't know, mate, I just think it's pretty fuckin' odd, young guy like you. You ought to be on a beach somewhere, sowing your oats. People shouldn't waste their talent on people who don't deserve it. Why not write a book about Jesus?'

'I think someone did that already.'

'Can always write another. I'd read it.'

'Right, well, I'll bear that in mind for my next book.'

We roared on to the Harbour Bridge and slotted into the tight traffic. He turned to spend a few moments looking fully at the road, his left cheek twitching, and mumbled to himself: 'Yeah, well. . .don't care what anyone thinks of me. Don't care what anyone thinks.' Then he glanced back again: 'I'm only shittin' ya, mate, just firin' shit at ya.'

He dropped me at Lavender Bay as the clouds broke and he told me where to get some 'proper Aussie grub' for lunch. I thanked him, paid up and watched myself hand over a tip, then wandered through misting drizzle towards Wendy Whiteley's house, nursing a sense that if I ever saw him again it'd be as the subject of a news report concluding with the words 'before turning the gun on himself'. Whiteley shared his scepticism to a degree. She saw the worst of Litvinoff and felt protective towards Rowley, while also despairing of the effect that Litvinoff and her husband had on one another.

    'Well, he was demanding,' she growled. 'He was highly intelligent, obviously witty, angry, manic, demanding – and one of those men in my life was enough at once. So as part of the group he'd either have to be top dog, or he'd start interfering in everyone else's top dog priorities. Well, listen, the fucking whole world doesn't revolve around you. It's that weird mixture of megalomania and insecurity. Which I'm used to in people, but. . .' she grimaced. 'A difficult character.'

    Between the late 1960s and mid-1970s television viewers across the country tuned in for the Australian Broadcasting Corporation's 6.30pm *GTK* strand, which over the course of ten minutes allowed them to 'Get to Know' figures from the arts. On one occasion in early 1972 they got to know Brett Whiteley. A dolorous twang of pedal steel guitar moans as a handwritten caption explains the interview's circumstances: 'At 6pm on the 29th Febuary [*sic*] at the Bonython Gallery 52 Victoria Street Paddington the Brett Whiteley Exhibition *Portraits and Other Emergencies* will open. . .' The camera pans to a dark, hunched self-portrait in ink and then to a monochrome shot of an industrial-looking gallery space, large canvases hanging on the walls and laid on the floor, nothing else for an instant: until Whiteley flies into view clinging to a rope swing attached to the ceiling. He sails back and forth, dismounts and crashes down to sit cross-legged by assorted portraits of Francis Bacon, poring over them with a bashful grin, his lithe figure topped by a shaggy sphere of blond hair. By then he'd been associating with Litvinoff almost a year. Friends say his way of speaking had been noticeably influ-enced by Litvinoff's rhythms and vocabulary. In a programme titled *The Australian Londoners* filmed in 1965 he's impassioned but measured in his phrasing; now he's deploying language in flourishes that parallel the energy in his painting. He'd been tearing a wild streak through the art world for a decade. He and Wendy lived in London from 1960 to 1967, during which time he grew obsessed by the multiple stranglings committed by John Christie between 1943 and 1953 at 10 Rillington

Place, which was close to their home. ('Of the Australian painters, apart from Martin none of the others could afford to live in the King's Road,' she said. 'We were all in Ladbroke Grove, where there was cheap rent.') In 1961 the Tate Gallery bought his *Untitled Red Painting* that had been shown in a Whitechapel Gallery exhibition called *Recent Australian Painting*. At the launch party he got talking with Bacon, which sparked a series of conversations that shaped his thinking; Litvinoff would tell anyone who listened that they were conducted with Whiteley's foot jammed in Bacon's doorway, but the truth was that the pair sustained a long-term friendship coloured with occasional spats. Though Whiteley never owned a Bacon painting, Bacon briefly owned one of Whiteley's warped recreations of a Rembrandt self-portrait: after examining it for three weeks, he threw it away and told Whiteley that he considered it a failure. Their relationship recovered. Now, filmed three years later at the Bonython Gallery, Whiteley elaborated on how his work constituted an attempt to tackle the crisis in figurative art. Where Donald Cammell abandoned the discipline as moribund, Whiteley was, like Bacon and Freud, attempting to resuscitate its prostrate body after the barrage of blows levelled by film and photography. Australian painting existed in a lower state of confidence still, as he outlined to the *GTK* interviewer.

'I mean myself as an artist,' he said, or rather 'an *ard*'est' in Whiteley's soft Sydney drawl, 'I have a cavity and I have a culture.' His intention in this show was to fill Australia's cultural cavity by taking the masters of European art and 'paint[ing] them the way that one's seen them in relation to their work. . . While having the conversations with Francis,' he explained, he experienced hallucinatory moments in which he sensed that Bacon's spirit 'literally mirrored. . .my imagination', after which he 'left it for a few years and then I took it upon myself to do something about it. I've taken basically one formal element which is a drawing and then by using accident, which is Baconian, I've arrived at a sequence of images which gave a hint towards the kind of thing that I saw.'[1]

Whiteley continues to talk as the soundtrack switches to Bob Dylan singing 'I Shall Be Released'. After a succession of portraits of Bacon, along with similarly twisted renderings of Hitler and Mao, one by one the camera cuts between a selection of ink sketches and their sitters. His and Wendy's seven-year-old daughter Arkie, sitting piggy-back on her daddy's shoulders and tousling his hair. Wendy, with her wide eyes and sensual curved cheekbones and black hairband. Michael Hobbs, an art collector and patron to Whiteley. Litvinoff, jaw locked and jutting, expression cold and fixed, feral yet imperious: give him a toga and laurel wreath and he'd pass for a Roman emperor. *The rats are underneath the piles. / The Jew is underneath the lot.* Here he flips Eliot's aspersion on its head.

Litvinoff as featured in *GTK: Brett Whiteley.*

Whiteley's three-quarter-profile portrait captures him in chirpier form, the corner of his mouth hitched into a faint smirk and the suggestion of a sparkle in his eyes.

Brett Whiteley sketch of Litvinoff as featured in *GTK: Brett Whiteley.*

'The best paintings that were made,' Whiteley's saying as these images pass by, 'were Renaissance and around through that, and that was when painting was really up on the full bugle towards God. And slowly, slowly it's been knocked down. . .and it's now gone to the stage of "Is it still legitimately possible to take a poisonous ointment, paint, and smear it in some mean- ingful and tricky way on to a board so that it has immense spiritual and intellectual implications?"' The only way forward is to introduce a 'psycho- logical flash. . .drawn almost from the mystical area,' Whiteley explains, 'to be able to render, perfectly, the exact seen image of what the person's incar- nation is about'.

If Lucian Freud made plain his perception of what Litvinoff's incarnation was about, so did Whiteley: like George Melly, he saw him as a sacred monster. Other drawings of Litvinoff existed, such as 'an oriental scroll of him looking like a Zen monk, a hummingbird buzzing around his head' in Bruce Goold's description, and one drawn a while after this show of an unidentifiable figure fellating a reclining monk, captioned by Whiteley 'From David Litvinoff's story of Tangier'. Upstairs in the gallery was a large portrait of Bacon that 'had a shark's jaw and teeth fibreglassed to the board, then slashed with paint in a ferocious de Kooning-cum-Brett style frenzy', Goold added. Behind this was a reel-to-reel tape deck playing a recording of Whiteley and Litvinoff discussing Bacon, in which Litvinoff described their encounters in London: in Goold's recollection, comments such as '"When Francis went gambling he wore a purple shirt and when he went to the Colony Room Club he wore a grey shirt" – very trivial things'.

Whiteley went on to become one of Australia's most decorated artists. In 1978 alone he won the Archibald, Sulman and Wynne prizes, the country's three leading awards for artistic achievement, becoming the only person to do so in a single year. He diversified into sculpture and collage, following his inspiration wherever it led him, all the while grap- pling with addictions to alcohol and heroin. In 1990 he and Wendy divorced. Perhaps Litvinoff flashed through his mind that year when he gave another interview for a documentary about his life, titled *Difficult Pleasure*, which referred to his description of painting. This time he spoke in more sombre tones of being born with 'a very powerful gift, and there's a lot of gifted people. . .and I notice a lot of gifted people shipwreck'.[2] People gifted with wealth often 'run off the rails', those with high intelli- gence often end up isolated. All his heroes 'have been addicts', he says, 'and I'm an addict. And for the rest of my life I will struggle against the embracing of the mysterious self-destructive self-murder, the urge to deny, defy, wreck, ruin, challenge one's gift.'

The rest of his life only lasted another three years. Whiteley over-dosed on heroin in a beachside motel room in Thirroul, forty-two miles south of Sydney. He was fifty-three. Nine years after that Wendy lost their thirty-six-year-old daughter Arkie to cancer. 'I've wound up with the job of "look-ing after the flame",' she said, 'which sometimes gets a bit wearing, but it's inevitably a huge part of my life as I'm the last man standing in the family.'

Given her burdens, given the toll that becoming Whiteley's muse took – her own gifts as an artist became overshadowed by his career – and given Litvinoff's effect on Rowley, of whom she felt fond and protective, it was understandable that Wendy would lack patience with a character who avoided responsibility but, to her mind, drew little apparent pleasure from his freedom. She still lived in the same house and pointed to the door where, forty years earlier, Rowley would turn up from his home two streets away after trying repeatedly to explain to Litvinoff that there was no way forward for them.

'He was an odd mixture of a highly intelligent man who had had a rough and tough East End life,' she said. 'He could physically look after himself. But Rowley was very tall, very slender, and not homosexual. But fascinated with David, and David was making demands on him so he'd arrive over here in tears, and I would say to David, "Leave him," you know, "You can't bully someone into a relationship, David, for Christ's sake." And I'd get a bit of this "women are a pain in the arse" from him. He loved Brett. Brett the wild boy. And both of us had been friends with Francis Bacon, who fascinated David.

'He was just too much. There was no space left with David in the room. I used to think this about Brett a bit too and some other friends. . . that I actually was quite fond of, [who] made contributions in our lives: that they probably would [nowadays] have all been diagnosed with attention deficit syndrome and stuck on lithium, in which case they wouldn't have existed at all as they were. People with stretched emotions, over-the-top reactions to everything, probably very selfish and megalomaniac, who need to be at the centre all the time. And if that gets tipped in any way, then you get the rage. God knows, when he got angry, it was a *rage*. Very much like all the other things he did – it wasn't a small rage, it wasn't kept at the level of resentment. It was explosive and threatening and potentially violent. He didn't contain himself in any way, David.'

Unlike the taxi driver, though, she could see why he deserved to be written about. She could also see that doing so would be a recipe for frustration 'because he destroyed everything, didn't seem to keep any letters, or any evidence'. There was no point Brett ever giving Litvinoff one of his sketches of him because he would immediately give it away to someone else. No pages from the Lenny Bruce book ever materialised because 'David probably did what he did with everything – even if he'd written them, he probably read them and thought "This is not right", and burned them, or tore them up. That's the empty pit side of the megalomania, what appears to be completely selfish megalomania: nothing he ever did pleased him enough to be able to risk putting it out there.'

In her brusque way she touched a nerve. 'You've got heartstrings being pulled here,' she said. 'You want David to be probably less dangerous than he actually was. If you're going to get a proper picture of Litvinoff you're going to have to deal with that dark side of him, which was destructive – self-destructive, destructive of all relationships.'

You think you'd like him, she said, but by now I'd assimilated too many contradictory views to characterise my feelings so simply, and as I dug into his life's darkest places I found myself drifting into absurd speculation over the likely nature of an encounter with him: whether after due flattery he'd switch in a beat and jab me with questions that cut at my Achilles heel, or tie me to a chair for two nights then cut me loose to punish my indiscretion, or cut my face to make it look like his.

Cut, cut, cut. Time to change scene.

I took a train north out of Sydney to the town of Mooney Mooney, which sits on a peninsula jutting down into the wide Hawkesbury River in verdant country where green parrots reveal a flash of blue as they flutter from banana bushes. Spiders the width of my hand-span hung in webs festooned high across a riverside path. Juno Gemes and her husband, the poet Robert Adamson, live on a bluff in a house full of books and photographs and paintings, the enclosed air inhabited by the sounds of Bob Dylan and the primeval scent of river water. I remained jet-lagged throughout my stay and took to rising before dawn so I could sit on their veranda and watch the black wooded hills beyond the river tilt below the sun. Trills and screeches from the bushes, the slosh and ripple of a fish breaching the surface. Gleaming corrugations glided seawards past rickety wooden jetties jutting out from where sloping gardens met the riverbank, their old posts' reflections shimmering. I watched an ant navigate invisible cul-de-sacs across a cushion cover on a wooden chair beside me, then I looked over to the distant brightening hills. Within the woodland of Mooney Mooney lie rocks bearing ancient engravings of eels and Rainbow Serpents, sacred sites, ceremonial stones, allusions to the indigenous Darug people's understanding of creation and time and their lack of egoistic urge to delineate ownership of this land by erecting fences across it. 'We think they're behind us but they're beyond us,' said Juno. She was kindly (introducing me to numerous interviewees such as Marianne Faithfull and Wendy Whiteley), feisty, owlish with her silver bob, round spectacles and nocturnal habits; she'd rise late in the mornings and lie on her sofa to cast her mind back to Chelsea and the World's End in the 1960s and 1970s. We stirred up old memories, then she rested to let them settle. She arrived in late 1965 and worked her way into the heart of countercultural London, whether by orchestrating 'happenings' at the UFO club, writing for the *International Times*, staging performances at Joan Littlewood's Theatre Royal Stratford East, appearing in Yoko Ono's *Bottoms* film or sitting on stage for an hour while a screaming Ono wrapped her from head to foot in bandages. Unlike certain contemporaries such as Clive James and Germaine Greer she wouldn't become a household name in the UK, but back in Australia she became respected for a photographic career that served to document Aboriginal or, in her preferred term, Traditional people's lives and advocate their civil rights. After returning to Sydney, she took a room with her then-boyfriend, Mick Glasheen, in what would become the Yellow House and covered it with ancient texts of Aboriginal sacred stories and maps of Central Australia as an immersive preparation for creating their film *Uluru*, which would be drawn from reams of footage shot at the immense sandstone rock formation in the Northern Territory.

'After living for six months in the desert filming with Traditional Owners – camping in the desert each night under an arc of the starry sky so closely enfolding you, country where everything resonated with meaning – when I got back to Sydney, I had the most disturbing culture shock I've ever had after any trip,' she said. 'Suddenly people living on the eastern seaboard in apparent denial of their country's true history made no sense to me. There were two worlds here, two cultures both invisible to each other. People said I was talking in symbolic shorthand. There were only three people who appeared to understand me. They were Martin Sharp, Brett Whiteley and David Litvinoff. Every time I told stories to Litva about what I had learned from Traditional people out there he would say: "Man, this is just so fascinating! You have to write this down, man, just as you're saying. It's a revelation you are talking about! It would interest people worldwide." He'd be very insistent that that was what I had to do.'

She made it her life's work. It was a measure of her prolonged dedication to the cause that in 1985 she documented the ceremony that marked Uluru's title deeds' return to the Aboriginal people, and in 2008 she was one of ten people chosen to photograph the National Apology in Canberra, in which the prime minister asked their forgiveness for the generations of mistreatment they had endured. Litvinoff was instrumental to setting her on course, she said. They'd lived together for a time while he was in Lavender Bay, the memories of which she cherished: sitting on the harbour-side as dusk fell, with their feet dipping in the glistening water, swimming naked, smoking hash and drinking wine and laughing uproariously as they planned their futures. Since their days together in Chelsea she'd grown to feel a great camaraderie with him as a fellow seeker after new ideas and philosophical truths. She'd always been attracted to 'wiseguys', she said, not as in Mafiosi but worldly, deep-thinking men. Sixteen years older than her and wearing the physical and mental scars of two decades at the heart of London life, he fulfilled that role with panache.

'It had been obvious that he had survived very rough company. And so this astuteness that he had was partly from his own inner knowing about people, but was also from walking through almost every walk of life there was, which was very '60s – that's how it was, everything was open. He had this vast span of people that he'd interacted with quite deeply and knew well.

'I think he was a loner by nature, and he carried that with him. Some people were afraid of him, and some people were just immensely entertained by him and really adored him for what he brought to the situation. If he went for you. . .that was a merciless spectacle. Because whatever Achilles heel a person had, whatever hidden fear or weakness, he was on to it in a flash and he would drive it home. If he wanted to throw someone out to dry he really knew how to. And some people don't recover from that, and they don't forgive it. Whereas he would.' It was an attitude shaped by the Jewish East End, where no one minded their manners or pursed their lips: very different from the stereotypical buttoned-up white Anglo-Saxon Protestant Englishness of the time. 'That would be the flare-up of the moment, "I'm going to get you for saying that or doing that, and here it is

– take that!" and then the next time you see him it's over, move on. But not everybody could do that. I think some people liked him for that. Because if, after all, we were about throwing the floodgates open, and if we were seekers after the truth of any situation, "what's the truth about that situation?" – even if it's unpalatable, go there.'

This was Litvinoff as a teller of fundamental truths beside which his daily fabrications seemed inconsequential trifles.

'He thought on a large scale, with words he painted with a big brush. He was into the detail too. But the big picture came to him first. . . What makes this person tick? What are they really on about? What can they really do? How can I help them see what they are not seeing? The 1960s was a collaborative time. Friends naturally shared ideas and created together. I think it was a gloriously optimistic, inspired time: we wanted to change the world, to create new ways of doing everything. New ways of relating to each other. No one wanted to be held back by the past. Separating distinctions such as titles or any reference to class were thrown out the window. A new consciousness was made manifest across the world. Everyone was interested in creating a new dynamic visionary culture in Britain or wherever they were. Where does the truth lie? What are new ways for men and women to be free together? For men to be legally together? Every avenue of mystic enquiry was pursued. Every religious ideal was explored and interrogated. Was a tolerant, caring, just, peace-loving society really possible? These are the kind of questions we were asking. We each answered in whatever art form came to us, in art as in life. It was all one.

'I think he just really believed in people's rights to be free. To express themselves in whatever means they wanted to. Totally believed in sexual freedom, and the beauty of it, coming from a position that this is a beautiful way for human beings to interact, and to be free without any kind of censorship to say what they really believed and articulate their vision of the world, and to guard with your life that freedom. And to object absolutely strenuously to anyone who tried to put a stop on it. A humanist libertarian. And I do think that. . .I recognised a seer quality in him: in his mercilessness, in the astuteness of his perception, in the basic kindness of him, in his wish to help people. I saw a seer-like quality, that in this amusing court-jester-like character was something far deeper at work.'

They were scrutinisers of the whole strange, hilarious, fraught business of being human. Students of sacred sites, not through sympathy with religion but via a humanistic draw towards the concentration points on our memory-map of the British Isles. Now as they reunited in the country where Gemes grew up (she was born in Budapest but moved to Australia aged five) their friendship evolved into something deeper still.

'I felt so safe staying with him in North Sydney. He was happy, in love and so generous with his enthusiasm. It was like that for quite some time. That was really before Rowley turned it around in him. Suddenly Rowley backed off. He was around less. He started to protest that he wasn't really gay. That their sexual relationship was over.'

Litvinoff simply wouldn't accept it. How could the love of his life reject him? Nothing Rowley could say would get through: so he abandoned words and took action by turning up with his new girlfriend, an Iranian woman named Mahtub whom he said he intended to marry. Litvinoff's violence resurfaced: an altercation with someone in Patric Juillet's restaurant next to the Yellow House quickly escalated into his headbutting the man to the floor. Wendy Whiteley was there: 'It was an East End street-fighting kind of thing. He could have killed the guy. He just lost it – I don't know what was said to him but suddenly this guy was flat on the ground.' The ties to his friends began to fray as people found that the growing cost of having him around outweighed the pleasures. To a pessimist there is no blow more wounding than the sudden extinction of a hope that you've cautiously permitted yourself to cultivate, and Rowley's desertion had that effect.

'Litva was devastated,' Gemes said. 'It was so sad. He was inconsolable really. More drugs, more drink, more sadness. Gradually friends started to tire of him. Playing the joker with a broken heart was too much for many, no longer entertaining – for some now he became a nuisance. Needing more distraction, more attention, feeling lost.

'Brett and Martin and Joan, Martin's mother, all told me that the circles were closing, that it was time for Litva to move. So when I told him I was coming back to London, it was not surprising that he insisted that he wanted to come with me.'

Axel Sutinen said he 'knew he had been reluctant to return to London as he had previously told me that he was hounded by the notorious Kray brothers', but evidently he felt now that he had little to lose. Before his departure he took another trip out of Sydney, heading back again to Ian and Katie Reid's farm down south in the mining town of Captain's Flat.

The money he'd been lavishing on friends and drugs a few months earlier had all gone, and he needed to fund his next move.

When a writer doesn't write, a music collection can function as an oblique autobiography; moreover one more honest than Litvinoff would likely have penned. Two hundred reel-to-reel tapes, comprising more than two months' audio, amount to a vast sound collage that both mimicked and in turn shaped his interior. They form a transect of his consciousness that reveals his preoccupations and sympathies, his friendships and familial relationships, clues to his sexuality and ethnicity and, in his recorded conversations, jagged dashes of the personality his friends try to describe. Mick Jagger's younger brother, Chris, viewed the habit as part of Litvinoff's fascination with humanity: 'He was one of the first guys probably interested in archiving the spoken word.'³ Snippets emerge unheralded amidst hard bop, trad and modern jazz: Art Blakey and the Jazz Messengers are hollering through 'Nica's Tempo', alto sax and trumpet asserting the theme, when they're interrupted by a click and then Litvinoff's voice. A soft-spoken Jamaican man called Steve is getting the John Ivor Golding treatment. It's the verbal equivalent of a finger jabbed in the sternum, Pinter without the pauses. Litvinoff's opening barb: 'Now, Steve, can you say something that's at all interesting?'

'Like what?'

'Could you confess to all the crimes you've committed? You would? What crimes have you committed then? Have you robbed anyone?'

'What?'

'Are you letting down the Jamaican ideal in London?'

'No. . .'

'*What?*'

'Yes, yes. . .'

'You are? Have you been living off immoral earnings lately?'

'I've never lived on immoral earnings.'

'Not lived on them, have you lived *off* them?'

'No.'

Another burst, Blakey's saxophonist Jackie McLean letting rip for ten seconds.

'Now, Steve, what is your opinion of the music you've just heard?'

'Well, David, my feeling about the music, I like jazz and it's something I've always liked, and I reckon this is the sort of music you should sit and listen to.'

'Yes. . .*where*?'

'At home, of course, at home. Sort of after-hours music.'

'After-hours music. And what's your ambition in life?'

'My ambition in life is to become a priest.'

'A priest? Hahahahaha! And convert people? Well why do you go around poncing your way around London if that's your ambition?'

'I'm not a ponce.'

'Not a *good* one. What *are* you?'

'I'm just. . .'

He trails off. Laughter from both men, one with a nervous edge. Click: Sam Dockery's taking the piano solo now, and the Messengers blast on through their 1957 album *Drum Suite* without further interruption. Having shipped the tapes to Sydney, Litvinoff then hauled them to Katie and Ian Reid's home, which housed a transient population of bohemian characters from the city who fancied spending some time working on the land. As an aspiring singer-songwriter Katie was dazzled by Litvinoff's knowledge of music and his storytelling abilities. She wasn't sure whether to believe him, but he told her that a striped jacket he owned at the time was the same one Dick Van Dyke wore in *Mary Poppins*. She didn't care in any case: regardless of his stories' veracity Litvinoff's entry into her life felt akin to 'a ray of sunshine, a multicoloured ray of sunshine, like a rainbow'. Together they worked through the track listings on the tape cases to produce a comprehensive alphabetical catalogue, beginning with Cannonball Adderley, Herb Alpert, Louis Armstrong, taking in a recording he played her of him giving someone speech therapy – some boyfriend back in London who'd somehow been left brain-damaged – and ending after hundreds of pages with Johnny Winter and the Who's *Live at Leeds*. In between are the *Basement Tapes* copy with which he helped re-route Clapton's career, a sound collage made by Keith Richards, Brian Jones' Moroccan field recordings, Rolling Stones out-takes from their Muscle Shoals sessions. The collection's diversity was testament to his initiative and dedication, as Nigel Waymouth explained. 'He would record my collection, he used to buy or borrow albums and give them away, and then he did this thing where he would write away to the States and they sent him the albums from odd sources. Let's say the Smithsonian, the Library of Congress. He wasn't lazy. Not mentally lazy either. He would make it his business.'

Some of the tapes had duplicates in London and Wales; not all, but enough to accept the idea of leaving them in Australia if it would put some cash in his pocket. He sold the collection to Ian Reid for $2,000 and left his most substantial physical legacy on one side of the world before departing for the other.

Conversations with a Sydney taxi driver, part two: to Kingsford Smith Airport from Wirian, Bellevue Hill, where I'd returned to collect seven of the reel-to-reels, which Reid had loaned to Sharp and Sharp had now loaned to me for my research. This driver was a sixty-something over-weight Middle Eastern man with a throaty, high-pitched voice.

    'Where are you from?' he asked.

    'England.'

    'From Wigan?'

    'No. . .'

    'I have friend in Wigan. He doesn't talk like you.'

    'Oh. No, he's probably more. . .erm. . .where are you from?'

    'I am Palestinian. You know my country, Palestine?'

    'Yes.'

    'The country you gave to *the Jews!*'

    'Mmm. What do you think the best answer is to the situation there?'

    'An earthquake. Destroy the place and start again.'

    'Mmm. . . Failing that?'

    'We just keep fighting until they get tired and go away.'

    His taxi sped along the freeway, its nose a yard behind the car in front. I had a plane to catch and a selection of precious tapes to keep safe all the way to London. At the airport I handed over another tip before heaving my bags on to a trolley. We did not discuss David Litvinoff.

He and Juno didn't fly direct to London. They did as he had suggested to Albie Thoms on camera and stopped in Bali. Litvinoff had 'scored some grass within five minutes', Juno remembered. She stayed with a Brahmin family at Sanur in a simple hut by the sea, whereas he preferred a small hotel nearby. When her hosts invited her to a three-day ceremony in the Princes Temple in Ubud, her interest in anthropology and sacred cere-monies meant she had no hesitation in accepting. That night at dinner Litvinoff announced some exciting news. Mick and Bianca Jagger were on the island, staying in the penthouse suite of the Hyatt hotel down the road from where Juno was living.

He told her that they'd been invited to visit after dinner – 'We'll go up and snort some coke and have a good time,' and Juno replied: 'No, I'm going up to this ceremony.'

'And he laid into me: "Oh, you are so exasperating! You're such a fucking idiot sometimes, you know? How could you possibly choose to go to a Balinese ceremony rather than see them?"' They continued rowing after the meal as they walked along Sanur Beach in the dark, Litvinoff tearing into her: '"You're such a fucking fool, you drive me mad!" He kept on laying into me about how I never did what was good for me, I made impossible choices. He was really furious with me... And he did really hurt me. So I actually wandered off into an opium den for three days. I didn't see him again in Bali. I stayed my course and he stayed his course.'

The next time they saw one another it was in London, where Ricky Levesley still sat moaning in a care home's wheelchair.

Chapter 11

The Caretaker

'Some people call me a hobo, some call me a bum
Nobody knows my name, nobody knows what I've done'
Bessie Smith, 'Young Woman's Blues'

There came loose, unaffiliated days in which neither he nor the young decade had an established direction. He drifted, lacking purpose. The Lenny Bruce book had gone, and with it any chance of cultivating a publisher's trust. *Performance* had provided no entrée to film-making. Many of his peers from the mid- to late 1960s had moved on in some respect. Eric Clapton was mired in heroin addiction; Donald Cammell was embroiled in his doomed attempt to follow *Performance* with *Ishtar*, which was again to star Mick Jagger; Jagger, along with his bandmates, was barely in Britain now. The radical threat to social order they purportedly posed had revealed itself as a rugged individualism that, finally, rejected little more than the notion that one's life is entwined with those of less affluent fellow citizens, a mutuality traditionally demonstrated by paying income tax. Christopher Gibbs had come into some money and left town for Davington Priory in Kent, while maintaining a pied-à-terre in Cheyne Walk. Like his suburbanised brothers, many of Litvinoff's friends had settled down. He was best man at the weddings of Julian Lloyd and Victoria Ormsby Gore, where his speech entertained an audience including Nick Drake, and Nigel Waymouth and Nicky Samuel, the latter at Chelsea Town Hall where he kept the guests amused like a true *badchen*, teasing the bride and groom, interrogating the registrar: 'So tell me, how many homosexual couples have you married?' When the laughter faded away he too often found himself alone. The only urgent project on returning from Australia had been to direct himself towards a friend's spare bedroom. Nigel Waymouth invited him to live at 52 Glebe Place, Chelsea, an invitation he accepted, though he spent much of his time away in Wales and Shropshire.

'David reading': a sketch from the early 1970s by Nigel Waymouth.

He tried to travel to India, perhaps overland on the increasingly well-worn hippie trail, for he wrote Sandy Lieberson a letter (undated) from the Tehran International Hotel: 'What am I doing here? What happened to India was I was refused permission to enter Bahrain (anti-Zionist paranoia) so split with beautiful Arab who's taking me to the mountains tomorrow.' He attempted to maintain the friendships he'd developed during his year in Sydney, and on 23rd August 1972 he fed a blue airmail letter into his type-writer at Glebe Place and hammered out a missive to Albie Thoms, having first drawn deeply from two of his favoured sources of stimulation.

Dearest Albie, Having just taken a monstrous snort from the proffered golden spoon, and had a blast of equally preposterous proportions from the obligingly proffered toke, I reach for my quill for the obligatory bullshit. Heah goes man. . . Your letter to hand. Full of nice vibes. Yes do make Bali if and when. It's a stone groove. Full of cunts, maybe. But BEAUTIFUL cunts definitely. Hope all your various entrepreneurial hustles on movies sort themselves out. Hope to see them someday soon, yes? Well man, it's summertime here and the livin' is easy. . . . Ha Ha. I've been in Shropshire - that magical border country of Wales and England - for the past two months with the Harlech boys and girls, the latter all nicely pregnant from the stalwart efforts of some pretty assorted courtiers from the Anglo-American Kenneth Anger/M. Jagger/A. Warhol axis. Not as bad as it sounds as I've been making a very cool little number with a cat called Jay Johnson who used to be Andy's* dude (Jay's brother Ed† now fills that sinecure I understand). . .

How is Bruce? I think of him and tell very tall tales of him in London, obtaining much largesse at dinner whilst so doing. Have you his address? I'd love to write to him. I've also heard from Rowley. I still dig him as a person as much as I ever did I think. I believe he's off to Greece very soon, and if he comes to London that would be really terrific. Please take some trouble with him if you ever see him, will you, Albie? Thanks. . .

Did you see that stuff in *Rolling Stone* recently about Mick's birthday party in New York with ZaZa Gabor, Dylan, Capote, Radzywill, Warhol et al? Makes you think doesn't it man why the scene's fucked up (or, worse, maybe even really FUCKED). Yes my dears it's all Cocaine, Champagne and more pain. The state of mind of people like Clapton, [Joe] Cocker and the English Rock thing is so fucked up with smack and coke and mercury and whatever else is deemed to be cool at any given time that it's no wonder the vibrations from that thing colour so much of what's happening here. Still man why waste your own life moaning about the wrongs of other people's lives as Thoreau, Catullus or Richard Neville said. Anyway. . .it weren't me babe. . . Much Love & Peace - Dave.

---

*   Andy Warhol.
†   Actually Jed, rather than Ed. Jay Johnson's twin brother was later killed in the TWA800 aeroplane crash near New York in July 1996, and Jay took over the running of his interior design company.

Forty years on Jay Johnson didn't recall any affair; he conceded that in his inebriated state during the early 1970s a one night stand was possible, but he would have remembered anything more enduring. Instead his abiding memory of Litvinoff was quite different. 'I was staying in London at Catherine Tennant's place on Bramerton Street in Chelsea and happened to be reading Nietzsche's *Thus Spoke Zarathustra* and he walked in, ripped it out of my hands and started to tear it up and accused me of being anti-Semitic. He was in a complete paranoid rage. Myself, I was speechless. It made quite an impression.'

His temper began to darken many such relationships. Catherine Tennant and her husband Mark Palmer found Henrietta Moraes* a cottage in Montgomeryshire called the Den and Litvinoff lived there with her for a while, but it didn't work: they were too similar, too tempestuous, and they drove one another mad. She kicked him out, he moved on.

After leaving him at Wheelers it was two years before I saw Frank Harlech again. This time I drove with Patrick Kennedy to north-west Wales to hear what more he had to say, and capture his memories on camera for Patrick's film. Glyn Cywarch hides within a lush valley clustered with ancient oaks, stately beeches and Scots pines, lending it a closeted air heightened by its owner's disdain for the modern world. It is a Jacobean home in hefty irregular chunks of grey stone, with transomed and mullioned windows and a slate roof with three great dormers that overlook the neat lawn, through which a path leads to a tall gatehouse with an archway just wide enough for a coach and horses. Within the gatehouse are a woodshed and a worn stone staircase that twists up to a library and billiards room. Carved in two small shields above the top corners of the house's entrance are the numerals '16' and '16'; and to step through into the elongated drawing room instilled a profound sense of transportation into a time of greater stillness and silence. A heavy mustard-coloured greatcoat lay draped over the back of a chair by an antique desk, on which Harlech laid open a leather-bound edition of John Worlidge's *Systema Agriculturae, being the Mystery of Husbandry Discovered*, 'mystery' in its archaic sense of a craft, 'discovered' as in 'revealed'. Inside the cover was the date 1681 and the flowing inked signature of Sir Robert Owen, Harlech's distant forebear, from whom he and the intervening generations had inherited a strong sense of patrician duty towards their land and tenants. The portraits of Sir Robert and other ancestors peered down from the William Morris oak-leaf-papered wall, which

---

*   The artists' model well known for her depictions by Francis Bacon and Lucian Freud.

also supported five long shelves packed with hundreds more such volumes. Smoky garlands of cobwebs drooped between the old picture frames and wall-mounted brass light fittings: they 'keep the flies down', Harlech explained. At the other end of the room he kept a summer fire burning in the hearth, above which was an ornate plaster carving of the family crest and Adam and Eve in the Garden of Eden, dated 1638. He moved between a low chair there and the open doorway, his animated face lit by turns with the ochre glow of firelight and the pale wash of daylight, talking all the while of the days when Litvinoff was there. He took us through rooms and outbuildings in which the air felt glutinous with centuries of family history, running a finger down dusty man-telpieces, straightening the pictures. Victorian maritime prints, a painting of the 'Godolphin Arabian', the famous stallion that sired a line of thoroughbreds and after being walked to Britain by a Georgian ancestor was, according to the surrounding inscription, 'allowed to have refrefh'd ye Englifh Blood, more than any Foreign Horfe ever Yet Imported'. Brooks's stationery, mildewed letters, Holyhead tide tables, copies of *Auto Trader* in piles on desks and sofas. He showed us a monk's bench with three small hearts neatly carved on one arm, the mysterious origin of which caused Litvinoff to twist the sacred into the profane: probably one for each time the celibate occupant masturbated over the thought of the person he loved, he concluded. Hanging on the stone wall in one of the outbuildings was a framed black-and-white photograph of a sturdy local tough guy astride a motorbike, with a slight, pliant-looking woman riding pillion: Harlech said it embodied everything Litvinoff despised about male chauvinism. The story went that Litvinoff exacted his own justice by seducing the woman and taking her to a hotel, and had to disappear the next morning when the town's men found out.

Between here and Brogyntyn the Ormsby Gores' hospitality gave Litvinoff precisely what he needed, just as it did for Eric Clapton in the same period. Back at Wheelers, Harlech had described one of his most vivid memories of those early 1970s days, this time at Brogyntyn. In his late teens he was overseeing the estate; as Clapton put it, 'running a farm that barely broke even, and. . .doing it virtually single-handed'.[1] While helping Harlech out and trying to come off heroin Clapton was 'up at dawn, working like a maniac, baling hay, chopping logs, sawing trees and mucking out the cows. . . In the meantime, Frank was swanning around doing stuff with trucks and mechanical devices. He fancied himself as a trader, and loved to talk about the massive deals he was doing with people for lorries and tractors and things.' The situation and Harlech's convivial company proved a tonic, he said. 'Frank did something very important for me. He helped me to feel good about myself again. . . He was very loving and very kind to me, and best of all he seemed to have no agenda. I think he truly liked my company and just accepted me for who I was.'

Litvinoff's situation was a little different – rather than shake a heroin habit he was trying to keep himself away from harm – but there were great similarities. Despite Harlech being less than half Litvinoff's age, he and his family came to represent sanctuary, and as Litvinoff had shown in Australia on the Reids' farm, contrary to his reputation for being workshy, he was willing to repay friends' hospitality with hard labour, for instance by shovelling earth, pushing a wheelbarrow or scything undergrowth.

A break from farm work with Frank Ormsby Gore at Brogyntyn.

'He knew he was safe in my house,' said Harlech. 'And I said: "Those old greenhouses have still got good foundations. If we dig them out I'll put a couple of galvanised sheds up and put the machinery under-cover. You can make a start. You get a pick and shovel and you dig, and shift the earth with a barrow." Anyway, this is an absolute classic. There'd been a bit of trouble down at Brogyntyn Hall, which the Postmaster General, the GPO, had a ninety-nine-year lease on. And 374 personnel, mostly moved from Dollis Hill in north London. Nine hundred and thirty phone lines go in and basically destroy a Grade I mansion. The wires coming through the floorboards like spaghetti. The oak floorboards were wrecked. However, in the meantime, in the stables next door, me and D. L. were working away on our sheds. And it was taking his mind off worry, and worry, and bloody more worry, pushing this barrow up this ramp.

'It was a very hot day. Bare feet. No shorts. A filthy T-shirt. A red hanky and a Turkish titfer. At which point a Rover 3.5 jam sandwich appears with two officers. And they got out of their patrol car, doffed their hats to me and came swaying over, and David walked up to the patrol car, an officer on each side, everything dangling out, nothing on below the waist, and came up to these two officers and laid down the law, big time. And the faces on those officers. . . "So sorry to disturb you, sir! Very sorry, there must be some mistake, we'll take up our enquiries with the estate office!"

'Hand on hips. Fag in mouth. "You'd better get back to what we pay you for." Real bravado.'

One of the policemen got back in the car, but Litvinoff was leaning against the other door with his waist against the window, which was wound all the way down. 'And then I saw that he'd left his cock resting on the top of the door, and the policeman inside was looking completely aghast. They drove off very quickly after that.'

Harlech thought it typical: outrageous, fearless, uninhibited. Litvinoff was 'a guy who gave an incredible amount of pleasure to people, even people he hated or didn't know.' This prompted a sudden divergence into an anecdote about Lucian Freud. 'We had a little *boisson* in the Colony Club, as one does. Lucian was there. Litvinoff said something, Freud replied: "You will never speak to me like that. . .you are trash!"

'Litvinoff stood up and said: "Lucian, just on the stairs – just on the stairs." He meant not to go outside, let's just step out of the room,' to the famously dingy flight of steps that ran down to the entrance on Dean Street. 'The beef was, when you get down to it. . .now, [Freud's] got his grand exhibition* and he's brown bread. [But back then] he grassed on David. He was tighter than a cat's tongue with the Kray boys, Lucian was. David felt totally betrayed by Lucian. He did make a

---

*   This was in March 2012, during Freud's posthumous retrospective at the National Portrait Gallery.

statement to the police about the association with Freud and the Krays.*
Remember, he fucked off to Australia and disappeared with me to north
Wales. It was about four and a half years [between this incident in the
Colony Room circa 1973 and its origins around the time of Litvinoff's
flight to Llanddewi Brefi]. But Lucian wasn't going to let it drop, like a
bone in a dog's mouth, saying that David had tried to frame him of associating himself with the underworld, and that they had profited from
that, from the sale of his pictures. . .' He trailed off. 'Litvinoff basically
loved music. He didn't love life. He was disappointed by his religion.'

He had long ago traded orthodox religion for an idiosyncratic belief
system and morality of his own devising, one drawn from his own experiences: he believed in love and art and music rather than his people's God,
until he became agnostic in this religion too. There was nothing left to
believe. There is no one so bereft as a disillusioned humanist. Here at Glyn
Cywarch, Harlech projected the same blend of amusement and sadness
when remembering his old friend as he had over lunch in St James's. In the
still of the late night they would hear the shipping forecast; then as early as
he rose the next day, Litvinoff would be up already. At 5am he'd be sucking
on a roll-up in the sharp morning air while listening to the radio, exhaling a
billow of smoke and mist. A glance upward and a smile in greeting: 'Isn't the
World Service wonderful, Frank?' On Sunday mornings they might catch
the early train down to London and head for Speakers' Corner in Hyde
Park, where Litvinoff would stand enthralled by the arrayed radicals and
doom-mongers and proselytisers, reading the atmosphere and attuning
himself to the popular mood, then fire a barrage of precise questions that
left his targets in knots and surrounding members of the crowd in fits of
laughter. They took a day trip up to Blackpool with Nigel Waymouth, and
Waymouth visited them at Brogyntyn, where he took a series of photographs capturing Litvinoff in rustic mode: caressing a donkey and a goat,
looking tender, though his face had grown almost sculptural in its divots and
striations; wandering through a meadow like a yokel; gesturing towards
Frank, who's perched on the back of a Dodge trailer looking towards camera
with a vague Romantic languor. While Harlech embodied the kind of

---

*   If he did, it eluded the requests I made to the Metropolitan Police under the Freedom of
Information Act, a process akin to asking someone to search for a needle in a haystack and
being repeatedly asked for more specific instructions as to where in the haystack they ought to
search.

aristocratic youth that Litvinoff found attractive, their friendship was forged in a love of music and long conversations about ethics – would you convict the fireman who stoked the train to Treblinka, Litvinoff mused – and history and where they sensed society was heading. The slum clearances in the East End left him saddened, Harlech said: not through any sentimental tie to the damp, lice-ridden tenements of Fuller Street or elsewhere, but by what was emerging in their place. Horizontal runs of poky terraces with neighbouring backyards made way for vertical blocks that seemed a recipe for alienation and social dysfunction, where grandmothers on the twelfth floor were only likely to encounter fellow occupants on the concrete staircase or in the urine-scented lift when it happened to be working. He could see a society moving away from intimacy in the name of progress, human connection withering in a more mediated and alienated world, and this troubled him.

At Brogyntyn.

Litvinoff in a meadow at Brogyntyn.

With Frank Ormsby Gore at Brogyntyn.

* * *

They visited Philip Yorke at Erddig Hall, his vast stately home near Wrexham, with Frank's sister Victoria, her husband, Julian Lloyd, and their friend Martin Wilkinson. Yorke was the last in a 240-year-long line of squires of Erddig, all of whom were named either Simon or Philip. He was an endearing character, then in his late sixties, who rode a penny-farthing, played the musical saw, gave magic lantern lectures, dressed only in second-hand clothes and never threw anything away. He was racked with worries that the nearby colliery was undermining his house and lived most of his time in the servants' hall, where the great table lay littered with tins of food, papers and broken radio equipment, and there was never any meat or alcoholic drink to be seen other than a bottle of sherry for visitors. Litvinoff was glad to add him to his collection of amusing eccentrics.

Martin Wilkinson, Litvinoff, Frank Ormsby Gore and Victoria Lloyd at Erddig.

At the end of 1972 they saw in the New Year in Morocco, Wilkinson recalled. 'He was acting as the caretaker of Christopher Gibbs' house in the Ourica Valley near Marrakech – well actually, rival *gardien*, as there was an old Berber couple doing the same thing, and a Marrakech hustler from the city also attempting to play the role. David had great fun in seeing him off, kind of beating his chest with loud proclamations of: "*Moi, vous savez, je suis JUIF!*" In other words, "I know a thing or two about you Moors." I think he saw himself as a cross between Paul Bowles, Joe Orton and Lady Hester Stanhope.* As always, hysterically amusing and self-mocking at the same time. Or maybe it was Rimbaud in Africa.'

In Tangier.

---

*   The Georgian socialite turned adventurer who, in 1815, undertook the first major excavation of an archaeological site in the Holy Land.

The guardian role was one that he had come to perform for his younger friends, whether seeing off the ranks of what he termed 'hippie stormtroopers' who'd outstayed their welcome at Brogyntyn or, as John Pearse remembered, acting as 'a strong mother hen-like presence' at Nigel Waymouth's home in Glebe Place, 'barring all visitors, and placing a sign on the door: "Art at Work – Go Away"'.

They visited Bishop's Castle in Shropshire, where Litvinoff glimpsed a half-timbered house's fireplace through a front-room window and marched Wilkinson and another friend inside to give an impromptu lecture on the decorative style, then marched them out again, leaving the bewildered owner open-mouthed. 'It was a bravura performance, even by his standards, with lots of lip-pursing and "Hmmmm. . ." noises as he examined the fireplace. He had two roles going on: genuine architectural expert to the householder (and to himself) and stand-up comedian to us.'

Waymouth and Litvinoff flew from Elstree out to the Dordogne in a light aeroplane with Merlin Hay, son of Sir Iain Moncreiffe-of-that-Ilk, and met up there with the Blunden sisters. Caroline Blunden remembered 'David sitting on a picnic rug in the middle of the French countryside offering mugs of wine to everyone' and that they stayed in an old house they named '*Au Prince Noir*', as the facade bore a plaque saying that the Black Prince had billeted his soldiers there in the fourteenth century. They visited Cadouin and wandered around the twelfth-century abbey and its ornate late-medieval cloisters, where Litvinoff slumped himself down on the stone bishop's seat, looking crushed, propped up only by his bones: head resting on his fist, elbow on the throne's arm, his slat of a mouth set grimly flat, brow furrowed and eyes half closed, 'his gaze fixed blankly into the future or the past or whatever it is that the present eventually becomes',[2] as Geoff Dyer wrote of a sculpted soldier on a First World War memorial. Above him a winged angel and a bearded man peer down, their small honey-toned faces exuding curiosity and benevolence, but he seems determined to ignore them. It is rare that a photograph of him should contain no tension, no sense of his image trying to wrest itself loose. He looks inert now. The social chameleon adapting to a background of stone. His expression in such medieval context suggests a *memento mori*: a reminder that behind his face's customary twitch and jabber, there lay the stillness of his skull.

Litvinoff at Cadouin Abbey in 1973.

The signs had been there a while for those who spent sustained periods in his company. 'He would get the blues from time to time,' Waymouth said. 'David didn't like parties. He would turn up for five minutes and leave. I remember one time there was a big fashionista thing at the roof garden of Derry & Toms, and he almost broke down, he was miserable and almost crying. I said: "What's the matter, David?" We left. I was with Fiona, my girlfriend. We took him home and he was better. Things crashed in on him. He would get gloomy. Not often, but it happened.'

Then one day back at Glebe Place he asked Waymouth a question. 'How would you do it?'

'Do what, David?'

'If you were going to commit suicide, how would you do it?'

Waymouth had no answer. He wouldn't do it. The moment passed and Litvinoff seemed to brighten again. 'He had this manic depressive side like Hemingway,' Waymouth said, 'especially in the machismo: "I can even top myself".'

While his friends sympathised, living with him became more trouble than they could bear. There were vintage moments still, such as when he and Waymouth were travelling on the Tube and Litvinoff reached his stop, at which he suddenly kissed his friend and announced for all the carriage to hear: 'Thanks for last night, and please don't tell anyone my cock tastes salty,' before stepping to the platform and leaving Waymouth with all his fellow passengers' eyes on him; but the retrospective amusement such times engendered became outweighed by the difficulties his presence brought. Chris Jagger lost Waymouth's camera and was making little apparent effort to find it, so Litvinoff reassured him that he would handle the matter. His method was simple: the next time the three men were together, he suddenly punched Chris Jagger on the jaw. That was the moment that Waymouth decided he was too much. While Litvinoff was away Waymouth moved his belongings out of the flat and moved his girl-friend Fiona in. When Litvinoff returned he was furious. They had little more to do with one other.

Certain of his Australian friends caught up with him again in London. Juno Gemes bumped into him on the King's Road and their row in Bali was forgotten. Albie Thoms visited in 1973 and Litvinoff arranged a screening of *Sunshine City* in Sandy Lieberson's office; he remained close to Lieberson, who put Litvinoff up for a month at his family home in Islington after he left Glebe Place. 'We snorted some cocaine before setting off,' Thoms recalled, 'walking via Hyde Park, with Litva chatting all the way, and we seemed to get there within minutes, such was the disorientation caused by the drug and Litva's flights of fantasy. We dropped in on his old friend Christopher Gibbs in his West End antique shop, where Litva discoursed convincingly on antiques, and then it was hard to shut him up while I showed the film to Sandy, with Litva claiming he had not realised I had had the camera on during his five-minute rave.'

Martin Sharp was back in town too. Eric Clapton seemed to have got himself together after his stint at Brogyntyn and 13th January 1973 marked his return to the public gaze with a concert at the Rainbow Theatre in Finsbury Park. Sharp and Litvinoff attended together, though a policeman stopped their car en route: 'David just held him there and just talked his way through,' Sharp said. 'The policeman's face at the window, and David leaning down, and manoeuvring his way through by identifying the person's home town, I think: taking the uniform off to the person underneath.'

They attended another concert together around this time, one as different as it is possible to imagine. Litvinoff persuaded Sharp to accompany him and Christopher Gibbs to Canterbury Cathedral to see the countertenor Alfred Deller, the burly, bearded singer whose extraordinary voice once prompted a German woman to approach him after a performance with the question: 'You are eunuch, Herr Deller?' His reply: 'I am sure you mean unique, madam.' As Sharp described it, Deller 'would sing with his incredible high voice like a child. I made a cassette tape of that concert and I gave it to Tiny. David was on at me saying something to the effect of "Well, folks, I've done my best". It was like a strange statement that he made to the recorder. Like a statement of resignation in a way. It seemed to be like an aside to the tape recorder, to the future.'

Tim Whidborne's last dealings with Litvinoff had been to clear up the mess at St George's Court and pay his overdue rent after he departed for Llanddewi Brefi. Now Litvinoff reappeared five years later with some promising news. 'He suddenly called on me,' Whidborne said, 'in a studio I had in Glebe Place, Chelsea, one afternoon, and I let bygones be bygones, while he told me that, being broke, he had found employment as the housekeeper for. . .Christopher Gibbs, who had a medieval priory near Faversham in Kent. His job was to get the place ready with food and drink and rooms prepared for Christopher and his guests to enjoy at weekends.'

Gibbs had been a substantial figure in Litvinoff's life for the past decade, and something of a role model: a well-read, well-travelled aesthete with a dazzling breadth of knowledge and social connection, adventurous in his drug use,* comfortable with his homosexuality, self-assured, always knowing the thing to do. If being in his friend's informal employ tweaked the balance of their relationship, at least the role suited his love of hosting and entertaining. It seemed that, having been ejected from his previous domestic scenarios in Australia and London, he had landed on his feet.

Some insist that it should be 'Albany', no definite article, and that to call it 'the Albany' marks you out as a social interloper, though this seems something of a false shibboleth that says more about people's need for

---

* Keith Richards wrote in his autobiography that Gibbs was the only person he knew who kept a phial of amyl nitrate by his bedside to snort immediately on waking in the morning, behaviour that took even Richards aback.

perceptible threshold markers within the British class structure. After Henry Holland converted the neo-classical Melbourne House into sixty-nine apartments in 1802, the trustees deemed that it would be known as 'Albany', but throughout the nineteenth century the latter version was common, being preferred by Charles Dickens and Oscar Wilde among others. Hugh Trevor-Roper uses 'the Albany' in a 1959 letter to the American historian Wallace Notestein,[3] and Trevor-Roper was not a man prone to imprecision in such matters. According to the *Survey of London*, 'the present resolute omission of the article seems to spring not so much from awareness of correct usage as from a sense, about the beginning of the twentieth century, that "the Albany" sounded "like a public house"', this information coming in the 1950s from William Stone, an elderly life-long proprietor known as the 'Squire of Piccadilly'.[4]

Regardless, it is one thing to know the preferred styling, another to be deemed eligible to live there. Gibbs' suitability was never in doubt. Though he was expelled from Eton for being 'generally totally impossible' as he once put it, it was there that, strutting around sporting a monocle and silver-topped cane with blue tassels, he set himself upon the path that would lead by the mid-1960s to his position as the acknowledged dandy king of bohemian London, the man of wealth and exquisite taste who dressed the inner sancta of the pop aristocracy in what became his signature style: exotic wall hangings, cushions, rugs, jewellery and a plethora of curious, distressed *objets d'art* culled from his expeditions to North Africa and the East, a taste acquired in his first adventures to those parts in the late 1950s. 'The Gibbsian Moroccan manner',[5] as Donald Cammell termed it, was to be seen in Brian Jones' home at Courtfield Road and in Turner's mansion in *Performance*, and is apparent in Gibbs' residences in Piccadilly and Tangier. After slipping through Albany's darkened red-brick frontage, with its looming pediment high above the white-columned entrance, you tell the liveried porter whose 'set' you wish to visit and he telephones ahead: then you cross a ropewalk to the apartments and feel yourself a thousand miles from central London. In a newspaper article Gibbs advised readers to imagine 'a monastery, but one in which the customary Trinity has been replaced by secular devotions – exacting taste, the pleasures of life and a romantic nostalgia for England's past'.[6] Its hushed elegance has appealed to writers from Graham Greene and Aldous Huxley back to Lord Byron, whose lover Lady Caroline Lamb crept into his set in 1815 dressed as a pageboy; women have been permitted to live there since the 1880s. Children younger than fourteen are not. Pets, whistling and musical instruments are banned, applicants on the interminable waiting list are thoroughly researched, and in a rare instance in 2011 of a set going to public market rather than being discreetly transferred to a suitable party, the asking price was £2 million. I arrived flustered at being late, but Gibbs received me with concern rather than irritation, setting me at ease as he poured a mint tea and reclined in his chair in a crepuscular green sitting room in which his kilims and sculptures flickered in the light of a small fire.

'It's a very long time ago,' he warned. 'As you're probably well aware, memory is a kind of moveable feast and a very tricky animal. I was reading this book, which I commend to you, by Mary Warnock, about memory. I think it's something like, after two months you can't remember anything accurately. . .'

In her book *Memory*, Baroness Warnock advises against understanding her subject 'as a "storehouse", in which things that may come in handy later are put away: a kind of attic or junk-room',[7] and in seeking to 'cast off Cartesian dualism' she proposes that we conceive not a dichotomy but a continuum between 'habit memory' and 'conscious memory':[8] that is between, say, knowing how to ride a bicycle and describing one's interactions with a friend half a century ago. There is a sense, she argues, 'in which memory and imagination overlap and cannot be wholly distinguished. Both consist of thinking of things in their absence.'[9] This business of recalling what is no longer before us has innate problems, for 'memory is not merely something which we deliberately evoke, but it is also something that comes charged with emotion and is highly prized'.[10]

Her ideas are complemented by the research of Chris French at the Anomalistic Psychology Research Unit at Goldsmiths College, who reports that '[m]emory researchers have always recognised that memory does not, as is often assumed, work like a video camera, faithfully recording all of the details of anything we experience. Instead, it is a reconstructive process which involves building a specific memory from fragments of real memory traces of the original event but also possibly including information from other sources.'[11] Though I did not know at that time how pertinent Gibbs' caveat would prove, the whole quest, I later grew to understand, amounted to an investigation into memory. Litvinoff was a fictionaliser who now existed in memory, and memory itself usually contained a seed of fiction: the prospects of consolidating his ghost could only rest on identifying overlaps between his associates' recollections, all the while negotiating territorial rivalries on the fields. Some tried to view him with analytical detachment, others only through the filter of their own relationship, needing to be perceived as closer to him than other people; memory became politicised, at times corrupted. Some memories were worn smooth with handling, others jagged and fresh, having lain unsummoned in the mind's depths for decades until I made contact. The sense grew that, however freighted they might be, memories remain but negligible fragments plucked from the roaring torrent of time, akin to leaves caught on a grille in the gutter while it pours down into the darkness; yet they are all we have, all we are, all the more precious for their scarcity. Memory operates under perpetual tension: the only way to cope with life is to learn what to forget; the only way to feel one has an identity is to remember. Litvinoff couldn't forget his past: he was too intelligent, ultimately too honest.

'I think it was 1970,' Gibbs continued, 'when I inherited some money, because I never had any; all my life we sort of had £482 a year. . .and I bought this place in the country, Davington Priory, in Faversham which is now owned by Bob Geldof. So David came and installed himself there.' He arrived in late 1973. 'And I was happy to have him, and I used to come down from London. This house was actually stuck on to the church and had a door that went straight into the church, so Litvinoff used to jump about in there at night. And there was a window upstairs that looked down into the church so you could see in. We had a sauna almost next door to the window.'

Davington Priory, Faversham.

The Priory was built in 1153 abutting the church and became a Benedictine nunnery. It had fallen into disuse by the Reformation, thus avoiding demolition in the Dissolution of the Monasteries. In the nineteenth century it became home to a stained glass artist named Thomas Willement, whose restoration left a legacy of medieval-style wall-paintings and glowing coloured panes. Litvinoff had a small bedroom with a wide dormer overlooking an ornamental garden. His possessions were few, he needed little space. It had its own intimate charm. Gnarled and cracked wooden bedposts, and beams laid into the ceiling; plain white walls greyscaled with diffuse daylight. Before he drew the curtains and retired to bed, he would have seen the night sky segmented into squares and hexagons by the leaded windows.

'He lived very simply, he never had any money,' Gibbs said. 'Sometimes when he got hold of a bicycle he'd go on these rather amazing shoplifting excursions. I'd mention something and David would leap on a bike and come back: "Here it is, man."

'"Where did you get it from?"

'"Nuffin' to do wiv you where I got it from." He was able to live on very, very little. I loved David but I didn't have a sensual relationship with him at all. I was endlessly amused and delighted and annoyed by him, and he was a sort of handsome, lively fellow, but that wasn't part of it.

'Ricky was someone that David was mad about,' he said. By the time Litvinoff reached Davington, Levesley was, in Gibbs' words, 'a wrecked creature. David looked after him and carried him about. I was never actually quite sure if David was partly responsible for his condition.'

During the first half of 1974 the Lucian Freud painting now known as *Man in a Headscarf* temporarily left the Astor family's hands, and while Litvinoff settled into Davington his likeness glanced away from visitors to the Hayward Gallery, before travelling to Bristol, Birmingham and Leeds in a touring exhibition of Freud's work. In his essay introducing the exhibition catalogue, the critic John Russell noted that 'The question "What can painting still do?" runs in tandem with the question "How much can one know of another human being?". For ten years and more [during which period he painted *Man in a Headscarf*] Lucian Freud answered both questions in terms of a tight, primarily linear form of expression which on many occasions was quite startlingly exact.' Russell added that most of these paintings were small, quoting Freud as saying

'Lifesize looks mean'. 'It was as if he could only arrive at maximum intensity by scaling the image well below the true dimensions of what was being portrayed. Possibly, also, certain things had to be writ small, lest they should get out of hand.'[12]

They coexisted well for a time, helped by Gibbs' frequent trips away on business, but Litvinoff grew bored and restless again. Sometimes he shuttled up to the city, usually managing to evade the ticket inspector on the train into Victoria, but he had grown tired of London. When Gibbs returned, he often found that Litvinoff had been driven half mad by the solitude, and like many 'people who spend a lot of time alone you simply can't stop them talking – he couldn't anyway. And so it was jabber jabber jabber jabber jabber. And then he made various friends in the neighbourhood.'

'He drifted away, David. . .' That was Sandy Lieberson's perspective. To others he hoved now into sharp focus. 'No one knows who I am,' he whispered to Jacqueline Hitchcock. At this time in his life she grew to know him as well as anyone. She was a couple of years older and widowed already, with four daughters. Her husband, Vincent Hitchcock, had found fame as the first English bullfighter; *El Ingles*, the Spanish called him. They had lived together in Madrid but now she was in a cottage opposite Davington Priory, and had left her previous career as a journalist to become a schoolteacher. The first time they met, Litvinoff was typically importunate: 'Could you lend me £100?' he asked. 'David, where on earth do you think I'm going to get £100 from?' she replied. But they grew close and she came to see him as a 'really lovely man' who was 'often talking about being discontented about not doing anything'. They often took trips together, whether walking down to the nearby Stonebridge Pond and looking for shapes in the mud ('David usually saw penises'), or driving out in her car: sometimes to the nearby Howletts Zoo, founded by John Aspinall, whom Litvinoff knew from his gambling days, once for tea with Aspinall's mother, Lady Osborne, she of the illicit payments to tame policemen, and often over to Seasalter, a village on the coast. They would walk the sea wall, crunch along the shingle shore, look out beyond the silvering wooden groynes to the North Sea, Litvinoff gazing towards the Isle of Sheppey and eulogising. 'His conversation went from the holy to the satanic.' On one occasion they brought the visiting Ricky Levesley, whom Litvinoff left unattended in the car with the door open 'to get some sea air' while they set off for their walk.

Martin Sharp and his friend Nell Campbell had helped pick Levesley up from his institution. Sandy Lieberson lent them a prop van from *Stardust*, the film he was then producing, and they collected him with Litvinoff and drove to the Priory. 'David seemed genuinely tender to Ricky,' Sharp said. 'David told us that Ricky had swallowed the contents of Brian Jones' drug cabinet, hence his condition.'

Gerry Goldstein spent time with Levesley at Davington too, caring for him and pushing him around in his wheelchair, but they stopped visiting after growing terrified of Litvinoff's rages. The Priory became a gothic theatre for such performances, in which his self-assigned role had shifted from the wise fool to something altogether angrier, sadder, irremediably darker. He began to spend lengthening spells in his room. Time's texture had grown abrasive. The days chafed and dragged. When he ventured into London the tales he told were rooted ever-deeper in the past; then in the hungover mornings he'd scrutinise his battered face in the reflected light of the bathroom mirror, trying to find the optimum arrangement of thinning hair across balding pate. It needn't be that way; some happier souls can find solace in the falling away of what once seemed all-important, finding that with maturity all the mind's fervid commingled particles of joy and regret and hope and grief associate into a stable structure. In George Melly's last years, Litvinoff's once-priapic old friend welcomed his loss of libido as a liberation akin to 'being unchained from a lunatic'.[13] The city had changed: the early editions of the *Soho Clarion*, a residents' magazine established in December 1973 by the Soho Society, warned often that Soho was disappearing, just as people were saying at the same time of Spitalfields. A photographer named Ian Berry documented the last throes of the Jewish East End at the Whitechapel Gallery in 1972, an exhibition reprised in 2011, at which time Berry recalled 'a certain palpable feeling of sadness that was in the air, the sense that one wave of immigrants was being supplanted by another. It was just becoming a multi-racial, but mainly Asian community, and the old Jewish community was in terminal decline. You could see the sadness in their faces, in their demeanour. That's what I remember most.'[14]

Soho and Spitalfields echo to the same call today, the process of disappearance being inherent in the dynamism that lends them their allure.

To one who demanded control of his life, the prospect of dying in a time and place of his choosing had a strong appeal. He could continue in life's blind backward descent, only ever guessing at the moment of impact, experiencing now and again the illusion that in freefall one is actually floating, even ascending; or he could take hold of the matter. Suicide normalises itself. It becomes an available option, then a fixation, then the destination as a mind contemplates its own inevitable extinction and resolves to expedite the process.* It is, according to Albert Camus in *The Myth of Sisyphus*, the only serious philosophical problem. As the Greek king heaved the boulder up the mountain, so Litvinoff pushed forward daily the latter boundary of his existence, his 'queer shoulder to the wheel'.[15] Camus identified suicide as a response to a realisation of life's absurd quality, a perception heightened in devastating instants when all roles and meaning deconstruct and '[i]t happens that the stage sets collapse',[16] and one to which his preferred reaction was revolt. Litvinoff had revolted since childhood and at forty-six years old he was fundamentally tired. Gibbs noticed a 'dulling and dimming'. His fiftieth birthday began to loom. He'd told his brothers he didn't wish to reach that age. He was not a man one could imagine in his dotage, grey flecks of stubble encrusting the high-water line in the bathroom sink, a blanket over his knees, queuing weekly for his pension, fumbling for his bus pass. He told Waymouth he didn't want to become an *alter kocker*,† moping around, getting in other people's way.

John Pearse: 'My last encounter with Litvinoff is at a party with Christopher Gibbs. He sidles up to me, puts his face close to mine: "I'm gonna tell you something." Clasps his forehead trying to recall for what seems like an eternity. Forgets and moves on.

'Nigel [Waymouth] played endless reels of his blues tapes. Litvinoff would introduce tracks in the slurred voice of an insomniac at the end of his tether. Broke and getting old. I guess he was. . .'

---

*   In a 1995 essay David Foster Wallace described this diminution of scope to a vanishing point in heartbreaking fashion, noting 'how as time gains momentum my choices will narrow and their foreclosures multiply exponentially until I arrive at some branch of all life's sumptuous branching complexity at which I am finally locked in and stuck on one path and time speeds me through stages of stasis and atrophy and decay until I go down for the third time, all struggle for naught, drowned by time. It is dreadful.' He committed suicide thirteen years later. *A Supposedly Fun Thing I'll Never Do Again*, by David Foster Wallace (Abacus, 2012), pp. 267–8.

†   Yiddish, roughly meaning 'old buffer', though literally meaning 'old shitter'.

* * *

Once in mid-1974 he cycled in fury across Regents Park to find Kenneth
Anger, who had cursed him. Litvinoff told Gerry Goldstein that he
'straightened him out', beating Anger and yelling in his face, 'Don't put
fucking spells on me!'* Gerry had a grainy photograph from this time, a
second one of Litvinoff with a bike. Around seventeen years on and a mile
south-west of Hans Crescent, he's standing in Camera Place – having read
it as a designated location for photography – in profile rather than straight
on, and the earlier jauntiness has given way to a kind of irate resignation.
He looks ravaged and irascible. The scene is little changed today: the same
russet buildings, black railings, street sign, only the trees a little taller, the
parked cars newer and Litvinoff not there.

In Camera Place, London SW10.

On a trip into town in early 1975 he caught up with Juno Gemes.
She found herself in a testing situation in that she had become pregnant in
a relationship that hadn't worked out, but she had no doubt about wanting

---

*   Mentioned by Gerry Goldstein in a filmed interview with Patrick Kennedy. Perhaps
understandably Anger did not respond to my attempts to contact him.

to have her baby alone. 'In an early flush of feminism I thought this was possible,' she said, 'despite the warnings of my friends Catherine Tennant and Georganne Downes that I had gone too far out on a limb on this one.'

Knowing of her situation when they met for coffee on the King's Road, Litvinoff presented her with a solution that left her stunned.

'I've got it all worked out, man,' he said. 'I'm going to organise everything. You, darling, are going to have the most fabulous birth experience, right? I've got it all lined up. I'm going to get the Queen's gynaecologist, you'll give birth in a four-poster bed. Henrietta Moraes is going to announce our engagement in the *Irish Court Circular*. Then we'll get married and go live in Wales. You, baby and me. Perfecto. . .what do you say?'

What could she say? She was taken aback and charmed too. Another friend had made a similar offer – a measure of the era's supportive ethos, she said – but Litvinoff's seemed very carefully considered.

'What strikes me,' she said forty years later, 'is that he was so protective, thoughtful and affectionate in his plan, yet there was an edge of panic there too. My antennae were sharp at the time. It's painful to reflect on, but on another level most likely he was saying: "We can save each other – we have done it before, we'll do it again." That was the undercurrent to it.

'I was a fiercely independent young woman who couldn't say "yes" to anyone. Now I had my protective animal instincts up. I was eight months pregnant. My first priority was to protect my child. Could I really manage with a new child and David alone in Wales? The best answer I could come up with was to plead for some time: "David, that's really so beautiful of you, let me fully consider it."

'I said to David: "We told Nicky Samuel just now that we'd come to her wedding party* at Christopher's in a few days. Let's meet there, we can go on afterwards, I'll answer you then." It was the best I could do at the time. We stayed in the coffee shop for another hour or so, making light of things, catching up, laughing at each other's stories. David was curious about everything, and tender company that afternoon. I was very moved by him too; we did love and care for each other in our own way. Yet there was an edginess to him that was not his usual kind of edginess. The

---

*   They'd seen Nicky earlier in the cafe. She and Nigel Waymouth had divorced and she married Ken Lane in New York in 1975. Christopher Gibbs gave a wedding party for them when they returned to London at his home at Cheyne Walk.

undercurrent to it may have been that he needed a safe haven. We'd been that for each other before, why shouldn't we do it now? His concern for me and my child was genuine. What he suggested made total sense to me. I just didn't know if I could do it. How could I could trust that it would be okay for the three of us alone in Wales?'

Gemes attended the wedding party at the full term of her pregnancy, resplendent in a long floral silk gypsy dress lent to her by Ossie Clark. She looked out for Litvinoff but he didn't appear. Friends plied her with joints and champagne, and joked that if she gave birth it would make it a party to remember. At 5am she went into labour and that afternoon she gave birth to her son at Middlesex Hospital, accompanied by her mother and Georganne Downes. She spent the coming weeks closeted in the enclosed world of new parenthood, concentrating on caring for her baby and never suspecting that she had seen her friend for the last time.

His behaviour at Davington was becoming too much. He'd give away Gibbs' clothes, and 'go through my drawers all the time; you'd find him examining the stubs in your chequebook, complaining about how much you were spending on suits or in Italian restaurants'.[17] Gibbs called Nigel Waymouth to say that he didn't know what to do, and Waymouth empathised: he knew well 'that manipulative psychological pressure that David could put on you because he wasn't providing anything except his charm. It wasn't an easy exchange.' After a time Gibbs settled on what seemed a solution.

'I eventually said to him: "Look, I just can't have you here full-time, you will drive me insane. What you can do if you want, you can move into this cottage down by the pond", which I owned, and I said "You can have it as long as you like and stay there". Anyway, that wasn't what he wanted.'

The weekend of 5th and 6th April 1975 saw Gibbs travel to Scotland to visit his brother. Litvinoff invited his fifteen-year-old nephew David Levy to visit, just as the ninety-five-year-old Emanuel Litvinoff remembered, explaining that he wanted to give him some gifts as he would be going away for a long while. The younger David arrived to find his uncle subdued, and later departed with some records, an electric razor, a tab of LSD and his cassette recorder (which with hindsight seemed 'such an obvious indicator that he wasn't going away, as he told me. While you could imagine him travelling light, he was never without music.'). Afterwards

Litvinoff asked Jackie Hitchcock if they could have Sunday lunch, and she cooked salmon. They discussed his friend Simon Scuddamore, a young actor whose parents came from Faversham, and who on other occasions had joined them for a meal. Litvinoff gave her some LPs that he had taped for himself. All seemed much as normal until they parted.

'We usually kissed on the cheeks, but this time he got hold of my face by the hands and kissed me on the lips, and said: "See you." I can see him walking away now. . .he was wearing a raincoat. It was odd, and I followed him up the road, just to watch him go into the Priory gates. It was in the afternoon; daylight, it wasn't dark. And I thought there was some-thing wrong and I called out to him: "You all right, David?"'

She watched him cross the road and go through the Priory's dark wooden gates, his hunched figure receding up the long curved driveway until he slipped out of view.

Whatever else may have occurred in the coming hours we can picture the following instants. He walked through the ornamental garden and the ornate wooden porch into the house. He wrote a note telling the cleaners, Doreen and Joan, that he would be sleeping late and did not wish to be disturbed, and left it on the kitchen table. He walked along the pammented hallway and up the fourteen worn wooden steps of the twisting staircase with its carved lion finials on the bannister, passed the window that looks down into the Church of St Mary Magdalene and St Lawrence, slipped a note for Gibbs into the pocket of a shirt in a wardrobe, then trod the long narrow corridor to his little bedroom, turned the brass knob and clicked the door closed behind him. He unscrewed his bottles of butobar-bitone and Mogadon and swallowed a large quantity of pills washed down with water, leaving the glass and a couple of dozen Mogadon tablets on a chair by the bedside. He climbed into bed, lay back and drew the covers up to his chest.

Ken Judges was the gardener at Davington then and remained so for another thirty-five years until his retirement. He returned to the Priory on Tuesday, 8th April, to find Gibbs' cat in an agitated mood, bustling and wailing outside the drawing room bay window. (You mean it sensed something was wrong? I asked. No, he said. It was very hungry, it hadn't been fed.) He found the note on the table. He walked upstairs and along the corridor. He knocked on the door, then hammered on it: 'Mr Litvinoff?'

Then he tried the handle, turned and pushed it and saw Litvinoff's ashen face, and knew there was no need to check for a pulse.

'He was a delightful, charming, fascinating, mildly deranged – occasionally totally deranged – starter-up of people,' said Gibbs. 'A prodder and goader and winder-upper. He was a stranger to conventional morality, but he certainly wasn't a stranger to love and loyalty, which is more important to my mind. He had fairly elastic ideas about what's yours and what's mine, and one of the things he did, just before he killed himself, he removed my life membership card of the National Trust and gave it to a neighbour in Faversham. He left me a letter which I didn't find for about two years.' Gibbs happened to retrieve the shirt from the wardrobe for the first time since Litvinoff's death, and a piece of paper fluttered to the floor. 'It wasn't a letter saying "I'm sorry I've done this".' It was just matter of fact, he said, a set of instructions regarding Litvinoff's belongings. 'There were some tapes that had to be sent to somebody in Australia, some boy he was passionate about – Rowley Davidson.'

All these years on Litvinoff lingered in his mind, remaining a palpable absence. Gibbs would have loved to see him every few days, just not to have him as a constant presence in his home. 'I wasn't used to having somebody living in close quarters with me, especially not somebody who barely drew breath.' As he walked me out of Albany through a central courtyard surrounded by flowerbeds and shrubs, he said: 'I dreamed about him the other night, you know. . . . I still feel like he's going to pop up again from behind those bushes, and tell us it was all just a joke.'

I cast my mind back to earlier that day at Wheelers, when the afternoon was waning and the dining room near-empty, the waiters glancing now and then towards our table. We'd drained the bottle of wine between us and Frank Harlech was on to a double brandy, speaking slower now, more deliberately. He turned his chair towards me, fixed me in the eye. His nose bore a divot on the bridge, the whites of his eyes were yellowing, but somewhere in that face remained the sweet intent of the boy who sat beside Macmillan.

'So why did he do it?' he asked. 'This extraordinary man. Why would he kill himself? What do *you* think?'

'Some people think he felt guilty. He hadn't done what he could have with his life. You can feel guilty about things you have done, and about things that you haven't done,' I replied, the answer feeling quite profound at the time.

'Well that's true,' said Harlech. 'But, still. . . I remember talking to George Melly once. . .he said: "Don't you miss old Litvinoff, Frank?"

"'Course I do."

"*Why'd he go and kill himself?*"'

Harlech didn't know any better than Melly. Most people were equally shocked – if self-loathing was part of his shtick, none of them felt it had been quite so acute – though Wendy Whiteley was not. 'I just thought it was par for the course, it was bound to happen. Litvinoff was an accident waiting to happen, all the way along. And the fact that he actually took control of that situation was probably very much part of his personality. He'd come to the end of people going, "Look, it's all right, David, we'll put up with you."'

She picked up on an unspecified guilt concerning Ricky Levesley, the tenth anniversary of whose alleged attempted murder by overdose was approaching at the time of Litvinoff's overdose. She sensed that 'he felt responsible for what had happened to Ricky: then he'd pissed off and done his own life, and then he went back from here [Australia] and thought "I'm going to go and see him", and started to take on a semi-caretaking role, but there was nothing he could do, it was all too late. And he couldn't even pick up the pieces of his own life and reconnect; this person was long gone. Already. It was too late. And that would have been pretty devastating. That as responsible as he may have felt, there was nothing he could do.'

James Fox always thought of Litvinoff with great fondness but by this time he was geographically and mentally far removed from any scenario in which their paths might cross again. After *Performance* he 'saw Donald in about 1971 or 1972' and 'tried to see Mick when I was in Australia but he was a bit aloof'. After his religious conversion he went to California as a member of the Navigators, an evangelical Christian organisation, and 'with my newfound faith I probably burned a few people off because I was not very sensitive about things. What's honest is that David was definitely not the sort of person you would meet without a context. I found the context of Dylan, because I was very interested in Dylan at that time myself, connected us, and in the days of Soho and *Performance*. So you needed a context with David. I don't know whether that was part of the reason he must have felt an outsider.

'One feels for him so much,' Fox said. He saw 'that outer level of giving pleasure to others and obviously receiving a lot of pleasure, but there's a deep need that isn't satisfied by that. So I didn't know him in that personal way but just in a strong contextual way.

'I did *so* like him. Yes I did. . . If it [Litvinoff's death] was '75 I probably was insulated, I probably didn't even read the obituaries. And one is so blooming selfish that I wouldn't have heard it from a friend, I just wasn't in touch. So I now feel about him dying [and] those last years absolutely quite bad; one now is better able to understand people, one now feels that that surface was also covering up a deep, deep level of need. But I don't think I would ever have been able to meet his needs myself as a friend, so in a sense I can't regret anything.'

Sandy Lieberson was deeply upset by his loss, even if they'd grown apart a little by then. 'I couldn't see it coming. Most people who take their lives, you don't know it's coming. It was a total shock when I found out that David had killed himself. It was a shock for Christopher Gibbs, he was very angry. Didn't like the idea that David had done it in his house.' Gibbs said he was more sad than angry; certainly not as angry as some of the Litvinoff brothers.

'He was getting old,' said Lieberson. 'He wasn't old, but he was getting old, he felt old. He would complain about that occasionally.' The coroner's notes suggest that he might have had gout. 'He was feeling maybe a little bit irrelevant. And in a way he had missed an opportunity with *Performance* and the Lenny Bruce thing. . . I would say it was a combination of a lot of things. You know, it's the ultimate act, suicide. A lot of people committed suicide in the 1960s and '70s, one way or the other. Usually through drugs, but there were a few others as well. It was, I think, part of the era.'

Bob Geldof bought Davington Priory in 1983. He had never heard of Litvinoff at the time, nor that there had been a death in the smallest bedroom eight years earlier. Even before he learned of it he noted the scene's resemblance to that of a famous Pre-Raphaelite portrayal of a suicide.

'That particular bedroom I think is the most romantic in the house,' he said, 'largely because it always struck me as being very similar to the one in which the young poet Chatterton is depicted as having killed himself, also by swallowing a poisonous draft, in the beautiful and famous painting in the Tate, *The Death of Chatterton*. I thought of that long before I knew of Litvinoff.'

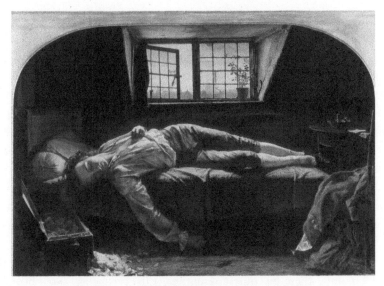

The Death of Chatterton by Henry Wallis.

In all likelihood Litvinoff knew Henry Wallis's painting, which was unveiled to immediate acclamation at the Royal Academy's 1856 Summer Exhibition, its frame inscribed with lines from Christopher Marlowe's *The Tragedy of Dr Faustus*: 'Cut is the branch that might have grown full straight, And burned is Apollo's laurel bough.' It shows the seventeen-year-old Thomas Chatterton splayed over a bed after taking arsenic, his auburn locks, white blouse and blue trousers gleaming in the soft light of a leaded dormer window. If Litvinoff knew the room's suitability as the setting for an act he'd already decided to commit, then his death befitted the manner in which he lived: referential, knowing, bleakly ironic, an existence framed by quotation marks, Susan Sontag's understanding of camp taken to its loneliest place. His was not a branch that might have grown full straight: but if it was gnarled and twisted, hollowing on the inside, still it might have blossomed again in later life. 'I had sensed that before in him, I guess, that possibility of immense depression,' said Martin Sharp.

'But I was looking forward to his old age, I really was. I was looking forward to that hopefully. But maybe people like that can't become that. When the passions of life have left them, they're alone. I wrote a little verse when David died, just a few lines:

When the jester was no longer king, the curtain had to fall.
He stepped out into the night, he stepped out for us all.

'A little verse I wrote for David, because he was a very valuable person who it was impossible for society to support well enough. The most sensitive people, we can't support them enough and we lose them, because they're too important. . . It's a failure of society, like Brett Whiteley as well. It's a failure that these people can't achieve old age, and that sort of maturity where their enormous wisdom can be shared.

'I felt David was a real giver: he loved connecting people and helping life flow. But there was no one who could give to him when he really needed it. He needed to be cared for and there was no one there for him.'

Geldof explained that the bedroom had first been inhabited by the family's nanny, then his oldest daughter, Fifi Trixibelle. 'No ghosts to report, I'm afraid,' he added. Why would there be? Any honest search for them should conclude with a realisation more discomforting than any spectre: ghosts do not exist. Everyone disappears. The river keeps flowing. The only spreading ripples on the surface once we've slipped under are our works, others' memories, our stories.

The funeral was held on 13th April at Rainham Cemetery, on the Essex marshes, where his parents were buried. Many people remember being there but insist they were among a small gathering; there is something about the cemetery's vast desolate expanse that would make any funeral seem ill-attended. Julian Lloyd was chided by Christopher Gibbs for bringing flowers: "Flowers are for *goy* funerals!" Of course Christopher knew the form.'

After Litvinoff's body was received from the Medway Hospital in Gillingham, a Mr Welt of the Federation of Synagogues had carried out the *taharah*, the preparation for interment, ritually washing him and wrapping him in a white shroud. Nicolette Meeres, his dancing partner from his Soho days, remembered the cantor singing beautifully, mourners being handed a spade at the graveside, scattering soil down a six-foot drop, the casket disappearing by increments. Marianne Faithfull travelled there with Gibbs and Robert Fraser. As their limousine turned out of the cemetery gates into Upminster Road, she recalled a sudden outburst from Gibbs: 'Well, I hope we never have to go through that again! And certainly not with *you*, Marianne.' She'd been close to the grave herself in the previous few years, sleeping rough, developing a heroin habit, but was beginning to re-emerge. 'My terrible moment was kind of over then, actually, and I remember feeling when Chrissie said that, "You impertinent fuck! You can't assume that!"

'He was so funny and so witty and so wonderful, I just fell in love with him, and was in love with him until he died. He hadn't achieved at all what he might have done. Being everybody's jester and good luck charm really wasn't enough for him. The thing of having a beautiful house. . . I think he was very envious of Christopher.

'I think he was very important, because he was a bit older, and he knew a lot. I think his life with all of us was like an escape from his real life, which was the East End and thugs and danger. We weren't dangerous and nobody would hurt him, we laughed at his jokes. . .he teased me a lot, I loved it, he knew me very well.

'We are all impoverished by losing David from our lives. I always think, in a way, when somebody commits suicide, they are punishing you. It's a very hostile act. There's no getting away from that.'

None of the Rolling Stones attended the funeral. They had an imminent American tour and besides, they had moved on from the days when Litvinoff figured in their thinking. Someone I'd interviewed, an old friend of the band, kindly asked their manager whether Jagger or Richards would discuss him. It seemed worth a try: another friend had related how he'd been 'a goldmine' for them. Litvinoff himself had written of them in familiar terms that show he was more than just another 'hanger-on' of the sort that Richards dismissed in their drugs trial. (Sandy Lieberson: 'They hung on to *him*! They were always inviting him to things.') The answer was no. 'Apparently the word is that they were never actually that close to him.' As the Greatest Rock'n'Roll Band in the World pushed ever onwards Litvinoff became one of the corpses left lying on the roadside, along with Gram Parsons, Brian Jones and Meredith Hunter. Recalling his days touring with the Stones and hanging out with Jagger and Richards in 1973 and 1974, the music journalist Nick Kent observed that though 'they were lords of all they surveyed, the hideous spiral of fame they'd both been riding rough-shod over had fucked with their souls badly'.[18] He noticed Jagger's accent mirror half a dozen others' as he worked a room, watched him perform a bewildering array of roles in the perpetual one-man-show that his celebrity had become: 'the leering hedonist, the repellent aristo-crat, the working class "oik" with a social edge, the concerned family man, the life and soul of the party, the "don't approach me" prima-donna, the narcissistic old queen, the ruthless businessman, the loving husband, the rapacious adulterer. There was really no limit to the masks he'd don.'[19] When Kent confronted him over the apparent discrepancy between the power and solidity of his position and his nebulous personality, Jagger reflected for a silent moment. 'I just enjoy changing personality,' he concluded. 'Honestly, I feel I've got to be very. . .uh. . .chameleon-like just to preserve my own identity.'[20] It was a trait – partly a survival technique, partly an actor's pleasure in exploring diverse personae – that Litvinoff had acquired long before Jagger and Richards met him. As their egos grew more delicate, it seems also that they had less tolerance for the unsolicited, unvarnished truths that were his speciality. 'He was very fearless,' said Faithfull. 'I think that's why he made enemies. Not just in the gangster world, but probably Lucian Freud and Mick Jagger too. He would say what he thought and didn't care about their egos. Which is fatal with people like that.'

Afterwards Barnet Litvinoff received the mourners at his home in Hampstead. Faithfull's then-boyfriend, Oliver Musker, remembered two of the brothers apologising profusely to Gibbs for David's poor manners in committing suicide in his house. He also remembered a poignant remark by Emanuel Litvinoff.

'At the wake, Manny said: "I'm so pleased that so many of you turned up." I said: "What do you mean? Of course we'd turn up." He said: "David always said to me his friends didn't like him."'

Then the party disbanded, the wider family back to suburbia, the friends to Chelsea, Shropshire and Faversham, the single overlap between their worlds remaining enclosed beneath a mound of earth in the Essex marshes.

Two weeks after Litvinoff's death Christopher Gibbs received a visitor at Davington Priory. The doorbell rang and waiting there was a young man, who said: 'Is Mr Gibbs in?'

He replied: 'I'm Mr Gibbs.' The visitor said: 'No, you're not Mr Gibbs. Mr Gibbs is a small bloke with a big nose. He told me to come round this afternoon and we'd have some tea and listen to some music.'

It was a strange and unsettling incident. Gibbs and Oliver Musker discussed it later. 'Christopher and I were talking about this, and I said to Christopher: "I think David did this on purpose",' Musker said. 'He knew he was going to commit suicide and he'd made this arrangement about a week earlier, and it was a deliberate act.' If so this was Litvinoff's final barb at a man who seemed to have it all, executed with typical precision from the grave. Then he was gone.

Chapter 12

Beyond the Grave

'And now let's talk about more cheerful things. Tell me, what
news is there about the cholera in Odessa?'
Sholem Aleichem, 'Hodel', trans. Julius and Frances Butwin*

The inquest took place on 15th May 1975, at Sittingbourne Coroners'
Court. Of the family, his brothers Phil and Frank Levy and Barnet Litvinoff
attended. W. Jervase Harris, the coroner for North Kent, took submissions
from Ken Judges and Jacqueline Hitchcock, the last people to see him
alive, and consultant pathologist John Leslie Dales, who had performed
the post-mortem examination. In the coroner's clerk's rushed scrawl the
salient points among their contributions are rendered as follows:

Frank Levy: *Numerous jobs, never kept them for long
periods - he couldn't settle. Very interesting person
but not very responsible. He went abroad to Australia
for a time. Kept in touch with us. He had relationships
with opposite sex but they didn't last. As far as I
could see he had no particular worry. None that you
could put your finger on. He never suggested at any time
he would take his own life. If I had to select anyone
out of my family I would pick him but I still couldn't
think he could do it. His financial position always
bleak. He used to help at Davington Priory. No pay. A
friend of person at Davington Priory. I didn't know Drs
had prescribed drugs. I can't help you over that.*

Ken Judges: *He kept himself to himself at times.
I didn't get to know him very well. I perhaps didn't*

* As collected in *The Penguin Book of Short Stories*, ed. Emanuel Litvinoff.

see him for several days but I knew he was in the house. He would stay in his room. He could be very pleasant. He could also get irritated and annoyed if things didn't go right. He told me he thought got gout & he told me his nerves were bad. He would sometimes be like this in morning & then be pleasant in the afternoon. Friday subsequent to death I last saw him. I checked at 5pm to see if he was back because he had been away on the Thursday and Mr Gibbs would be away the w/end. He said he would be there for the w/end.

Jackie Hitchcock: *I have known dec'd since Christmas before last – about 16 months. I knew he was staying at Davington Priory. This is just across the road from us. He came and had meals with our family. He introduced young David as his son.* He didn't seem unusual on 6/4/75. He gave us some records but this was not unusual as he had taped them. He never mentioned at any time he would take his life. He was so full of life.*

The pathologist confirmed that the cause of death was barbiturate overdose. He found powder on the lungs and oesophagus and in the stomach. '*Large quantity taken at same time. Died before he had absorbed all the tablets. No marks of violence. Butobarbitone is a sedative and could be prescribed.*' When the coroner delivered a verdict of suicide Barnet Litvinoff shouted 'No!', but to no effect.

The notes form a bleak coda to such a varied and fabled life, but their purpose was as a document rather than a story. The stories would exist in the ether rather than on paper.

We are all storytellers. We all have our stories to tell. Justifications and explanations that we create to elucidate to ourselves how we emerged from the morass of the past and stumbled into the present. The stories we tell others may differ. We are all editors. We elide, emphasise, excise the chaff to create plausible narratives. We adapt our performance for our audience and venue. We squeeze ourselves free of the past's grip while carrying sufficient memories to construct a satisfying tale. This pertains to cities as

---

*   His nephew David Levy, his brother Frank's son.

much as the individuals who form them. Litvinoff's ghost was pressed into service as a storyteller who helped London understand itself, one who could explain how in the 1960s a merger of criminality and bohemia and resurgent post-war energy spawned a hybridised city whose frantic spin hurled some protagonists into the stratosphere and others into a vortex. Litvinoff's stories survived his death, were liberated by it: without any tether to the physical world they bred amongst themselves and created mongrels. There are a dozen variants on the Kensington High Street balcony-dangling affair roaming the streets now, likewise the tale that Frank Harlech titled 'The Cock and the Coppers'. In other renditions Litvinoff is entirely naked, covered with ash from a bonfire he has been tending, dragging on a joint and offering it to the officers as a 'herbal cigarette' that he's smoking for medicinal reasons to help with his cough. They cannot all be true, but all are true of his character. Litvinoff's posthumous myth became constructed on this nebulousness, this intangibility: the man who laughed, the man who disappeared.

By the mid-1980s, investigators of London's animating energies took note. Iain Sinclair began to grow obsessed. There were rumours of a journal, the so-called 'Litvinoff's Book', in which its author had disclosed the true workings of the 1960s, and associated rumours that had his death as murder at the hands of shadowy figures who believed he was about to expose them. Perhaps there was a seed of truth in the novelist Robin Cook's claim, prompted by discussing his appearance in Sinclair and Christopher Petit's film *The Cardinal and the Corpse* alongside Emanuel Litvinoff: 'Used to know [his] half-brother David quite well. He managed to kill himself. Which was probably just before he would have been murdered.'[1]

Gerry Goldstein confirmed to Sinclair that 'when we were living in the country he was writing bits of stuff down',[2] but there was no book. A likelier candidate for such a dossier emerges in the form of Ricky Levesley's diary, the document of his and Litvinoff's criminal dealings that Levesley's mother apparently refused to submit to the prosecutor because it would have left him prone to reprisals. Gerry must have been aware of this at the time, even through his fug of heroin addiction. If this was 'Litvinoff's Book', how fitting that the document most associated with him was written by someone else. The graphic novelist Alan Moore, who also featured in Sinclair and Petit's film, purloined its title for a song rich in oblique allusions to Litvinoff's connections with the Krays:

There's a tall tale of two cities, and it's all in double-dutch
Some two-bit hustler double-crossed the heavenly twins
One with his lily-white boys (They're too-too and he's too soon;
*   too much)*
The other brother would have doubled up and quit for just two
*   pins*
But with deuces wild the Jack was aced, decked by the old
*   one-two*
When he threw snakes-eyes they were holding all the cards
Down Casenove Road, where first offenders find their second
*   chances few*
There's Bobbies bicycling, two by two, towards New Scotland
*   Yard.*
So like two Hierophants dispensing double visions, double talk
The dopplegangsters, living by their binary code,
Lead Jack Spot, Rachman and Lord Boothby in a two-step
*   Lambeth Walk*
Off to a Looking-Glass House (two up, two down) back in Vallance
*   Road*
But there's two sides to every story and the door to every cell
Two wrongs to every right; two backs to every beast
And now they've looked at life from both sides it's a sentence
*   hard to spell:*
Double your money in the City, but you'd better think twice
*   down East*
And the muscle is bunched in the Carpenter's Arms
In their opposite corners sit Justice and Crime
But in matters of grievance or bodily harm
They're like peas in a pod, or the sides of a dime.

'I first brushed against the spectral absence of David Litvinov [*sic*] in 1992 when I was one of the wrangled freaks contributing to Iain Sinclair and Chris Petit's majestic *The Cardinal and the Corpse*,' Moore wrote.

The film's central conceit was that of a number of book-obsessive fanatics searching for marginal or possibly non-existent tomes in the shops and markets of the East End. One of the lost books was attributed to David Litvinov. . .[who] had reportedly compiled a journal that incidentally documented the casual links between crime, show-business, government and the aristocracy. Litvinov had disappeared, or had been disappeared, perhaps because of the sensitive information in his putative book, and only existed now as a credit line on *Performance* and as an intriguing East End enigma. Even David's half-brother, the author and East End chronicler Emanuel Litvinoff who appeared in *The Cardinal and the Corpse*, had no information.

I cast my mind back to watching the film with Sinclair at the outset of my research. He uttered quiet chuckles at its black flashes. Driffield, an extrovert book-dealer of London legend, disclosed a secret intention to enclose the entire capital in a circular wall of books. A deadpan Tony Lambrianou recalled Ronnie Kray getting laughs in the pub by using a midget as a ventriloquist's puppet: 'Ron's sense of humour was something different.' Only Gerry and Pat discussed Litvinoff, and they had little of substance to say on camera.

'It was a mystery with no apparent solution,' said Moore, 'and as such it rattled around in my mind for the next year, at some point during which I wrote the song "Litvinov's Book", initially for the band I was with at that time, The Emperors of Ice Cream.' After Sinclair published *Rodinsky's Room*, with its extracts from the Golding tapes and a few of Gerry Goldstein's recollections, Moore considered the case solved,

although, of course, figures like that are not depleted in mystery for as long as they are fascinating to us. We can, after all, always speculate. Was one of those two boys dancing under coloured lights to the Beach Boys' "Good Vibrations" just prior to the murder of Jack McVitie actually David Litvinov? Was that why the secrecy, even after all those years? The Colonel was still alive in Broadmoor back then, of course, sending warning messages to former lieutenant and fellow *Cardinal and the Corpse* alumnus Tony Lambrianou, so perhaps it was all still too fresh. For my own part, when I came to write the "1969" section of my *League of Extraordinary Gentlemen* series with Kevin O'Neill, since a large part of the plot was focused upon events similar to those in *Performance*, I took the opportunity to include a few cryptic references to David Litvinov in both that and the previous volume. I think I did this to indicate to those interested parties among the readership that if you prise up just some minor flagstone of culture, you are likely to be surprised by the richness and strangeness of the life that writhes beneath.

This posthumous interest evolved in tandem with a growing appreciation of *Performance* born of the perspective gained from two decades' distance and precipitated in particular by Cammell's suicide in 1996 by gunshot to the head, replicating Turner's fate. His death spurred a flurry of retrospective literature and a documentary, *Donald Cammell: the Ultimate Performance*, that also combined to kindle Litvinoff's reputation. From often being attached solely to the better-known Roeg, *Performance* became understood as thematically more indebted to Cammell's milieu, and the corollary was that Litvinoff began to seep into the proliferation of texts addressing the film. Increasingly the facts began to interchange among themselves. In a film book's entry on *Performance* Litvinoff became an 'Old Etonian fascinated with the gangster milieu',[3] while numerous writers took relish in mentioning that Ronnie Kray had pushed a sword through his mouth, some adding that Kray had twisted it for added effect. As mentioned earlier, *The Krays* fixed this myth in celluloid 'reality'.

Colin MacCabe's 1998 book for the BFI was the first substantial appraisal, Mick Brown's for Bloomsbury in 1999 the next. Jonathan Meades treated him with amused disdain in an essay on Christopher Gibbs – a 'piece of very rough trade', 'the scion of a liberal Jewish Highgate family' (Sinclair on this: 'In effect, he becomes his brother's son'; in life Litvinoff cast his brothers' sons as his own), who 'topped himself' at Davington.[4]

More than anyone, it was Sinclair who intensified Litvinoff's mythology, not least through his thwarted efforts to deconstruct such mythology and solidify Litvinoff's ghost. He felt compelled to return to the subject, most substantially in *Rodinsky's Room* but also in *Dining on Stones*, *London: City of Disappearances* and *Lights Out for the Territory*.

I thought back often to my conversations with Sinclair at the beginning of my search, when, like some unwisely deployed volunteer detective learning on the job, I had little understanding of what I was investigating. The questions invoked by excavating a life arose entangled with questions concerning the nature of time, and memory, and knowledge. I remembered Sinclair's intuition that, just like David Rodinsky, Litvinoff lived in a landscape where 'there is a very strong sense of plural time, of being able to reach it and lose it'. More than once I felt an illusory sensation of knowing Litvinoff, of having threaded the story into the fabric of the deep past and pulled the loop tight to the present; and then the instant was gone, and I was left only with the dull physical sensation of holding a reel-to-reel tape case, a frantically typed letter, a photograph. But it felt real, believe me.

I interviewed a hundred people and in the course of my research had assistance from a further 150. I crossed the world, traversed the UK several times, found my way back into London after a period of enforced separation. I tried to track down everyone I could. The quest was never finished, only abandoned. There are bound to be people I've missed, those who feel aggrieved that I didn't hear of them, those who feel aggrieved that a man who damaged or somehow sullied their lives is so fondly remembered by others. 'The deification of David Litvinoff,' sneered an Australian artist and film-maker named George Gittoes, when I spoke to him on the telephone from Wirian. 'I couldn't stand the man. Others were overawed by him but I saw through that.' Sometimes I shared that disdain for my subject, but ultimately the fluctuating esteem in which I held him was quite irrelevant: what mattered was whether he was interesting and significant, and only the most partisan observer would deny that he was both.

Of the characters in Litvinoff's story as it's told here, several have since left us. The Krays, Lucian Freud and George Melly are all gone, of course. Bobby Buckley died in mysterious circumstances in the 1970s. He was adjudged to have accidentally overdosed on heroin but his friends David and Patrick Fraser were sceptical: 'There was always a smell about it,' reckoned David, who said that Buckley didn't use heroin and suspected instead that it was a murder made to look like an accidental death. Martin Sharp died of emphysema eighteen months after my visit, aged seventy-one. Albie Thoms' cancer was in remission when I met him but it returned soon after. He died in November 2012, also aged seventy-one. Rowley Davidson and his wife Mahtub died young of AIDS some years before I began work. Andy Garnett received a generous obituary in the national press in July 2014,[5] and Frankie Fraser rather more (though less complimentary) coverage when he died aged ninety that November. Had Litvinoff reached old age too, would he have found happiness? Perhaps. Marianne Faithfull found herself at a similar juncture and eventually flourished.

'Why does *anyone* commit suicide?' she asked in response to my enquiring why she thought he did so. 'Because they can't bear it. But that feeling does pass. I've tried to commit suicide and I've never managed it. And I'm so glad I didn't.

'I felt deprived of seeing Dave age and become probably happier, because all those difficult desires and impulses do go away, in time. That is a great relief, and something like that might have happened to Dave. I think it happens naturally as you get older. It just stops mattering.'

As for whether he would have transformed his talents into a physical legacy, it is a counterintuitive question. He did produce a legacy. If he was a performer and a procurer, he was also a curator. Professional curators do not leave behind a body of work, only a CV charting their visionary gatherings of diverse objects that placed together stimulated new connections, ideas, memories in gallery visitors. Litvinoff was a rogue curator who aggregated obscured music, books, facts, lies, stories and people, and embarked on a project of relentless sharing with the intention to brighten the gallery of life. He succeeded. Martin Sharp saw this with typical clarity.

'He had nothing to leave apart from what he'd done, who he'd connected to whom,' he said. 'Those were his gifts.'

* * *

'Life is a passing shadow, say the Scriptures. The shadow of a tower or a tree; the shadow which prevails for a time? No; even as the shadow of a bird in its flight, it passeth from our sight, and neither bird nor shadow remains.'

The Talmud

Tease through a tangle of broad grey ribbons of tarmac until one straightens and stretches into Upminster Road North, then growl through half a mile of exasperated traffic before trading congestion for solitude at a stroke: one twist through a high stone gateway and you're inside a silent citadel of the Jewish dead, or a 'house of the living'. The first burial took place in 1872 but Rainham Cemetery's transformation into a necropolis began in the mid-twentieth century with the passing of the generation who had fled the Tsarist pogroms: born in 'Warsaw, Kishinev, Kiev, Kharkov, Odessa', landed in Whitechapel, then displaced again in death, shunted to the periphery to merge into the mulch of this Essex interzone between suburb and wilderness, this outer edge of London's spreading grey stain, where kebab shops leak meaty odours towards the dull green marshes and car dealers flog ten-year-old Vauxhalls beneath a broad mouldering sky.

Surveyed from the car park on a damp late afternoon in February, the burial ground resembled a scene Caillebotte might have painted had he shifted his gaze from Paris to Essex. Monochrome marble headstones filtered through flat grainy light, water in the air and on the ground, brooding clouds threatening more. I put on a *yarmulke* and picked up a prayer book outside a small office occupying the far end of a winged building that also houses the ceremonial hall and the visitors' toilets. A sign on the door warned of a hazard attendant on visiting the graves: the small but ever-present risk of suddenly finding oneself underground too. 'Please be aware and take care whilst walking among the memorials. Subsidence of the ground can occur at any time and whilst the ground staff do their upmost [*sic*] to prevent this, unfortunately holes do appear without warning.'

I set forth down the 250-metre-long concrete road that bisects the cemetery and found the area to which the caretaker had directed me when I telephoned that morning, then left the path to take tentative steps between the densely cluttered rows of gravestones. Beyond a high brick perimeter wall stood tall leafless trees in charcoal silhouette. The marsh-land offered little else to distract the eye between the graveyard and the misty pylons and copses that crinkle the horizon, above which low grey cumuli piled up like a mirage of mountains. Traffic hummed along the Upminster Road, but within the deserted cemetery it was just me and twenty-five thousand dead people. If the subsidence meant that some caskets were less firmly enclosed than others, perhaps this explained the subtle but unmistakable scent of putrefaction loitering in certain quarters. With a faint nausea I tiptoed around the L-shaped conjunctions of upright and flat gravestones, most in grey with black engraving, but some rendered in black marble with gold script, counting to myself as I stole along. Here I was now: section B, row 40, grave number 35. . . A pale rain-streaked slab, the upper half bearing sparse Hebrew lettering and the lower English:

In Loving Memory of
ROSE LEVY,
DAUGHTER OF JACOB MICHAELSON OF ODESSA,
DIED 22ND FEB. 1947
AGED 54.
DEEPLY MOURNED
BY HER DEVOTED HUSBAND

SOLOMON
HER EIGHT SONS, DAUGHTER,
SON AND DAUGHTERS-IN-LAW,
GRANDCHILDREN, RELATIVES AND FRIENDS,
BUT THY ETERNAL SUMMER SHALL NOT FADE.

I'd have been more surprised if I'd found Litvinoff where I expected him to be. I edged my way between forgotten memorials, murmuring apologies to sundry Caplans, Kaufmans, Goldbergs and Diamonds as I skipped over them, my shoes accumulating clags of marshland mud. And there near the end of the row, just as I'd become more concerned with avoiding others' graves than finding his, stood a dirty dark grey marble slab bearing a simple legend in almost indecipherable black capitals, so weathered that I'd already wandered past it without realising.

IN EVERLASTING MEMORY OF DAVID LITVINOFF.
SON OF THE LATE SOLOMON & ROSE LEVY.
BORN 3RD FEBRUARY 1928. DIED 8TH APRIL 1975.
SADLY MISSED BY HIS FAMILY AND FRIENDS.
SHALOM DAVE.

The clouds were darkening, cold gusts weaving around the headstones and into me, ghosts' hands kneading at my chest. In silence I scanned the prayer that the book indicated was suitable for 'an adult male':

'O Lord who are full of compassion, who dwells on high – God of forgiveness, who are merciful, slow to anger and abounding in loving kindness, grant pardon of transgressions, nearness of salvation, and perfect rest beneath the shadow of Your divine presence, in the exalted places among the holy and pure, who shine as the brightness of the firmament, to_____ who has gone to his eternal home. We beseech You, O Lord of compassion, remember unto him for good all the meritorious and pious deeds which he wrought while on earth. Open unto him the gates of righteousness and light, the gates of pity and grace. O shelter him for evermore under the cover of Your wings; and let his soul be bound up in the bond of eternal life. The Lord is his inheritance; may he rest in peace. And let us say, Amen.'

I laid a stone on Litvinoff's grave and paused a few moments until the clouds began to break, droplets dappling the long grey strip that led back to the car park, then gathering in muddy hollows, draining into the marshland and coursing now down the concrete; raindrops striking puddles in concentric bursting circles that intersected and vanished, geometric beauty in the gutters. I strode back kicking mud from my shoes, laid the prayer book on its shelf by the office and drove away, wondering as I left which of its lines would have made Litvinoff laugh the loudest.

Notes

Introduction

1 Jonathon Green, *All Dressed Up: The Sixties and the Counterculture*, p. 179.
2 Eric Clapton, *The Autobiography*, p. 92.
3 Clare Peake, *Under a Canvas Sky: Living Outside Gormenghast*, p. 210.
4 George Melly, *Owning Up: The Trilogy*, p. 490.
5 Colin MacCabe, *Performance (BFI Film Classics)*, p. 25.
6 Rachel Lichtenstein and Iain Sinclair, *Rodinsky's Room*, p. 135.
7 Iain Sinclair, *White Chappell, Scarlet Tracings*, p. 177.
8 MacCabe, p. 25.

Chapter One – A Modest Unassuming Young Hebrew Boy

1 Museum of London interview with Emanuel Litvinoff by Hannah Berman.
2 Ibid.
3 Joseph Roth, *The Wandering Jews*, trans. Michael Hofmann, pp. 109–10.
4 Museum of London interview with Emanuel Litvinoff.
5 Emanuel Litvinoff, *Journey Through a Small Planet*, p. 21.
6 *Night Waves* interview with Emanuel Litvinoff.
7 Patrick Wright's Introduction to *Journey Through a Small Planet*, p. xvii.
8 Emanuel Litvinoff, p. 32.
9 Ibid., p. 35.
10 Ibid., p. 36.
11 Ibid., p. 56.
12 Ibid., p. 65.
13 http://discovery.nationalarchives. gov.uk/details/rd/0b3812c8-f787-4ce7-9d02-c9aba70e55la
14 Sophie Parkin, *The Colony Room Club 1948–2008*, p. 2.
15 Museum of London interview with Emanuel Litvinoff.
16 *Sunshine City* directed by Albie Thoms.
17 George Orwell, 'Antisemitism in Britain', first published in the *Contemporary Jewish Record*.
18 Betty Miller, *Farewell Leicester Square*, p. 108.
19 Daniel Farson, *Limehouse Days: A Personal Experience of the East End*, p. 2.
20 Melly, quoted in 'London: The swinging Sixties', *Independent*, 30th October 2005.
21 Andy Garnett, *Memories of a Lucky Dog*, p. 48.
22 Anthony Blond, *Jew Made in England*, p. 197.
23 George Melly, *Slowing Down*, p. 192.
24 Letter to Andy Garnett, loaned to author.

Chapter Two – Mirrors and Mergers

1 Sebastian Smee, *Freud at Work*, p. 28.

2 Melly, *Owning Up: The Trilogy*, p. 49.

3 Smee, p. 28.

4 William Feaver, Lucian Freud and Frank Auerbach, *Lucian Freud*, p. 28.

5 Geordie Greig, *Breakfast with Lucian*, p. 84.

6 John Russell, introduction to *Lucian Freud: Exhibition Catalogue*, p. 17.

7 Sebastian Smee, *Lucian Freud*, p. 34.

8 Smee, *Freud at Work*, p. 28. It is unclear whether Freud meant from Litvinoff's kitchen at home or a workplace.

9 The lot notes are online at: http://www.christies.com/lotfinder/lot/lucian-freud-man-in-a-headscarf-1478482-details.aspx?intObjectID=1478482.

10 Lucian Freud, 'Some Thoughts on Painting', *Encounter*, July 1954, pp. 23–4.

11 Garnett, p. 48.

12 Julian Maclaren-Ross, *Collected Memoirs*, p. 301.

13 *Spectator*, 14th July 1955, p. 7.

14 Billy Hill, *Boss of Britain's Underworld*, p. 28.

15 Paul Rogerson, 'Book review: *Gangland Soho* by James Morton', *Law Society Gazette*, 14th December 2010.

16 James Morton, *The Mammoth Book of Gangs*, pp. 320–1.

17 John Pearson, *The Profession of Violence*, pp. 96–7.

18 Garnett, p. 61.

19 Michael Block, 'Double lives – a history of sex and secrecy at Westminster', *Guardian*, 16th May 2015.

20 Garnett, p. 62.

21 Bernard Kops, *Shalom Bomb: Scenes from my Life*, pp. 24–5.

22 Ibid., p. 50.

23 Ibid., p. 51.

24 Francis Wheen, *Tom Driberg: His Life and Indiscretions*, p. 72.

25 Christopher Hitchens' review of *Tom Driberg: His Life and Indiscretions* by Francis Wheen, in *London Review of Books* vol.12 no. 9, 10th May 1990.

26 *Daily Express*, Saturday 19th January 1957, p. 6.

27 *Daily Express*, Friday 25th January 1957, p. 8.

28 Saul Bellow, 'A Father to Be', in *Mosby's Memoirs and Other Stories*, p. 138.

29 William Feaver, *Lucian Freud*, p. 13.

30 William Feaver, interviewed in *Lucian Freud: Painted Life*, BBC Two, 18th February 2012.

31 Feaver, Freud and Auerbach, *Lucian Freud*, p. 28.

Chapter Three – The Man Who Laughed

1 Joan Wyndham, *Anything Once*, p. 62.

2 Dave Robins, 'Notting Hill: the Three Villages', in *International Times 30*, 3rd May 1968.

3 Ed Glinert, *The London Compendium: A Street-by-street Exploration of the Hidden Metropolis*, p. 462.

4 Shirley Green, *Peter Rachman*, p. 233.

5 Leslie Payne, *The Brotherhood*, p. 13.

6 Reported in the *Daily Telegraph*, 1st June 1964.

7 Daniel Farson, *Soho in the Fifties*, p. 95.

8 Daniel Farson, *The Gilded Gutter Life of Francis Bacon*, Chapter Six, 'Addicted to Soho'.

9 Douglas Thompson, *The Hustlers: Gambling, Greed and the Perfect Con*, Chapter Six, The Long Legs of the Law.

10 Payne, p.67.

11 Fergus Linnane, *London: The Wicked City – A Thousand Years of Vice in the Capital*, pp. 340–1.

12 'Princess to Ballet – Fiancé in Debut', *San Antonio Light*, 1st March 1960, p. 11.

13 Rebecca and Sam Umland, *Donald Cammell: A Walk on the Wild Side*, p. 46.

14 Paul Willetts, *Members Only*, p. 113.

15 Payne, p. 19.

16 Mim Scala, *Diary of a Teddy Boy: A Memoir of the Long Sixties*, p. 50.

17 *The New London Spy: A Discreet Guide to the City's Pleasures*, ed. Hunter Davies, p. 166.

18 Greig, p. 196.

19 *Lucian Freud: Painted Life*.

20 Ibid.

21 John Pearson, *The Cult of Violence*, p. 98.

22 *The New London Spy*, p. 170.

23 Fawcett, Chapter Five, 'Having a Quiet Drink at the Hammer Club'.

24 Micky Fawcett, *Krayzy Days*, Chapter Five, 'Having a Quiet Drink at the Hammer Club'.

25 Ibid.

26 Ibid.

27 Bert Wickstead, *Gangbuster: Tales of the Old Grey Fox*, p. 97.

28 Ibid., p. 98.

29 Fawcett, Chapter Five, 'Having a Quiet Drink at the Hammer Club'.

30 Scala, p. 56.

31 Melly, *Slowing Down*, p. 192.

32 Shawn Levy, *Ready Steady Go: Swinging London and the Invention of Cool*, p. 49.

33 Anthony Haden-Guest, 'The Party Hard Gangsters of '60s London', *Daily Beast*, 1st August 2015.

34 Fawcett, Chapter Five, 'Having a Quiet Drink at the Hammer Club'.

35 Albert Donoghue and Martin Short, *The Krays' Lieutenant: Their Chief Henchman and Final Betrayer*, p. 105.

36 Ibid.

37 *The Krays: The Final Word*, directed by Aubrey Powell and produced by Geoff Foulkes.

38 Mick Brown, *Mick Brown on Performance*, p. 109.

39 Victor Hugo, *The Man Who Laughs*, Book the Second, Chapter One.

40 MacCabe, p. 83, fn. 8.

41 Pearson, *The Cult of Violence*, p. 108.

42 Umland and Umland, p. 100.

43 *Vanity Fair*, vol. 53, 1990, p. 225.

44 Greig, p. 196.

45 Ibid.

46 Ibid., p. 151.

47 Ibid.

48 Martin Gayford, *Man with a Blue Scarf*, '11th May 2004'.

49 Bertrand Russell, *The Autobiography of Bertrand Russell*, p. 194.

50 Russell's introduction to *Lucian Freud: Exhibition Catalogue*, p. 17.

51 *Independent*, 24th, June 1998.

Chapter Four – I Always Use a Cut-throat Razor

1 Barry Miles, *Paul McCartney: Many Years from Now*, p. 189.

2 Ibid., p. 87.

3 George Melly, *Revolt Into Style: The Pop Arts in Britain*, p. 87.

4 Christopher Anderson, *Mick: The Wild Life and Mad Genius of Jagger*, p. 68.
5 Lichtenstein, *On Brick Lane*, p. 235.
6 Richard Levesley, *Into My Veins*, Introduction, 'This is how it all started'.
7 Ibid.
8 Ibid.
9 Ibid.
10 Ibid.
11 Ibid.
12 Ibid.
13 Ibid.
14 Ibid.
15 Ibid.
16 Ibid.
17 Ibid.
18 Ibid.
19 Ibid.
20 Miles, p. 134.

Chapter Five – Gaily Coloured Posters and Gaily Coloured People

1 Max Décharné, *King's Road*, p. xxi.
2 Nikolaus Pevsner, *The Buildings of England: London*, vol. II, p. 100.
3 Nesta Macdonald, *The History of the Pheasantry 1766–1977*, p. 22.
4 Philippe Mora, 'Culture Shock: Australians in London in the Sixties', in *Art Monthly Australia*, December 2002–February 2003, p. 8.
5 Levy, pp. 248–9.
6 Clapton, p. 79.
7 Ibid., p. 92.
8 Paul Scott, *Motherless Child: the Definitive Biography of Eric Clapton*, p. 81.
9 Clapton, p. 93.
10 Fawcett, Chapter Three, 'At Home with the Krays'.
11 During a talk at the New Writing Types conference, the Assembly House, Norwich, 10th–14th November 2004.
12 W. H. Auden, *The Dyer's Hand and Other Essays*, p. 10.
13 Clapton, p. 94.
14 Ibid, p. 93.
15 Ibid.
16 Pinter quoted in *Paris Review: Playwrights at Work*, ed. by George Plimpton and introduced by John Lahr, p. 262.
17 Lichtenstein and Sinclair, p. 146.

Chapter Six – A Diabolical Liberty

1 Philip Norman, *The Stones: The Acclaimed Biography*, p. 223.
2 Simon Wells, *Butterfly on a Wheel: The Great Rolling Stones Drugs Bust*, pp. 104–5.
3 Ibid, p. 106.
4 Décharné, pp. 202–3.
5 Welles, p. 187.
6 Tony Sanchez with John Blake, *Up and Down with the Rolling Stones*, p. 8.
7 Ibid, p. 40.
8 Ibid, p. 41.
9 'The great art-fake game', *Sunday Times*, 2nd April 1967, p. 41.
10 In Litvinoff and Golding's recorded telephone conversation from September 1968, as featured throughout Part One of this book.
11 Duncan Campbell, 'Obituaries:

Reggie Kray', *Guardian*, 2nd October 2000.

12 *The Krays: The Final Word.*

13 Leonard Read with James Morton, *Nipper Read: The Man Who Nicked the Krays*, p. 131.

14 Ibid., p. 93.

Chapter Seven – How to Lose Friends and Influence People

1 Richard Schickel, 'A Completely Worthless Film', *Life* magazine, vol. 69, no. 14, 2nd October 1970, p. 6.

2 Marianne Faithfull, *Faithfull: An Autobiography*, p. 154.

3 MacCabe, p. 24.

4 'The disappearance of Ginger Marks' on Fraser's website, www.madfrankiefraser.co.uk/frankiefraser.htm?story/marks.htm~mainframe.

5 Donoghue, p. 195.

6 'The disappearance of Ginger Marks' on Fraser's website.

7 Donoghue, p. 208.

8 Jimmy Evans and Martin Short, *The Survivor: Blue Murder, Bent Cops, Vengeance, Vendetta in 1960s Gangland*, p. 203.

9 Ibid.

10 Ibid., pp. 203–4.

11 Ibid., p. 204.

12 *Donald Cammell: The Ultimate Performance*, directed by Kevin Macdonald and Chris Rodley (1998).

13 Evans, p. 204.

14 Donoghue, pp. 79–80.

15 *Donald Cammell: The Ultimate Performance.*

16 Ibid.

17 Ibid.

18 Ibid.

19 Clapton, p. 104.

20 Rebekah Wood, 'The Acid House', article in *Neon* magazine of March 1998, pp. 108–13.

21 *Donald Cammell: The Ultimate Performance.*

22 William S. Burroughs, *The Soft Machine*, p. 25.

23 Pearson, The Cult of Violence, p. 109.

24 Peake, p. 210.

25 Ibid., pp. 211–12.

26 Ibid., p. 210.

27 Ibid.

28 Ibid., p. 211.

29 Ibid., p. 213.

30 Wood, 'The Acid House'.

31 Andrew Barrow, *Quentin and Philip: a Double Portrait*, p. 212.

32 *Donald Cammell: The Ultimate Performance.*

33 MacCabe, p. 51.

34 Mick Brown, *Performance: Pocket Movie Guide 6*, p. 34.

35 Faithfull, pp. 154–5.

36 David Thomson, 'Film Studies: Was this the most prententious film ever made?' *Independent*, 9th May 2004.

37 Jean Genet, *The Thief's Journal*, trans. Bernard Frechtman, p. 9.

Chapter Eight – Celticlimboland

1 Kenneth Grahame, *The Wind in the Willows*, p. 93.

2 Zalman Shneour, *Restless Spirit:*

Selected Writings, trans. Moshe Spiegel, pp. 13–14.
3 Geoff Ballinger, 'David Litvinoff and the Teifiside Blues', BBC website.
4 Lyn Ebenezer, *Operation Julie*, p. 26.
5 John Ivor Golding, 'Urological Nurturement', *Oz*, no. 24: 'The Beautiful Freaks' October–November 1969, pp. 6–7.
6 'Dog Owner Fined', *Cambrian News*, 15th May 1970.
7 Hampton Hawes and Don Asher, *Raise Up Off Me: A Portrait of Hampton Hawes*, p. 28.
8 *The New London Spy*, p. 224.

Chapter Nine – The Extraordinary David Litvinoff

1 Audiotape of recordings from within the Yellow House conducted by Aggy Read and Albie Thoms, loaned to the author by Albie Thoms.
2 'Street of Dreams', The Horse Hospital website.
3 *No Direction Home*, directed by Martin Scorsese.
4 Paul Buck, *Performance: A Biography of the Classic Sixties Film*, p. 32.

Chapter Ten – Face Dancer

1 *GTK: Brett Whiteley*, Australian Broadcasting Corporation, February 1972.
2 *Difficult Pleasure: A Film About Brett Whiteley*, directed by Don Featherstone.
3 *Teifiside Blues*, produced by Geoff Ballinger and presented by Euron Griffith.

Chapter Eleven – The Caretaker

1 Clapton, p. 158.
2 Geoff Dyer, *The Missing of the Somme*, p. 76.
3 Hugh Redwald Trevor-Roper, *One Hundred Letters From Hugh Trevor-Roper*, ed. by Richard Davenport-Hines and Adam Sisman, p. 71.
4 *Survey of London*, vol. XXXI–II.
5 Cammell's treatment for *The Performers*, as quoted in *Mick Brown on Performance*, p. 86.
6 Christopher Gibbs, 'Corridors of Power: Albany in Central London has been a secretive refuge of the elite – until now', *Independent*, 1st June, 2013.
7 Mary Warnock, *Memory*, p. 6.
8 Ibid., p. 14.
9 Ibid., p. 12.
10 Ibid., p. 14.
11 French quoted in 'False memory planted in mouse's brain' by Alok Jha, *Guardian*, 25th July 2013.
12 John Russell's introduction to *Lucian Freud: Exhibition Catalogue*, p. 18.
13 *Brewer's Famous Quotations*, ed. Nigel Rees, p. 437.
14 Berry quoted in 'The big picture: Whitechapel 1972' by Sean O'Hagan, *Observer*, 6th March 2011.
15 Allen Ginsberg, *Howl and Other Poems*, p. 43.
16 Albert Camus, *The Myth of Sisyphus*, trans. Justin O'Brien, p.18.
17 Brown, *Mick Brown on Performance*, p. 111.
18 Nick Kent, *The Dark Stuff: Selected Writings on Rock Music 1972–1995*, pp. 134–5.

19 Ibid., p. 135.
20 Ibid., p. 144.

Chapter Twelve – Beyond
the Grave

1 'A tough old cookie' by Chris
Peachment, *Independent*, 16th
August 1992.
2 Lichtenstein and Sinclair, p.148.
3 Peter Wollen, '*Performance*' in *Film:
The Critics' Choice*, ed. Geoff
Andrew, p. 264.
4 Jonathan Meades, *Peter Knows
What Dick Likes*, p. 70.
5 Adrian Hamilton, 'Andy Garnett:
Leading figure of the 1950s London
set who later helped develop one of
Britain's most innovative engin-
eering firms', *Independent*, 29th July
2014.

Dramatis personae

All unreferenced quotations in this book are taken from the author's own interviews and correspondence. All with endnote references are from other sources.

Kenneth Anger: occult film-maker known for titles such as *Lucifer Rising* starring his friend Donald Cammell.

Pietro Annigoni: Italian modern realist artist who painted the Queen's portrait in 1954–5 and 1969.

John Aspinall: organiser of gambling parties whose court victory helped trigger the 1960 Betting and Gaming Act.

Sam Bienstock: American photographer who met DL at the Yellow House, Sydney.

John Bindon: criminal and actor who played Moody in *Performance*.

Caroline and Jane Blunden: twins who met DL in Bali while travelling there together.

Lord (Robert) Boothby: Conservative peer whose friendship with Ronnie Kray caused scandal in mid-1960s London.

Michèle Breton: actor who played Lucy in *Performance*.

Bobby Buckley: gambler and later croupier at Esmeralda's Barn who became the subject of Ronnie Kray and DL's rivalry.

Michael 'Dandy Kim' Caborn-Waterfield: leading member of the Chelsea Set and founder of the Ann Summers chain of sex shops.

David Cammell: associate producer of *Performance*, co-directed by his older brother Donald.

Donald Cammell: friend of DL's from 1950s Chelsea onwards who co-directed *Performance* with Nic Roeg.

Derek Cattell: visitor to Cefn-Bedd with his blues record collector friend Jim Vyse.

Julian Cayo Evans: friend of DL's in Llanddewi Brefi, leader of the Free Wales Army.

Eric Clapton: guitarist who came to know DL while living at the Pheasantry in the King's Road.

Jack 'Spot' Comer: London gangster who collaborated with Billy Hill until their acrimonious split.

George Cornell: Richardson brothers' associate shot dead by Ronnie Kray.

Nicky Cramer: King's Road flower-child and a 'hanger-on' to the Rolling Stones.

Raymond Daniel: photographer who lived in Llanddewi Brefi during DL's time there.

Rowley Davidson: DL's boyfriend in Sydney.

Cledwyn Davies: farm labourer in Llanddewi Brefi.

Johnny Davies: associate of the Krays and Micky Fawcett, with whom he went into hiding at Ashburn Place.

Gail Davis: DL's niece, daughter of his oldest half-brother, Abraham Litvinoff.

Stefan de Fay: owner of Esmeralda's Barn nightclub after the death of Esmeralda Noel-Smith.

Albert Dimes: 'Italian Al', bookmaker and associate of gangland boss Billy Hill.

Deborah Dixon (now Roberts): Texan model and girlfriend of Donald Cammell.

Albert Donoghue: enforcer for the Krays' firm from 1964 onwards.

Tom Driberg: founder of the *Daily Express*'s 'William Hickey' column and Labour MP, friendly with Ronnie Kray.

John Dunbar: gallerist and artist who was married to Marianne Faithfull.

Lyn Ebenezer: journalist and author who met DL in Llanddewi Brefi.

Paul Elvey: courier and radio engineer whom the Krays asked to kill Jimmy Evans, and later a witness for their prosecution.

Goronwy Evans: Unitarian minister in Tregaron near Llanddewi Brefi.

Jimmy Evans: gangster who formed the model for Chas Devlin in *Performance*.

Daniel Farson: writer and television presenter well known for chronicling Soho life.

Micky Fawcett: associate of the Kray twins who ran long firm frauds on their behalf.

Freddie Foreman: notorious south London gangster implicated in the murders of Tommy 'Ginger' Marks and Frank Mitchell.

George Foreman: Freddie Foreman's brother who was shot and injured by Jimmy Evans.

James Fox: actor who knew DL from early 1960s Soho and played Chas Devlin in *Performance*.

Frank Fraser: infamous south London gangster best known as an enforcer for the Richardson brothers.

Robert Fraser: aka Groovy Bob, one of Swinging London's most prominent art dealers.

Lucian Freud: eminent artist whose 1954 portrait of DL sparked a feud between the two men.

Andy Garnett: Old Etonian member of the Chelsea Set and one of DL's housemates at Cheyne Walk in mid-1950s.

Juno Gemes: Hungarian-born Australian artist and photographer, friends with DL in London and Sydney.

Christopher Gibbs: influential antiques dealer, interior designer and dandy, who invited DL to live at Davington Priory.

David Gittleman: friend of DL's in late 1950s and early 1960s London.

John Ivor Golding: Welsh itinerant who inveigled himself into the Pheasantry, possible model for Harold Pinter's Mac Davies in *The Caretaker*.

Gerry Goldstein: one of DL's closest friends, and housemate at St George's Court.

Pat Goldstein: book dealer with her husband Gerry.

Bruce Goold: artist at the Yellow House in Sydney.

John Griffiths: owner of a dairy herd at Gogoyan Farm in Llanddewi Brefi, and DL's near neighbour.

Mair Griffiths: dairy farmer at Gogoyan with her husband John.

Billy Hill: self-proclaimed 'Boss of Britain's Underworld' who worked with and then split from Jack 'Spot' Comer in the 1950s.

Jacqueline Hitchcock: friend of DL's in mid-1970s in Faversham, Kent.

Chris Jagger: musician, younger brother of Mick Jagger.

Mick Jagger: lead singer of the Rolling Stones.

Brian Jones: multi-instrumentalist founder of the Rolling Stones.

Ken Judges: gardener at Davington Priory.

Patrick Kennedy: actor, writer and film-maker who began creating a documentary about DL in the early 2000s.

Bernard Kops: playwright and poet whose first success came with *The Hamlet of Stepney Green*.

Charlie Kray: gangster older brother of Ronald and Reginald Kray.

Reginald and Ronald Kray: twin brothers who rose to become the most famous underworld figures in 1960s London.

Anne Lambton: daughter of Lord Lambton who met DL in late 1960s Chelsea.

Philip Laski: dubious art-dealing friend of DL's from early 1950s Chelsea onwards.

Richard (Ricky) Levesley: DL's boyfriend from 1963 until summer 1965.

David Levy: DL's nephew, son of his brother Frank Levy.

Frank Levy: Solomon and Rose Levy's fourth child, DL's younger brother.

Gerald (Jack) Levy: DL's older brother.

Margaret Levy: DL's sister-in-law, married to his brother Philip.

Philip Levy: DL's youngest brother.

Solomon Levy: DL's father.

Sonya Levy: DL's sister.

Jonny Lewis: Australian photographer who met DL in Sydney.

Lynn Lewis: Fleet Street journalist who interviewed DL while researching Peter Rachman and the Krays.

Sanford 'Sandy' Lieberson: talent agent turned film producer for *Performance*.

Abraham Litvinoff (Alf Lister): son of Maksim and Rose Litvinoff, oldest of DL's half-brothers.

Barnet Litvinoff: third oldest of DL's half-brothers, respected historian and biographer.

Emanuel Litvinoff: second oldest of DL's half-brothers, eminent author, poet and civil rights activist.

Maksim Litvinoff: DL's mother Rose's first husband and father of his four older half-brothers.

Miles Litvinoff: DL's nephew, son of his half-brother Barnet Litvinoff.

Pinchus Litvinoff: youngest of DL's four half-brothers.

Rosa Litvinoff: DL's niece, daughter of half-brother Pinchus.

Sarah Litvinoff: DL's niece, younger daughter of his half-brother Emanuel.

Vida Litvinoff: DL's niece, older daughter of his half-brother Emanuel.

Julian Lloyd: photographer who befriended DL at the Pheasantry in the King's Road.

Tommy 'Ginger' Marks: accomplice of Jimmy Evans shot dead by Freddie Foreman in 1965.

Hew McCowan: baronet who ran the Hideaway club in London's West End.

Jack McVitie: aka Jack the Hat, gangland figure murdered by Reggie Kray in 1967.

Nicolette Meeres: artist who painted DL and socialised with him in Soho and Chelsea.

George Melly: jazz singer and author who knew DL from the early 1950s onwards.

Brian Messitt (aka Masset): friend of DL's in early 1960s Chelsea.

Rose Michaelson (later Litvinoff, later Levy): DL's mother.

Barry Miles: co-founder of *the International Times* and the Indica Gallery.

Frank 'the Mad Axeman' Mitchell: gangland character sprung from Dartmoor prison by the Krays and then murdered at their behest.

Anne Moore: DL's niece, daughter of his half-brother Abraham Litvinoff.

Philippe Mora: Australian film-maker and artist who met DL at the Pheasantry.

Henrietta Moraes: muse to artists including Francis Bacon and Lucian Freud.

Oliver Musker: antiques dealer and boyfriend of Marianne Faithfull.

Raymond Nash (né Nakachian): Lebanese nightclub manager and associate of Peter Rachman.

'Iron Foot' Jack Neave: 'King of the Bohemians' in 1950s Soho.

Richard Neville: Australian writer, co-founder of *Oz* magazine.

Neil Oram: playwright who ran the Soho beatnik cafe the House of Sam Widges.

Francis Ormsby Gore: now Lord Harlech, friend of DL's in London and Wales from the late 1960s to mid-1970s.

Jane Ormsby Gore: friend of DL's along with then-husband Michael Rainey, older sister to Julian, Victoria, Alice and Francis Ormsby Gore.

Julian Ormsby Gore: eldest son of the fifth Lord Harlech.

Victoria Ormsby Gore (now Lloyd): friend of DL's, daughter of the fifth Lord Harlech.

Anita Pallenberg: actress and model who starred in *Performance* alongside Mick Jagger and James Fox.

Sir Mark Palmer: owner of English Boy model agency and traveller of rural Britain in gypsy wagons.

Rob Parrett: teenager in Llanddewi Brefi whom DL befriended.

Leslie Payne: Kray twins associate who helped manage their fraudulent business interests.

John Pearse: tailor who co-founded Granny Takes a Trip.

John Pearson: author of the Kray twins' biography *The Profession of Violence*.

Clare Peake: daughter of Mervyn Peake who met DL while dating Gerry Goldstein.

Suna Portman: model and socialite prominent among the Chelsea Set in the late 1950s and early 1960s.

Andrew Powell: owner of Cefn-Bedd, DL's cottage in Llanddewi Brefi.

Brigadier Patrick Powell: rent-collector on his son's behalf during DL's tenancy at Cefn-Bedd.

Peter Rachman: slum landlord infamous for his squalid properties in Notting Hill.

Leonard 'Nipper' Read: policeman who led the Kray twins' successful prosecution for murder.

Ian Reid: farmer and property-owner, benefactor to the Yellow House in Sydney.

Keith Richards: lead guitarist with the Rolling Stones.

Charlie and Eddie Richardson: brothers who came to rule the south London underworld during the 1960s.

Sir John Richardson: art historian and friend of Lucian Freud's from 1940s onwards.

Nicolas Roeg: film director who made his debut co-directing *Performance* with Donald Cammell.

Alec Roitman: neighbour of the Litvinoffs at Fuller Street Buildings in the 1920s.

Freddie Rondel: enforcer for Peter Rachman known as 'Freddie the Earbiter'.

Nicky Samuel: model and artists' muse married to DL's friend Nigel Waymouth.

'Spanish' Tony Sanchez: underworld fixer and Keith Richards' drug dealer.

Emilio 'Mim' Scala: theatrical agent and author, co-founder of the Scala Browne Associates agency.

David Schneiderman: aka 'the Acid King', mysterious drug dealer suspected of involvement in the Rolling Stones' Redlands bust.

Johnny Shannon: former boxing trainer and market stallholder turned actor who played Harry Flowers in *Performance*.

Martin Sharp: Australian pop artist who met DL in mid-1960s Chelsea.

Alexander 'Shura' Shihwarg: poet and restaurateur, friend of DL's in late 1950s and early 1960s.

Iain Sinclair: author who explores his fascination with DL in books such as *Rodinsky's Room*.

'Mad' Teddy Smith: playwright and associate of DL and the Kray twins.

Antoinette Starkiewicz: artist at the Yellow House, Sydney.

Axel Sutinen: Finnish artist at the Yellow House.

Mark Sykes: socialite and organiser of *chemin de fer* parties in 1950s and 1960s London.

Asher Tarmon (né Arthur Tremberg): mentor at Habonim wartime hostel in Devon.

Catherine Tennant: astrologer married to Sir Mark Palmer.

Charlie Thomas: roguish art dealer in 1960s Chelsea.

Albie Thoms: Sydney-based underground film-maker who made *Sunshine City*.

Caroline Upcher: secretary in the film production office during the making of *Performance*.

Douglas Villiers: businessman friend of DL's who ran the Soho nightclub La Discotheque.

Nigel Waymouth: pop artist who co-founded vintage fashion boutique Granny Takes a Trip.

Timothy Whidborne: artist who trained under Annigoni, and friend of DL's from 1953 onwards.

Brett Whiteley: Australian painter whom DL knew at the Yellow House and later in London.

Wendy Whiteley: artist and muse, married to Brett Whiteley, knew DL in Sydney and London.

Martin Wilkinson: writer and landowner, friend of DL from mid-1960s onwards.

Joan Wyndham: writer and restaurateur, friend of DL's along with her husband Shura Shihwarg.

Philip Yorke: the last squire of Erddig Hall, a vast stately home near Wrexham.

Bibliography

Ackroyd, Peter, *London: The Biography* (London: Vintage Books, 2001).

Adamson, Robert and Gemes, Juno, *The Language of Oysters* (Sydney, NSW: Craftsman House, 1997).

Aftel, Mandy, *Death of a Rolling Stone: The Brian Jones Story* (New York: Delilah Books/Putnam, 1982).

Aleichem, Sholem, *Selected Stories of Sholem Aleichem* (New York: The Modern Library, 1956).

Anderson, Christopher, *Mick: The Wild Life and Mad Genius of Jagger* (New York: Gallery Books, 2012).

Andrew, Geoff, ed., *Film: The Critics Choice* (London: Aurum Press, 2001).

Auden, W.H., *The Dyer's Hand and Other Essays* (New York: Random House, 1962).

Babel, Isaac, *The Complete Works* (New York: W. W. Norton and Company, 2005).

Barrow, Andrew, *Quentin and Philip: A Double Portrait* (London: Pan Books, 2004).

Bellow, Saul, *Mosby's Memoirs and Other Stories* (Harmondsworth: Penguin, 1971).

Bergson, Henri, 'Laughter: an Essay on the Meaning of the Comic', trans. Cloudesley Brereton and Fred Rothwell (London: Macmillan, 1914).

Blond, Anthony, *Jew Made in England* (London: Elliott and Thompson, 2004).

Boothby, Robert J., *Boothby: Recollections of a Rebel* (London: Hutchinson, 1978).

Borrow, George, *Wild Wales: Its People, Language, and Scenery* (London: John Murray, 1862).

Boyd, Joe, *White Bicycles: Making Music in the 1960s* (London: Serpent's Tail, 2007).

Brod, Max, *The Biography of Franz Kafka*, trans. G. Humphreys Roberts (London: Secker and Warburg, 1947).

Brown, Mick, *Mick Brown on Performance* (London: Bloomsbury, 1999).
—*Performance: Pocket Movie Guide 6* (London: Bloomsbury, 2000).

Bruce, Lenny, *How to Talk Dirty and Influence* (New York: Fireside/Simon and Schuster, 1992).

Buck, Paul, *Performance: A Biography of the Classic Sixties Film* (London: Omnibus Press, 2012).

Burroughs, William S., *The Soft Machine* (New York: Grove Press, 1992).

Cammell, Donald, *Performance* (London: Faber and Faber, 2001).

Camus, Albert, *The Myth of Sisyphus*, trans. Justin O'Brien (London: Hamish Hamilton, 1955).

Cassady, Carolyn, *Off the Road: Twenty Years with Cassady, Kerouac and Ginsberg* (London: Black Spring, 2007).

Cassady, Neal, *The First Third & Other Writings* (San Francisco: City Lights, 1981).

Clapton, Eric, *The Autobiography* (London: Arrow Books, 2008).

Clark, Ossie and Rous, Henrietta, *The Ossie Clark Diaries* (London: Bloomsbury, 1998).

Clarkson, Wensley, *Bindon: Fighter, Gangster, Actor, Lover – the True Story of John Bindon, a Modern Legend* (London: John Blake, 2005).

Cohen, Derek and Heller, Deborah, *Jewish Presences in English Literature* (Montreal: McGill-Queen's University Press, 1990).

Cohen, John, ed., *The Essential Lenny Bruce: His Original Unexpurgated Satirical Routines* (St Albans: Panther Books, 1975).

Cohen, Rich, *Tough Jews* (London: Jonathan Cape, 1998).

Cohn, Nik, *Today There Are No Gentlemen: The Changes in Englishmen's Clothes Since the War* (London: Weidenfeld and Nicolson, 1971).

Collins, Ronald and Skover, David, *The Trials of Lenny Bruce: The Fall and Rise of an American Icon* (Naperville, Illinois: Sourcebooks MediaFusion, 2002).

Davies, Hunter, ed., *The New London Spy: A Discreet Guide to the City's Pleasures* (London: Corgi Books, 1967).

Davis, Angela Y., *Blues Legacies and Black Feminism: Gertrude 'Ma' Rainey, Bessie Smith, and Billie Holiday* (New York: Vintage, 1999).

Décharné, Max, *King's Road* (London: Weidenfeld and Nicolson, 2005).

Deighton, Len, *London Dossier* (Harmondsworth: Penguin, 1967).

Donoghue, Albert and Short, Martin, *The Krays' Lieutenant: Their Chief Henchman and Final Betrayer* (London: Smith Gryphon, 1995).

Dyer, Geoff, *The Missing of the Somme* (Edinburgh: Canongate, 2012).

Ebenezer, Lyn, *Operation Julie* (Tal-y-bont, Ceredigion: Y Lolfa, 2010).

Eliot, T. S., *Selected Poems* (London: Faber, 2009).

Englander, David, ed., *A Documentary History of Jewish Immigrants in Britain 1840–1920* (Leicester: Leicester University Press, 1994).

Evans, Jimmy and Short, Martin, *The Survivor: Blue Murder, Bent Cops, Vengeance, Vendetta in 1960s Gangland* (Edinburgh: Mainstream Publishing, 2002).

Evans, Mike and Palmer-Edwards, Paul, *The Art of British Rock: 50 Years of Rock Posters, Flyers and Handbills* (London: Frances Lincoln, 2010).

Faithfull, Marianne, *Faithfull: an Autobiography* (New York: First Cooper Square Press, 2000).

Farson, Daniel, *The Gilded Gutter Life of Francis Bacon* (London: Vintage Books, 1994, Kindle edition).

—*Limehouse Days: A Personal Experience of the East End* (London: Michael Joseph, 1991).

—*Soho in the Fifties* (London: Michael Joseph, 1987).

Fawcett, Micky, *Krayzy Days* (Brighton: Indepenpress, 2013, Kindle edition).

Feaver, William, *Lucian Freud* (New York: Rizzoli International Publications, 2007)

Feaver, William, Freud, Lucian and Auerbach, Frank, *Lucian Freud* (London, New York: Tate Publishing, Abrams 2002).

Ficacci, Luigi, *Francis Bacon 1909–1992: Deep Beneath the Surfaces of Things* (Cologne: Taschen, 2010).

Fishman, William, *The Streets of East London* (London: Gerald Duckworth & Co., 1979).

Foreman, Freddie and Lambrianou, Tony, *Getting it Straight: Villains Talking* (London: Pan Books, 2001).

Foster Wallace, David, *A Supposedly Fun Thing I'll Never Do Again* (London: Abacus, 2012).

Fox, James, *Comeback: an Actor's Direction* (Grand Rapids, MI: W. B. Eerdmans, 1983).

Freud, Lucian, 'Some Thoughts on Painting' (*Encounter*, July 1954, pp. 23–4, accessible at http://www.unz.org/Pub/Encounter-1954jul-00023).

Freud, Lucian, et al., *Lucian Freud: Painting People* (London: National Portrait Gallery, 2012).

Garnett, Andy, *Memories of a Lucky Dog* (London: Turnham Press, 2011).

Gayford, Martin, *Man with a Blue Scarf* (London: Thames and Hudson, 2010, Kindle edition).

Gemes, Juno, *Proof: Portraits from the Movement 1978–2003* (Canberra: National Portrait Gallery, 2003).

Genet, Jean, *The Thief's Journal*, trans. Bernard Frechtman (London: Penguin Books, 1967).

Ginsberg, Allen, *Howl and Other Poems* (San Francisco: City Lights Pocket Bookshop, 1956).

Glinert, Ed, *The London Compendium: A Street-by-street Exploration of the Hidden Metropolis* (London: Penguin, 2004).

Gowing, Lawrence, *Lucian Freud* (New York: Thames and Hudson, 1984).

Grahame, Kenneth, *The Wind in the Willows* (London: Methuen's Modern Classics, 1933).

Gray, Michael, *Hand Me My Travelin' Shoes: In Search of Blind Willie McTell* (London: Bloomsbury, 2007).

—*Song & Dance Man III: The Art of Bob Dylan* (London and New York: Continuum, 2000).

Green, Jonathon, *All Dressed Up: the Sixties and the Counterculture* (London: Jonathan Cape, 1998).

—*Days in the Life: Voices from the English Underground 1961–1971* (London: Pimlico, 1998).

Green, Shirley, *Peter Rachman* (London: Michael Joseph, 1979).

Greig, Geordie, *Breakfast with Lucian* (London: Jonathan Cape, 2013).

Hawes, Hampton and Asher, Don, *Raise Up Off Me: A Portrait of Hampton Hawes* (New York: Thunders Mouth Press, Distributed by Publishers Group West, 2001).

Hill, Billy, *Boss of Britain's Underworld* (London: Naldrett Press, 1955).

Hirsch, Marianne, 'The Generation of Postmemory' (*Poetics Today*, vol. 29 no. 1, pp. 103–28, 2008).

Hugo, Victor, *The Man Who Laughs* (Public domain Kindle edition).

Julius, Anthony, *Trials of the Diaspora: A History of Anti-Semitism in England* (New York: Oxford University Press, 2012).

Kafka, Franz, *The Diaries of Franz Kafka: 1910–23*, trans. Martin Greenberg and Hannah Arendt (Harmondsworth: Peregrine Books, 1964).

Kelland, Gilbert, *Crime in London* (London: Grafton, 1987).

Kent, Nick, *The Dark Stuff: Selected Writings on Rock Music 1972–1995* (New York: Da Capo Press, 1995).

Kops, Bernard, *Shalom Bomb: Scenes from my Life* (London: Oberon Books, 2000).

Kerouac, Jack, *On the Road* (London: Penguin Books, 1991).

Kray, Charles and McGibbon, Robin, *Me and My Brothers* (London: HarperCollins, 1997).

Kray, Ron, *My Story* (London: Pan Books, 1994).

Lazaroms, Ilse Josepha, *The Grace of Misery: Joseph Roth and the Politics of Exile, 1919–1939* (Leiden: Brill, 2012).

Levesley, Richard, *Into My Veins* (Bloomington: AuthorHouse, 2011, Kindle edition).

Levy, Shawn, *Ready Steady Go: Swinging London and the Invention of Cool* (London: Fourth Estate, 2002).

Lichtenstein, Rachel, *On Brick Lane* (London: Penguin, 2008).

Lichtenstein, Rachel and Sinclair, Iain, *Rodinsky's Room* (London: Granta, 2000).

Linnane, Fergus, *London: The Wicked City – a Thousand Years of Vice in the Capital* (London: Robson Books, 2007).

Litvinoff, Barnet, *The Burning Bush: Antisemitism and World History* (London: Fontana, 1989).

Litvinoff, Emanuel, *Journey Through a Small Planet* (London: Penguin, 2008).

—, ed., *The Penguin Book of Jewish Short Stories* (Harmondsworth: Penguin Books, 1979).

MacCabe, Colin, *Performance (BFI Film Classics)* (London: BFI Publishing, 1998).

MacDonald, Ian, *Revolution in the Head: The Beatles' Records and the Sixties* (London: Pimlico, 1995).

Macdonald, Nesta, *The History of the Pheasantry 1766–1977* (London: self-published, 1977).

Macfarlane, Robert, *The Old Ways* (London: Penguin, 2012).

Maclaren-Ross, Julian, *Collected Memoirs* (London: Black Spring Press, 2004).

Marks, Dennis, *Wandering Jew: The Search for Joseph Roth* (London: Notting Hill Editions, 2011).

Mayhew, Henry, *Mayhew's Characters* (London: Spring Books, no date).

McIlvanney, Hugh, *McIlvanney on Boxing: An Anthology* (London: Stanley Paul, 1982).

Meades, Jonathan, *Peter Knows What Dick Likes* (London: Paladin, 1989).

Melly, George, *Revolt into Style: The Pop Arts in Britain* (Harmondsworth: Penguin Books, 1972).

—*Owning Up: The Trilogy* (London: Penguin, 2006).

—*Slowing Down* (London: Penguin, 2006).

Melnick, Jeffrey P., *A Right to Sing the Blues: African Americans, Jews, and American Popular Song* (Cambridge, Mass.: Harvard University Press, 1999).

Mezzrow, Milton and Wolfe, Bernard, *Really the Blues* (London: Jazz Book Club by arrangement with Secker and Warburg, 1959).

Miles, Barry, *London Calling* (London: Atlantic Books, 2010).

—*Paul McCartney: Many Years from Now* (London: Secker and Warburg, 1997).

Miller, Betty, *Farewell Leicester Square* (London: Persephone Books, 2000).

Mora, Philippe, 'Culture Shock: Australians in London in the Sixties' (*Art Monthly Australia*, December 2002–February 2003).

Morton, James, *The Mammoth Book of Gangs* (London: Robinson, 2012).

Musil, Robert, *Young Törless*, trans. Eithne Wilkins and Ernst Kaiser (Harmondsworth: Penguin, 1961).

Neville, Richard, *Playpower* (London: Paladin, 1971).

Norman, Philip, *The Stones: The Acclaimed Biography* (London: Pan, 2002).

Nowra, Louis, *Kings Cross: A Biography* (Sydney: NewSouth Publishing, 2013).

O'Leary, Laurie, *Ronnie Kray: A Man Among Men* (London: Headline, 2002).

Orwell, George, 'Antisemitism in Britain' (*Contemporary Jewish Record*, April 1945).

Parkin, Sophie, *The Colony Room Club, 1948–2008: A History of Bohemian Soho* (London: Palmtree Publishers, 2012).

Payne, Leslie, *The Brotherhood* (London: Michael Joseph, 1973).

Pearson, John, *Notorious: The Immortal Legend of the Kray Twins* (London: Arrow, 2011).

—*The Profession of Violence: The Rise and Fall of the Kray Twins* (London: HarperCollins, 1995).

—*The Cult of Violence* (London: Orion Books, 2002).

Peake, Clare, *Under a Canvas Sky: Living Outside Gormenghast* (London: Constable, 2011).

Pevsner, Nikolaus, *The Buildings of England: London*, vol. II (Harmondsworth: Penguin, 1952).

Phillips, Mike, and Phillips, Trevor, *Windrush: The Irresistible Rise of Multiracial Britain* (London: HarperCollins, 1998).

Pinter, Harold, *The Caretaker* (London: Faber and Faber, 1961).

—*Art, Truth and Politics: The Nobel Lecture* (London: Faber and Faber, 2006).

Plimpton, George, ed., *The Paris Review: Playwrights at Work* (New York: Modern Library, 2000).

Polano, H., trans., *The Talmud: Selections from that Ancient Book* (London and New York: Frederick Warne and Co., 1888).

Read, Leonard and Morton, James, *Nipper Read: The Man Who Nicked the Krays* (London: Little, Brown, 2001).

Richards, Keith, *Life* (London: Weidenfeld and Nicolson, 2010, Kindle edition).

Rosten, Leo, *The Education of Hyman Kaplan* (London: Constable and Robinson, 2012, Kindle edition).

—*Hooray for Yiddish!* (London: Elm Tree Books, 1983).

Roth, Joseph, *The Wandering Jews*, trans. Michael Hofmann (London: Granta Books, 2001).

Russell, Bertrand, *The Autobiography of Bertrand Russell* (London: Routledge, 2014).

Russell, John and Freud, Lucian, *Lucian Freud* (London: Arts Council of Great Britain, 1974).

Salamander, Rachel, and Chorin, Schalom, *The Jewish World of Yesterday, 1860–1938: Texts and Photographs from Central Europe* (New York: Rizzoli, 1991).

Sanchez, Tony and Blake, John, *Up and Down with the Rolling Stones* (London: Blake Paperbacks, 1991).

Scala, Mim, *Diary of a Teddy Boy: A Memoir of the Long Sixties* (Surrey: Goblin Press, 2009).

Scaduto, Anthony, *Bob Dylan* (London: Helter Skelter, 2001).

Scott, Paul, *Motherless Child: The Definitive Biography of Eric Clapton* (London: Headline Publishing Group, 2015).

Shneour, Zalman, *Restless Spirit: Selected Writings*, trans. Moshe Spiegel (New York: Thomas Yoseloff, 1963).

Short, Robert, *Dada & Surrealism* (London: Laurence King Pub, 1994).

Sinclair, Iain, *Lights Out for the Territory* (London: Penguin, 2003).

—*White Chappell, Scarlet Tracings* (London: Granta Books, 1998).

Smee, Sebastian, *Freud at Work* (London: Jonathan Cape, 2006).

Smee, Sebastian and Freud, Lucian, *Lucian Freud* (Cologne and London: Taschen, 2007).

Sontag, Susan, 'Notes on Camp' (*Partisan Review*, vol. 31, no. 4, pp. 515–30, 1964, accessed at http://www9.georgetown.edu/faculty/irvinem/theory/sontag-notesoncamp-1964.html).

Sounes, Howard, *Down the Highway: The Life of Bob Dylan* (London: Black Swan, 2002).

Symons, A. J., *The Quest for Corvo* (Richmond, Virginia: Valancourt Books, 2014, Kindle edition).

Thompson, Douglas, *The Hustlers: Gambling, Greed and the Perfect Con* (London: Pan Macmillan, 2008).

Trevor-Roper, Hugh Redwald, *One Hundred Letters From Hugh Trevor-Roper*, ed. Richard Davenport-Hines and Adam Sisman (Oxford: Oxford University Press, 2014).

Umland, Rebecca A. and Umland, Samuel J., *Donald Cammell: A Life on the Wild Side* (Godalming, Surrey: FAB Press, 2006).

Warnock, Mary, *Memory* (London: Faber and Faber, 1987).

Webb, Billy, *Running with the Krays* (Edinburgh: Mainstream Publishing, 1993).

Wells, Simon, *Butterfly on a Wheel: The Great Rolling Stones Drugs Bust* (London: Omnibus Press, 2011).

West, D. J., *Homosexuality* (Harmondsworth: Penguin, 1960).

Wheen, Francis, *Tom Driberg: His Life and Indiscretions* (London: Chatto and Windus, 1990).

White, Jerry, *Rothschild Buildings: Life in an East End Tenement Block, 1887–1920* (London and Boston: Routledge & Kegan Paul, 1980).

Wickstead, Bert, *Gangbuster: Tales of the Old Grey Fox* (London: Futura, 1985).

Williams, Richard, *Long Distance Call* (London: Aurum Press, 2000).

Willetts, Paul, *Members Only* (London: Serpent's Tail, 2010).

Wisse, Ruth R., *The Schlemiel as Modern Hero* (Chicago: University of Chicago Press, 1971).

Wyndham, Joan, *Anything Once* (London: Flamingo, 1993).

Zangwill, Israel, *The King of Schnorrers* (London: William Heinemann, 1931).

Zweig, Stefan, *The Invisible Collection / Buchmendel* (London: Pushkin Press, 1998).

Newspaper articles, magazines and pamphlets:

'Six Days to Sunday: Jew-Baiting in Ridley Road' by D. L., *Jewish Standard*, 3rd June 1949.

'Young Jewish Poet's New Play' by David Levy, *Jewish Standard*, 29th July 1949.

'"AN ORGY" AS MAYFAIR NECKS IN DOCKLAND', *Sunday Pictorial*, 13th May 1956, p. 3.

'William Hickey', *Daily Express*, Saturday 19th January 1957, p. 6.

'William Hickey', *Daily Express*, Friday 25th January 1957, p. 8.

'About this portrait: The man in it rows with Freud' by 'William Hickey', *Daily Express*, 25th March 1958, p. 3.

'Princess to Ballet – Fiancé in Debut', *San Antonio Light*, 1st March 1960, p. 11.

'Pop Stars and Drugs: Facts That Will Shock You', three-part series, *News of the World*, January–February 1967.

'Drug Squad Raids Pop Stars' Party', *News of the World*, 19th February 1967, p. 1.

'The great art-fake game', *Sunday Times*, 2nd April 1967, p. 41.

'Notting Hill: the Three Villages' by Dave Robins, *International Times 30*, 3rd May 1968.

'Performance' photo spread, *Films and Filming*, March 1969, pp. 33–5.

'Urological Nurturement' by John Ivor Golding, *Oz* no. 24: 'The Beautiful Freaks', October–November 1969, pp. 6–7.

'A Completely Worthless Film' by Richard Schickel, *Life Magazine*, vol. 69, no. 14, 2nd October 1970, p. 6.

'Nothing Queer about Johnny Shannon' by Christopher Ford, *Guardian*, 23rd January 1971, p. 7.

'Must Soho Die?', *Soho Clarion*, no. 1, December 1973, p. 1.

Bricks and Mortar: The Buildings of Tower Hamlets, London: Directorate of Community Services London Borough of Tower Hamlets, 1975.

Tower Hamlets in Photographs: 1914–1939. London: Tower Hamlets Central Library, 1980.

'Lucian Freud: The Unblinking Eye' by Marina Warner, *New York Times Magazine*, 4th December 1988.

'Lights, camera. . .decadence' by Mick Brown, *Telegraph Magazine*, 3rd June 1995, pp. 24–30.

Museum of London interview with Emanuel Litvinoff by Hannah Berman, 22nd January 1998.

'The Acid House' by Rebekah Wood, article in *Neon* magazine of March 1998, pp. 108–13.

'You ask the questions: Frank Fraser', *Independent*, 24th June 1998.

'Fall of the House of Harlech' by Angela Pertusini and Hugh Davies, *Daily Telegraph*, 22nd June 2000.

'Obituaries: Reggie Kray' by Duncan Campbell, *Guardian*, 2nd October 2000.

'Film Studies: Was this the most pretentious British film ever made?' *Independent*, 9th May 2004.

'London: The swinging Sixties', *Independent*, 30th October 2005.

'Book review: *Gangland Soho* by James Morton', *Law Society Gazette*, 14th December 2010.

'The big picture: Whitechapel 1972' by Sean O'Hagan, in *Guardian*, 6th March 2011.

'Curse of Harlechs hits again', *Daily Mail*, 17th March 2011.

'Corridors of Power: Albany in central London has been a secretive refuge of the elite – until now' by Christopher Gibbs, *Independent*, 1st June 2013.

'False memory planted in mouse's brain' by Alok Jha, *Guardian*, 25th July 2013.

Survey of London, vol. XXXI–II (London: London City Council, 1963) http://www.british-history.ac.uk/report.aspx?compid=41481#n98.

'David Litvinoff and the Teifiside Blues' by Geoff Ballinger, on BBC website, http://www.bbc.co.uk/blogs/wales/entries/9e8918d9-93ad-3e07-bb37-1793e68ed8bc.

'Street of Dreams', on the Horse Hospital website, http://www.thehorse-hospital.com/past/kinokulture-past/street-of-dreams/.

'Double lives – a history of sex and secrecy at Westminster', *Guardian*, 16th May 2015.

'The Party Hard Gangsters of '60s London', by Anthony Haden-Guest, *Daily Beast*, 1st August 2015.

Films and television programmes:

Soho Goes Gay (British Pathé newsreel issued 14th July 1955).
Clubs Galore! (British Pathé newsreel issued 22nd December 1958).
Echoes of London: Soho Nights 1958 until 1962, YouTube video accessible at https://www.youtube.com/watch?v=yAM8KqzXkmU.
The Australian Londoners, dir. Stefan Sargent (Channel Nine Australia, 1965).
Trouble in Molopolis, dir. Philippe Mora (Arthur Boyd/Eric Clapton, 1969).
Performance, dir. Donald Cammell and Nicolas Roeg (Warner Bros., 1970).
Villain, dir. Michael Tuchner (Anglo-EMI, 1971).
Report from the Yellow House, Sydney Channel Ten News, 31st March 1971.
GTK: Brett Whiteley, Australian Broadcasting Corporation, date unknown (February 1972).
Sunshine City, dir. Albie Thoms (Sydney Film-makers Co-operative, 1973).
Something Old, Something New, Something Borrowed, Something Blue, dir. Albie Thoms (Australian Broadcasting Corporation, 1976).
Withnail and I, dir. Bruce Robinson (HandMade Films, 1987).
The Krays, dir. Peter Medak (Fugitive Features, 1990).
The Cardinal and the Corpse, dir. Christopher Petit (Koninck/Channel 4, 1992).
The Krays: The Final Word, dir. Aubrey Powell (WEA International, 2001).
No Direction Home, dir. by Martin Scorsese (Paramount, 2005).
UBU Films: Sydney Underground Movies 1965–70, dir. John Clark, David Perry, Aggy Read, Albie Thoms *et al.* (Contemporary Arts Media, 2011).

Radio:

Emanuel Litvinoff in conversation with Patrick Wright on *Night Waves*, broadcast on BBC Radio Three on 4th April 1995.
Teifiside Blues, produced by Geoff Ballinger and presented by Euron Griffith, first broadcast on BBC Radio Wales on 19th April 2013.

Acknowledgements

Attempting to write about such an elusive character as David Litvinoff would be impossible without substantial help from kind-hearted people. I've been lucky enough to meet many in the last five years. I would like to thank. . .

Paul Buck, an authority on *Performance* who put me in touch with some key interviewees.

David Cammell, for his encouraging enthusiasm that Litvinoff's story should be told, and his vivid and detailed recollections.

Eric Clapton, who in granting such a considered and insightful interview shifted this book from an idea to a reality. Many thanks also to his assistant, Cecil Offley, and to his manager, Michael Eaton, for granting permission to quote from Clapton's autobiography.

In Llanddewi Brefi, Raymond and Olwen Daniel: Ray for sharing his memories, Olwen for finding Litvinoff's court case news report at the University of Aberystwyth archives; also Lyn Ebenezer for his stories and for searching his records for information on Litvinoff's time in the village; and Rosemary Northover and Miles Willis for showing me around Cefn-Bedd.

Micky Fawcett, who gave a thoughtful and funny interview, patiently answered various follow-up enquiries about his dealings fifty years ago with Ronnie Kray, David Litvinoff and Bobby Buckley, and let me quote extensively from *Krayzy Days*, which is the best criminal memoir I've read. His son Michael Fawcett has been a great help too.

William Feaver for his guidance on Lucian Freud's dealings with Litvinoff and on obtaining the rights to reproduce *Man in a Headscarf (The Procurer)*.

James Fox for giving two substantial, reflective interviews and for putting me in touch with Johnny Shannon.

At Jonathan Cape, Dan Franklin for his faith in me and for his wise editorial suggestions, and to Clare Bullock for her meticulous and sensitive copy-editing.

Bob Geldof for his trustfulness in allowing a stranger into his home, and Ken Judges for guiding me around and answering my questions.

Juno Gemes, without whom this book would not exist. When I first approached a couple of Litvinoff's London friends they only consented to talk once she had sounded me out: all else unfolded from there. In Australia she housed me and took me to visit Bruce Goold and Mick Glasheen, whom I also thank for their time, and arranged my stay with Martin Sharp. Later she connected me to several more otherwise unreachable people. I greatly appreciate her kindness, encouragement, perceptive comments on my manuscript and all-round efforts on my behalf.

Christopher Gibbs, who answered my many questions with unfailing good humour and a vivid and eloquent turn of phrase.

Lord Harlech for hosting me at Wheelers and Glyn Cywarch and speaking so entertainingly about his old friend.

Matthew Hamilton, my brilliant literary agent at Aitken Alexander Associates, for his sterling work on my proposal and belief in Litvinoff's story.

Patrick Kennedy, my fellow obsessive pursuer of the Litvinoff mythology; our conversations about the man and his era clarified my thoughts. I am most grateful for his intelligent observations and having access to his filmed interviews.

Martin Levy, who provided valuable information on the Litvinoff/Levy family history and directed me towards many useful resources. I appreciate his kindness in helping me access the notes from Litvinoff's inquest. Likewise his father, Philip Levy, who summoned rich memories of his and David's childhood. One of this book's pleasures has been growing acquainted with them and other members of the Litvinoff/Levy family, among them Gail Davis, Mike Flockhart, David Levy, Aaron Litvinoff, the late Emanuel Litvinoff, Miles Litvinoff, Rosa Litvinoff, Sarah Litvinoff and Anne Moore. My thanks to them all.

Sandy Lieberson, who gave a thoughtful interview, some fine photos and kindly loaned his letters from Litvinoff.

Julian Lloyd, who repeatedly dug deep into his memory banks and gave some touching insights into his old friend's more vulnerable side. I'm delighted to feature Julian's photographs and thank him and Karena Hutton for their assistance with this.

Dan Meller, my dear cousin and friend. This book derives entirely from his suggestion that I should read *Rodinsky's Room*. Since then I have greatly valued his perpetual enthusiasm, pertinent suggested reading and astute close analysis of an early draft.

Philippe Mora, a fount of perceptive insights, amusing stories and great photos.

James Morton, a courteous and generous source of information on the London underworld, whose books proved a regular reference point.

Clare Peake, for enabling me to meet Gerry Goldstein and checking the section of my manuscript describing that meeting.

Rowan Pim, for everything, but especially her sensible editorial suggestions and all the times she held the fort while I undertook research trips.

My parents, Claudia and Malcolm Pim: Mum in particular for finding an important Lucian Freud exhibition catalogue, Dad for introducing me to the Bertrand Russell quotation concerning atheism, both of them for their constant support and love over the years.

Mim Scala, for his colourful recollections, readiness to answer numerous questions and putting me in touch with several hitherto unreachable contacts.

Iain Sinclair, for sparing time for an interview back in 2010 and then loaning the Golding and Laski recordings, two important early developments in my research.

Nigel Waymouth, for his perceptive insights and vivid stories shared over lunch, coffee and by email from the very beginning to the end; he also gently corrected some silly errors in my manuscript and copied some superb photographs. His and Louis Waymouth's kindness in loaning their collection of Litvinoff-compiled reel-to-reels greatly enriched my understanding of his musical tastes.

The patient and kind-hearted Timothy Whidborne, whose letters invariably included some telling detail that helped to fill a gap in the narrative.

Martin Wilkinson, a fascinating source of anecdotes and insights into Litvinoff's later years, and also of some fine illustrations.

Ashleigh Wilson, author of the Brett Whiteley biography *Art, Life and the Other Thing* (Melbourne: Text Publishing, 2016), for reading the Australia chapters and making useful suggestions.

Simon Wells, a great help on all matters Redlands-related – his book *Butterfly on a Wheel: the Great Rolling Stones Drugs Bust* (Omnibus Press, 2011) is definitive on that subject.

Last but certainly not least, my good friend Paul Willetts, who from this book's conception to completion has suggested people to interview, research material to explore and general improvements to my manuscript. His biography of Julian Maclaren-Ross (*Fear and Loathing in Fitzrovia*, Dewi Lewis Publishing, 2003) is a model of how to record a seemingly untraceable life and if I have succeeded at all in emulating that feat, then I owe much to his generous guidance.

I regret that several of my most important interviewees did not live to see this book published. It was a privilege to know Andy Garnett, Martin Sharp and Albie Thoms: each went above and beyond in their support of my research, and I remember them with fondness and gratitude. Similarly Richard Levesley must have summoned up much courage to contact the biographer of a man whom he blamed for ruining his life. Precisely what occurred between him and Litvinoff will now never be known, but I appreciate him and his wife Mary taking time to give me their account.

Sincere thanks also go to Chris Bailey, Mark Bond-Webster and Jeremy Noel-Tod, each of whom critiqued my manuscript, giving encouragement and suggesting intelligent amendments. I valued Mark's advice that I should explore how Litvinoff's Jewishness and sexuality combined to shape his character. Any errors that remain are my responsibility alone.

I was the fortunate beneficiary of a generous grant from the Authors' Foundation that allowed me time to write and covered some of my research expenses, and for which I'm very grateful.

I'd also like to thank the following authors for permitting me to quote at length from their work: Mick Brown, Eric Clapton, Micky Fawcett, Andy Garnett, Marianne Hirsch, Anthony Julius, Nick Kent, Shawn Levy, Colin MacCabe, Clare Peake, Iain Sinclair and Patrick Wright.

Finally I'm grateful to all of these people, each of whom helped me to tell Litvinoff's story: Stuart Anderson, Guy Sangster Adams, Brian Angel, Geoff Ballinger, Andrew Barrow, Clive Bettington at the Jewish East End Celebration Society, Sam Bienstock, Caroline Blunden, Jane Blunden, Jo Boothby, Kateri Butler, Michael Caborn-Waterfield, Derek Cattell, Joanna Cohn, Caroline Coon, Anthony Dalton, Cledwyn Davies, Max Décharné, Jeff Dexter, Helen Donlon, Mark Donnelly, Albert Donoghue, Stephen Dorril, John Dunbar, Paul Elvey, Goronwy Evans, Marianne Faithfull, David Flatau, David Fraser, the late Frankie Fraser, Patrick Fraser, Esther Freud, Joel Gausten, Martin Gayford, Alec George, The Gentle Author, David Gittleman, Marc Glendening, Gerry Goldstein, Jonathon Green, Geordie Greig, Chris Gribble, Mair Griffiths, Nic Groombridge, Anna Guthrie, Mark Guthrie, Georgina Hale, Linda Hallett, Richard Handford, Trevor Heaton, Jacqueline Hitchcock, Virginia Ironside, John Jack, Eric Jackson, Mick Jackson, Piers Jackson, Chris Jagger, Derek James, Jay Johnson, Bernie Katz, Bernard Kops, Chris Lambrianou, Anne Lambton, Lucinda Lambton, Tony Landaw, Sylvia Laws, Henry Layte (www.thebookhive. co.uk), Emma Lee, Mandy Leggate, Bob Le-Roi, Nemone Lethbridge,

Joshua Levine, Margaret Levy, Jonny Lewis, Lynn Lewis, Victoria Lloyd, Mary McClory, Jonathan Meades, Colin MacCabe, Chris and Andrew Manley (www.norwich-computers.co.uk), Ian Maund (www.sandybrown-jazz.co.uk), Nicolette Meeres, Diana Melly, Barry Miles, Sam Mitchell, Mike Molloy, Alan Moore, Francis Morland, Suna Morrissey, Oliver Musker, Lara Narkiewicz, the late Raymond Nash, Neil Oram, Jane Ormsby Gore, Mark Ottaway, Sir Mark Palmer, Sophie Parkin, Lilian Pizzichini, Rob Parrett, John Pearse, John Pearson, Laura Pim, Suna Portman, Andrew Powell, Tim Powell, David Praed, Andy Prevezer, Stuart Purves at Australian Galleries, Ian Reid, Rupert Reid, Sir John Richardson, John Rigbey, Deborah Roberts, Stash Klossowski de Rola, Laurence Romance, Paul Rousseau, Nicky Samuel, Peter Sargent, Johnny Shannon, Katie Sharp, Sandy Sharp, Anthony Sharples, Alexander 'Shura' Shihwarg, Tony Shrimplin (www.themuseumofsoho.org.uk), Pete Smith, Steve Snelling, Sue Spooner, Caroline Stafford, David Stafford, Antoinette Starkiewicz, Annabelle Steele, Phil Sutcliffe, Axel Sutinen, Tom Sykes, Mark Sykes, Catherine Tennant, David Thomson, Douglas Thompson, Tony Thorne, Jim Tobin at St George's Court, Angelica Tremblay, Cathi Unsworth, Caroline Upcher, Douglas Villiers, Tom Viney, Peter Walsh, Dickie Weight, Marcus Werner Hed, Neil White, Wendy Whiteley, Eric Williams, James Williams, Ashleigh Wilson, David Wright and Tom Zelmanovits.

Lines from *Howl and Other Poems* © Allen Ginsberg 1956, used by permission of The Wylie Agency (UK) Limited.

All extracts from David Litvinoff's letters to Sandy Lieberson remain the sole and exclusive property of Sandy Lieberson and are reproduced here by his kind permission.

Lines from 'To T. S. Eliot', as reproduced in *Journey Through a Small Planet* by Emanuel Litvinoff (Penguin Classics, 2008) are reproduced by kind permission of the Estate of Emanuel Litvinoff and Penguin Books.

Owning Up: The Trilogy by George Melly (© George Melly, 2006)/ Reprinted by permission of A.M. Heath & Co. Ltd.

Revolt Into Style: The Pop Arts in Britain by George Melly (© George Melly, 1972) reprinted by permission of A.M. Heath & Co. Ltd.

The lyrics of the song 'Litvinov's Book' are the copyright of Alan Moore and reproduced by his kind permission.

Antisemitism in Britain by George Orwell (© George Orwell, 1945) reprinted by permission of Bill Hamilton as the Literary Executor of the Estate of the Late Sonia Brownell Orwell.

Index

Entries in *italics* indicate illustrations, paintings and photographs.
DL indicates David Litvinoff.